D1718834

Development and Territorial Restructuring
in an Era of Global Change

Development and Territorial Restructuring in an Era of Global Change

*Theories, Approaches and
Future Research Perspectives*

Edited by

Élisabeth Peyroux
Christine Raimond
Vincent Viel
Émilie Lavie

WILEY

First published 2023 in Great Britain and the United States by ISTE Ltd and John Wiley & Sons, Inc.

ISTE Ltd
27-37 St George's Road
London SW19 4EU
UK

www.iste.co.uk

John Wiley & Sons, Inc.
111 River Street
Hoboken, NJ 07030
USA

www.wiley.com

Library of Congress Control Number: 2022950068

British Library Cataloguing-in-Publication Data
A CIP record for this book is available from the British Library
ISBN 978-1-78630-653-1

Contents

Chapter 8. Artisanal and Small-scale Gold Mining and Territorial Development in Africa: A Difficult Equation 141

Anna DESSERTINE, Raphaëlle CHEVRILLON-GUIBERT, Laurent GAGNOL,
Julie BETABELET, Lamine DIALLO, Robin PETIT-ROULET, Edith SAWADOGO,
Tongnoma ZONGO and Géraud MAGRIN

Chapter 9. New Approaches to City–Countryside Relations 161

Martine BERGER and Jean-Louis CHALÉARD

**Chapter 10. Using Scientific Modeling for Adaptation of Agriculture
to Climate Change: A Political and Organizational Challenge**   181
Malika MADELIN and Évelyne MESCLIER

**Chapter 11. Hydrogeography: Towards a Systemic Analysis in
the Context of Global Changes, from Watershed to Spillway Basin.**   201
Vincent VIEL, Émilie LAVIE, Guillaume BROUSSE, Benoît CARLIER, Luc MICHLER,
Mathilde RESCH, Gashin SHAHSAVARI and Gilles ARNAUD-FASSETTA

Acknowledgments

This book is based on research conducted by the UMR Prodig. We would like to thank all contributors for participating in this collective and fruitful endeavor. We would also like to thank the reviewers of the first versions of the chapters for their valuable comments and suggestions: Frédéric Bertrand, Armelle Choplin, Hubert Cochet, Emeric Lendjel, Jérôme Lombard, Benjamin Lysaniuk, Malika Madelin, Géraud Magrin, Karine Peyronnie, Alain Piveteau, Anne Julia Rollet, Yohan Sahraoui and Julie Trottier.

Finally, we would like to acknowledge the contribution of Jean Menut in proofreading and editing the bibliographical references and extend our thanks and appreciation to Catherine Valton for her contribution to the maps and the formatting of the illustrations.

Introduction

Linking Environment and Development at a Time of Global Changes: A Challenge for Geography and Social Sciences

Scientific challenges

The Anthropocene is a challenge for research in the humanities and social sciences, and more particularly for geography. Both must tackle numerous issues, including that of thinking jointly about development and the environment. This implies exploring global changes and their impacts on territories taking into consideration territorial and environmental governance on various decision-making scales.

Overcoming disciplinary divides and opening up new epistemological perspectives

The notion of global changes is increasingly used to account for all the changes observed since the second half of the 20th century: climate change, degradation of natural resources, demographic transition, worldwide urbanization, economic globalization and global migration. These global changes make the analysis of the links between environment and development more complex. On the one hand, they imply crossing societal and environmental issues by mobilizing the humanities and social sciences as well as natural sciences to analyze the interactions between biogeophysical systems and human activities. On the other hand, they imply a cross-scale analysis (international, regional, national, local) and to pay

Introduction written by Élisabeth PEYROUX, Christine RAIMOND, Vincent VIEL and Émilie LAVIE.

attention to contexts of development (from the richest countries to the margins of the world system) to account for the diversity of physical manifestations, political responses and socio-spatial dynamics of these changes (Lombard et al. 2006).

Geography, the discipline mostly represented in this book, is well positioned to meet the challenges of a systemic approach to our world through its attention to spaces, places and scales, to the relations between societies and their environment, to territories and contexts. By taking part in a renewed dialogue between disciplines and studies around several key objects or concepts geography can also make a significant contribution to help decipher the factors and effects of global changes on territories.

While the spatiality of processes or "the spatial referents of actions, experiences and imaginaries" is becoming a "shared perspective" for many disciplines (Volvey et al. 2021, p. 34), geography pays particular attention to how territories are constructed and appropriated, their lability, and to spatial arrangements rather than spatial structures (Stock et al. 2021). It takes into account the power relationships underlying the exploitation of resources, governance or territorial integration strategies by highlighting their spatial implications (inequalities, fragmentation, polarization).

Similarly, in a context of growing concern about the effects of climate change, many disciplines are taking up environmental issues (Chartier and Rodary 2016) and contributing to the broadening of the notion (by including biodiversity, water and air quality, interactions between non-human and human components). Geographers, who have been catching up with this trend more recently, try to overcome the disciplinary divides and open up new epistemological perspectives to rethink the interface between societies and the environment.

Initially addressed by physical and then human geography, environmental studies have diversified by embracing the human–nature relationship. Many current approaches dealing with the environment build on constructivist approaches in geography (Georges 1971; Bertrand and Bertrand 2002) and beyond, in the social sciences. These have challenged the dichotomy between nature and culture, the division between the physical and the social, or between the physical and the cultural realms (Baviskar 2003; Latour 2014). The work on globalized resources, apprehended as a social construction, notably based on Raffestin (1980), also participated in this opening of geography to constructivist approaches (Magrin et al. 2015a). The environment, resulting from the interactions between physical, chemical, biological and social processes, becomes a hybrid and complex object for the social sciences, which calls for inter and multidisciplinarity (Rakoto Ramiarantsoa et al. 2012; Chartier and Rodary 2016; Dufour and Lespez 2020). As a social construct, it requires scientists to consider the interactions between development, planning and conservation policies, and geographers to help conceptualize their spatialization. The need to conserve resources upstream of productive activities and to impact them as little as possible downstream, the emergence of the notion of the commons, as well as ethical questions related to rights of access to resources, also raise questions about desirable futures and their underlying values (Ogé 2014, 2016).

The attention paid to the environment and the fact that geography is increasingly borrowing from anthropology and sociology have also played a role in renewing approaches to risks and crises associated with global changes (Sierra 2020). Moving away from a narrow focus on context (as with objectivist and culturalist approaches to risk) they now seek to identify the "overall dynamics", emphasizing representations, strategies, discourses and the construction of viewpoints (Coanus 2020, p. 738), and mobilize new concepts (fragility, vulnerability) (Sierra 2020). Taking into account the systemic nature of the risks linked to global change implies thinking about complexity, multiscalarity and temporality (Raimond et al. 2019). This means taking into account the "highly evolving systemic effects" of climate change in a context where the paradigm of uncertainty as theorized by Beck (1986), is being reinforced by the worsening of environmental degradation and the link between health crises and environmental crises (Cramer et al. 2020, p. 6).

Constructivist and critical approaches also challenge the notion of development traditionally attached to the study of "developing" countries. This takes place through deconstruction and decentering.

The term development has long been based on an economic approach (GDP growth and wealth inequality) and a modernist and linear Western vision of progress based on the economic take-off modeled by Rostow (1962). It was based on the idea that countries will "catch-up" and shift from "underdeveloped" countries to "developing" countries, including LDCs ("Least Developed Countries"), then to "emerging" or even "developed" countries. This understanding is part of a long history (colonial, then linked to development aid and current geopolitical issues) that has seen many theoretical approaches (from modernist to dependency approaches, from tropical geography to Third World geography). This is being challenged by a plurality of perspectives carried by postcolonial critical approaches and subaltern studies and more recently by post-development studies (Rist 2007; Ziai 2013, 2015; Dubresson 2020; Koop 2021).

This goes along with alternative thinking to the productivist conceptions of growth and economic development of the 1970s and 1980s, as promoted by neoliberal doctrines, as well as with by broader conceptions of development that integrate qualitative and relational indicators (Inequality-adjusted Human Development Index, well-being of populations, approaches in terms of capabilities).

The role of certain actors (women, indigenous and local communities, NGOs, diasporas) has more recently been integrated into social science research (Smouts 2005), which has opened up questions of equity and social justice. Country typologies have become more complex as development models conceived in the North have stumbled over national realities (Chaléard and Sanjuan 2017). New economic categories ("emerging" countries, "high-, middle- or low-income" countries), the relevance of which are debated (Piveteau et al. 2013), have been proposed attesting to the blurring of rankings and development trajectories (Chaléard 2014).

This paradigm shift in studies of development and global changes is currently reshaping the analysis of the links between the environment and development within geography (from "preservationism" to "exploitationism", from regulation by resource use to "neo-populism" that emphasizes human agentivity) (Haan 2000, p. 360). The concept of "sustainable development", which emerged in the 1980s, aimed to reduce the tensions and incompatibilities between environment and development, that is between economic growth and the conservation of natural resources. A useful conceptual tool for some (Emelianof 2007), a communication tool devoid of scientific meaning for others (Tsayem-Demase 2011; Chartier and Rodary 2016), the notion of sustainable development has been criticized for its ambiguity (origin, definitions, objectives), its empty rhetoric and its association with the market economy and capitalism (Theys 2014). Not only are modernist and universal values and principles being questioned, but also the very notion of development has been replaced in recent years by the notion of transition (Magrin and Ninot 2020), which involves rethinking questions of trajectories and temporality.

This notion of transition has been gradually replaced by the term "sustainability" in a societal and epistemological context strongly impacted by the debate on climate change and the Anthropocene (Felli 2015). This has been prompted by environmental crises (Bonneuil and Fressoz 2013), economic uncertainties and socio-economic problems that emerged in the post-2008 recessionary period, which some refer to as a polycrisis (Swilling and Annecke 2012). It goes hand in hand with the vanishing idea that the world is predictable and that a return to normality after a crisis is possible (Gunderson and Holling 2001): the linear development based on Rostow and the idea of a "stationary regime", carried by the notion of sustainable development, are undermined in a context where "structural uncertainties" are recognized and a "world of limits" acknowledged a situation that resilience approaches try to account for (Bonneuil and Fressoz 2013, pp. 39–42; Reghezza-Zit and Rufat 2015). Sustainability is situated in a broader context of social responses to global warming: it is expected to foster "ecological awareness" (Arias-Maldonado 2013, p. 429). In addition to recognizing that the category "natural" is no longer relevant, it takes greater account of the complexity and changing nature of environmental dynamics that impact human life and therefore the nonlinear dynamics of the human–natural system (Peyroux et al. 2014). Sustainability studies pay attention to practices, policies and actions. However, this concept, which mixes "scientific judgments, moral values and ideological positions" (Arias-Maldonado 2013, p. 433), remains debatable. Sustainability is seen as a "powerful idea" but a "vague concept" (Arias-Maldonado 2013, p. 428), a "strange theoretical abstraction that has nothing to do with our daily lives" ("the politics of never getting there") (Foster 2008, p. 66).

There is an ongoing debate about the relevance of other concepts (such as ecosystem services) (Arnauld de Sartre et al. 2014) as well as about the notion of Anthropocene (Cynorhodon 2020). The latter challenges our analytical frameworks (Latour 2014): by reformulating human agentivity in terms of moral and political responsibility, by reopening the classical question in anthropology "of what is common and specific in the different ways of inhabiting the earth" (Latour 2014, p. 7), by seizing all disciplines by the "urgency of doing something" and by questioning the "political relevance" of the work of researchers. More generally, it redefines "spatial and temporal coordinates as well as the right kind of agentivity" (Latour 2014, p. 16).

The decentering that is taking place concomitantly with this deconstruction in the field of geography, and more broadly in development studies, is part of a larger movement that challenges the vision of progress as certain, linear, sequential and based on the models of Western societies. It also questions the fact that developing countries will "catch up" with Western countries, recognizing that "leapfrogging" and bifurcations are possible (Ninot and Peyroux 2018; Magrin and Ninot 2020). This decentering also takes place in the scientific and operational field by recognizing asymmetries between various types of knowledge (Western, indigenous, vernacular, lay, scholarly and expert), by calling for stronger integration and involvement of different actors (Stock et al. 2021), which are now gaining momentum in the participatory science and open science movements.

From development to "transitions"

The concept of transition has tended to replace the concept of sustainable development in research and in certain public policies since the 2000s, although international institutions maintain their interest in "sustainability" (such as the 2015 Sustainable Development Goals, see above). Transition is generally understood dynamically as the passage from one state to another over time. Research focuses on the nature of changes, the dynamics of evolution, temporalities and increasingly on how to guide these transitions.

Initially, the term transition was used to refer to demographic, economic, urban and political transitions over the long-term (e.g. demographic transitions in Latin America, post-Soviet transitions in Eastern Europe or post-apartheid transitions in Southern Africa), emphasizing the interdependence of transition processes (Beucher and Mare 2020). In the environmental field it has taken several forms and adopts different epistemological positions.

The term transition, as it has been used since the 2000s, is part of the quest for a new societal model for Western capitalist countries impacted by the multiple crises of the early 21st century (Koop 2021). For Padovani and Lysaniuk (2019), studying transitions means defining upstream the "states" of the system and then analyzing the time of the transformation from one system to another. The change of state can be unexpected or planned and scheduled, which implies managing it. They for that matter consider the transition as a "period", the passage from one state to another, an intermediate state, a process between two ends within a constantly changing system (Padovani and Lysaniuk 2019, p. 10). This approach to transition builds on the notion of "recrystallization" by K. Lewin, an American psychologist. Coudroy de Lille et al. (2017) add that there is a difference between change – which is a form of continuity – and transition, which they define as "mutation in the course of a linear process that can be repeated in the form of cycles" (Padovani and Lysaniuk 2019, p. 10). For these authors, because of the dynamics involved, the transition implies a systemic rather than an analytical analysis: in their view, it is appropriate to study the "generating force of change from the initial state", the disequilibrium, and the emergence of a new state that corresponds to the final phase of the transition (Padovani and Lysaniuk 2029, p. 11).

Valeagas (2020) considers the transition as a fundamental reconfiguration rather than a simple adjustment. He calls for distinguishing transitions as defined by the observation of past or current phenomena (demographic, democratic) and transitions that are the result of an intention, "a watchword prescribing practices" as illustrated by the ecological transition (Valeagas 2020, p. 780) or the environmental transition that is being institutionalized through public policies (Beucher and Mare 2020).

Ecological and societal transition is at the heart of a specific interdisciplinary field (sustainability transition studies), which is reflected in the structuring of networks, academic institutions and journals (Peyroux et al. 2014; Koop 2021, p. 326). Some trends in sustainability transition studies focus on the analysis of socio-ecological or socio-technical systems (in terms of niches or regimes) in an often sectoral perspective (energy, water, transport). They are distinct from transition approaches in the field of urban studies, which take more into account issues of agentivity, power and learning (Baud et al. 2021). The notion of resilience is one of the concepts that helps us rethink transitions (such as vulnerability or adaptation) (Reghezza-Zit and Rufat 2015; Beucher and More 2020). For some, this concept is of particular interest to geographers to study the links between environment and development, for example, the resilience of socio-ecosystems (Lemoalle and Magrin 2014; Raimond et al. 2020). For others, its transposition from the field of ecology to that of the social sciences raises epistemological and normative problems (Metzger and Peyroux 2016).

Approach and objectives: understanding the complexity and diversity of the links between the environment and development from a territorial perspective

Given the increasing complexity of both the processes under consideration and the analytical frameworks that are needed, the objective of this collective work is to provide some analytical lenses for a deeper and renewed understanding of the links between environment and development. It focuses more particularly on the challenges posed by global changes at various territory levels. Rather than trying to find a consensus shared by a research team, the aim is to show, through a diversity of approaches and objects, how recent geography research deals with the issues identified above.

This collective book builds on the research work of a joint research unit, the UMR Prodig (Research Center on Developmental and Environmental Dynamics; Centre national de la recherche scientifique (CNRS), Université de Paris 1 Panthéon-Sorbonne, Institut de recherche pour le développement, Université Paris Cité, AgroParisTech, Sorbonne Université), conducted over the past 15 years on the links between the environment and development in Northern and Southern countries in the field of social sciences. Between 2014 and 2018, a research seminar was organized to clarify how researchers positioned themselves in the above-mentioned debates, and more specifically on how they addressed the dynamics of territories in the face of global changes. The objective was to highlight the theoretical, empirical and methodological contributions, bringing together authors who did not necessarily collaborate. The 14 resulting chapters have been discussed and reworked to cover three entry points (frames of reference, empirical research objects and the relationship between science and society), which now constitute the structure of this book. They therefore provide syntheses of research covering one or two decades as well as research avenues.

The objective of this book is to show how geography, a major discipline in the UMR, handles a diversity of objects (i.e. cities, transportation, food, agriculture, energy, mining activities, coastlines, watersheds), using different methodologies (qualitative and quantitative approaches, modeling, in situ measurements) and different fieldwork methods (surveys, observation). It also engages in a dialogue between disciplines or fields (geography, political ecology, heritage studies, urban studies). Finally, it locates the research results in the advances of social sciences and natural sciences, including the geosciences, and within the diversity of knowledge production (basic research, action research, expertise).

This work thus gives an account of how geography is currently being practiced in the shifting field of social sciences (Clément et al. 2021), how it addresses the debates highlighted above, in dialogue with other disciplines, and how it is anchored in a diversity of terrains (Africa, Latin America, Europe).

Our objective is not to collectively and unanimously define the two key terms (environment and development) or even to propose a unified approach to the interactions between the environment and development, but to show how we construct research objects that articulate these two dimensions by mobilizing different approaches and methodologies, all in the context of global changes the effects of which are being felt in ecosystems and territories.

The common point of these contributions is to address these relations between the environment and development through three types of interactions: society/physical environment; space/time scales; Northern/Southern countries. They underline the importance of the collaborations between the UMR Prodig and other research institutes in France and internationally (North and South), as well as with civil society organizations. They also show how research is shaped by the establishment of structures that support inter-UMR exchanges (notably Labex Dynamite, Collège international des sciences du territoire – CIST), collaborations with partners in the South (mixed international laboratories – LMI of the IRD, international research groups – GDRI of the CNRS and the IRD) and exchanges within area studies (scientific interest groups – Groupement d'intérêt scientifique on Latin America and Africa research in France).

Most of the contributions are based on an interdisciplinary approach that covers the disciplines represented in the UMR (human and physical geography, agronomy, agro-economics, political science, sociology, economics and urban planning) and beyond. They include other social sciences as well as natural sciences (biology, ecology, geology) and physical sciences. Some of the contributions are based on a transdisciplinary, participatory approach, integrating administrative authorities and civil society in companion modeling. This approach recognizes the diversity of information and knowledge production and dissemination through social networks and open data, for example, the rapid circulation of expert and non-expert knowledge. This goes along with more open debates with civil society, as well as with controversies (e.g. the contestation of the concept of nature and of the extent of climate change) that challenge the legitimacy of different forms of knowledge. This book also provides the opportunity to question our analytical, modeling and predictive capacities and their limits, particularly with regard to anticipating and measuring the long-term impacts of climate change.

Finally, by highlighting the interactions between urban development, risk management, production systems, and the protection of nature and biodiversity this collective book brings together issues that are often dealt with separately in the literature. Focusing on the fieldwork, both from a qualitative and a quantitative point of view, provides a detailed account of the processes at work, highlighting the diversity of contexts in terms of the physical and environmental manifestations, the political responses and the spatial dynamics of global changes.

Moreover, to deal with the relations between development and the environment, we adopt a cross-cutting perspective on territorial restructuring, paying attention to the construction and circulation of norms and structures of power relations. Looking critically at instruments, categories and representations, as well as modes of regulation and governance leads to a better understanding of the power relationships between actors and the way they contribute to socio-economic and socio-spatial discrimination and inequality. Studying the production and circulation of North/South and South/South models (Magrin et al. 2015b) shows how different fields of policy making connect and interact, ranging from the social construction of problems to the creation of spaces for deliberation, from modes of governance to the emergence of new referentials for public action.

This overview of research is not exhaustive: some topics addressed in the UMR, or certain geographical areas, could not be included in this book, although they contribute to the construction of our knowledge and to our comparative and interdisciplinary approaches: this includes analytical and methodological issues in relation to poverty in Europe (Ribardière et al. 2014), access to urban resources in a migratory context (Ribardière 2017), territorial recompositions and the circulation of international models in Asian cities (China, Japan, Southeast Asia) (Franck and Sanjuan 2015), public health issues in Europe and the South (Lysaniuk and Durrafour 2013; Lysaniuk and Tabeaud 2015), health–society–environment interactions in the Indian Ocean (Herbreteau and Taglioni 2015), comparative agricultures in the South (Cochet et al. 2018), the use of environmental geographic information in Latin America (Gautreau and Noucher 2013; Gautreau 2021), simulation and modeling applied to environmental issues in France (Delbart et al. 2015; Bétard et al. 2016) or in Southern countries (Bécu et al. 2014), geopolitics and territorial issues of the illicit drug economy in Southeast Asia (Chouvy 2013, pp. 1–28), or political issues around water in the Middle East (Brooks and Trottier 2020), to name the main ones.

Presentation of the book

The 14 chapters gathered in this book are divided into three parts. The first part composed of four chapters, examines the continuities or the shift of paradigms in a context of profound transformation of our societies, be it linked to the environmental changes observed in recent decades or to the rapid mutations linked to the diffusion of new technologies. The second part proposes seven themes – and therefore seven chapters – to discuss the effects of such changes on territories, representations and practices. Finally, in the third part, three chapters focus on the positions that we can adopt (e.g. research-action, expertise) to better understand the complexity of social relationships and their spatial inscription in a changing world.

The first part questions the frames of reference in which our research is embedded. What are the paradigms that bring us together and/or challenge us? Which models are being debated? The chapters underline how new paradigms are combined with old ones or replace each other: sustainable development and sustainability, sustainable development and resilience, development and transition. They take into account the circulation and transfers of models that are accelerating and diversifying today. Indeed, they are no longer limited to the application to the South of models developed in the North.

Chapter 1 discusses the relevance of the Northern models and their replicability in the South with a focus on food transition. Christine Raimond, Cécile Faliès, Angèle Proust and Bernard Tallet question whether it should be considered as a universal notion, a predictive model or a mere concept . This analysis is based on the fieldwork that has been carried out for a long time by members of UMR Prodig in developing and emerging countries in Africa, Asia and South America. It sheds light on heterogeneous situations from an historical, social, economic and political point of view. The authors highlight the importance of places and links between agricultural production and consumption, as well as the importance of asymmetrical power relations between actors and the ways in which they unfold in the highly diverse territories of the South. Therefore, this chapter first demonstrates that beyond the apparent global standardization of the model that it suggests, the food transition model is less universal than it seems. Then, it demonstrates that the trajectories are shaped not only by socio-economic factors, but also by political and cultural issues and the mobilization of actors in favor of fairer food systems.

Chapter 2 highlights the relevance of the concepts of risk and crisis to study the link between urban environment and development issues. These concepts, analyzed at different spatial and territorial scales, allow rethinking the relationships between society and the environment. They allow us to grasp paroxysmal situations that bring into play the multiple interactions between physico-chemical, biological and social dynamics in a geosystem. Based on the work carried out in South America and Tunisia, Alexis Sierra, Anaïs Béji, Axelle Croisé, Cyriaque Hattemer, Pascale Metzger, Marie Pigeolet and Irene Valittuto demonstrate that the spread of discourse on the crisis from one city to another and from one scale to another is the work of local actors. These actors project a distant crisis onto their own territory, according to their own approach to risk, which translates into controversies about the nature of development and the local environment.

In Chapter 3, Élisabeth Peyroux and Pascale Metzger look into the growing role of the environment in development policies. Based on a broad bibliographical synthesis in the field of urban research, the authors describe the way in which approaches to the city have evolved, from a mainly politico-economic reading to works integrating environmental issues, from both physical and political perspectives. They underline the epistemological challenges facing urban research. They also show the paradoxes and challenges facing research on the "sustainable city", between local innovations and global governance, and present some research avenues which, by opening up to new objects and new issues, are making the city an increasingly complex and hybrid object.

Chapter 4 argues that the pluralization of actors, categories and heritage elements requires going beyond the monumental, artistic and scientific dimensions of heritage. It proposes examining, with an alternative approach influenced by Southern theories, what constitutes a heritage practice in the cities of the South, whether or not it relates to heritage institutions. By crossing the results of surveys conducted in Valparaiso and Yaoundé, Sébastien Jacquot, Marie Morelle and Muriel Samé Ekobo propose a critical approach to the usual theoretical frameworks of "patrimonialization" or "heritage". They reveal the presence of an "infra-heritage", designating practices of preservation and transmission that are neither recognized by public policies nor formally qualified in heritage terms by the individuals or groups concerned, but which are key to understanding urban transformations.

The second part deals with shared research objects among Prodig researchers. Working on a wide variety of fields and themes helps to overcome a certain number of obstacles in the analysis of the interactions between environment and development. Our research objects contribute to a better understanding of the dynamics of environments and societies through a systemic approach and in the context of climate change, from physical processes to uses (resources, food, energy, transport, urban services). Questions regularly addressed are those of protection, degradation or exploitation (heritage, food, agricultural, energy, natural resources) issues of access to collective services (urban services, infrastructure, transportation), as well as those related to regional integration and associated public policies.

In Chapter 5, Angélique Palle and Yann Richard continue the reflection begun in the first part of this chapter on transition issues. They question the conceptual and political frameworks that underpin the objective of energy transition, which the EU has made a priority in numerous speeches and official documents in response to global change. By underlining the complex challenges related to scales within this policy framework, the authors question whether this transition is compatible with European energy integration, as it was conceived in the 1990s around the liberalization of energy markets. After showing that the European energy transition is situated at the crossroads of a multiplicity of research fields (the social and political construction of spatial scales, governance, regional integration and the construction of Europe), the authors describe the way in which the EU (as an institution) understands the notion of energy transition as political positioning, an economic strategy and an instrument of power. Finally, they identify the spatial construction models towards which the ongoing regional integration is moving the European energy space based on a series of spatial models.

Chapter 6 addresses the issue of transport in Africa and the way it shapes territories. Jérôme Lombard, Nora Mareï and Olivier Ninot propose taking a critical look at the developments, political orientations and societal choices that have guided the organization of transport networks, as well as their effects at different scales. They note a growing disconnection between the geographical scales of transport in Africa: while African countries are increasingly better connected to the world by various networks, including those of transport, it is still difficult, if not impossible, to travel by road between certain parts of national territories and in certain urban districts, particularly in capital cities. They demonstrate the major role played by national and supranational public policies, as well as the programs of international donors, in promoting transport corridors and metropolitan regions to the detriment of non-hierarchical and looser networks in less dense areas. At the end of this chapter, the authors propose several ways to consolidate the place of local territories within globalization.

Chapter 7 aims to better understand the role of digital tools in accessing transport services. Kei Tanikawa Obregón, Lisa Coulaud and Olivier Ninot propose, from a dual epistemological position – socio-technical systems and the circulation of models – a discussion on the transposability of intelligent mobility models. ICT (Information and Communication Technologies) participate in the definition of new forms of urban governance of large cities in the South. Based on research located in Mexico City, Accra and Dakar, the authors discuss the urban fabric and development models taking into account the role of informality in accessing individual and collective transport services. This chapter shows that despite the innovations promised by ICT, the economic system is not undergoing a real transformation. In this context, the transition to a new model can only be made by taking informality into account in the organization of transport networks.

Chapter 8 sheds light on the ways in which the formalization and territorialization of gold mining in Africa are put in place in order to question their socio-economic and environmental effects on development at the local level. Based on the fieldwork carried out in a wide variety of countries in the northern part of Africa, Anna Dessertine, Raphaëlle Chevrillon-Guibert, Laurent Gagnol, Julie Betabelet, Lamine Diallo, Robin Petit-Roulet, Edith Sawadogo, Tongnoma Zongo and Géraud Magrin discuss the hypothesis that the current period is characterized by a tension between the repression of gold panning in favor of industrial mines and the State's takeover of an artisanal sector that is being mechanized, producing contrasting effects in terms of development and environmental impacts. After describing the different forms of emergence or re-emergence of the gold resource, this chapter questions the power issues that govern its regulation. Finally, it discusses the relationship between its exploitation and the development of territories.

Chapter 9 provides a synthesis of renewed approaches dealing with relations between cities and the countryside, in a context of accelerated metropolization and globalization. Martine Berger and Jean-Louis Chaléard deconstruct the idea that there is a gradient between urban and rural spaces and highlight the inequalities and solidarities between cities and the countryside. Through personal research and doctoral supervision in a wide variety of fields in the South and North, the authors demonstrate the recent evolutions of the relations between cities and the countryside, with their similarities and their disparities, between interactions and tensions. Thus, while the North has a contact zone called peri-urban, the South generally sees a vast and plural periphery expanding. The agricultural question allows for discussion about complementarities, mobility, solidarity and inequalities.

Chapter 10 looks at the political and organizational challenges of using climate models for agricultural adaptation to climate change. Malika Madelin and Évelyne Mesclier discuss the hypothesis that the current structuring of climate change data tends to produce simplified information on a global scale with a focus on a few variables. This leads to an adaptation paradigm that favors equally simple and global discourses and the dissemination of a number of "good solutions" at the expense of others. Based on a comparative approach between France and Peru, the authors demonstrate that although scientific models are increasingly precise, they vary according to the territories, with equally varied uses. They suggest consideration of two scales, that of the States and their representation of vulnerabilities, and that of the farmers who translate national policies in a highly heterogeneous manner.

Chapter 11 concludes this thematic section with a discussion of the way in which watershed functioning is apprehended. Anchored in a naturalistic approach to processes, hydrogeography has been able to evolve thanks to the contributions of close critical approaches such as political ecology or critical physical geography.

Integrated research on watersheds highlights the complexity of the social, political and economic processes that drive them. Past, present and future trajectories are linked to climatic contexts or to environmental management practices, particularly those related to soil (e.g. urbanization, intensification or agricultural abandonment). Vincent Viel, Émilie Lavie, Guillaume Brousse, Benoît Carlier, Luc Michler, Mathilde Resch, Gashin Shashavari and Gilles Arnaud-Fassetta demonstrate that the so-called natural processes that drive the functioning of watersheds are strongly anthropized. The authors argue that the epistemological and methodological contexts have made it possible to refine the understanding of the complexity of the processes, leading to a rethinking of the management of hydrosystems.

The third part highlights the approaches, methods and sources used within Prodig and the way in which they participate in the different modes of knowledge production. Among our competences, there is first of all the collective capacity to combine advanced analysis of environmental changes with social, political and economic changes at different scales using both quantitative (field metrology, statistics, cartographic and spatial data processing) and qualitative methodologies (mainly field surveys). Second, our field-centered approach goes along with a diversity of geographical areas (on four continents, in gray areas that are difficult to access for security reasons) and work in partnership. The research brings together, in varying proportions, the collection of existing data (which is hampered by a lack of human resources!), the creation and coupling of quantitative and qualitative data, modeling, data processing, the development of methodological tools (including collaborations with Géotheca/Université Paris Cité and the Spatial Center) and spatial analysis. Finally, a last competence of the UMR is based the a posteriori valorization, in forms as diverse as the frequent participation in expert appraisals and/or the diffusion of research results via Géoportail.

Chapter 12 proposes an analysis of the ecological transition in France via the example of coastal zone management. Frédéric Bertrand and Brice Anselme draw on the synthesis of results from a decade of research on paradigm shifts in state management policies. They highlight a contrasted assessment of the ecological transition of the French metropolitan and ultra-marine coastlines, which have not succeeded in finding an intermediate position between weak and strong sustainability models. The authors thus show that adaptive responses to global change depend on the local combination of multiple factors, such as the mobilization of existing legal tools, the evaluation of costs and benefits, the valuation of long-term benefits, the methods of communication and consultation, and the restoration of coastal areas released for protection purposes (e.g. depoldering).

Chapter 13 analyzes the way the IPCC (Intergovernmental Panel on Climate Change) is functioning and how its results and publications are used. After recalling the context of the creation of the IPCC, whose emergence appears to be an historical process of gathering and making available scientific work from various disciplines and covering various fields, Hubert Cochet and Jean-Claude Bergès highlight the discrepancy between the richness of databases gathered by the IPCC experts and their recommendations, on the one hand, and the sometimes, somewhat simplistic use made of it by certain scientific teams for political promotion purposes, on the other hand. To do this, they use the example of the adaptation of Tanzanian agriculture to climate change, which shows that the partial use of the IPCC results from Volume 1 of the fifth report can lead to conclusions that are the antithesis of those advocated by many experts who participated in the drafting of Volume 2 of the same report or those put forward by other research communities involved in these issues.

Chapter 14 concludes this collection of chapters with the synthesis of a not so common research practice: expertise. Based on their experience in this area around Lake Chad, Géraud Magrin, Charline Rangé, Audrey Koumraït Mbagogo, Abdourahamani Mahamadou, Jacques Lemoalle and Christine Raimond emphasize that expertise constitutes one of the instruments of the political work of researchers, which allows them, at a time when access to the field through the usual channels is difficult, to influence the balance of power at the heart of the process of selecting ideas that precedes and/or justifies action. The authors thus show that the knowledge and messages produced through expertise essentially affect the sponsors (international donors), but that ideas also circulate beyond them to national decision-makers or society, according to complex infusion processes. Networks of research/experts/investigators/donors are then structured and form a hybrid complex where research and expertise are embedded, likely to feed research work. The North/South asymmetry that is becoming more pronounced, however, poses limits in terms of the legitimacy of the ideas put into circulation.

References

Arias-Maldonado, M. (2013). Rethinking sustainability in the Anthropocene. *Environmental Politics*, 22(3), 428–446.

Arnauld de Sartre, X., Oszwald, J., Castro, M., Dufour, S. (2014). *Political ecology des services écosystémique.* Peter Lang AG, Bern.

Baud, I., Jameson, S., Peyroux, É., Scott, D. (2021). The urban governance configuration: A conceptual framework for understanding complexity and enhancing transitions to greater sustainability in cities. *Geography Compass* [Online]. Available at: https://onlinelibrary.wiley.com/doi/10.1111/gec3.12562 [Accessed 15 September 2021].

Baviskar, A. (2003). For a cultural politics of natural resources. *Economic and Political Weekly*, 38(48), 5051–5055.

Beck, U. (1986). *La société du risque. Sur la voie d'une autre modernité.* Aubier, Paris.

Bécu, N., Raimond, C., Garine, E., Deconchat, M., Kokou, K. (2014). Coupling environmental and social processes to simulate the emergence of a Savannah landscape mosaic under shifting cultivation and assess its sustainability. *Journal of Artificial Society and Social Simulation*, 17(1) [Online]. Available at: https://www.jasss.org/17/1/1.html [Accessed 30 September 2021].

Bertrand, C. and Bertrand, D. (2002). *Une géographie traversière. L'environnement à travers territoires et territorialités*. Arguments, Paris.

Bétard, F., Dansurand, G., Poiraud, A., Viette, P., Kuhnel, A. (2016). Multifinality in geoheritage inventories: A cross-cutting approach of geotourism and geoconservation issues in the "Causses du Quercy" Regional Natural Park (Lot, SW France). In *Actes du congrès international – Les inventaires du géopatrimoine*, Cornée, A., Egoro, G., De Wever, P., Lalanne, A., Duranthon, F. (eds). Soc. Géol. Fr., Toulouse.

Beucher, S. and Mare, M. (2020). Cadrage épistémologique de la notion de transition en sciences humaines et sociales et en géographie. *Bulletin de l'Association de Géographes Français*, 2020–4, 383–394.

Bonneuil, C. and Fressoz, J.B. (2013). *L'événement anthropocène. La terre, l'histoire et nous*. Le Seuil, Paris.

Brooks, D. and Trottier, J. (2020). Moving water from last to first in the Middle East peace process. *International Journal of Water Resources Development*, 37(4), 741–745.

Chaléard, J.L. (2014). Réflexions de géographe sur des mots autour du développement. In *Communication au "séminaire central"*. UMR Prodig, Paris.

Chaléard, J.-L. and Sanjuan, T. (2017). *Géographie du développement. Territoires et mondialisation dans les Suds*. Armand Colin, Paris.

Chartier, D. and Rodary, E. (eds) (2016). *Manifeste pour une géographie environnementale : Géographie, écologie, politique*. Presses de Sciences Po, Paris.

Chouvy, P.-A. (ed.) (2013). *An Atlas of Trafficking in Southeast Asia. The Illegal Trade in Arms, Drugs, People, Counterfeit Goods and Natural Resources in Mainland Southeast Asia*. IRASEC, London/Bangkok.

Clément, V., Stock, M., Volvey, A. (eds) (2021). *Mouvements de géographie. Une science sociale au tournant*. Éditions Universitaires de Rennes, Rennes.

Coanus, T. (2020). Risque. Epistémologie. In *Dictionnaire critique de l'Anthropocène*, Cynorhodon (ed.). CNRS, Paris.

Cochet, H., Ducourtieux, O., Garambois, N. (2018). *Systèmes agraires et changement climatique au sud. Les chemins de l'adaptation*. Editions Quae, Versailles.

Coudroy de Lille, L., Rivière-Honegger, A., Rolland, L., Volin, A. (2017). Notion à la une : Transition. *Géoconfluences* [Online]. Available at: http://geoconfluences.ens-lyon.fr/informations-scientifiques/a-la-une/notion-a-la-une/notion-transition [Accessed 15 September 2021].

Cramer, W., Criqui, P., Guégan, J.F., Le Treut, H., Lebel, T., Lecocq, F., Le Roux, X., Malijean-Dubois, S. (2020). La recherche sur les changements globaux à l'épreuve de la Covid-19 [Online]. Available at: http://www.bruno-latour.fr/sites/default/files/139-AAA-Washington.pdf [Accessed 15 September 2021].

Cynorhodon (2020). *Dictionnaire critique de l'Anthropocène*. CNRS, Paris.

Delbart, N., Dunesme, S., Lavie, E., Madelin, M., Goma, R. (2015). Remote sensing of Andean mountain snow cover to forecast water discharge of Cuyo rivers. *Journal of Alpine Research*, 103(2).

Dubresson, A. (2020). Développement. In *Dictionnaire critique de l'Anthropocène*, Cynorhodon (ed.). CNRS, Paris.

Dufour, S. and Lespez, L. (2020). *Géographie de l'environnement : La nature au temps de l'anthropocène*. Armand Colin, Paris.

Emelianof, C. (2007). La ville durable : L'hypothèse d'un tournant urbanistique en Europe. *L'information géographique*, 71, 48–65.

Felli, R. (2015). La durabilité ou l'escamotage du développement durable. *Raisons politiques*, 60, 149–160 [Online]. Available at: https://doi.org/10.3917/rai.060.0149 [Accessed 15 September 2021].

Foster, J. (2008). *The Sustainability Mirage: Illusion and Reality in the Coming War on Climate Change*. Earthscan, London.

Franck, M. and Sanjuan, T. (eds) (2015). *Territoires de l'urbain en Asie. Une nouvelle modernité ?* CNRS, Paris.

Gautreau, P. (2021). *La Pachamama en bases de données : Géographie politique de l'information environnementale contemporaine*. Éditions de l'IHEAL, Paris.

Gautreau, P. and Noucher, M. (2013). Gouvernance informationnelle de l'environnement et partage en ligne des données publiques. Politiques et pratiques de l'opendata environnemental (Amérique du sud – France). *Introduction au numéro spécial de la revue. Networks and Communication Studies*, 27(1–2), 5–21.

George, P. (1971). *L'environnement*. PUF, Paris.

Gunderson, L.H. and Holling, C.S. (2001). *Understanding Transformations in Human and Natural Systems*. Island Press, Washington, DC.

Haan, L.J. (2000). The question of development and environment in geography in the era of globalization. *Geo Journal*, 50, 359–367.

Herbreteau, V. and Taglioni, F. (2015). Interactions santé-sociétés-environnement : Étude du paludisme et de la leptospirose à Mayotte. Report, IRD/Ministère de l'Outre-mer, 2012–2015, IRD, 46.

Koop, K. (2021). La géographie du développement a perdu le Nord et alors ! Plaidoyer pour une géographie des transitions sociétales. In *Mouvements de géographie. Une science sociale au tournant*, Clément, V., Stock, M., Volvey, A. (eds). Presses Universitaires de Rennes, Rennes.

Latour, B. (2014). Anthropology at the time of the Anthropocene – A personal view of what is to be studied. *Lecture at the American Anthropologists Association Meeting*, Washington, 1–16 [Online]. Available at: http://www.bruno-latour.fr/sites/default/files/139-AAA-Washington.pdf [Accessed 30 August 2021].

Lemoalle, J. and Magrin, G. (eds) (2014). Le développement du lac Tchad : Situation actuelle et futurs possibles. Synthesis report, Contributions intégrales des experts, 66.

Lombard, J., Mesclier, É., Velut, S. (eds) (2006). *La mondialisation côté Sud. Acteurs et territoires*. IRD, Paris.

Lysaniuk, B. and Durrafour, F. (2013). L'apport des SHS dans un programme de santé publique : L'exemple de la géographie et de l'approche SMA dans Tolimmunpal. *Communication au séminaire de l'UMR 216 MERIT*, Paris.

Lysaniuk, B. and Tabeaud, B. (2015). Les santés vulnérables des Suds. *L'Espace Géographique*, 14, 229–244.

Magrin, G. and Ninot, O. (2020). Transitions et développement en Afrique : Un continent d'incertitudes. *Bulletin de l'Association de Géographes Français*, 2020–4, 395–411.

Magrin, G. and Thibaud, B. (2020). L'Anthropocène sous les tropiques : Tropicalité et développement à l'heure des changements globaux. *Belgeo*, 3 [Online]. Available at: http://journals.openedition.org/belgeo/42708 [Accessed 5 October 2021].

Magrin, G., Chauvin, E., Lavie, E., Perrier-Bruslé, L., Redon, M. (2015a). Introduction. Les ressources, enjeux géographiques d'un objet pluriel. In *Ressources mondialisées. Essais de géographie politique*, Redon, M., Magrin, G., Chauvin, E., Lavie, E., Perrier-Bruslé, L. (eds). Publications de la Sorbonne, Paris.

Magrin, G., Mesclier, E., Piveteau, A. (2015b). Quand les Suds investissent dans les Suds : Un basculement aux contours encore indistincts. Introduction au dossier. *Autrepart*, 76(4), 203–228 [Online]. Available at: https://horizon.documentation.ird.fr/exl-doc/pleins_textes/divers19-12/010069035.pdf [Accessed 5 October 2021].

Meztger, P. and Peyroux, É. (2016). Comment la résilience s'impose à la pensée et à l'action : Usage rhétorique et effets politiques dans la planification urbaine à Johannesburg et la gestion des risques au Rímac (Lima). *XXXIIèmes Journées ATM de LILLE. Catastrophes, vulnérabilités et résiliences dans les pays en développement*, Lille.

Ninot, O. and Peyroux, É. (2018). Révolution numérique et développement en Afrique : Une trajectoire singulière. *Questions Internationales*, 90.

Ogé, F. (2014). L'environnement comme nouveau facteur d'incompréhension et de tension entre les cultures. Communication au "séminaire central", UMR Prodig, Paris.

Ogé, F. (2016). La résurgence des biens communs : Passerelles pour articuler environnement et développement ? Communication au "séminaire central", UMR Prodig, Paris.

Padovani, F. and Lysaniuk, B. (2019). *Les gestions des transitions. Anticiper, subir, réagir, planifier*. L'Harmattan, Paris.

Peyroux, É., Scott, D., Baud, I., Jameson, S. (2014). Spatial knowledge management and participatory governance: Rethinking the trajectories of urban, socio-economic and environmental change and the politics of "sustainability" in Southern cities, Final analytical framework. Report, Chance2Sustain EADI.

Piveteau, A., Rougier, E., Nicet-Chenaf, D. (eds) (2013). *Emergences capitalistes aux Suds*. Karthala, Paris.

Raffestin, C. (1980). *Pour une géographie du pouvoi*. Litec, Paris.

Raimond, C., Sylvestre, F., Zakinet, D., Abderamane, M. (eds) (2019). *Le Tchad des Lacs. Les zones humides sahéliennes au défi du changement global*. IRD Editions, Paris.

Raimond, C., Mbagogo, A., Madjigoto, R., Zakinet, D. (2020). Le lac Fitri (Tchad) face à la montée des insécurités. Repenser la gouvernance d'une zone humide autour d'un pouvoir local fort. In *Conflits et violences dans le bassin du lac Tchad*, Chauvin, E., Baroin, C., Seignobos, C. (eds). IRD Editions, Paris.

Rakoto Ramiarantsoa, H., Blanc-Pamard, C., Pinton, F. (2012). *Géopolitique et environnement. Les leçons de l'expérience malgache*. IRD Editions, Paris.

Reghezza-Zit, M. and Rufat, S. (eds) (2015). *Resilience Imperative: Uncertainty, Risks and Disasters*. ISTE Press, London, and Elsevier, Oxford.

Ribardière, A. (2017). Du Oaxaca à la ville de Mexico : L'accès aux ressources urbaines. *EchoGéo*, 40 [Online]. Available at: http://journals.openedition.org/echogeo/14961 [Accessed 29 September 2021].

Ribardière, A., Bonerandi-Richard, E., Martin, M., Merchez, L. (2014). La pauvreté dans l'espace européen : Grilles de lecture. In *La pauvreté en Europe. Une approche géographique*, Bonerandi-Richard, E. and Boulineau, E. (eds). Presses Universitaires de Rennes, Rennes.

Rist, G. (2007). *Le développement. Histoire d'une croyance occidentale*. Presses de Sciences Po, Paris.

Rostow, W.W. (1962). *Les étapes de la croissance économique*. Le Seuil, Paris.

Sierra, A. (2020). Risque. Histoire du concept. In *Dictionnaire critique de l'Anthropocène*, Cynorhodon (ed.). CNRS, Paris.

Smouts, M.C. (ed.) (2005). *Le développement durable : Les termes du débat*. Armand Colin, Paris.

Stock, M., Volvey, A., Clément, V. (2021). Conclusion générale. In *Mouvements de géographie. Une science sociale au tournant*, Clément, V., Stock, M., Volvey, A. (eds). Presses Universitaires de Rennes, Rennes.

Swilling, M. and Annecke, E. (2012). *Just Transitions: Explorations of Sustainability in an Unfair World*. Juta, Cape Town and United Nations University Press, Tokyo.

Theys, J. (2014). Le développement durable face à sa crise : Un concept menacé, sous-exploité ou dépassé ? *Développement durable et territoires*, 5(1) [Online]. Available at: http://journals.openedition.org/developpementdurable/10196 [Accessed 24 September 2021].

Tsayem-Demase, M. (2011). *Géopolitique du développement durable*. Presses universitaires de Rennes, Rennes.

Valeagas, F. (2020). Transition. Ecologie. In *Dictionnaire critique de l'Anthropocène*, Cynorhodon (ed.). CNRS, Paris.

Volvey, A., Stock, M., Calbérac, Y. (2021). Spatial turn, tournant spatial, turnant géographique. In *Mouvements de géographie. Une science sociale au tournant*, Clément, V., Stock, M., Volvey, A. (eds). Presses Universitaires de Rennes, Rennes.

Ziai, A. (2013). The discourse of "development" and why the concept should be abandoned. *Development in Practice*, 23, 123–136.

Ziai, A. (2015). Post-development: Premature burials and haunting ghosts. *Development and Change*, 46(4), 833–853.

PART 1

How to Rethink Frames of Reference: Paradigms, Models, Epistemological and Theoretical Foundations

The Food Transition, a Unique Model?

1.1. Introduction

If, since the beginning of the 2000s, the concept of transition has often replaced the concept of sustainable development (Loorbach 2010; Falque et al. 2017), it is because it proposes a sequence of methods and expected effects that make it more concrete and therefore more likely to be generalized (Godelier 1990; Hopkins 2008). Whether the transition is "imposed" by a stress or a disaster, or proposed as part of a public policy, the question of managing from a prior state to a second state is posed according to a temporality and modalities of support that affect territories and populations more or less brutally (Padovani and Lysaniuk 2019).

Among its many variations, the food transition retains attention because, as a "total social fact", food calls for a broad multidisciplinary approach between human sciences (anthropology, geography, sociology, history) and nutritional sciences (de Garine 1988), as well as for taking into account the conditions of production (agronomy, ecology) and distribution (economy, logistics), which have changed considerably in the context of globalization. Depending on countries' levels of development (more or less advanced development, emerging and developed (Chaléard and Sanjuan 2017)), the inequalities in access to food and the awareness of the negative externalities of contemporary food systems, the food transition directly questions the links between the environment and development and how they are taken into account in the food policies and programs implemented in its name.

The food transition is an evolutionary model used since the 2000s. It is based on the assumption that diets are changing as a result of lifestyles, and on the global scale observation of a rapid evolution in eating habits as a result of globalization,

Chapter written by Christine RAIMOND, Cécile FALIÈS, Angèle PROUST and Bernard TALLET.

urbanization and income growth (Collomb 1989). As household incomes rise, there is a tendency for households to reduce their consumption of staple grains in favor of animal products, fruits and vegetables.

The model is based on three successive periods, linked to those of the demographic transition: the end of famine, then dietary diversification and the decline in physical activity, and finally the reversal of these trends and a rebalancing of the diet (Popkin 1993). Born in the North as an explanatory model a posteriori of certain trends, is this model relevant and applicable in the South and can it serve as a basis for food policies or programs to help the desired advancement of phase 3? Beyond an easy expression to account for changes in food systems, is it relevant to use the same expression to cover very different evolutionary dynamics depending on the country's level of development? The use of the same expression to designate the reduction in the proportion of protein in the diet of developed countries, the provision of basic food needs in the least developed countries, or the explosion of obesity and cardiovascular diseases in emerging countries, raises questions about the application of this model to many contrasting situations, particularly from the point of view of the scales of analysis, the stakeholders at work and the political underpinnings of the actions undertaken in favor of the food transition.

Research conducted by UMR Prodig on agricultural production processes and urban–rural relations (ANR PeriSud, PeriMarge, Plantadiv) and doctoral research (Le Gall 2011; Faliès 2012; Raton 2012; Leloup 2018; Proust forthcoming) have shown the importance of the places and links between agricultural production and consumption, as well as the importance of asymmetrical power relations between stakeholders in very diverse territories in the South. This diversity of situations and issues raises questions about the food transition, between a universal and predictive model, just like the demographic transition, or a simple concept to be analyzed in the light of heterogeneous situations from the historical, social, economic and political points of view.

Based on this experience in developing countries (Sahelian Africa) and emerging countries (Chile, Brazil, Mexico, India), as well as complementary bibliographic research, this chapter aims to analyze the use of this food transition model considering inequalities and the need for social equity in terms of food (quantity and quality), both in developed and emerging countries as well as in developing countries. We show, based on the challenges of the food transition and the apparent global uniformity it suggests, that this model is less universal than it seems and, above all, that beyond the socio-economic aspects that define the succession of the three phases, political and cultural issues shape the trajectories and mobilizations of stakeholders for fairer food systems.

1.2. The food transition to the test of temporalities and territories

According to J.L. Rastoin (2018), humanity is experiencing its fifth food transition, after the transition from the use of fire to prepare food (culinary techniques and commensality), that of domestication and the appearance of agriculture (agricultural production), then the appearance of large cities and the division of labor (professional specialization), and finally the Industrial Revolution (agrifood and globalization). The last transition started in the 1990s with the awareness of the negative externalities of contemporary food and agricultural systems and refocused food systems on the local aspect. Even more recently, new slogans call for a "food transition" which replaces a food system based on supplies in large distribution channels with a system based on more equitable and healthier local distribution channels. We return here to the different meanings that the food transition takes.

1.2.1. *An expression built on the demographic transition model*

The term transition is always associated with a qualifier that gives it its field of application: demographic, economic, epidemiological, urban, migratory, energy, food or landscape transition. All these expressions use the word transition to designate the passage from one regime, or one mode of operation, to another, and this takes place over time. The reference example remains that of the demographic transition, which is very much in use in geography. Adding to this is the more recent trend of ecological transition which refers to a change in consumption patterns, as well as to public policy production and distribution.

According to P. Collomb (1989), the demographic transition is characterized by a first phase of decreasing mortality and increasing population, which is accompanied by an increase in food needs and, in some cases, by famines. The second phase observes a decline in the birth rate, which leads to a slowdown in population growth and then, in a third phase, a balancing of the pattern between births and deaths. The food transition model is built on this demographic transition model and is concomitant with it.

The food transition model is reinforced by urban transition. This marks an inversion of the relationship between rural and urban population, with first a strong growth in migratory flows to the cities, then a drop in the migratory balance and finally a natural increase in the intra-urban population (Cosio-Zavala and Lopez Gareri 2004). Population increase in the city is accompanied by a change in lifestyles and diets, with in particular an increase in meat intake. By reorganizing relationships with the countryside and food supply methods, the urban transition marks a profound change in the functioning and management of territories, as well as in food practices (Steck 2006) which accelerate the process of food transition.

Beyond the demographic and urban transitions, the work of nutritionist Barry Popkin has had a significant influence on food studies and the definition of the food transition. His nutritional transition model became widely known in the 1990s. It is used to apprehend the transformations of food practices linked to migrations and the passage from a traditional rural society to a developed and urbanized society.

The model is described by Popkin (1993) in three phases:

– An end to the famine following an increase in the average income of households, resulting in an increase in the consumption of cereals and, more specifically, of the so-called "superior" cereals (wheat and rice), having benefited from agricultural progress marked by an increase in yields.

– Dietary diversification, with a decrease in the consumption of cereals and an increase in sugars, saturated fats and animal proteins, especially meat. This evolution is coupled with a decrease in physical activity and has as main consequences changes in stature as well as the emergence of diseases (e.g. high blood pressure or high cholesterol).

– The third phase observes the beginning of a reversal of the trends of the preceding phase.

These developments go hand in hand with changing eating habits, an increasing consumption of animal products and industrially processed foods. This observation sums up – excessively – phase 2, while waiting for the reversal of the trend that heralds phase 3. From this evolutionary diagram, we can see that the definition stricto sensu corresponds to the increase in the protein and fat contents of animal origin in a diet. This seems to be corroborated by the trends towards uniformity in dietary patterns Rastoin and Ghersi (2010).

1.2.2. *A multi-speed transition*

In developed countries, the last dietary transition corresponds to the nutritional transition described by Popkin which took place over two centuries, starting with the agricultural revolution of the 18th and 19th centuries (which reduced the frequency of famines in Europe) and the Industrial Revolution. With the rise of manufactured goods, professional specialization and urbanization following World War II, consumption patterns evolved. Agro-industrial production became intensified for standardized urban consumption. It led to major nutritional imbalances which tended to stabilize with consumer awareness of a healthier diet.

Depending on the development trajectory and the rate of urbanization, the transition to phases 2 and 3 is more or less rapid and takes place at contrasting rates. In Egypt, for example, phase 2 occurred in the 1980s, when abundant energy availability encouraged increasing urbanization (Galal 2002). In Vietnam, it was later (Pulliat 2017, p. 63, Figure 1.1):

> Between 2002 and 2010, in urban areas, meat consumption increased from 21.6 to 25.2 kg per person per year, seafood consumption from 14.4 to 16.8 kg [...], while rice consumption decreased [...]. The consumption of dairy products, almost in existence before the opening to international trade, is spreading and benefits from an enhanced image among consumers – they are considered important for children's health.

Surveys conducted in developing countries (Delpeuch and Maire 2004; Jacobi et al. 2010) show that obesity and chronic food-related diseases are gaining ground. These countries are rapidly beginning a transition from phase 1 of "famine relief", (from which all have not yet fully emerged), to phase 2 of "degenerative diseases". While there are changes in diet at work as a result of rising standards of living, these are also the result of the extension of globalized forms of distribution (supermarkets, distribution firms, etc.) which disseminate standards and types of low-quality, high-calorie products that cause significant deficiencies, with very accessible pricing policies (Fumey 2007). Malnutrition is no longer only caused by large quantities of undiversified products, as in phase 2 of the food transition in industrialized countries, but it is also the result of public policies. These policies are largely inspired by an economic model that promotes low wages in the industrial sector in order to maintain the comparative advantage of low labor costs, especially in industries geared towards exporting to the global market. Mexico with the rise of the "*maquiladoras*" (low-cost labor industries) presents a caricature of this dual mechanism of wage restraint and access to low-cost food (Tallet 2012). A key element is the promotion of low-cost food imports and the distribution of low-quality products. Thus, new consumption patterns are imposed and supported by the development of highly profitable domestic and foreign agro-industrial industries.

Some countries that are gradually overcoming food insecurity problems are facing chronic food-related diseases, regardless of the phase the country is in. The cities are the first to be affected by these changes, due to their exposure to massive imports of manufactured food products and to the active advertising and marketing of food groups. Sedentary lifestyles and a decrease in daily physical activity (employment and leisure), diets high in energy, fat and free sugars, the emergence of fast food, carbonated and/or alcoholic beverages: all of these factors, along with smoking and urban lifestyles, contribute to the greater frequency of chronic diseases such as diabetes, cardio or cerebrovascular diseases and certain cancers, as well as to excessive weight and obesity which are often early markers (Salem and Fournet 2020).

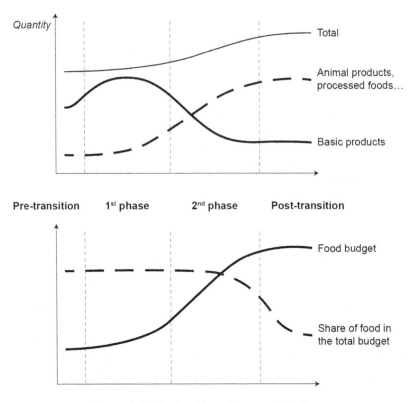

Figure 1.1. *The food transition model in three phases for the case of Vietnam (Pulliat 2017)*

The idea of an inevitable succession of the three phases of the model is undermined since the limits of phase 2 (obesity and related diseases) can be observed in poor populations that have not yet entered it. Many countries are still in phase 2, with no prospect of moving on to phase 3 and to the return to a more balanced diet that it heralds. There is even a diffusion of the phase 2 food model, linked to the mass of the poor or low-income population and "easy" eating habits. In low- and middle-income countries, we observe the coexistence of two types of malnutrition (from both deficiency and excess), with the coexistence of problems of under and overnutrition (Delpeuch and Maire 1997; Finney Rutten 2010). This is the case in Brazil, where the "multiplicity of hunger" was denounced in the 1950s by the thinker Josué de Castro (1951).

1.2.3. *Uniformity challenged by cultural and dietary habits*

In very densely populated countries with strong cultural diversity, such as India or China, the food transition model works poorly (Landy 2009). India, for example, is a largely vegetarian country for which a transition to a predominantly meat-based diet is difficult to envisage. Can a model be considered valid if a country of 1.1 billion inhabitants is excluded from it?

In these countries, the food transition is not thought of on a national scale, but rather on the scale of regions or specific categories of the population. In India, the transition is taking place among the urban middle classes, who are the first to change their eating habits (Landy 2009), as it is in emerging countries where new consumption patterns are being observed with a middle class concerned about its eating practices (Paddeu 2012). In the South and Northeast Indian states, levels of meat consumption are much higher than those in the Center and Northwest. This difference is not related to higher individual income but rather to the proportion of Muslims, Christians or members of the "lower castes" compared to the "high castes". In other words, it is not economic variables but rather cultural and political variables that explain meat consumption levels in India. There is therefore nothing mechanical about the "nutritional transition" model (Landy 2009). This "Indian exception" shows a steady decline in calorie and protein intake from animal sources since the 1980s (Deaton and Drèze 2009), with less than 5 kg per person per year (Landy 2009), well below the world's average of 43 kg and the 54 kg consumed by neighboring China.

The theoretical homogenization of food, often criticized (Bricas and Seck 2004), is to be linked to the market and the cost of raw materials. While the increase in sugar and fat consumption is one of the factors explaining the explosion of obesity worldwide, it has only been possible because the price of these two commodities has fallen over the last 40 years. Ultra-processed food, with its "hidden" fats and sugars, is a major contributor to some of the ills of the food transition. Conversely, cultural preferences persist in food choices and guide food systems along their own, regionalized trajectories (Rastoin 2018).

The food transition model seems to be less universal than the demographic transition model to which it is often compared. Popkin developed it on the basis of mainly economic and social factors rather than political ones, which we propose to reconsider here given the influence of certain political decisions observed at national and international levels in the food transition.

1.3. The confrontation of a linear model to the diversity of public food policies

Faced with the diversity of situations, public policies target very different objectives by playing on food supply and demand without directly addressing issues related to income and poverty at the heart of the notion of transition, on the one hand, nor those of the balance of power existing between stakeholders of production, marketing and consumption, on the other hand. The widening of inequalities observed during the 20th century, between countries and within each country, blurred a simplistic interpretation of the food transition and the public policies designed in its name. We base this demonstration on the example of countries at varying levels in each of the three phases of the food transition, while emphasizing the emergence of new questions.

1.3.1. *Public policies and food to respond to situations of food shortage*

This scenario brings together countries that are mostly in phase 1, marked by chronic deficits in agricultural production and very low incomes that only allow access, when possible, to food at low prices and with little diversity. In these developing countries, public policies mainly aim to improve the food situation of the poorest populations. Two paths are favored: increasing the supply, through agricultural policies aimed at increasing production and through food aid (school canteens, acute periods of crisis), and access to food for the poorest populations, especially in cities where the risks of social unrest are greatest and most destabilizing for the governments in place (Roudard 2002).

Public policies aimed at increasing agricultural production were mainly inspired by the experience of European countries after World War II. Food policies focused on securing supplies and promoting the green revolution model (Bonnefoy and Brand 2014) in order to rapidly increase agricultural production and emerge from the crisis.

The policies for food self-sufficiency applied in Africa following the great droughts of the 1970s and 1980s aimed to develop food production that was better adapted to drought on the basis of varietal research, intensive agriculture based on the use of inputs (fertilizers and pesticides) and modernization of agricultural equipment (animal and mechanized traction). This agricultural model thus required an increase in capital and caused a significant differentiation between family, employer and entrepreneurial farming systems (Cochet 2011), which competed and sought to add value to their products on the market. The liberalization of economies imposed by structural adjustment policies from the 1980s did not cause the collapse of the agricultural sector that some had predicted, but neither did it lead to the virtuous circle of development which was expected (Coulter and Onumah 2002), or major progress on food security, as shown by the paradox of Sikasso in Mali where growing agricultural production in the cotton-growing area was concomitant with widespread child malnutrition (Dury and Bocoum 2012). Poverty traps still exist with situations of chronic malnutrition (Janin 2010) or crisis areas where food aid is still needed more or less regularly. The revival of agricultural policies following the "hunger riots" of 2008 aims to support a "second-generation" agriculture, which is modernized and intensive and requires little labor. However family farming, still representing the largest part of the rural world, has great difficulty adopting this. The future of this rural population, which is growing rapidly on the African continent, is a major development challenge for the 21st century.

In parallel with these agricultural policies, developing countries have policies aimed at improving access to food for the poorest populations, particularly in cities. Access to low-cost food has quickly become a priority, thanks to customs policies that abolish import taxes on certain basic agricultural products: the poor countries of the Sahel (Mali, Burkina Faso, Niger, Chad) as well as those more advanced in the development process, such as Senegal and Cameroon, for example, have implemented these policies since the 1970s following the great famines linked to droughts. Continuing to the present day these policies have ensured social harmony in countries that are very poor and rapidly urbanizing. At the same time urbanization, has rendered them closely dependent on international markets, as the 2008 crisis revealed (Janin 2008).

The juxtaposition of these two policies aiming to both intensify agriculture and to control low food prices contributes to keeping countries in an inextricable situation summarized in the "food price dilemma": the opportunity to increase the protection of African agriculture by raising customs duties, to support more robust agri-food sectors and better compensate producers, and therefore their food security, would penalize the poorest (often urban) consumers by increasing prices on local markets and would slow down the participation of African family farming in global value chains (Debar and Tapsoba 2019).

In the fight against this injustice for producers the Via Campesina movement, particularly in Latin America, mobilized and proposed, during the Food Summit organized by the FAO in 1996, the concept of food sovereignty which refers to "the right of populations, their States or Unions to define their agricultural and food policies without dumping on third countries"[1] (Thivet 2012). It includes the defense of local production, the access of farmers to land, seeds and water, the right of farmers to protect themselves against agricultural imports at too low a price and

---

1 http://viacampesina.org.

consequently to practice agricultural prices linked to production costs, in order to live with dignity. Food sovereignty thus means the integration of populations in agricultural choices, without being opposed to trade but wishing it to be fairer. These principles of equity were reaffirmed in December 2018 by the United Nations Declaration on the Rights of Peasants adopted after 20 years of mobilization bringing together 160 peasant organizations in 73 countries.

The principles of food sovereignty underline the political dimension of food systems so as to integrate differentiated choices according to stakeholders and territories, and also the defense of alternative models. This approach is far from a standardizing definition that is implicit in the term food transition.

1.3.2. *Public policies to address current imbalances and build sustainability in developed countries*

In contrast to the poorest countries, countries in phase 3 of the food transition are focusing their policies in part on health and sustainability objectives, thus joining the concerns of wealthier populations for a healthier diet. In this context, the food transition concerns all the stages between production and consumption: an agriculture using methods that respect the environment and human health, processing methods that create direct links between farmers and consumers, easier access to diversified food for all, reduced distance and fewer intermediaries between producers and consumers, and consumers who are enlightened about the benefits of a diet that is less meaty, of quality, local and seasonal.

In France, for example, a component of the national food policy encourages territorial food systems (*systèmes alimentaires territoriaux*, SATs), broken down into regions (PRAs) and territories (PATs) that refocus on the local, around consumers and their health and environmental concerns. This refocusing was initiated by consumers' sudden consciousness of the importance of the highly variable quality of food and its consequences on their health, on the one hand, and of their dependence on potentially failing supply networks, because they depend on numerous intermediaries over long distances, on the other (Rastoin 2018). These developments leave a place for local authorities and intercommunalities that are asserting themselves in the governance of territorialized food systems. They reveal a new segmentation of the "agri-food arena" (Bonnefoy and Brand 2014) in which the major economic and political stakeholders (professional organizations, agribusinesses, commercial groups) are only marginally involved, their interests being located elsewhere. This new arena therefore needs to be included in the networks of powers and competences that are expressed at different scales, the articulation of which remains to be explored. Crises of multiple origins and their consequences on health, product availability and consumer access are all shocks that test the linearity of global food systems and lead politicians, producers, distributors and consumers to rethink their objectives.

Also in France, the law "for the balance of commercial relations in the agricultural and food sector and a healthy, sustainable and accessible food for all" (Egalim) adopted in 2018, although significantly behind the general states held in 2017, advocates an agricultural and food transition on a national scale, by in particular, proposing a better distribution of added value between producers and intermediaries. This law is the first to consider agricultural policy in conjunction with food policy through producer price and product quality standards, as well as through specific programs, such as collective catering aimed at promoting local supplies of diversified foods, organic products as well as the reduction of the meat portion in the meals offered. The objectives of the law are therefore defined to support the reduction of animal protein intake in the diet and to favor quality and local products. However, it has not managed to limit the influence of the major players of the agri-food sector, whether it be in the field of agricultural production, where phytosanitary companies are still very present (see the lobbying on the use of glyphosate or neonicotinoids), or in the field of marketing standards (such as Lactalys in the dairy industry) and consumption standards (see the report on the use of nitrite salts in industrial charcuterie and the proposed law, Commission des affaires économiques, 2021).

Even in a sector where they were not pioneers, that of the marketing of organic farming, retail actors impose themselves both in display and volumes sold. Supermarkets occupy an increasingly important place in the food distribution chain. Six international purchasing centers operate at European level. In Chile, in 2020 and in 10 of its stores in the central region of the country, the Jumbo brand set up a section of "fresh, healthy, additive-free, quality and traceable food". Indeed, two benchmarking studies, one in 2018 on meat consumption and the other on the quality of food, show that two-thirds of Chileans are ready to make changes in their lifestyle. For its part, the Líder group, a subsidiary of Walmart, has been offering a "zero waste" action since 2018. These actions are taking place alongside those of the legislator who is taking up the issue of obesity and childhood obesity, in particular with the 2017 law which passed after five years of parliamentary debates and which left time for the agri-food industry to adapt: it prohibits the marketing of toys included in food products and imposes the labeling of foods rich in saturated fats, sugars, sodium and calories.

These major industrial stakeholders have imposed themselves on the food landscape in the course of the 21st century, and not only in the countries of the North, as the example of Chile shows, with a major role in defining production, marketing and consumption standards. Their role and positioning in the changes to come are questionable. For example, the Carrefour Foundation stated on its website in September 2020 that it was committed to the food transition for "healthier food that is sustained by healthy and sustainable agriculture". These developments illustrate the place taken by these new driving forces in the ecological, health and food transitions.

1.3.3. *In emerging countries, meeting contradictory challenges to reduce precariousness*

Some countries with a large urban domestic market, a long history of industrialization, a useful and high potential agricultural area and a large population are difficult to place in the food transition phases. This is the case in particular for some BRICS (Brazil, Russia, India, China, South Africa), where very poor populations in a situation of chronic food insecurity are juxtaposed with very wealthy populations who have the same health requirements and sustainability objectives as in countries in the North.

In Brazil, the policies to fight poverty in the 1990s included food issues. The Zero Hunger program (*Fome Zero*) was created in 2003 under the presidency of Lula to ensure food security, particularly in Northeast Brazil and in the favelas of large cities such as Rio de Janeiro and São Paulo. The aim was to organize the distribution of basic baskets (*cestas básicas*), food vouchers and subsidies for food production. However, in 2004, the Brazilian Institute of Geography and Statistics (IBGE) showed that only 4% of the Brazilian population was malnourished, while 10% suffered from obesity and 30% were overweight (Pero 2012). The *Fome Zero* program, which strengthens generalized access to food and accompanies phase 2 of the food transition, falls very short of guaranteeing the quality and nutritional intake needed by populations. Subsequent programs seek to promote access to better quality food in localized areas, such as the National School Feeding Program (PNAE), which encourages public institutions – schools, hospitals – to buy from small agricultural producers and to prepare balanced meals (FAO 2018).

In India, the federal food policy has consisted mainly, since the 1960s, of encouraging production (green revolution for cereals, then white revolution for milk[2] (Atkins 1989)) while building up public stocks to be distributed to the poorest. However, the contrasting situations between federated states, which may be neighbors, generate conflict situations that reveal internal inequalities (Racine 2015). In 2016, for example, a water war broke out within Karnataka. On one side

2 The White Revolution (Operation Flood) is one of the largest dairy development programs in the world. It was implemented from 1970 onwards by the Indian Dairy Corporation and aimed at stimulating Indian milk production to satisfy domestic demand and thus create a territorialized food system (Atkins 1989).

Bangalore metropolis, with an urban identity as a high technology hub, marked by new food fashions is a major consumer of water. On the other side the more rural state of Tamil Nadu produces irrigated rice, on which part of the country depends for its food consumption[3]. The scale of the conflict and the criticism of the Supreme Court's 2018 verdict show the imbalance of power between urban and rural stakeholders, who are, however, interdependent in a highly territorialized food system. Other conflicts involve peasant movements, such as that of Punjabi farmers against the Farms Bills, the laws adopted by the Narendra Modi government in September 2020 which commit to a profound liberalization of the agricultural sector (Bhattacharya and Patel 2021). This farmers' revolt was joined by tens of thousands of consumers, as well as farmers from other regions and other sectors of the economy such as truckers, leading to a blockade of the capital New Delhi. In January 2021, the Supreme Court suspended the reform to restore social peace. In this case, we see a convergence of the struggles of consumers who have demands in terms of quality or quantity, with those of producers who, after decades of adaptation to imposed models, are starting to resist.

These countries with dense and contrasting populations, where many agricultural producers confront the dominant actors of globalization, as well as informed and militant consumers, thus face the most contradictions. The balance of power and the outcome of what can be violent conflicts is uncertain, as either the peasant world continues to be marginalized or they are victorious in the name of equity which is difficult to defend. Under these conditions, we can imagine the challenge of defining global and coherent public policies.

1.3.4. The new questions posed to the food transition model by health crises

In 2021, two factors were particularly relevant to the food transition: the multiplication of zoonoses (infectious diseases of vertebrate animals transmitted to humans) and the development of challenges to the dominant systems of agricultural production and food distribution.

At the end of the 20th century, it was no longer production crises that forced food policies, but food health crises (contaminated milk, mad cow disease) that revealed the separation between the normative sector of food security and that of agricultural supply (Bonnefoy and Brand 2014). In the case of Sanlu milk contaminated with melamine in China, the health scandal was based on profound modifications of production practices (industrialization of the dairy industry and

---

3 https://www.lemonde.fr/asie-pacifique/article/2016/09/15/a-bangalore-en-inde-la-crise-de-l-eau-degenere-en-emeute-urbaine_4998285_3216.html.

addition of a toxic product) and consumption (powdered milk for migrant children), making the quality of the product and the intoxication of children by the milk "unacceptable" (Keck 2009). The disjunction between food standards and production is also shown by two other zoonoses: "mad cow" (bovine spongiform encephalopathy), which revealed the use of animal meal to increase the growth of cattle, and avian flu (avian influenza), which was disseminated by the confinement of industrial sectors and the transport of live animals in very large commercial food networks. These two crises have raised consumer awareness of the ambivalent relationship between humans and animals, which are considered as both suppliers of goods and potential carriers of threats (Keck 2008). In France, the creation of the French Agency for Food Safety (*Agence française de sécurité sanitaire des aliments*) in 1999 has since assessed the risks of dissemination of pathogens from production to consumption and has led to improved food traceability.

The global pandemic of Covid-19 reveals, in particular, the contrasts between territories and population types. With the limits imposed on mobility, the consequences on short and long-distance distribution channels are major (IPBES-Food 2020) and reaffirm the need to put the territory at the center of food policies. Sanitary measures have led to an acceleration of ongoing dynamics, such as the increase in demand for product traceability (local, organic, environmental factors, associations for the maintenance of a farming agriculture (AMAP) and quality labels) and e-commerce devices (including fruit and vegetables and in developing countries as shown by the experience of Yelemani in Burkina Faso[4] which has set up a delivery service on the WhatsApp application for the distribution of organic and local vegetable baskets to their customers). Locally, pre-existing networks of actors have even shown a great capacity to adapt, for example, in Lyon where the supply structure has remained in the midst of a pandemic (Lanciano 2020). However, for urban populations that are deficient and dependent on the informal economy, the consequences are very serious and reveal an increase in food insecurity (Basquin Fané 2020). The situation is particularly catastrophic in emerging countries where no social security system is in place to mitigate the sudden drop in the middle classes and where metropolitanization accelerates the spread of infectious diseases (Verdeil 2020).

1.4. Conclusion

The food transition model has shown its relevance for studying food changes in the countries of the North, with nuances depending on the social, cultural and regional groups to which it applies. The questioning of the theory of the standardization of dietary patterns in favor of diversification and enrichment based

---

4 https://www.suco.org/circuits-courts-et-approvisionnement-local/.

on local products is increasingly widely accepted (Soula et al. 2020) and is expressed in the diversity of territorialized food systems and cultural identities. It calls into question the temporal dimension of the notion of food transition, which assumes a linearity in the succession of the three phases, while reaffirming the close links between food and agricultural production in order to think about the sustainability of these systems. Thus, some local stakeholders (consumers, producers) are shaking up top-down power games, particularly during food crises, which constitute sounding boards.

The profound disruptions of food systems brought about by zoonoses and protest movements meet those caused by local actors, whether in the field of production or in that of consumption in favor of healthy products in local distribution channels. Despite the scale and duration of the contestations that question the dominant systems (technocratic model of the green revolution, globalization and the circulation of food over very long distances), their historical scope raises questions. Are these the outbursts of actors who have been defeated in the power struggles that oppose them to powerful private sector stakeholders and ministerial spheres, or on the contrary, are they the harbingers of a more fundamental revolution of the current system?

The food transition is not a universal model: it does not have a linear course and it does not stand up to the test of the field in the countries of the North nor the South. To understand the evolution of food, we must take into account, in addition to population growth, urbanization processes and income levels, the links between the conditions of food production (in volume and quality, ensuring a decent income for producers) and the accessibility of products desired by consumers. In this context, where environment and development are closely linked, the question of food justice calls for the territorialization of food systems, particularly in marginal metropolitan areas (Hochedez and Le Gall 2016). These questions are becoming central to the consideration of issues specific to the Anthropocene.

1.5. References

Atkins, P.J. (1989). Operation Flood: Dairy development in India. *Geography*, 74(3), 259–262.

Basquin Fané, H. (2020). Impacts de la crise Covid-19 sur la sécurité alimentaire en Afrique subsaharienne. *CFSI*, 7.

Bhattacharya, S. and Patel, U. (2021). Farmer's agitation in India due to audacious farm bill of 2020. *International Journal of Research in Engineering, Science and Management*, 4(1), 35–37.

Bonnefoy, S. and Brand, C. (2014). Régulation politique et territorialisation du fait alimentaire : De l'agriculture à l'agri-alimentaire. *Géocarrefour*, 89(1–2), 95–103 [Online]. Available at: https://journals.openedition.org/geocarrefour/9424 [Accessed 31 August 2021].

Bricas, N. and Seck, P.A. (2004). L'alimentation des villes du Sud : Les raisons de craindre et d'espérer. *Cahiers d'Agriculture*, 13(1), 10–14.

de Castro, J. (1951). *La géopolitique de la faim*. Éditions sociales, Paris.

Chaléard, J.L. and Sanjuan, T. (2017). *Géographie du développement. Territoires et mondialisation dans les Suds*. Armand Colin, Paris.

Cochet, H. (2011). *L'agriculture comparée*. Editions Quae, Versailles.

Collomb, P. (1989). Transition démographique, transition alimentaire II. De la logique démographique à la logique alimentaire. *Population*, 44(4–5), 777–807.

Commission des Affaires Économiques (2021). Rapport d'information sur les sels nitrités dans l'industrie agroalimentaire. Report 3683, Commission des Affaires Économiques [Online]. Available at: https://www.assemblee-nationale.fr/dyn/15/rapports/cion-eco/l15b3731_rapport-information#_Toc256000054.

Cosio-Zavala, M.A. and López Gareri, V. (2004). Concentration urbaine et transition démographique. *Cahiers des Amériques latines*, 47, 63–70 [Online]. Available at: https://journals.openedition.org/cal/7757 [Accessed 31 August 2021].

Coulter, J. and Onumah, G. (2002). The role of warehouse receipt systems in enhanced commodity marketing and rural livelihoods in Africa. *Food Policy*, 27, 319–337.

Deaton, A. and Drèze, J. (2009). Food and nutrition in India: Facts and interpretations. *Economic & Political Weekly*, 44(7), 42–65.

Debar, J.C. and Tapsoba, A.F. (2019). Les protections à l'importation sur les produits agricoles. État des lieux et enjeux pour l'Afrique subsaharienne. *Fondation pour l'agriculture et la ruralité dans le monde*, 12(24), 1–24.

Delpeuch, F. and Maire, B. (1997). Obésité et développement dans les pays du Sud. *Médecine Tropicale*, 57(4), 380–388.

Delpeuch, F. and Maire, B. (2004). La transition nutritionnelle, l'alimentation et les villes dans les pays en développement. *Cahiers Agricultures*, 13(1), 23–30.

Dury, S. and Bocoum, I. (2012). Le "paradoxe" de Sikasso (Mali) : Pourquoi "produire plus" ne suffit-il pas pour bien nourrir les enfants des familles d'agriculteurs ? *Cahiers Agricultures*, 21(5), 324–336.

Faliès, C. (2012). Espaces ouverts et métropolisation entre Santiago du Chili et Valparaiso : Produire, vivre et aménager les périphéries. PhD Thesis, Université Paris 1 Panthéon-Sorbonne, Paris.

Falque, A., Lubello, P., Temri, L. (2017). Introduction. In *Systèmes agroalimentaires en transition*, Lubello, P. (ed.). Éditions Quae, Versailles.

FAO (2018). Nutrition et systèmes alimentaires. Report, Groupe d'experts de haut niveau sur la sécurité alimentaire et la nutrition du Comité de la sécurité alimentaire mondiale, Rome [Online]. Available at: http://www.fao.org/3/I7846FR/i7846fr.pdf [Accessed 27 January 2021].

Finney Rutten, L.J. (2010). Poverty, food insecurity, and obesity: A conceptual framework for research, practice and policy. *Journal of Hunger & Environmental Nutrition*, 5(4), 403–415.

Fumey, G. (2007). La mondialisation de l'alimentation. *L'information géographique*, 71, 71–82 [Online]. Available at: https://www.cairn.info/revue-l-information-geographique-2007-2-page-71.htm [Accessed 31 August 2021].

Galal, O.M. (2002). The nutrition transition in Egypt: Obesity, undernutrition and the food consumption context. *Public Health Nutrition*, 5(1), 141–148.

de Garine, I. (1988). Anthropologie de l'alimentation et pluridisciplinarité. *Écologie humaine*, 6(2), 21–40.

Godelier, M. (1990). La théorie de la transition chez Marx. *Sociologie et sociétés*, 22(1), 53–81.

Hochedez, C. and Le Gall, J. (2016). Justice alimentaire et agriculture. *Justice spatiale*, 9 [Online]. Available at: https://www.jssj.org/article/justice-alimentaire-et-agriculture/ [Accessed 31 August 2021].

Hopkins, R. (2008). Le manuel de transition. De la dépendance au pétrole à la résilience locale. *Ecosociété*, 216.

IPBES-Food (2020). Le Covid-19 et la crise dans les systèmes alimentaires : Symptômes, causes et solutions potentielles. Communication, April, 12.

Jacobi, D., Buzelé, R., Couet, C. (2010). Peut-on parler de pandémie d'obésité ? *La Presse Médicale*, 39(9), 902–906.

Janin, P. (2008). Crise alimentaire mondiale. Désordres et débats. *Hérodote*, 4(131), 6–13 [Online]. Available at: https://www.cairn.info/revue-herodote-2008-4-page-6.htm [Accessed 31 August 2021].

Janin, P. (2010). Faim et politique : Mobilisations et instrumentations. *Politiques africaines*, 3(119), 5–22 [Online]. Available at: https://www.cairn.info/revue-politique-africaine-2010-3-page-5.htm [Accessed 31 August 2021].

Keck, F. (2008). Risques alimentaires et maladies animales. L'agence de sécurité sanitaire des aliments, de la vache folle à la grippe aviaire. *Médecine Science*, 24(1), 81–86 [Online]. Available at: https://www.medecinesciences.org/fr/articles/medsci/full_html/2008/02/medsci2008241p81/medsci2008241p81.html [Accessed 31 August 2021].

Keck, F. (2009). L'affaire du lait contaminé. *Perspectives chinoises*, 106, 96–101.

Lanciano, E. (2020). Lyon : Le confinement, une parenthèse propice aux innovations sociales dans l'alimentation ? *The Conversation* [Online]. Available at: https://theconversation.com/ lyon-le-confinement-une-parenthese-propice-aux-innovations-sociales-dans-lalimentation-146710 [Accessed 27 January 2021].

Landy, F. (2009). India, "Cultural Density" and the model of food transition. *Economic and Political Weekly*, 44(20), 59–61 [Online]. Available at: https://www.epw.in/journal/2009/ 20/discussion/india-cultural-density-and-model-food-transition.html [Accessed 31 August 2021].

Le Gall, J. (2011). Buenos Aires maraîchères : Une Buenos Aires bolivienne ? Le complexe maraîcher de la Région métropolitaine à l'épreuve de nouveaux acteurs. PhD Thesis, University of Buenos Aires, Buenos Aires.

Leloup, H. (2018). Les agriculteurs de l'agglomération de Lima : Des acteurs territoriaux au défi des attentes de la ville. PhD Thesis, Université de Paris 1 Panthéon-Sorbonne, Paris.

Loorbach, D. (2010). Transition management for sustainable development: A prescriptive, complexity-based governance framework. *Governance: An International Journal of Policy, Administration, and Institutions*, 23(1) [Online]. Available at: https://onlinelibrary. wiley.com/doi/full/10.1111/j.1468-0491.2009.01471.x [Accessed 31 August 2021].

Paddeu, F. (2012). L'agriculture urbaine dans les quartiers défavorisés de la métropole New-Yorkaise : La justice alimentaire à l'épreuve de la justice sociale. *VertigO*, 12(2), 1–26 [Online]. Available at: https://journals.openedition.org/vertigo/12686 [Accessed 31 August 2021].

Padovani, F. and Lysaniuk, B. (2019). Introduction. In *Les gestions des transitions*, Padovani, F. and Lysaniuk, B (eds). L'Harmattan, Paris.

Pero, V. (2012). Bolsa Família : Une nouvelle génération de programmes sociaux au Brésil. *CERISCOPE Pauvreté* [Online]. Available at: http://ceriscope.sciences-po.fr/pauvrete/ content/part4/bolsa-familia-une-nouvelle-generation-de-programmes-sociaux-au-bresil?page= show [Accessed 27 January 2021].

Popkin, B.-M. (1993). Nutritional patterns and transitions. *Population and Development Review*, 19(1), 138–157.

Proust, A. (forthcoming). Nourrir São Paulo par ses marges : Dynamiques et enjeux socio-spatiaux de l'agriculture périphérique à l'échelle métropolitaine. Geography PhD Thesis, Université Paris 1 Panthéon-Sorbonne, Paris.

Pulliat, G. (2017). Métropoles émergentes et alimentation : Une lecture croisée. *L'information géographique*, 81, 54–74.

Racine, J.-L. (2015). Géopolitique de l'agriculture indienne. *Hérodote*, 156, 29–49 [Online]. Available at: https://www.cairn.info/revue-herodote-2015-1-page-29.htm [Accessed 31 August 2021].

Rastoin, J.-L. (2018). Accélérer la transition vers une alimentation durable par un changement de paradigme scientifique et économique et des politiques publiques innovantes. *Systèmes alimentaires/Food Systems*, 3, 17–27.

Rastoin, J.-L. and Ghersi, G. (2010). Théorie et méthodes d'analyse du système alimentaire. In *Le système alimentaire mondial : Concepts et méthodes, analyses et dynamiques*, Rastoin, J.-L. and Ghersi, G. (eds). Éditions Quae, Versailles.

Raton, G. (2012). Les foires au Mali : De l'approvisionnement urbain à l'organisation de l'espace rural : Le cas de la périphérie de Bamako. PhD Thesis, Université Paris 1 Panthéon-Sorbonne, Paris.

Roudard, L. (2002). L'alimentation dans le monde et les politiques publiques de lutte contre la faim. *Mondes en développement*, 117, 9–23.

Salem, G. and Fournet, F. (2020). *Atlas mondial de la santé*. Autrement, Paris.

Soula, A., Yount-André, C., Lepiller, O., Bricas, N. (eds) (2020). *Manger en ville : Regards socio-anthropologiques d'Afrique, d'Amérique latine et d'Asie*. Editions Quae, Versailles, 172.

Steck, J.-F. (2006). Qu'est-ce que la transition urbaine ? Croissance urbaine, croissance des villes, croissance des besoins à travers l'exemple africain. *Revue d'économie financière*, 86, 267–283.

Tallet, B. (2012). Les relations villes/campagnes : Nouveaux contextes, nouvelles configurations ? In *Population, mondialisation et développement. Quelles dynamiques ?* Cambrézy, L. and Petit, V. (eds). La Documentation française, Paris.

Thivet, D. (2012). Des paysans contre la faim. La "souveraineté alimentaire", naissance d'une cause paysanne transnationale. *Terrains & Travaux*, 20, 69–85.

Verdeil, E. (2020). La métropolisation, coupable idéal de la pandémie ? *The Conversation* [Online]. Available at: https://theconversation.com/la-metropolisation-coupable-ideale-de-la-pandemie-135226 [Accessed 27 January 2021].

Development and Urban Environment Through the Prism of Risk and Crises

2.1. Introduction

The aim of this chapter is to show that risk and crisis analysis is a means of questioning each of the notions of development and the urban environment. It is based on the research experiments of the *Institut de recherche pour le développement* (French Institute of Research for Development) and the UMR Prodig for over 20 years, in Latin America and more recently in Tunisia, particularly in cooperation with the municipalities of Quito and Lima, as well as with the Peruvian and Tunisian civil protection agencies.

The proposed approach is above all geographical, as we insist on the contribution of spatial and territorial dimensions as well as multiscalar dimensions, as these questions are dealt with by a good number of disciplines. It is also pragmatic, as it goes beyond the positivist/constructivist alternative (Dussouy 2010), a theoretical opposition that does not stand up to the empirical approach and situated research, especially when it is produced with local partners. While we approach risks and crises as a construct, particularly a political and social one, in which historical processes and the confrontation of representations are central, we analyze these issues through specific situations and actions. This is why the methodology adopted involves a detailed study of risk and crisis management processes. This one has a territoriality that we identify through the census and the geo-referencing of actions, the reconstruction of their chronology, the confrontation with other spatialities and other chronologies, in particular that of disruptive phenomena and their modeling

Chapter written by Alexis SIERRA, Anaïs BÉJI, Axelle CROISÉ, Cyriaque HATTEMER, Pascale METZGER, Marie PIGEOLET and Irene VALITTUTO.

produced by the Earth sciences, and with that of urban development and its stakes. This management also mobilizes principles, knowledge, representations of the urban environment and its dynamics, specific to a given territory, which can be understood through interviews accompanied by mental maps, semantic and lexical analysis of expert reports as well as the press. This management is the result of the actions of specific actors, some of whom are partners in the research and levers for our participatory observation practice. Crisis management in particular is conceived as a test in which an argument and power relations are deployed in the flow of action, testifying in this to a pragmatic approach in the sociological sense of the term (Nachi 2006).

In this chapter, we prioritize crisis over risk. In order not to discuss these widely debated notions in detail, we posit from the outset that risk is a situation of anticipation of a crisis, and therefore an abstract reality resulting in the representation of a major loss in connection with the triggering of a hazard (natural, technological, biological, social, etc.). The value of the loss can be quantified, giving the risk a probabilistic connotation. However, this precise quantification effort is often not made. Each social group or each actor gives it an unequal value and arbitrates between potential losses. The consensus around a major loss, defining a common issue, tends precisely to build a major risk. In this, the risk is relative, its management, an arbitration and its study a means of identifying what has value for a given urban society. A crisis is, for its part, a moment of major disruption that we circumscribe to the emergency, a period of acceleration of time compared to daily life. It is not to be confused with a disaster but includes it, sometimes preceding it during the alert, sometimes extending to the post-disaster recovery phase. This emergency situation is a situation of very great uncertainty, marked by amazement (Gilbert 1992). It thus constitutes a test (Boltanski 2009) which, in our opinion, makes it possible to identify the dominant knowledge on the urban environment such as the balance of power at work in a given society and the development issues that mobilize it.

We apply this conceptual tool to the urban environment that we consider as the material, historical and territorial result of the modes of production and consumption of common goods such as soil, water or air (Metzger 1994). This approach allows us to "restore the irreducibly social, political, economic, legal and technological dimension of the environment, while raising the question of the modalities of development" (Metzger 2020). Being marked by density and diversity, the city concentrates the issues and the complexity of their interactions, the systemic effects are amplified, and consequently the uncertainties, including for researchers as well. From the point of view of the global environmental crisis, the urban environment represents a form of "reduced meta-population and meta-ecosystem model to answer theoretical questions about the resilience of ecological systems" (Barles et al. 2020, p. 143). Since risks and crises are a means of rethinking the relations between society and the environment, studying crises in the city is a means of understanding paroxysmal situations that bring into play the multiple interactions between physical–chemical, biological and social dynamics, in a space thus apprehended as a particularly artificial geosystem (Beroutchachvili and Bertrand 1978).

Our general objective is thus to show the interest of approaching the crisis to make the link between urban environment and development issues.

2.2. Crisis and development: a paradigm shift

Approaching the city by the crisis directly interrogates the question of development because it approaches the relationship that society has with its future in a different way. Since its emergence as a scientific paradigm, the notion of development has been used to analyze the situation and dynamics of formerly colonized regions of the world (Latin America, Africa, Asia-Pacific), unable to meet the growing needs of their populations and suffering from external and internal relations of domination (Lacoste 1965). Development is therefore part of an emancipated vision of these regions of the world. At the same time, this notion has also contributed to forging tools, actions and practices leading to the improvement of living conditions (Sen 1999). This is why, in this sense, the notion of development is inseparable from the idea of progress, in which the future is envisaged in a quasi-teleological manner, as a constant improvement in living conditions. Thus, in the developmentalist period (from the 1950s to the 1970s), "underdevelopment" was mainly analyzed structurally and in terms of basic trends (Nurkse 1953; Furtado 1966), but little in terms of paroxysmal phenomena and disruptions particularly environmental or technological in nature. Certain crises, essentially political, sometimes economic, have generally only served to establish sequencing and punctuate a narrative (Lacoste 1965). It is thus remarkable to observe that Yves Lacoste, in the 1960s, in his initial analysis of the concept of underdevelopment (Lacoste 1967) among the 12 criteria that allowed him to define underdevelopment, the strong sensitivity to shocks, external or internal, which we have since called vulnerability, did not appear. As a geographer trained in the classical school, he clearly reaffirmed the need to take into account the relationship between societies and environmental data in order to grasp what (under)development is, but he did not, however, mention the impact of disasters, whether of natural, industrial or even health origin. In other words, the environmental crisis was not yet on the development research agenda. This situation changed in the 1970s.

Economically and socially, the first oil shock (1973) and its consequences were very significant. They seem to illustrate the alert triggered earlier by the first United Nations conference on the environment in Stockholm (1972) and the Meadows report, "The Limit to Growth", by revealing a crisis of resources and questioning both the current mode of development and the faith in technical progress that would constantly allow for the substitution of resources. This report and this summit envisage the future differently, by establishing prospective scenarios and by setting a critical horizon around the years 2020–2030. A few major natural (Bhola cyclone or earthquake in Peru in 1970) and industrial catastrophes (Torre Canyon 1967; Seveso 1976) hit the headlines and initiated an ever-growing list of tragedies, including the Armero lahar (Colombia), the Mexico City or Armenia earthquake, and the Lake Nyos eruption (Cameroon), which justified the setting up of the International Decade for Natural Disaster Reduction (IDNDR 1990–1999). From an epistemological point of view, the combination of these disasters, which have become benchmark events, and the resulting international (or global) mobilization, has led to an increase in the number of studies in this field. For the Latin American region, the *Red des Estudios sociales en prevención de Desastres* (La RED) is an emblematic translation, with the creation of a journal, *Desastres y Sociedad*, and a collection of 26 books, two-thirds of which occurred during the IDNDR. This network of researchers and experts produces a real epistemic community that, following Anglo-American authors such as Kenneth Hewitt, Ian Davis and Piers Blaikie, tackles relationships to the environment through disasters, questioning a *naturalizing* reading of them. Through its slogan, *los desastres no son naturales* (disasters are not natural), it insists in particular on the conditions of development in their occurrence (Mascrey 1993).

2.3. Converting disorder into a problem and uncertainty into a risk

Since the 1970s, the succession of crises has produced widespread uncertainty that undermines the positivist and teleological vision of development and has led some researchers to consider development from the point of view of risk.

The research of Antony Giddens, and even more so of Ulrich Beck, testifies to this reversal of perspective. The modernity crisis that they point out by mobilizing the notion of risk changes the relationship to the future. It can also be translated into a development crisis which is itself beginning to be questioned (Sachs 1978). Jean Gallais, whose work was at the crossroads of tropical geography and development, underlines in *Tropiques, terres de risques et de violences* (1994) the double dialectic between crisis and development: a series of scourges hit poor countries and these scourges feed a vicious circle representing an obstacle to development. Avoiding any determinism, he shows that it is partly the choices of development that lead to the crisis and not a zonal position.

The change of perspective formalized in these academic works is also formalized in the operational sphere. A sign of an era that is more neo-modern than post-modern, risk becomes a performative notion and enters into the criteria of (sub)development as evidenced by the "country risk"[1]. This indicator, forged in the United States in the financial sphere, remains a rational attempt to classify countries according to their capacity to secure investments. Its use, which appeared at the end of the 1960s, became widespread in the 1970s as developing countries saw their public debt grow (Gaillard 2015). Initially synonymous with sovereign risk, country risk is assessed in terms of a country's ability to repay its debt. Gradually, the calculation of country risk is incorporating the entire range of threats that a country may face, by now including environmental hazards. Like gross domestic product (GDP) or the human development index (HDI), this indicator is synthetic and translates a development situation in a quantitative, supposedly objective and scientific manner. However, unlike GDP and the HDI, country risk has a directly forward-looking aim and seeks to reduce an uncertainty that has become general and growing. This process has led us to approach risk management policies at other scales. Powerless in planning and controlling urban expansion, urban actors perceive the future of the city as particularly uncertain. To deal with it, they can identify a small number of sufficiently recognized and shared threats to try to mobilize all city dwellers. The cognitive approach, which aims to reduce uncertainty by calculating risk (Casteigts 2013), thus has its political counterpart through the transition from an uncertain situation to the construction of a representation of the future catastrophe, a performative representation which thus becomes an instrument of government from which the thought of the city is developed, all the more relevant as urban society is fragmented (Sierra 2015a).

Another reductive logic has been operating since the 1970s. While in 1983 Kenneth Hewitt denounced the representation of a geography of disasters similar to "an archipelago isolated misfortunes" (Hewitt 1983, p. 12), the combination of the vulnerability paradigm (as the propensity of people and property to become fragile in the face of a shock) and that of the Anthropocene (as an era in which humanity is the driving force of global change), has constructed a logic linking the crises together. The report "Our common future" (1987), with its title revealing this new relationship with the future, thus encourages us to establish the principle of a crisis,

1 Post-modernism envisions the contemporary world as marked by a generalized uncertainty. The risk-country, by transforming uncertainty into a synthetic index, translates rather a rationality proper to modernity.

both of development (economic and social) and environmental crises: "these are not separate crises: an environmental crisis, a development crisis, an energy crisis. They are all one" (Brundtland 1987, p. 20). With the notion of sustainability, development seems to be driven less by a positivist vision of continuous progress than by the idea that a major crisis must be avoided, "as if the predestined horizon of progress could only be followed by the predestined horizon of disaster" (Revaud d'Allonnes 2012, p. 140). The global environmental crisis that experts have been highlighting and that has marked national Earth summits since the Stockholm summit has called into question the modes of development at work and led some authors to question the very idea of development (Rist 1996; Latouche 2003). It seems to us to be one of the main driving forces of the emergence of a "world-society", i.e. a global imagining that creates links between the planet's populations (Lessard 2003; Lévy 2015).

2.4. Distant crisis, present-day risk

To approach this history of development through the notion of crisis is thus a way of grasping a triple ambiguity, of objects, temporalities and spatial scales, the three being very closely intertwined. The first ambiguity is what turns the crisis into both a diagnosis and an experienced situation: the Meadows and Bruntland reports diagnose an untenable (or unsustainable) development and predict a future catastrophe, so that the crisis is both the evaluation of a *critical* situation and the disruption of the environment. This ambiguity is intrinsic to the history of the term, the Greek *krisis* designating the moment of judgment in the face of a disease. This ambiguity is of direct interest to us because the crisis depends on who defines it and how. It is an eminently political moment, because the one who makes the diagnosis puts themselves in the position of having to justify, propose and act. Faced with rupture phenomena that leave time for an alert, this diagnosis clearly precedes the catastrophe but already creates the disturbance. We have seen this, for example, with the announcement of an El Niño year in Ecuador in 1998, or in the face of the spread of the Covid-19 in March 2020, both in the Andean countries and in Tunisia. In both cases, the President of the Republic and the local authorities diagnosed the crisis even before the arrival of the rains or the virus. In both cases, the level of development to *cope* was questioned, information on national and local resources had to be mobilized, and a demonstration of power was staged that led to an assumption of responsibility.

In doing so, the second ambiguity is that the crisis is both present and future. It is both the moment of diagnosis, of the public and widely shared denunciation of a crisis situation, and the future moment of the catastrophe. And between these two moments, the term crisis covers a more or less long duration, which Myriam Revault d'Allonnes speaks of as "a long time without promise" (Revaud d'Allonnes 2012, p. 14), leading to a confusion of temporalities. It is in this ambiguity that the risk is inscribed and that the present representation of a future catastrophe is constructed. To define risk in a given urban environment means mobilizing knowledge, resources and "acting to ensure that something that has not yet happened does not actually happen". This sentence, stated by the Director General of Planning of Quito, during an interview in 1996, meant that risk management is difficult to justify in the absence of a recent or nearby disaster.

Hence, the reflection on the third ambiguity: in moving *from* crises to *the* global crisis, any local crisis reflects a global approach to environmental and development issues. Each local or regional crisis is not only the symptom of a local situation: it serves as a warning for the whole planet, showing a global risk that becomes a common horizon. The process of a risk's emergence, analyzed in Lima between 2008 and 2012, was an opportunity to show that not only does every crisis in a city become a symptom of the global crisis, but also that every crisis in a place participates in the construction of the risk in other places on the planet, thus articulating the local scales where the crisis takes place, and the global scales where the risk spreads, more or less eclipsing the intermediate scales. Any crisis in one place thus becomes a test for the urban actors of Lima and pushes them to act because they are not only spectators of the distant crisis must also directly face what is from then on a risk for their own society. It thus operated a transformation of the distant crisis into present risk, with what that represented of demonstration of powers.

Thus, in a context where the number of risk studies has contributed to forging the perspective of a seismic "big one", local and national authorities have been confronted with the occurrence of the disasters of Port-au-Prince and Concepción (Chile) in 2010 and Japan in 2011. Instead of evading them and considering them as distant, they used them to assert a local risk. This test allowed them to apply the precautionary principle, which has become an internationally valued principle of action, and to demonstrate their power by assuming future danger. The Concepción earthquake of February 2010 was used as an argument by President Alan García to launch an action plan and a revision of the legislation on crisis management and risk management. On March 11, 2011, nine weeks after taking office, the mayor of the Lima metropolis (Susana Villarán) seized the tsunami alert related to the earthquake in Japan to assume new decentralized powers. Despite the distance (more than 15,000 km from the epicenter), she decided to evacuate the beaches and close the coastal road (the *Costa Verde*). Very firm, she insisted that "although the impact should not be strong, no preventive measure is exaggerated in this case, given that Peru is in a seismic zone" (statement to the media on March 12, 2011). The national police force and civil protection applied this decision according to the rules of crisis management which placed the mayor at the top of the decision-making process.

Given the nature of the threat, this alert was also an instrument to place the various municipalities under her authority. In both cases, the analysis of public action showed that space is a power issue, making crisis management a real question of urban geopolitics. Alan García's action plan was reflected in the acceleration of the transformation of old city centers, in line with the 2009 law on the renewal of urban centers. Susana Villarán's decision demonstrated her authority both over the entire urban area, beyond the boundaries of each municipality[2], and over facilities such as the main roads and parks, which she could make accessible or inaccessible.

The use of a crisis that occurred thousands of kilometers away as an instrument of urban government is all the more effective as the experts and the press have drawn an analogy between the territories. These two sources seem to us to be essential for analyzing the link between development and the urban environment through risk and crises. Experts have a decisive role as intermediaries, helping to disseminate the risk and to place it on the political agenda, particularly through multilateral or bilateral development aid. They have a strong influence on national and local institutional actors and relate to an ideology that transcends urban projects through normative discourse (Allal 2010; Koop and Amilhat Szary 2011). Thus, foreign cooperation agencies such as the Swiss Agency for Development and Cooperation, the Japan International Cooperation Agency (JICA),and the *Agence française pour le développement* (AFD) are involved in risk studies or civil protection programs, both in Lima for the first two and in Tunis for all three. As for the press, it is not limited to reporting on the disruptions and actual damage, where it takes place. It also contributes to projecting the reader into the universe of possibilities, by making a link between distant disasters and the local urban environment. The following analysis is a testimony to this. It is the result of a work carried out in 2012 from the systematic census of press articles of a national reference newspaper, *El Comercio,* published in the month following the earthquake in Port-au-Prince (2010) and in the six months following the disasters in Concepción (2010) and Japan (2011). This study establishes the construction of risk in Lima from crises that occurred elsewhere in the world (Figure 2.1).

If the analogy between disaster-stricken cities and Lima is labile with Port-au-Prince in 2010, it is much better established and embodied in the Limenian territory, with the two other crises. Thus, following the earthquake in Concepción, Chile, 37 articles make a direct link with the Peruvian capital. This link has three dimensions: either reflexive to evoke actions of prevention and preparation in Lima, or bijective in relation to an aid provided in Chile and the presence of a Limenian interest in Concepción, but, in three quarters of the cases, it is directly comparative

---

2 The metropolitan municipality of Lima has a limited power due to the strong autonomy of the municipalities of districts and the consequent fragmentation of the agglomeration.

and analogical between the two cities, projecting Lima in an equivalent crisis. This comparative discourse leads, on the part of the journalists, to particular urban spaces considered susceptible to be affected. In order to establish this Limenian geography of the crisis, the geographical information (places, neighborhoods, municipalities) extracted from the articles was reduced to the scale of the municipalities (*distritos*) of the agglomeration (Figure 2.2).

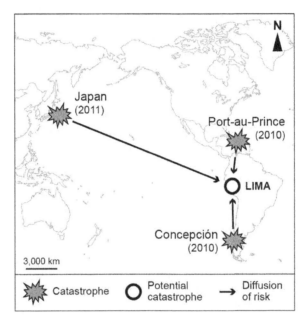

Figure 2.1. *Territorialization of the Chilean crisis (Concepción earthquake) in Lima. For a color version of this figure, see www.iste.co.uk/peyroux/development.zip*

Overall, the analogy between the cities is made possible by the similarity of the geographical situations: coastal and on the oceanic plate's subduction zone under the continental plate. However, the comparison does not only concern the natural conditions and dynamics, but also the mode of development and production of the city: as many articles state that Lima is more vulnerable than the Chilean city in terms of its occupation and organization. The articles point out the absence of preventive action, of "risk culture", of an emergency alert system, the bad state of the constructions, notably in the two historic centers of Lima and of its port Callao. A distant crisis therefore offers not only a horizon at risk but also the occasion to question local development, with a fear that is all the more acute because the Limenians consider the Chilean cities to be a source of order (Protzel de Amat 2011).

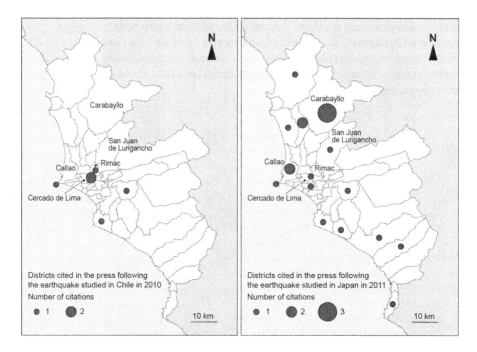

Figure 2.2. *Projection and territorialization in Lima of the Japanese and Chilean crisis, by analogy constructed via the press (data source: El Comercio Peru - national press) Authors: A. Sierra and P. Peña 2012. For a color version of this figure, see www.iste.co.uk/peyroux/development.zip*

The municipalities of the Limenian coast thus appear to be more exposed than during the Chilean crisis. However, cartography also reveals major issues: Callao is distinguished by the presence of the two main gateways to the country, the port and the international airport, which would be directly affected. And the highlighting of the municipality of Carabayllo testifies to the point of caricaturing this diffusion of risk: the Peruvian metropolis is so assimilated to Fukushima that the press commented on the existence of a nuclear reactor that few people knew then. And for good reason, according to the website of the Instituto Peruano de Energía Nuclear, the Racso center (or El Huarangal) is not an energy production plant, as in Japan, but a small reactor used to produce radiopharmaceuticals for medical imaging, for diagnostic purposes. Nevertheless, the parallel made the headlines and encouraged civil protection to launch impact studies around this site, as well as to denounce the urban expansion, by self-construction, which places city dwellers in the immediate vicinity of the plant. On this last point, the cartography testifies not only to the existence of natural and technological threats, but also to a strong vulnerability.

Following the Concepción earthquake, the old centers of Lima and Callao were cited both for the precariousness of habitat, made up of slums, and for architectural value and heritage, a local issue. Following the Japanese crisis, this vulnerability was much more pronounced in the peripheries. It was an opportunity to point out the informality of housing (from central slums to illegal occupation of more peripheral land), non-compliance with standards and the lack of control of urban expansion linked to self-construction in the most popular districts. The media, which relayed the opinion of experts and authorities, therefore broadcast a double representation: the city was under the threat of an earthquake followed by a tsunami and a nuclear incident, but the effects would be more serious than elsewhere because self-construction and informal occupation of the old central buildings have produced greater vulnerability. Admittedly, this propensity of the Latin American city, as an unequal city marked by poverty, to amplify the effects of disruptive events is in line with the social approach to urban risks deployed by La RED (Fernandez 1996). However, the vulnerability of the poorest was reversed here into a vulnerability of the city and the Japanese crisis reactivated relations of domination to the detriment of the margins (Sierra 2015a).

2.5. Representation of the origins of the crisis: globalization of local power relations

The globalization of risk, which proceeds by analogy of urban environments, was based, in the previous cases, on a similarity of the natural conditions of development. On the contrary, the Peruvian capital was compared to urban environments that were more economically prosperous. Is there also a globalization of vulnerabilities? The preceding reflections, based on Latin American cities, lead us to two observations: on the one hand, the existence of an inversion whereby a vulnerable population represents the vulnerability of the city in the event of an exceptional disruptive event; on the other hand, the assimilation of spaces at risk to urban margins (Sierra 2009). Are these conclusions valid elsewhere? In order to answer these questions, we have chosen to analyze the urban crisis in another region of the world, marked by a different culture and a different political history, while having, according to the HDI, a similar level of development. Tunis offers an interesting point of comparison. As a national metropolis like Lima, the slightest disruption has systemic effects at different scales, according to the risk-capital principle, which states that the geographic concentration of issues produces a major risk (Sierra 2015b). According to the interviews initially carried out (November 2018, March–April 2019), the reading of civil protection reports (March–April 2019) and the French-speaking press (*La Presse*, *Le Temps*, *Réalités*, *Naawat*), Tunis is subject to hazards recognized both by crisis management actors and city dwellers, including floods and fires. The floods that have occurred over the past two decades have been the occasion of crises that demonstrate a close similarity in the definition of risk areas between the Tunisian capital and the Peruvian metropolis. The sources cited were also used to build timelines that parallel the media events and serve as a reference, with the actions taken to protect themselves from flooding. In that, we mobilized a methodology elaborated in 1999–2000 to understand the territorialization of risk management policies in Quito. The following analysis will mobilize this research carried out in Ecuador[3], because the points of comparison with Tunis are quite remarkable.

The first similarity is the existence of crises that create a break in the vision of the urban environment. While floods are seasonal in Tunis and floods of a catastrophic nature have appeared in scientific literature since the beginning of the 20th century, it is the floods of the last 20 years that serve as an argument for action.

Two events are particularly cited in expert reports and mentioned in the media: the 2003 floods in Tunis and those of 2018 in Nabeul (on Cap Bon). The former thus justify the launch of numerous studies and the revision of the Town Planning Code. We had already made this observation in Quito for morphoclimatic accidents: it is not the most deadly or the most destructive that constitute the argument for action, nor is it all the studies, expert opinions or scientific analyses which serve as a reference, but those which relate to the northwest of Quito and which are part of the logic of a treatment of the urban margins of this part of the city (Sierra 2020). In Quito, two accidents in 1983 justified the classification of slopes as "protective wood" and imposed the idea of risk. More than a rupture, these accidents accelerated a process in the making, but, from the heuristic point of view, these reference accidents have a great advantage of revealing the stakes of local development. From this point of view, with admittedly a time lag, the similarities are striking. During the crises linked to the floods in Tunis, three issues appeared, identical in all respects to the construction of the risk of morphoclimatic origin in Quito: mobility, the sanitation system and above all the control of informal urban expansion. The disruption of mobility was a symptom of the crisis, a loss that allowed for immediate diagnosis for all city dwellers and that gave the impression of both exceptionality and novelty. The press reported a general discourse in which global change offered a quickly intelligible key to explanation, widely used by local authorities and city dwellers, avoiding questioning the mode of development and the conditions of mobility of the city. However, with massive urban sprawl, the spectacular increase in the car fleet and the growing need to move, the slightest intense rain has disruptive effects on all of these cities.

---

3 In fact, from the methodological point of view as well as from the point of view of approaches, the research carried out in Quito was at the origin of the research carried out in the framework of the PACIVUR program from 2006 to 2012 in Lima.

Figure 2.3. *The rich city of the developers also produces risk: construction on flood-prone soils on the banks of the northern lake of Tunis in 2019 (upper photo); and building on dead cliffs classified as red zones from a seismic point of view (lower photo). Author: Sierra, 2019, Tunis (above ph.). Sierra, 2012, Lima (lower photo) For a color version of this figure, see www.iste.co.uk/peyroux/development.zip*

The issue represented by the sewerage system is more complex because we are dealing here with an object that has three statuses: it is affected by floods that saturate and damage it; it is a factor creating runoff and flooding of roads because, according to commentators, it cannot carry rainwater away; finally, it is a central development issue because it supports hygiene, which can be considered a common asset of the urban environment (Metzger 1994). This ambivalence makes it a key element in crisis diagnosis. It is for this type of urban object that we have coined the notion of amphibole (Sierra 2020). This term is useful to be able to designate a disorder, an ambiguity, embodied in an object of the urban environment which constitutes at the same time an element of threat or intensification of a threat. It is a factor of urban vulnerability, which it accuses, while being itself affected and having to be protected because of being considered necessary to the functioning or the development of the city. Finally, its potential loss participates in the definition of the risk itself. It is therefore an object of the diagnosis and prognosis of the crisis at the same time as it accentuates its uncertainty.

Finally, the floods in Tunis are an opportunity to highlight the power relations that cross most cities in the South to the detriment of the urban margins (Lopez 2008; Sierra and Tadié 2008). Precarious neighborhoods are not only affected, vulnerable spaces and therefore symptoms of the crisis, but are also the cause of it. The urbanized areas around the two sebkhas (floodable and salty depressions), made up of popular neighborhoods, partly self-built, are represented as one of the major causes of flooding. Certainly, urban expansion producing urban soil on land subject to hazards ipso facto creates risk. What is more surprising is that the catastrophic events occurring in Tunis, as in Quito or Lima, are rarely the occasion to point the finger at the modern factory of the city, that of developers and planning. However, whether in Tunis or Lima, the modern city produced by developers is also built outside the rules of planning and on land subject to hazards (Figure 2.3). In Tunis, the production of urban soil also takes place on the naturally floodable banks of the lake, this being the case since French colonization (Barthel 2006; Ammar 2010). Housing estates under construction require pumping, revealing their propensity to be flooded. These projects nevertheless remain showcases of modernity, a medium for urban utopia as the recent Tunis 2030 project shows[4]. Nothing in the press (nor, moreover, in the expert reports to which we are allowed access) makes it a vulnerability of the city.

The crises are thus an opportunity to show the ambiguity of the notion of vulnerability and the pitfalls of a development whose only objective is to avoid or surmount these paroxysmic moments. The poorer a population is, the more vulnerable it is considered to be (Blaikie et al. 1994), and precarious neighborhoods thus constitute territories of vulnerability for themselves. Approaching risk through vulnerability has the merit of going beyond the exceptional hazard approach, which leads to a sectoral and technical response (Hewitt 1983), to emphasize the underlying social conditions and even the daily lives of populations and the "forgotten people of development" (Gaillard 2007). However, it is undoubtedly the whole paradigm of risk that pushes us to focus on the exceptional moment and

---

4 The A'sima project, subtitled "for a resilient city" (sic), is a mega real-estate project involving Saudi financing planned on the shores of Lake Tunis and involving their polderization.

therefore the crisis. The phenomenon of rupture remains the identifier of the crisis in which a society projects itself and against which it is mobilized. The recurring question asked to the researcher when he works on the crisis in the city is not "which crisis: natural? Industrial? Sanitary?". Even if we consider that the crisis must be approached through vulnerability, it is still evaluated according to the phenomenon of rupture. In the cases discussed, designating precarious, poor and self-built neighborhoods as vulnerable to a particular hazard leads to making them the weak point of the urban system and becomes a "given" (Schutz 2007) that can be mobilized independently of the available data. It is as if what is vulnerable in itself (poor neighborhoods) represents, in a dominant way, a vulnerability for the rest of the city. Conversely, the modern city of developers does not constitute, in these dominant representations, a space at risk, even when it is exposed to natural threat.

2.6. Conclusion

The spread of the crisis from one city to another and from one scale to another is the result of local actors who project the distant crisis onto their own territory, according to their own approach to risk, resulting in controversies with regard to development and the local environment. The crisis is then an opportunity to question and denounce the local relationship of the population to its environment and the local modalities of the urban fabric. This denunciation is therefore both environmental (occupation of land subject to physical dynamics) and bearing on the methods of development (non-regulatory urbanization and self-construction). The argumentation and the controversies then deployed testify to the international and interscalar diffusion of the crisis but through the prism of local issues, certain experts with multiple hats, being the relay actors. They lead to actions or even a mobilization that makes this crisis obvious. In the urgency of the event, however, controversies and actions tend to obscure some of the responsibilities at the expense of the most vulnerable city dwellers and territories: treating these vulnerabilities as a priority appears, in the eyes of the authorities and in fact of great majority of city dwellers, as a rational means of reducing uncertainty in the conduct of the crisis. Is it not indeed logical, according to the current paradigm of development built around risk, to focus attention on what is vulnerable? In this situation where the analysis lacks hindsight, this orientation seems to us to rather proceed from an exacerbation of local power relations and from a representation in which an approach to vulnerabilities and a vision of urban disorder are intertwined: what "is" vulnerable becomes what "makes one" vulnerable.

These power relations are then part of a diversity of spaces, territories and places, a set of neighborhoods or infrastructures that must be "redeveloped", "rehabilitated", "renovated" or attempted to be controlled. In this sense, crisis management becomes, including at the urban and infra-urban scales, a geopolitical issue. The crisis as an opportunity and justification for the treatment of certain spaces is part of this "catastrophe optimism" (Rosario 2007) aimed at stimulating a new urban order. Public authorities are not the only ones concerned: the actors of humanitarian action, for example, transform emergency intervention into a "projectorship" (Lombart et al. 2014), thus becoming in turn actors of the urban fabric. In Lima, following the ENSO phenomenon, denominational organizations forged alliances with the inhabitants and the municipalities to this end: the diocese of Lurín had a church built in a peripheral area affected by the disaster, while the *"young conquerors"* adventists proposed a development plan in another working-class neighborhood on the outskirts of Lurigancho-Chosica. This urban geopolitics of the crisis then translates into an interweaving of territorialities within which a diversity of stakeholders (from public authorities, national or local, to NGOs, via cooperation agencies and religious organizations) act in the name of development and a relationship to the environment consisting of order. Finally, if diagnosing a crisis is a political act, building an end to or a way out of the crisis is another whose geopolitical dimensions, both in terms of development and the environment, remain to be analyzed.

2.7. References

Allal, A. (2010). Les configurations développementistes internationales au Maroc et en Tunisie : Des policy transfers à portée limitée. *Critiques internationales*, 2010/3(48).

Ammar, L. (2010). *Tunis, d'une ville à l'autre, cartographie et histoire urbaine 1860–1935.* Nirvana, Tunis.

Barles, S., Paddeu, F., Abbadie, L., Thébault, E., Lehec, E. (2020). L'urbain, un objet socioécologique. In *Pour la recherche urbaine*, Adisson, F., Barles, S., Blanc, N., Coutard, O., Frouillou, L. (eds). CNRS, Paris.

Barthel, P.A. (2006). Aménager la lagune de Tunis : Un modèle d'urbanisme et de développement durable ? *Autrepart*, 2006/3, 129–146.

Beroutchachvili, N. and Bertrand, G. (1978). Le géosystème ou "système territorial naturel". *Revue géographique des Pyrénées et du Sud-Ouest*, 49/2, 167–180.

Blaikie, P., Cannon, T., Davis, I., Wisner, B. (1994). *At Risk: Natural Hazards, People Vulnerability and Disasters.* Routledge, London. doi: 10.4324/9780203428764.

Boltanski, L. (2009). *De la critique. Précis de sociologie de l'émancipation.* Gallimard, Paris.

Bruntland, G. (1987). Report of the world commission on environment and development: "Our common future". Report, United Nations, New York.

Casteigts, M. (2013). Risques, développement durable et transactions discursives. *Pensée plurielle*, 33–34(2–3), 117–129 [Online]. Available at: https://doi.org/10.3917/pp.033. 0117.

Dussouy, G. (2010). Pragmatisme et géopolitique. Les opportunités méthodologiques d'une retrouvaille épistémologique. *L'Espace Politique*, 12, 2010-3 [Online]. Available at: https://doi.org/10.4000/espacepolitique.1752 [Accessed 29 June 2021].

Fernandez, M.A. (1996). *Ciudades en riesgo*. USAID-La RED, Quito.

Furtado, C. (1966). *Développement et sous-développement*. PUF, Paris.

Gaillard, N. (2015). Le concept de risque pays. Politique étrangère. *Été*, 2, 161–172 [Online]. Available at: https://doi.org/10.3917/pe.152.0161 [Accessed 29 June 2021].

Gaillard, J.C., Liamzon, C., Maceda, E. (2007). Retour sur les causes d'une catastrophe : Pourquoi plus de 1 600 morts aux Philippines fin 2004 ? *Mondes en développement*, 137, 35–50.

Gallais, J. (1994). *Les Tropiques. Terres de risques et de violences*. Armand Colin, Paris.

Gilbert, C. (1992). *Le pouvoir en situation extrême*. L'Harmattan, Paris.

Hewitt, K. (1983). The idea of calamity in a tecnocratic age. In *Interpretation of Calamities: The Risks and Hazards*, Hewitt, K. (ed.). Allen & Unwin Inc., Boston, MA.

Koop, K. and Amilhat Szary, A.L. (2011). Approche critique des modèles de développement territorial dans les Suds. *Information géographique*, 2011/4(75), 6–14.

Lacoste, Y. (1965). *Géographie du sous-développement*. PUF, Paris.

Lacoste, Y (1967). Le concept de sous-développement et la Géographie. *Annales de Géographie*, 76(418), 644–670 [Online]. Available at: https://doi.org/10.3406/geo.1967.15064 [Accessed 29 June 2021].

Latouche, S. (2003). *Décoloniser l'imaginaire. La pensée créative contre l'économie de l'absurde*. Parangon, Lyon.

Lessard, J.-F. (2003). Une société-monde en émergence: Analyse des matrices à la base de cette mutation sociale. *Cahiers de recherche sociologique*, 39, 259–274 [Online]. Available at: https://doi.org/10.7202/1002386ar [Accessed 29 June 2021].

Lévy, J. (2015). La société-Monde, une histoire courte. In *Histoire globale : Un autre regard sur le monde*, Testot, L. (ed.). Éditions Sciences Humaines, Auxerre.

Lombart, M., Pierrat, K., Redon, M. (2014). Port-au-Prince : Un "projectorat" haïtien ou l'urbanisme de projets humanitaires en question. *Cahiers des Amériques latines*, 75, 97– 124.

Lopez, J. (2008). La construction sociale du risque à Medellin (Colombie) : Gouvernance locale et représentations. PhD Thesis, EHESS, Paris.

Mascrey, A. (1993). *Los desastres, no son naturales*. Tercer Mundo, La RED, Bogotà.

Metzger, P. (1994). Contribution à une problématique de l'environnement urbain. *Enjeux et pratiques du développement. Cahiers des Sciences Humaines*, 30(4), 595–619.

Metzger, P. (2020). Environnement urbain. *Dictionnaire critique de l'Anthropocène*. CNRS, Paris.

Nachi, M. (2006). *Introduction à la sociologie pragmatique*. Armand Colin, Paris.

Nurkse, R. (1953). *Problems of Capital-Formation in Underdeveloped Countries*. Basil Blackwell, Oxford.

Protzel de Amat, J. (2011). *Lima imaginada*. Editorial Universidad de Lima, Lima.

Revaud d'Allonnes, M. (2012). *La crise sans fin. Essai sur l'expérience moderne du temps*. Le Seuil, Paris.

Rist, G. (1996). *Le développement : Histoire d'une croyance occidentale*. Presses de Sciences Po, Paris.

Rosario, K. (2007). *The Culture of Calamity: Disaster and the Making of Modern America*. University of Chicago Press, Chicago, IL.

Sachs, I. (1978). Ecodéveloppement : Une approche de planification in Économie rurale. *Écologie et société*, 124, 16–22 [Online]. Available at: https://doi.org/10.3406/ecoru. 1978.2551.

Schutz, A. (2007). *Essai sur le monde ordinaire*. Le Félin, Paris.

Sen, A. (1999). *Development as Freedom*. Oxford University Press, Oxford.

Sierra, A. (2009). Espaces à risque et marges : Méthodes d'approche des vulnérabilités urbaines à Lima et Quito. *Cybergeo: European Journal of Geography*, 456 [Online]. Available at: https://journals.openedition.org/cybergeo/22232 [Accessed 29 June 2021].

Sierra, A. (2015a). Transformer l'incertitude en risque : Un instrument de domination ? In *Espaces et rapports de domination*, Clerval, A., Fleury, A., Rebotier, J., Weber, S. (eds). Presses Universitaires de Rennes, Rennes.

Sierra, A. (2015b). La "capitale-risque" ou comment le statut de capitale participe à construire le risque. *Géocarrefour*, 90(2), 173–182.

Sierra, A. (2020). Des laves torrentielles naturelles, ou produites par les habitants ? L'histoire des expertises sur le risque à Quito (Equateur) à l'heure de l'Anthropocène. *Belgeo : Revue Belge de Géographie*, 3/202 [Online]. Available at: https://journals.openedition. org/belgeo/42986 [Accessed 29 June 2021].

Sierra, A. and Ortiz, D. (2012). Las periferias, ¿territorios de incertidumbre? El caso de Pachacútec, Lima-Callao, Perú. *Bulletin de l'Institut français d'études andines*, 41(3), 523–554.

Sierra, A. and Tadié, J. (2008). Introduction. La ville face à ses marges. *Autrepart*, 2008/1(45), 3–13.

City, Environment and "Sustainable Development": Critical Approaches and Renewal of Urban Research

3.1. Introduction

Since the 1970s, the environment has played an increasing role in development policies and in urban research. An interdisciplinary field of knowledge has opened up, accompanying the rise of "environmental issues" in the definition of public policies. The opening up of this field raises numerous questions of epistemology and positions within the social sciences. This chapter examines these questions based on a bibliographical synthesis in the fields of urban and economic geography, sociology and, more broadly, in both French and foreign (English and Spanish) urban studies, emphasizing the place of development and the environment in analytical frameworks.

Development emphasizes a triple register of interdependencies: temporal, of domains (economic, social, political, cultural, environmental) and spatial (Zuindeau 2008). Urban studies have thus increased the number of analytical approaches to better understand the functioning, production and governance of the city as well as the modes of living in their interactions with social, material, natural and technical processes. The renewal of urban issues is largely based on constructivist approaches to nature and the environment, and on radical and critical approaches which question ontological divisions (between nature and culture, humans and non-humans, subject and object) and propose new ways of understanding inequalities (political, social, socio-environmental). "Sustainable urban development", understood as a public policy which in its rhetoric aims at a structural transformation of production and

Chapter written by Élisabeth PEYROUX and Pascale METZGER.

consumption modes, has become an object of investigation, itself the bearer of new research objects ("ecological transition", "green growth") resulting from public policies.

Secondly, the term development refers to a particular link between politics and social sciences (Nederveen Pierterse 2010). A set of concepts and theories for some (Lafaye de Micheaux et al. 2007), a normative referential or an ideology shaped by the North–South relations for others (Rist 2007), development and its specific field ("development studies") are often equated with applied social sciences and phenomena observed "in the South". Their theoretical importance has been underestimated in a context where development has long been thought of in a linear fashion on the model of Western societies, a framework that is now being questioned.

Environmental issues also question the link between research and public policies. The borrowing or transfer of categories between these two domains shows the difficulty of constructing research problems and objects outside the categories of public action (Lemaire et al. 2020). Coupled with the evolution of the conditions of production of research, increasingly constrained by institutional demand, social sciences approach to the environment is trapped between interdisciplinarity and the words and issues imposed by public policies. The analysis of the articulation between development and environment in the field of urban studies therefore requires a twofold perspective: on the one hand, this involves retracing the emergence of a new field of knowledge and, on the other hand, showing how environmental issues, by imposing categories of analysis, shape scientific research, in particular that relating to "sustainable urban development".

This chapter first shows how approaches to the city have evolved from a primarily political–economic reading to works that integrate environmental issues, from both physical and political angles. It then outlines the paradoxes and challenges facing research on the "sustainable city", between local innovations and global governance. Finally, it presents some avenues for urban research which, by opening up to new objects and new issues, make the city an increasingly complex and hybrid object.

3.2. Economy and development: the political–economic approach to the city

Until the 1970s, apart from the work on urban–rural relations (see Chapter 9, "New approaches to urban-rural relations?"), urban research was essentially concerned with understanding the mode of production, operation and management of the city as an expression of the economic development model. What are now called "environmental constraints" were ignored, leading to a body of scientific literature that considered urban spaces not subject to the physical environment, except when speaking of the "site constraints" of physical geography.

3.2.1. *The city as an "engine of growth"*

In economic geography and in part of urban and regional geography, as well as in the literature from international organizations, the city has been analyzed as an "engine of growth". Its role in the organization of national and local production systems is studied, with particular attention to territorial forms of economic development (local production systems, industrial districts, technopoles) (Benko and Lipietz 1992; Castells and Hall 1994; Grosetti 2004). A functionalist vision of urban spaces predominates (the city and its hinterland, its productive, employment and supply basin, the enterprise and its "innovative environment"[1]). The spatial transformations of the city are associated with each major development model (Fordist, post-Fordist) (Storper and Scott 1989). In line with the reflections on the links between cities and capitalism (Lefevbre 1968; Castells and Hall 1994; Harvey 2004), the urban scale is taking precedence over the national scale in the analysis of the processes of capital accumulation. In a context of economic liberalization and financial deregulation at the international level, the work emphasizes the issues of privatization, decentralization and fiscal austerity, and the way in which cities, and more particularly metropolitan authorities, engage in competitive and territorial marketing strategies to attract investment and employment. These strategies are reflected in national land-use planning policies that play metropolises off against each other, thus participating in the fierce international competition between cities. The dominant actors in urban production (local governments, private actors, coalitions/networks of actors) become central objects of analysis of "urban neoliberalism" (Harvey 1989; Brenner and Theodore 2002; Arab et al. 2020).

The term "local economic development" used in both the North and the South expresses not only the promotion of economic growth based on local resources and actors, but also the promotion of local democracy through the decentralization reforms of the 1980s (Jaglin and Dubresson 1993; Dubresson and Fauré 2005). The term "territorial development", which was later coined, reinforces the idea of development within a given territory, with boundaries and organized social relations, and with particular social groups (Torre 2015).

---

1 The expression "innovative environment" refers to the importance given to the proximity between businesses and universities to explain economic dynamism and innovation (see "technopoles").

At the same time, echoing economic globalization, the reading of cities as territories linked to global flows of goods, capital, information and population is becoming increasingly important (Sassen 1991; Castells 1996). With the rise of newly industrialized and emerging countries, the place of the cities of the South in the international division of labor is changing. The urban hierarchy, which can be read on an international scale on the basis of competition as well as domination criteria (importance of stock markets, reputation of universities, quality of facilities and services, transport hubs, cultural reputation), is transcending the old North/South divide. This is reflected in national policies and in the evolution of urban planning: project-based urbanism is spreading, serving these same strategies, so as to attract jobs and investment, modernize the city and make it more competitive, in a context that demonstrates the international circulation of urban models, between the North and the South, as well as between cities in the South (Peck and Theodore 2010; McCann and Ward 2011; Peck and Theodore 2015; Peyroux and Sanjuan 2016).

In the 1980s, the critical literature focused on the need to find a compromise between economic and social issues (Turok 2007).

3.2.2. *Economic issues versus social issues*

In North American and European cities, the processes of social polarization, urban fragmentation, exclusion, inequality and gentrification of the "neoliberal" city are denounced, as well as the inability of social policies to regulate the tensions of capitalism.

In Asian and African countries, which are undergoing rapid urbanization (Franck and Sanjuan 2015; Goldblum et al. 2017; Jaglin et al. 2018), as well as in Latin America, the theory of dependency and "underdevelopment" was first mobilized to explain the persistence of poverty, the lack of infrastructure, the weakness of public authorities and the fragmentation of cities (Roy 2009). Research on the Latin American city questions the links between the dynamics of urbanization, the formation of post-colonial states and the economic model to follow in order to emerge from "underdevelopment" (Metzger et al. 2016). The inability of cities to absorb rural–urban migration, in terms of housing, facilities, services and jobs, has led to a generalized crisis: urban expansion based on self-building, illegality, informality, widespread under-equipment, lack of urban services, and poverty. Subsequently, approaches using a critical neoliberal lens take precedence.

In the 1980s and 1990s, the implementation of neoliberal policies in a context of economic globalization became the main driving force of urban transformations and their interpretation by research in urban geography and urban sociology, bringing with it notions, such as the hypertrophy of metropolises, socio-spatial segregations, privatization and fragmentation (Duhau 2012). The analysis of the processes of transformation of land use (renovation of historic centers, business districts, gated communities, new centralities, privatized public spaces, etc.) takes precedence over research on urban expansion, access to land and the production of low-cost, affordable housing. It is demonstrated that the whole city is becoming a market, with the development of low-cost private services (education, health) in working-class neighborhoods, the commodification of public spaces and the growing weight of real-estate developers as actors in urban production. This observation has also been made in Africa, particularly as a result of the circulation of entrepreneurial urban policy models (Miraftab 2007; Bénit-Gbaffou et al. 2012; Didier et al. 2013). The literature on city and structural adjustment shows how international organizations instrumentalize the "local". Thus, the promotion of decentralized urban management by the World Bank aims to profoundly modify the system of power by marginalizing central power, in favor of a discourse on the effectiveness of cities and local powers for promoting economic development (Osmont 1995, p. 282).

Scholars claiming to be part of the critical Southern turn movement (Choplin 2012; Edensor and Jayne 2012; Parnell and Robinson 2012) call for greater diversity of theoretical frameworks and a greater internationalization of urban theories, beyond North–South divides and approaches in terms of neoliberalism (Robinson 2006; Roy 2009). While some of the theories developed in the context of cities of the North are relevant to cities of the South, theories developed for cities of the South can also contribute to a better understanding of urban situations in the North, as in the case of informality (Jacquot and Morelle 2018) or socio-spatial segregation (Pfirsch and Semi 2016).

3.3. Urban research renewed by environmental issues

Environmental issues are renewing discourses and actors, representations and social practices, public policies and international norms, economic forms, social mobilization figures as well as new modes of governance (Theys 2002). These transformations are of particular importance in the city. They have led to an evolution in urban research, bringing along new issues as well as new ways of producing research, in a rather unclear epistemological context.

3.3.1. *Epistemological barriers and institutional constraints*

In France, social sciences have long resisted taking into account the environment (Henry and Jollivet 1998) as a new field of knowledge, due to a combination of both epistemological and institutional obstacles. Firstly, social sciences, which focus on "social facts", are epistemologically incapable of taking into account the "facts of nature" involved in the environmental issue (Boudes 2008; Kalaora and Vlassopoulos 2013), despite work on the nature–culture relationship. Indeed, social sciences, and especially sociology, have historically been constructed by claiming the autonomy of the social question against biological determinism and the natural environment (Kalaora and Larrere 1989; Boudes 2008).

3.3.1.1. A difficulty in defining the urban environment

The early institutionalization of the environment in the French administration (through the creation of the Ministry of the Environment in 1971) is another difficulty that resulted in both commissioned research and a demand for operationalization (Kalaora and Vlassopoulos 2013). Yet, historically, the social sciences are reluctant to respond to social demand, this approach being seen as a form of "misguidance" of the research (Castel 2009), or even as a role of' prince's advisor" to which they cannot comply (Dubar 2004). On the other hand, the pressure exerted by the demand for research on the environment, in parallel with the emergence of ecological movements, makes this question be perceived as a matter of ideology (Charles and Kalaora 2003; Boudes 2008). These arguments, are many cognitive and almost atavistic obstacles to an understanding of the environment by the social sciences, and have contributed to making the environment, particularly the urban environment, an object that has long been neglected and difficult to grasp for the social sciences, and more particularly sociology, leaving the institutional and civil society actors to appropriate this new theme (Boudes 2008).

Historically, the environmental issue first emerged in the 1960s–1970s as a social and political issue (Rudolf 2013), rooted in living environment issues and new forms of social mobilization, in a national and international context of awareness of the environmental limits of the growth model (Bonneuil 2017). The research occurred in fits and starts, pragmatically, producing a long list of themes and strands related to something referred to as the environment (Jollivet and Pavé 1993).

In most works, however, whether in geography or sociology (as well as in engineering and hard science), only one aspect of the urban environmental issue is dealt with (green spaces, waste management, transport networks, air pollution, urban climate, noise pollution, biodiversity in the city, new social struggles). This research does not claim to define the urban environment, which refers to the interaction between nature and society, i.e. to a set of interacting material and social elements in which societies evolve. Scholars in social sciences thus take note of the fact that "natural and ecological processes do not operate independently of social processes" (Kalaora and Vlassoupoulos 2013), a formulation that leaves "natural processes" at the heart of the environment. Working on urban environmental issues in the city should have made it obvious that it is no longer a natural environment. Yet, scholars continue to speak of environment as the natural environment, no effort has been made to conceptualize the environment differently.

This movement has led to research conducted under the label "urban environment", which refers globally to questions of "nature in the city", "risks" or "urban management" (Metzger 2017), in which we can include questions of governance and ecological inequalities (Theys 2002; Faburel 2010). The environment is seen as a set of phenomena caused by the interweaving of natural and social phenomena, irreducible to the field of the social alone (Kalaora and Vlassoupoulos 2013). The environment has thus come to question the paradigms of sociology insofar as it is a question of stating a "sociology that is not strictly social" (Boudes 2008).

Within this framework, political ecology highlights new forms of inequalities and injustice and provides an interpretation of the world and relations of domination transformed by the environmental question (Gautier and Benjaminsen 2012).

3.3.1.2. The city as a "socio-ecological" object, urbanization as a "socio-environmental" phenomenon

The confusion and profusion of terms used (ecosystem, metabolism, anthroposystem, urban ecology) underline the absence of a definition of the urban environment by the social sciences. But they can also be seen as efforts by urban research, not to define the urban environment, but to characterize and conceptualize the city through renewed approaches able to integrate materiality and natural objects and processes.

Many approaches attempt to understand the interactions between society and the environment, as understood by the natural sciences (the biosphere, nature, the "living"). However, "socio-ecological" approaches are relatively few in number when it comes to exploring the urban question despite interdisciplinary approaches (Barles et al. 2020). These approaches remain closely linked to a naturalistic conception of "ecosystems", as in the criticism of the term "resilience" (Davoudi 2012; Reghezza-Zitt et al. 2012) and confine analyses to a dualism between the social and environmental realms (Barles et al. 2020).

Urban political ecology, which emerged in the early 2000s from Marxist approaches, as a counterpoint to the urban ecology of the Chicago School (see a synthesis in Barles et al. (2020)), reinterprets the organization and function of the city by focusing on the political production of urban environments (Angelo and Wachsmuth 2014). It redefines categories ("nature", "culture", "humans" and "non-humans"), historicizes socio-environmental processes, reintegrates materiality ("socio-technical devices") and politicizes questions of sustainability by questioning the winners and losers of public policies (Barles et al. 2020). In line with work on the "right to the city" and "spatial justice" (Lefebvre 1968; Soja 2010; Morange and Spire 2019), it designates the urban environment as a crucial site of contestation of the regime of capitalist accumulation, following the example of the environmental justice movement.

The analytical frameworks of urban political ecology remain anthropocentric, however, and other avenues of research on human/non-human relationships and the relationship to living things deserve to be explored (Barles et al. 2020). Secondly, the studies focus on the city, considered as "the only analytical terrain of the urban environment", and not on urbanization as a process (Angelo and Wachsmuth 2014, p. 21). They elude non-city-centered urban processes and do not sufficiently consider everyday life.

According to Barles et al. (2020, pp. 158–159), there is "still a strong gap in addressing the articulation between contemporary urban capitalism and urban studies and urban ecological, technical and socio-environmental dynamics". The work on the interactions between global environmental changes and urban dynamics (Simon and Leck 2014), however, emphasizes transcalar issues in analyzing the consequences of urbanization: they show the consequences that a change in technology or a demand for resources in a city has on distant territories, for example, the exploitation of rare-earth metals necessary for the production of digital devices. This is in line with a re-theorization of the urbanization process as a global environmental phenomenon that takes into account aspects of urban processes not limited to the urban spaces (Angelo and Wachsmuth 2014).

3.3.2. *Paradoxes and challenges of the sustainable city*

3.3.2.1. *The sustainable city, between social innovations and the reproduction of relations of domination*

The global injunction to development and the question posed by climate change have transformed the management of the world, while reshaping scientific questions about the city around words imposed by public policies (Kalaora and Vlassoupoulos 2013). Indeed, sustainable development is going to become increasingly prevalent in thinking about urban development. It is the subject of consensus as well as multiple controversies, both in the scientific field and in the social world (Martin 2002; Rist 2007; Felli 2008). The paradox of sustainable development is that it is both a vehicle for social transformation and democratic openness at the local level, and an instrument for the reproduction of the social order and relations of domination on a planetary scale. Indeed, sustainable development and its urban version, the sustainable city, contribute to opening the field of the market economy to objects of the social and natural world (pollution rights, the living) that had remained outside this field, thus showing "the incredible aptitude of capitalism to revolutionize itself" (Rudolf 2013).

The sustainable city is at the origin of a multitude of local initiatives and new practices, involving new actors for the improvement of the living environment, health and the preservation of the environment. The territories, and the city in particular, are becoming places for experimenting "good practices", which constitute as many new objects for the social sciences. Green growth, "alternative technologies", "smart cities" (Henriot et al. 2018; Khan et al. 2018), participation, and the energy transition open up new perspectives for development while maintaining "growth".

The city as an object is being redefined both in its urban and local dimensions, with ever closer interconnection and ever greater tensions between social, economic and environmental dimensions.

The emphasis on economic development and urban regeneration in the 1980s and 1990s gradually gave way in the 2000s to policies aimed at making urbanization compatible with environmental concerns. Urban planning seeks to control the links between urban form and sustainability in a context of controversy over the correlation between the two (Laigle 2009). This is evidenced by discourses on the control of urban sprawl, the densification of urban centers, the extension of public transport networks, mixed-use developments, the energy renovation of the built environment and other so-called public policies in favor of environmental protection (Laigle 2009). The control of land by the public authorities is recognized as a key issue in urban planning policies. This vision of urban planning gives a central place to the link between urban planning and transport, which produces visible transformations with the aim of reducing car use (multimodal transport, pedestrianization, bicycle paths). These new urban policies are also embodied in "eco-neighborhood" projects, the second generation of which now incorporates smart city technologies. While these planning choices can improve urban quality, they also raise questions of social equity and environmental justice (Laigle 2009). The "green planning" or "greening" of public spaces, carried out in the name of "nature in the city", increases the value of land, as shown by the work on green gentrification in Barcelona and Brooklyn.

Since the 2010s, the "return of the local" also aims to reduce the ecological footprint of cities through the promotion of "short circuits", the "relocation" of economic activities and the development of urban and peri-urban agriculture, around "consuming less" and "consuming differently" associated with energy reduction (Semal and Szuba 2010). This movement refers to forms of local action, from below, at the scale of neighborhoods or cities, supported and popularized by the international movement of Transition Towns. These forms of local mobilization, on a territorial basis, are part of the international diffusion of new forms of local governance, such as participatory budgets.

The discourse on the post-carbon city promoted by local authorities or major operators also claims the "return of the local" by questioning the links between consumption, production and resources. The post-carbon city must "make the city productive again", supporting a virtuous metabolism. The notion of "circular and self-sufficient city" of the French Urbanism Construction Architecture Plan (*Plan urbanisme construction architecture*) (PUCA 2020), which takes up the approaches in terms of "short supply chain" and "urban metabolism", suggests a more virtuous urban development model, the advent of which has yet to be confirmed.

3.3.2.2. *The challenges and issues of the "city optimized by technology"*

Information and communication technologies (ICT) and digital technology reshape urban spaces, practices and services while promoting new development models (Douay 2018; Baraud-Serfaty et al. 2017; Beckouche 2019; Peyroux and Ninot 2019). Many areas of urban management are concerned: e-governance, monitoring and regulation of infrastructures, energy management, risk and crisis management. They are accompanied by a discourse of optimization through more efficient management and regulation of flows and activities, increased surveillance of public spaces, the production of new types of data for modeling urban processes and a discourse on citizen empowerment through open data and data transparency (Batty et al. 2012; Verrest and Pfeffer 2018). The critical literature, meanwhile, is concerned with the often simplistic and systemic view of cities that underlies the use of digital technology and the societal implications of surveillance technologies (Kitchin et al. 2017).

In the countries of the South, we note the rapid expansion of the use of cell phones and mobile applications (Ninot and Peyroux 2018). International organizations, in particular, consider that the digital economy has positive effects on productivity, growth, wealth and well-being, and offer developing economies the opportunity to "leapfrog" the steps that industrialized countries have taken. However, there is no consensus, and the diffusion of these technologies raises debates about the reinforcement of social and economic inequalities (Maiti et al. 2020) and their environmental impact. The "digital divide", at the heart of development policies, often posed in technical terms (infrastructure development, access, use and spatial distribution of ICT and digital equipment, promotion of access to digital content), hides the contradictions of development policies: for example, education and training, which are nonetheless necessary for digital literacy, are subject to budgetary austerity. The increased dependence of countries in the South on ICT operators and suppliers, as part of the "modernization 2.0" of the new "digital capitalism" promoted by the proponents of ICT4D (ICT for development), contributes to perpetuating the idea that "the diffusion of market forces is equivalent to development" (Nederveen Pieterse 2010, p. 170).

3.3.2.3. *Between pragmatism of local action...*

The sustainable city is the subject of empirical research on good governance and new public arenas, as well as on the conditions of acceptability of public policies (Theys and Emelianoff 2001). This new governance is conducted in a form of depoliticization and political disengagement (Emelianoff 2004; Rudolf 2013): it is a matter of implementing an ecological modernization that "holds out the prospect of overcoming the ecological crisis without breaking down", i.e. that does not call into question the relations of production and neutralizes social relations (Rudolf 2013). In the name of good governance and pragmatism, decentralization and participation are used to reduce down the management of the world to the local, and to point to the responsibility of individuals (Salles 2009; Quenault 2015). The naturalization of environmental problems in the sense of reducing them to physical, technical or management aspects at the local level (Reghezza-Zitt and Rufat 2015) allows us to only consider the causal factors that are considered "manageable" within the framework of sustainable development, i.e. locally and within the framework of neoliberal economics.

Thus, the "sustainable city", expressed in terms of compact city, mixed city, energy-efficient city, citizen-centric city, green city, smart city, resilient city, becomes a marketing argument for economic competition between territories, contradictory to the idea of planetary solidarity carried by the environmental issue. (Theys and Emelianoff 2001). Sustainable development implemented on a local scale tends to increase social and environmental inequalities. In concrete terms, while environmental degradation is a global issue, acting locally on local "environmental problems" often leads to externalizing the problems to neighboring territories (Theys and Emelianoff 2001; Felli 2016). Thus, the location of polluting activities in the poorest regions highlights the fact that the management of environmental risks operates by displacing them in function of relationships of domination. Under these conditions, environmental policies themselves produce inequalities and injustices (Theys and Emelianoff 2001; Emelianoff 2004; Felli 2016). This vision of the sustainable city operates on the local level of environmental management, which has the effect of disconnecting them from major social and political issues (production and consumption patterns, health, unemployment, security, etc.) (Reghezza-Zitt et al. 2012; Quenault 2015), while allowing for improvements in both the political field of local governance and on the local/living environment. Thus, the focus on "local innovations" tends to hide the reproduction of the economic model. But, in return, paying attention to the permanence of the system's trajectory can obscure the real social transformations it brings about.

This pragmatism of local action, which supports the role of the city in the ecological transition, makes it possible both to do without the criticism of the economic model (Rudolf 2013) and to decentralize environmental problems (Pestre 2011) by assuming a linear and univocal link between local action and global effect, in contradiction with the hypercomplexity and global interdependencies of environmental problems.

3.3.2.4. ...and overall environmental governance: towards urban climate governance

The issue of "global environmental governance", brought to the forefront by climate issues, takes further into account the context of uncertainty, interdependencies and hypercomplexity.

Environmental governance defines the environment as a global problem requiring global solutions. Cities, considered to be both the source of carbon emissions and greenhouse gases that produce climate change, and as the best place to reduce these emissions, are given a central place in the transition to post-carbon societies, as they are supposed to be better placed than states to reduce emissions and adopt mitigation and adaptation measures (Bulkeley 2010). Cities are becoming both the places and the actors of climate governance, as shown by the multiplication of transnational networks and alliances of cities dedicated to climate change and sustainable urban development (C40, networks of low-carbon cities, etc.) (Bulkeley 2010; Acuto 2013). The rise of cities in international development agendas (Sustainable Development Goals, New Urban Agenda) and in transnational networks goes along with a broadening of urban studies around new power relations.

Global environmental governance shifts the perspective from multi-level to transcalar governance (Bulkeley 2010) (see Chapter 5, "The European Union and the Energy Transition"). Transnational networks of cities and local governments are moving away from the classic territorial frameworks associated with a nested conception of scales, and a center-periphery vision. They are seen as new modes of coordination and governance based on horizontal political relationships. Breaking with the ontological division of "internal/external" at the foundation of the discipline of international relations (Compagnon 2013), they shake up the hierarchy of actors and open up new global public spaces. To speak of urban (rather than local) climate governance does not refer to a territorialized power scale, but to a space, a site, a territory where several actors may act who do not necessarily belong to this territorial level. This transcalar approach opens up a theoretical reflection on the "city political agency" in international affairs and global governance (Acuto 2013; Peyroux 2016), in particular the capacity of city-to-city networks, beyond the dissemination of "good practices", to create new "spheres of authority", capable of setting rules (Betsill and Bulkeley 2006).

This field opens up interesting avenues of research both for the field of international relations and for geography (Aust 2015): the international action of cities within networks and other instances of global governance poses the question of the particular form of non-state actors that cities and networks take on in international law, notably by constituting hybrid configurations of governance that associate local governments, private actors and transnational networks (Acuto 2013).

3.4. Conclusion

Analytical categories, discourses and policies fostered by environmental issues and the sustainable city have reconfigured urban research both in the North and the South. The integration of new objects (physical, technical and natural), coupled with political, economic and territorial changes, and the rise of the urban question in the environment/development relationship at local and international levels, has transformed the understanding of the city and urban spaces. Growth patterns, interdependencies between spaces and scales, and the relationship between the city and nature are being reframed, at the same time as new questions are emerging concerning the role of cities as actors in climate governance, the re-configuration of urban spaces and practices by digital technology, as well as the blurring of scales and relationships of domination.

This renewal of urban research is leading towards new epistemological foundations and theoretical frameworks, by disrupting the boundaries between research objects and by paradigm shifts within the social sciences (the society/nature divide, human/non-human, socio-ecological and trans-cultural approaches). At the same time, it seems necessary to open up to other disciplines (digital sciences, "hard" sciences, law and international relations, etc.) in order to account for the complexity of the objects, interactions and actors involved in the environment/ development problem. The multiple forms taken by the city/environment/ development relationship appear to be a promising direction for formulating a new understanding of the urban question.

Faced with the multiple contradictions of the sustainable city revisited from this angle, the scientific questioning is situated between two extreme positions. The first is to decipher the new dynamics, urban policies and discourses that make it possible to manipulate reality in order to make the neoliberal economic growth model seem sustainable (Felli 2014). This critical positioning implies going beyond the local level and the urban environmental issue to question the modes of production and consumption imposed at the global level. A second position is to consider that sustainable urban development contributes concretely to the transformation of the world. This is because its implementation and its "good practices", although limited and contingent, nevertheless make it possible to locally and concretely improve the "quality of the environment" and the living conditions of the inhabitants. This positioning suggests that changes in the world can be driven by the city, which is emerging as a global player and a space for political experimentation likely to transform the relationship between environment and development.

3.5. References

Acuto, M. (2013). *Global Cities, Governance and Diplomacy*. Routledge, London.

Angelo, H. and Wachsmuth, D. (2014). Urbanizing urban political ecology: A critique of methodological cityism. *International Journal of Urban and Regional Research*, 39(1), 16–27.

Arab, N., Bonnefond, M., Dris, Y., Lefeuvre, M.-P., Miot, Y. (2020). La production de la ville au prisme de ses acteurs et de leurs activités : Des recompositions à explorer. In *Pour la recherche urbaine*, Adisson, F., Barles, S., Blanc, N., Coutard, O., Frouillon, L., Rassat, F. (eds). CNRS, Paris.

Aust, P.A. (2015). Shining cities on the Hill? The global city, climate change, and international law. *The European Journal of International Law*, 26(1), 255–278.

Baraud-Serfaty, I., Rio, N., Fourchy, C. (eds) (2017). Qui paiera la ville (de) demain ? Étude sur les nouveaux modèles économes urbains. Report, Ibicy, Acadie, Espelia.

Barles, S., Abbadie, L., Lehec, E., Paddeu, F., Thébault, E. (2020). L'urbain, un objet socio-écologique ? In *Pour la recherche urbaine*, Adisson, F., Barles, S., Blanc, N., Coutard, O., Frouillon, L., Rassat, F. (eds). CNRS, Paris.

Batty, M., Axhausen, K., Giannotti, F., Pozdnoukhov, A., Bazzani, A., Wachowicz, M., Ouzounis, G.K., Portugali, Y. (2012). Smart cities of the future. *European Physical Journal*, 214(1), 481–518.

Beckouche, P. (2019). *Les nouveaux territoires du numérique. L'univers digital du sur-mesure de masse*. Editions Sciences Humaines, Auxerre.

Bénit-Gbaffou, C., Didier, S., Peyroux, É. (2012). Circulation of security models in Southern African cities: Between neoliberal encroachment and local power dynamics. *The International Journal of Urban and Regional Research*, 36(5), 877–889.

Benko, G. and Lepietz, A. (1992). *Les régions qui gagnent. Districts et réseaux : Les nouveaux paradigmes de la géographie économique*. PUF, Paris.

Betsill, M. and Bulkeley, H. (2006). Cities and the multilevel governance of climate change. *Global Governance*, 12(2), 141–159.

Bonneuil, C. (2017). Capitalocène, réflexions sur l'échange écologique inégal et le crime climatique à l'âge de l'Anthropocène. *EcoRev'*, 44, 52–60.

Boudes, P. (2008). L'environnement, domaine sociologique. La sociologie française au risque de l'environnement. PhD Thesis, Université Victor Segalen Bordeaux II, Bordeaux.

Brenner, N. and Theodore, N. (2002). Cities and the geographies of "Actually Existing Neoliberalism". *Antipode*, 33(3), 349–379.

Bulkeley, H. (2010). Cities and the governing of climate change. *Annual Review of Environment and Resources*, 35, 229–253.

Castel, R. (2009). *La montée des incertitudes*. Le Seuil, Paris.

Castells, M. (1996). *The Rise of the Network Society*. Blackwell Publishers Ltd, Oxford.

Castells, M. and Hall, P. (1994). *Technopoles of the World: The Making of Twenty-first Century Industrial Complexes*. Routledge, London.

Charles, L. and Kalaora, B. (2003). Sociologie et environnement en France : L'environnement introuvable ? *Écologie et Politique*, 27, 31–57.

Choplin, A. (2012). Désoccidentaliser la pensée urbaine. *Métropolitiques* [Online]. Available at: https://metropolitiques.eu/Desoccidentaliser-la-pensee.html [Accessed 28 June 2021].

Compagnon, D. (2013). L'environnement dans les RI. In *Traité de relations internationales*, Balzacq, T. (ed.). Presses de Sciences Po, Paris.

Davoudi, S. (2012). Resilience: A bridging concept or a dead end? *Planning Theory and Practice*, 13(2), 299–333.

Didier, S., Morange, M., Peyroux, É. (2013). The adaptative nature of neoliberalism at the local scale: Fifteen years of city improvement districts in cape town and Johannesburg. *Antipode*, 45(1), 121–139.

Douay, N. (2018). *Urban Planning in the Digital Age*. ISTE Ltd, London, and John Wiley & Sons, New York.

Dubar, C. (2004). Les tentatives de professionnalisation des études de sociologie, un bilan prospectif. In *A quoi sert la sociologie ?* Lahire, B. (ed.). La Découverte, Paris.

Dubresson, A. and Fauré, Y.-A. (2005). Décentralisation et développement local : Un lien à repenser. *Revue tiers monde*, 181(1), 7–20.

Duhau, E. (2012). La sociologie urbaine et les métropoles latino-américaines. *Sociologies* [Online]. Available at: https://doi.org/10.4000/sociologies.4193 [Accessed 3 June 2021].

Edensor, T. and Jayne, M. (2012). *Urban Theory Beyond the West: A World of Cities*. Routledge, London.

Emelianoff, C. (2004). L'urbanisme durable en Europe : A quel prix ? *Écologie & politique*, 21–36.

Faburel, G. (2010). Débats sur les inégalités environnementales. Une autre approche de l'environnement urbain. *Justice spatiale*, 2 [Online]. Available at: https://www.jssj.org/article/debats-sur-les-inegalites-environnementales-une-autre-approche-de-lenvironnement-urbain/ [Accessed 28 June 2021].

Felli, R. (2008). *Les deux âmes de l'écologie : Une critique du développement durable*. L'Harmattan, Paris.

Felli, R. (2014). Adaptation et résilience : Critique de la nouvelle éthique de la politique environnementale internationale. *Éthique publique*, 16(1) 101–120.

Felli, R. (2016). *La grande adaptation. Climat, capitalisme et catastrophe*. Le Seuil, Paris.

Franck, M. and Sanjuan, T. (eds) (2015). *Territoires de l'urbain en Asie : Une nouvelle modernité ?* CNRS, Paris.

Gautier, D. and Benjaminsen, T.A. (2012). *Environnement, discours et pouvoir*. Editions Quae, Versailles.

Goldblum, G., Peyronnie, K., Sisoulath, B. (2017). *Transitions urbaines en Asie du Sud-Est. De la métropolisation émergente et de ses formes dérivées*. Irasec/IRD Éditions, Mayenne.

Grossetti, M. (2004). Concentration d'entreprises et innovation : Esquisse d'une typologie des systèmes productifs locaux. *Géographie, économie, société*, 2(2), 163–177.

Harvey, D. (1989). From managerialism to entrepreneurialism: The transformation in urban governance in late capitalism. *Geografiska Annaler. Series B, Human Geography*, 71(1), 3–17.

Harvey, D. (2004). L'urbanisation du capital. *Actuel Marx*, 1(1), 41–70.

Henriot, C., Douay, N., Granier, B., Languillon-Aussel, R., Leprêtre, N. (2018). Perspectives asiatiques sur les Smart Cities. *Flux*, 114(4), 1–8.

Henry, C. and Jollivet, M. (1998). La question de l'environnement dans les sciences sociales. Programme Environnement Vie et Sociétés du CNRS. CNRS letter, Paris, 17.

Jacquot, S. and Morelle, M. (2018). Comment penser l'informalité dans les villes "du Nord", à partir des théories urbaines "du Sud" ? *Métropoles*, 22 [Online]. Available at: http://journals.openedition.org/metropoles/5601 [Accessed 28 June 2021].

Jaglin, S. and Dubresson, A. (1993). *Pouvoirs et cités d'Afrique noire, décentralisations en questions*. Karthala, Paris.

Jaglin, S., Didier, S., Dubresson, A. (2018). Métropolisations en Afrique subsaharienne : Au menu ou à la carte ? *Métropoles* [Online]. Available at: https://journals.openedition.org/metropoles/6065#:~:text=PDF-,M%C3%A9tropolisations%20en%20Afrique%20subsaharienne%20%3A%20au%20menu%20ou%20%C3%A0%20la%20carte,Chine%20ou%20de%20l'Inde [Accessed 28 June 2021].

Jollivet, M. and Pavé, A. (1993). L'environnement, un champ de recherche en formation. *Natures Sciences Sociétés*, 1(1), 6–20.

Kalaora, B. and Larrere, R. (1989). Les sciences sociales et les sciences de la nature au péril de leur rencontre. In *Du rural à l'environnement*, Mathieu, N. and Jollivet, M. (eds). L'Harmattan, Paris.

Kalaora, B. and Vlassopoulos, C. (2013). *Pour une sociologie de l'environnement. Environnement, société et politique*. Seyssel, Champ-Vallon.

Khan, S., Taraporevala, P., Zérah, M. (2018). Les villes intelligentes indiennes : Défis communs et diversification des trajectoires. *Flux*, 4(4), 86–99.

Kitchin, R., Coletta, C., McArdle, G. (2017). Urban informatics, governmentality and the logics of urban control. Working document, The Programmable City Working Paper, 25.

Lafaye de Micheaux, E., Ould-Ahmed, P., Mulot, E. (eds) (2007). *Institutions et développement. La fabrique institutionnelle des trajectoires de développement.* Presses Universitaires de Rennes, Rennes.

Laigle, L. (ed.) (2009). *Vers des villes durables – Les trajectoires de quatre agglomérations européennes.* Édition Recherche Puca, Paris.

Lefebvre, H. (1968). *Le droit à la ville.* Point, Paris.

Lemaire, N., Peyroux, É., Robineau, O. (2020). Circulation des modèles urbains : Acquis et perspectives de recherche interdisciplinaire et multiscalaire. In *Pour la recherche urbaine*, Adisson, F., Barles, S., Blanc, N., Coutard, O., Frouillou, L., Rassat, F. (eds). CNRS, Paris.

Maiti, D., Castellacci, F., Melchior, N. (2020). *Digitalisation and Development: Issues for India and Beyond.* Springer Verlag, Singapore.

Martin, J.-Y. (eds) (2002). *Développement durable. Doctrines, pratiques, évaluations.* IRD Editions, Marseille.

McCann, E. and Ward, K. (2011). *Mobile Urbanism: City Policymaking in the Global Age.* University of Minnesota Press, Minneapolis, MN.

Metzger, P. (2017). Connaissance et relations de pouvoir. Les sciences sociales, les risques et l'environnement. HDR Thesis, Université Grenoble Alpes, Grenoble.

Metzger, P., Rebotier, J., Robert, J., Urquieta, P., Vega Centeno, P. (eds) (2016). *La cuestión urbana en la región andina. Miradas sobre la investigación y la formación.* PUCE – FADA, Quito.

Miraftab, F. (2007). Governing post-apartheid spatiality: Implementing city improvement districts in cape town. *Antipode*, 39(4), 602–626.

Morange, M. and Spire, A. (2019). Le droit à la ville aux Suds. Appropriations et déclinaisons africaines. *Cybergeo: European Journal of Geography* [Online]. Available at: https://journals.openedition.org/cybergeo/32166#quotation [Accessed 28 June 2021].

Nerderveen Pieterse, J. (2010). *Development Theory. Deconstructions/Reconstructions.* Sage Publications Limited, London.

Ninot, O. and Peyroux, É. (2018). Révolution numérique et développement en Afrique : Une trajectoire singulière. *Questions Internationales*, 90.

Osmont, A. (1995). *La Banque mondiale et les villes. Du développement à l'ajustement.* Editions Karthala, Paris.

Parnell, S. and Robinson, J. (2012). (Re)theorizing cities from the global South: Looking beyond neoliberalism. *Urban Geography*, 33(4), 593–617.

Peck, J. and Theodore, N. (2010). Mobilizing policy: Models, methods, and mutations. *Geoforum*, 41, 169–174.

Peck, J. and Theodore, N. (2015). *Fast Policy: Experimental Statecraft at the Thresholds of Neoliberalism*. University of Minnesota Press, Minneapolis, MN.

Pestre, D. (2011). Développement durable : Anatomie d'une notion. *Natures Sciences Sociétés*, 19, 31–39.

Peyroux, É. (2016). Circulation des politiques urbaines et internationalisation des villes : La stratégie des relations internationales de Johannesburg. *EchoGéo*, 36 [Online]. Available at: http://journals.openedition.org/echogeo/14623 [Accessed 28 June 2021].

Peyroux, É. and Ninot, O. (2019). De la "smart city" au numérique généralisé : La géographie urbaine au défi du tournant numérique. *L'Information Géographique*, 83(2), 40–57.

Peyroux, É. and Sanjuan, T. (2016). Stratégie de villes et "modèles" urbains : Approche économique et géopolitique des relations entre villes. *EchoGéo*, 36 [Online]. Available at: https://doi.org/10.4000/echogeo.14642 [Accessed 28 June 2021].

Pfirsch, T. and Semi, G. (2016). La ségrégation dans les villes de l'Europe méditerranéenne. *Méditerranée*, 127, 5–13.

PUCA (2020). Appel à projet "La ville productive". Report, PUCA.

Quenault, B. (2015). De Hyōgo à Sendai, la résilience comme impératif d'adaptation aux risques de catastrophe : Nouvelle valeur universelle ou gouvernement par la catastrophe ? *Développement durable et territoires*, 6(3) [Online]. Available at: https://doi.org/10.4000/developpementdurable.11010 [Accessed 28 June 2021].

Reghezza-Zitt, M. and Rufat, S. (2015). L'adaptation en Île-de-France entre injonction et recyclage. Techniques et politiques de la société de l'incertitude. *Développement durable et territoires*, 6(3) [Online]. Available at: https://doi.org/10.4000/developpementdurable.11035 [Accessed 28 June 2021].

Reghezza-Zitt, M., Rufat, S., Djament-Tran, G., Le Blanc, A., Lhomme, S. (2012). What Resilience is not: Uses and abuses. *Cybergeo: European Journal of Geography* [Online]. Available at: https://doi.org/10.4000/cybergeo.25554 [Accessed 3 June 2021].

Rist, G. (2007). *Le développement. Histoire d'une croyance occidentale*. Presses de Sciences Po, Paris.

Robinson, J. (2006). *Ordinary Cities: Between Modernity and Development*. Routledge, London.

Roy, A. (2009). The 21st-century metropolis: New geographies of theory. *Regional Studies*, 43(6), 819–830.

Rudolf, F. (2013). De la modernisation écologique à la résilience : Un réformisme de plus ? *VertigO – La revue électronique en sciences de l'environnement*, 13(3) [Online]. Available at: https://doi.org/10.4000/vertigo.14558 [Accessed 28 June 2021].

Salles, D. (2009). Environnement : La gouvernance par la responsabilité ? *VertigO – La revue électronique en sciences de l'environnement* [Online]. Available at: http://journals. openedition.org/vertigo/9179 [Accessed 28 June 2021].

Sassen, S. (1991). *The Global City: New York, London, Tokyo*. Princeton University Press, Princeton, NJ.

Semal, L. and Szuba, M. (2010). Villes en transition : Vers le rationnement. *Silence*, 379.

Simon, D. and Leck, H. (2014). Urban dynamics and the challenges of global environmental change in the south. In *A Routledge Handbook on Cities of the Global South*, Parnell, S. and Oldfield, S. (eds). Routledge, London.

Soja, E.W. (2010). *Seeking Spatial Justice*. University of Minnesota Press, Minneapolis, MN.

Storper, M. and Scott, A.J. (1989). The geographical foundations and social regulation of flexible production complexes. In *The Power of Geography: How Territory Shapes Social Life*, Wolch, J. and Dear, M. (eds). Unwin and Hyman, Winchester.

Swyngedouw, E., Moulaert, F., Rodriguez, A. (2002). Neoliberal urbanization in Europe: Large-scale urban development projects and the new urban policy. *Antipode*, 34, 542–577.

Theys, J. (2002). La Gouvernance, entre innovation et impuissance. *Développement durable et territoires* [Online]. Available at: http://developpementdurable.revues.org/1523 [Accessed 28 June 2021].

Theys, J. and Emelianoff, C. (2001). Les contradictions de la ville durable. *Le Débat*, 113, 122–135.

Torre, A. (2015). Théorie du développement territorial. *Géographie, économie, société*, 3(3), 273–288.

Turok, I. (2007). The connections between social cohesion and city competitiveness. *OECD Territorial Reviews: Competitive Cities in the Global Economy*. OECD, Paris.

Verrest, H. and Pfeffer, K. (2018). Elaborating the urbanism in smart urbanism: Distilling relevant dimensions for a comprehensive analysis of smart city approaches. *Information, Communication & Society*, 22(9), 1328–1342.

Zuindeau, B. (2008). Environnement, développement durable, territoire : Enjeu d'équité, enjeu de régulation. HDR Thesis, Université des sciences et technologies de Lille, Lille.

4

Locating Heritage in the Cities of the South: Dialogue from Valparaiso and Yaoundé

4.1. Introduction

Since the 2000s, the North–South separation of urban studies has been regularly questioned by several authors, most often English-speaking (Leitner and Sheppard 2016; Roy and Robinson 2016; Jacquot and Morelle 2018). These authors not only encourage more work on cities of the South, but also going beyond the recurring opposition between "global" metropolises in the North and "crisis" megapolises in the South, in order to break with a normative vision of the city, its governance and its development (Roy 2009). Urban space and the concepts necessary for its analysis are thus becoming the objects of scientific controversy and new theorizations from the South; often under the influence of post-colonial approaches (Connell 2013) and by paying particular attention to the urban practices of "subaltern populations" (Roy 2011).

This turning point has been identifiable in heritage studies since the 1990s. Both heritage practices and heritage categories have been debated on global and continental scales, leading to an opening up and pluralization of the notion of heritage, starting from situations observed outside Europe (Harrison 2013). Heritage categories are being redefined by taking into account non-monumental heritages and an indigenous relationship to the traces of the past, following Aboriginal claims in Australia militating for the control of traces and interpretations of their past (Logan 2013). At the same time, the Nara document on authenticity (Icomos 1994) endorses the need to consider different forms of expertise in defining heritage, diversifying

Chapter written by Sébastien JACQUOT, Marie MORELLE and Muriel SAMÉ EKOBO.

the legitimate actors of patrimonialization. Moreover, critical approaches were fueled by the questioning, in the 1980s, of a strictly aesthetic and architectural vision of heritage, in favor of a broader understanding of the notion of culture, developed by UNESCO based on the contribution of ethnology (Gfeller 2015). These various movements converge in the relativization of the monumental, artistic and scientific dimensions of heritage, to the benefit of plural interpretations, including popular ones, emanating from dominated groups, detaching themselves from the "authorized narratives of heritage" (Smith 2006; Esposito Andujar et al. 2020). This pluralization of actors, categories and heritage elements invites an open examination of what a heritage practice is, in its relationship or not with the institutions that give heritage meaning.

This has led to changes in international heritage policies in the long-term, relativizing a diffusionist reading of the forms of heritage from the North to the South, and giving rise to new heritage categories based on reflections in the South: that of cultural landscape (Mitchell et al. 2011), and that of intangible cultural heritage (Smith and Akagawa 2009; Bortolotto 2011). We cannot therefore oppose a North and a South from a heritage point of view, while being wary of essentializing approaches to heritage by cultural areas (Winter 2012). As such, heritage studies would seem, like urban studies, to become "provincialized" (Chakrabarty 2009) in order to think about local singularities, the place of subaltern populations, as well as their effects in return on globalized approaches.

However, the decentralization carried out within urban studies has largely ignored that of heritage studies. Conversely, the decentralization of heritage studies has not relied much on the new urban approaches. This double indifference is due to the low level of recognition of heritage in certain cities in the South, particularly in Africa. Moreover, the heritage approaches carried out in these cities are mainly inscribed in hegemonic narratives that may euphemize or neutralize their colonial and postcolonial dimensions and meanings, to the benefit of a nationalo-centric interpretation (Monnet 1993; Labadie 2007), and at the expense of the narratives and attachements carried by the inhabitants. Finally, these approaches can be interwoven into urban projects, for the purpose of adding value or controlling urban uses and functions (Martinez 2016).

This chapter proposes to initiate a dialogue between urban studies and heritage studies in order to contribute to a critical approach (Winter 2013) to the usual theorical frameworks of heritage, starting from the cities of the South. We wish to discuss the notion and approaches to heritage from the contributions of urban studies that reconstruct the often informal practices of "subaltern populations" (Roy and AlSayyad 2004; Chatterjee 2009; Roy 2011), to identify infra-heritage practices. In turn, the study of these practices of transmitting and preserving elements of the past feeds into the analysis of relationships of attachment to a city in the wake of research conducted on urbanity (Gervais-Lambony 1994; Berry-Chikhaoui 2009). Heritage is often defined as "tangible or intangible legacies recognized by societies in order to be transmitted to future generations" (Veschambre 2007), involving heritage institutions. Conversely, we pay attention to heritages that are not or hardly the object of an institutional recognition. On the contrary, they reflect a specific relationship to the city, an affective or memorial one, leading to the perpetuation of social practices and the places. This specific relationship reveals an "infra-heritage" or a "heritage without appearing to be heritage", designating preservation and transmission practices that are not recognized by public policies, nor of a formal qualification in heritage terms by the individuals or groups concerned, but not without links to urban transformations. This approach is based on the notion of "heritage from below", which refers to the way in which the past is actualized through inhabitant memories and ordinary practices (Robertson 2015). This notion sometimes gives rise to a more restricted use, in a logic of strict opposition to the dominant heritageizations (Muzaini and Minca 2018). This approach is not essentializing: it does not postulate that heritage exists per se.

We conduct this exploratory reflection from the intersection of researches conducted in Valparaiso (Chile) and in Yaoundé (Cameroon)[1]. In both cases, a discrepancy can be identified between an official register of heritage and popular modes of attachment to places or urban practices. However, the national political context differs: the heritageization in Valparaiso takes place in a context of democratization, while that of Yaoundé unfolds in a context of authoritarian restoration starting in the 1990s (Morelle and Planel 2018). Looking at transmission and preservation practices in these different political contexts reveals the socio-political dimension of any heritage recognition action. It questions the place of the inhabitants, often in a precarious situation, in cities marked by major changes: very strong urban growth, environmental transformations, and increasing inequalities. In these contexts, we are interested in what the inhabitants wish to transmit and preserve to individuals and groups. While heritage has often been analyzed as an issue in the control of urban development, often in central spaces and carried by elites, taking an interest in infra-heritage practices makes it possible to generalize this question to all city dwellers, in the context of a globalized circulation of new conceptions and categories of heritage.

---

1 S. Jacquot conducted research in Valparaiso between 1999 and 2007, and again in 2011 and 2016. In Cameroon, this research is based on the inventory of the built heritage of Yaoundé jointly conducted by M. Samé Ekobo and M. Morelle in 2015, within the framework of the Paul Ango Ela Foundation, in response to a commission from the Cameroonian Ministry of Arts and Culture (Samé Ekobo and Morelle 2016), followed by research funded by the Sar-Dyn program of the Labex Dynamite "Mémoires plurielles et fabrique de l'Etat. Yaoundé" (2018–2019) by the three authors. These surveys are based on observations, interviews with residents, actors and experts, as well as documentary analysis.

In section 4.2, we will evoke the dominant heritage productions and the multiscalar modes of their institutionalization. These official and globalized heritage invite us to reflect, in section 4.3, on the conflicting emphasis or invisibilization of other forms of heritage, or even infra-heritage forms, as our investigations in Valparaiso and Yaoundé attest.

4.2. Heritagization: between dominant logics and the logics of domination

The public recognition of heritage in Europe is early (Choay 1992), in connection with the circulation of the architects and the town planners, and the organization of international congresses. This internationalization is also carried out by heritage policies in a context of colonial domination, as in Morocco (Girard 2006) or Sri Lanka (Blackburn 2011). This intersection between circulation, heritage and domination can still be questioned today, on several scales, by drawing up a brief inventory of heritage in the cities of the South, and by reflecting on the contemporary role of heritage in the South, between being an instrument at the service of a dominant narrative of the past and the integration of plural and local narratives.

4.2.1. Lesser recognition of the heritage of the cities of the South

The UNESCO World Heritage List constitutes a reflect of North–South inequalities in heritage recognition, while at the same time being an arena for debate about heritage categories and their supposed universality (Anatole-Gabriel 2016). Several inequalities run through it: Africa[2] is underrepresented, with only 9% of the 1,121 properties listed in 2019, compared to 47% for North America–Europe as a whole, 24% for Asia-Pacific, 12% for Central and South America, and 8% for the Arab States.

The place of urban heritage also appears to vary according to the area, between a strong recognition of urban heritage in Europe and in Central and South America, a progressive recognition from the 1990s onwards on the Asian continent (Esposito Andoujar et al. 2020), and a weak consideration in sub-Saharan Africa. In fact, few cities in Sub-Saharan Africa are listed as World Heritage Sites, such as Saint-Louis in Senegal (Toulier 2003). Does this echo the long urban denial that has marked the historiography of Africa (Coquery Vidrovitch 1993)? The urban elements that have been recognized as heritage in Africa remain largely cities with a recognized pre-colonial history, as in the medieval Sahel (Djenné in Mali) or in East Africa

---

2 Within the limits given to it by UNESCO without the Maghreb and Mashrek States, i.e. 50 states.

(Lalibela in Ethiopia) (Ouallet 2009; Bridonneau 2011). These processes of heritage-making vary in scope, in restricted urban perimeters, such as central and old districts (e.g. the Ville-Haute of Antananarivo is on the indicative list of Madagascar), or even a specific building (Fournet-Guérin 2005; Bosredon 2011).

Contrastingly, in Latin America, a large proportion of the heritage elements on the World Heritage List are urban ensembles, especially historical centers of colonial origin, from Quito or Lima to Havana, passing through Colonia del Sacramento or Salvador de Bahia, manifesting an imaginary continuity of the nation (Monnet 1999). The charter of Quito, since 1967, poses the idea of a Latin American heritage, integrating the urban elements of colonial origin.

Instrument of domination during the colonial period, heritage is reactivated by the globalized identification within the framework of the World Heritage Convention. Heritage strategies are also carried out in the name of international tourism, as encouraged by other institutions such as the World Bank or the Inter-American Development Bank (Gravari-Barbas and Jacquot 2014). Heritage identification and valorization are carried out mainly for the benefit of international tourists and their tastes and expectations, for example, in Benin (Coralli and Houénoudé 2013) or in Senegal, Ghana or Gambia (Sinou 2005).

If the various regions that compose the Global South are indeed part of the dynamics of the extension of heritage categories and intensification, the process of heritage-making is not homogeneous there. Both the recognition by UNESCO and the degree of heritageization of urban spaces appear to differ according to the continents and cultural areas[3]. This differentiation is also due to the singularities of the States and political contexts.

4.2.2. *Urban heritage in tension*

Heritage has long been linked to national politics, with heritage constituting one element constituting a collectively shared national imaginary, contributing to national adhesion (Anderson 1996). Heritage is then a support for the construction of a national narrative, through a State monopoly on the designation of monuments that function as commemorative places or national places of memory. This patrimonialization operates by national policies of identification and protection of buildings or elements. These heritage productions that serve official visions of history can be described as authorized heritage text (Smith 2006).

---

3 In the sense of UNESCO's division.

Thus, in Valparaíso, before the patrimonialization of the 1990s, the heritage identified in the city was a commemorative heritage of the glorious events of the nation's history, such as the monument to the heroes of the battle of Iquique. In Yaoundé, the Reunification Monument (1977), commissioned by the Cameroonian government to build a monopolistic discourse after the post-independence tensions, embodies state power, sovereignty and modernity, as well as the uniqueness of the country. Three decades later, the commissioning of an inventory of the capital's heritage still emphasizes the buildings, constructions from colonial times or modernist buildings of the 20th century, some of which house the headquarters of ministries (Samé Ekobo and Morelle 2016).

This state production of heritage takes place against a backdrop of memorial exclusions and "prevented memories" (Ricoeur 2000), through making certain accounts of the past invisible. For Cameroon, the denial of memory persists, in the wake of the mechanism of memory control that led to the destruction of the archives of the emancipation movements during the decolonization war (Mbembé 1986). It is also a tribalized and ethnicized rereading of these struggles that brings about a "compartmentalization of memories" (Stora and Jenni 2016)[4]. What remains today of the delegitimized and therefore underground narratives of this contested history (Mbembé 2013)? What place should be given to non-state memorial and heritage productions (Fouéré 2010), from songs of independence to more ordinary urban practices?

In addition, this construction of heritage in the service of a unique and controlled memorial narrative is part of a broader perspective than national construction. The formalized heritage legitimizes the values of certain social classes, renewing a dominant order (Aguilar 1982; Veschambre 2008). In Yaoundé, the terms of the order at the origin of the 2015 inventory invite the seizure of "hard" constructions (bricks, concrete, stones), for example, those from state orders (ministries) or those of elites (villas) on the basis of their architectural value, which participates in the legitimization of certain large families (Fouda 2014). In Chile, the inscription of the historic district of the port city of Valparaiso on the World Heritage List came after a long debate on what constitutes heritage, mobilizing the State services, the municipality, city groups, actors of emerging cultural tourism and architects. However, the narrative legitimizing this inscription, as developed in the application file[5], emphasizes the city's involvement in globalization of the second half of the 19th century, consecrating a particular version of the city's history. The spaces included in the inscribed perimeter (the port and commercial sector of the original site, the hills behind) include buildings built by the European cosmopolitan

---

4 The expression "memorial compartmentalization" coined for the Algerian and French situations can be transposed to Cameroon.

5 See https://whc.unesco.org/fr/list/959/.

bourgeoisie, located on the Alegre and Concepción hills, leaving aside the vernacular landscapes (Brinckerhoof Jackson 2003) that extend over the surrounding hills.

Thus, heritage designates a world order, as well as a national and social order, reflecting the biases of identification and enhancement. Faced with the denial and invisibilization of certain urban conservation and transmission practices, it is important to move beyond institutional mechanisms to identify more diversified heritage practices.

4.2.3. *Thinking differently about heritage-making*

Several works highlight heritage alternatives (Auclair and Hertzog 2015) constructed by social and associative mobilizations or by NGOs (Bourdin 1984; Fabre 2013), including in cities of the South (Orellana 2006). Even institutionalized heritage is subject to alternative uses and appropriations (Fabre and Iuso 2010).

These alternatives question the notion of heritage, its boundaries and content. Harrison (2013, p. 15) contrasts official heritage with non-official heritage, defined as "a broad range of practices that are represented using the language of heritage, but that are not recognized by official forms of legislation". The challenge is then to identify these unofficial and unregarded practices, in contexts of public control of what constitutes heritage. However, is it possible to think of heritage outside the logics of mobilization and recognition?

These questions invite us to leave the constructivist framework often mobilized to define heritage (Veschambre 2007), understood as the result of institutionalized approaches. Graham Fairclough's work on landscape allows us to pursue this idea. He proposes a reinterpretation of the notion by referring to the Faro Convention (2005) on the value of cultural heritage for society: heritage is what we inherit in a broad sense (its material dimension as much as its associated meanings), it is also constituted by the whole of the processes by which we "understand, contextualize, perceive, manage, modify, destroy and transform this inherited world" (Fairclough 2009, p. 29). He thus understands cultural heritage not as an institutionalized and consecrated outcome but as an ever-renewed process. This dynamic and open apprehension of heritage also gives rise to a re-reading of its meaning and scope: it is not only a narration of a past based on its "traces", vestiges and clues of the past remaining in an unintentional way (Veschambre 2008), but also an engagement in the present (Tornatore 2019a).

We can therefore hypothesize the existence of relations to objects, places or practices that can evoke a heritage-type relationship, even in the absence of an intentional heritage. We can also focus on the observation and understanding of urban practices in relation to traces of the past (Veschambre 2008), without limiting ourselves to official or explicit heritage claimed by collectives. In a certain way, the issue is to identify heritage on the margin of institutional categories and official recognitions, echoing theories on the arts of making from city dwellers, sometimes on a silent mode (Bayat 2010).

4.3. A daily relationship with the infra-heritage

What is the place of the inhabitants, both as subjects and as signifieds[6] (Jacquot 2015) in heritage-making? How can we identify alternative forms and modes to hegemonic forms of heritage-making? We pay attention to the use of the word "heritage" and to the controversies related to it, as well as to the ordinary uses that can be regarded as heritage, without nevertheless claiming this quality and category.

Stories and practices reveal popular forms of attachment to the city, constructed in a back-and-forth between past and present, sometimes to resist the threat of eviction and exclusion posed by development projects, and more broadly to resist the dynamics of urban growth associated with strong land and real-estate speculation. However, these forms of heritage, whether implicit or asserted, can also be used as a support for discourses of identity withdrawal, denying a right to the city (Morange and Spire 2019).

4.3.1. Heritage, beyond words: Valparaíso and Yaoundé

We are interested in the meanings, the uses as well as the absence of the word "heritage" in various national and social contexts. This corresponds to a close "pragmatic" and critical application of heritage developed by critical heritage studies (Smith 2006). However, we propose to identify alternative forms of heritagization beyond institutional logic or movements claiming heritage recognition. This allows us to discuss the openness of the notion of heritage, as well as to underline the place of inhabitant memories in the daily production of urban space.

In Valparaíso, the word "*patrimonio*" is explicitly used, beyond the experts and becomes a marker of public debates on the future of the city. While the heritage issue was not previously present as an urban theme, despite the inscription of some commemorative or public buildings in the register of national monuments, the candidacy for inscription on the World Heritage list opens a new discursive space and legitimizes a new way of conceiving the city and its transformations

---

6 That is, as characters in a narrative constructed through patrimonialization.

(development of cultural tourism, enhancement of new districts with gentrification dynamics, opening of the waterfront to new uses). However, this nomination is not consensual. It brings into play distinct visions of what constitutes heritage value. A first conception is based on a historical and urbanistic vision of heritage, based on the 19th century period and enshrined in the World Heritage listing in 2003. A second one relies on the landscape and more anthropological vision of heritage, more territorially open, initially carried by the municipal service in charge of heritage (*Unidad tecnica del patrimonio*) of the city and various associations (notably *Ciudadanos por Valparaiso*). It is based on the adaptation of urban forms to the topography, with buildings of limited size on the hillsides. The urban grid is explained in these heritage narratives both by the popular dimension of the city and by a form of self-limitation of heights, in order to preserve the rights to a view of the neighbors.

These debates lead to an extension of what makes heritage. Urban practices and landscapes are translated into heritage language, proposing a new way of stating a relationship to the city. The numerous independent businesses (food, clothing, hardware, bars), which constitute the commercial fabric of daily and popular life, or even stray dogs (target of public sterilization and elimination campaigns), are apprehended by city associations under the heritage perspective. These discourses and actions play with and subvert the dominant heritage values, showing other possible uses and meanings of urban spaces.

The controversy ultimately concerns the place of popular practices, rooted in everyday life, within the mechanisms of heritage recognition and preservation. While the prevailing heritagizations go hand in hand with the dynamics of gentrification and also legitimize them, the struggles to maintain popular practices take the detour of the heritage discourse, recycling imaginary images and expressions of a pre-existing relationship with the city (such as the musical, poetic and artistic works that are widely disseminated within the city). This revival of the heritage discourse for the purpose of resistance is also a heritage subversion, by widening the spectrum of what is considered as heritage, incorporating popular neighborhoods and practices and the landscape,. In other words, heritage is enlarged to intangible dimensions, beyond what is recognized in the World Heritage application. The notion of heritage thus becomes the mediator of a relationship to the city, a reflexive instrument allowing the translation of emotions and attachments to some of its elements, beyond a dominant narrative.

In Yaoundé, heritage policies and the way they mobilize the word "heritage" are limited to classical approaches that are not much challenged by public institutions. Indeed, despite the contributions of the law promulgated on April 18, 2013 governing cultural heritage in Cameroon, which encourages the consideration of intangible and community dimensions of heritage (Loumpet 2003), the term "heritage" remains largely the instrument of public institutions and is rarely applied to popular places, practices and narratives. In urban planning documents, reference to the notion of heritage is often confined to environmental issues, approached through the prism of vegetation and landscape (woodlands, water bodies and wetlands), for the purposes of tourism, recreation and science. In fact, heritage policy is only just emerging (the Heritage Department was created in the mid-1990s) and remains poorly developed (Samé Ekobo 2015).

However, the uses of the word "heritage", often reserved for the institutional sphere, cannot exhaust the manifestations of a city relationship of attachment and transmission, through the narratives of the past, the ways in which they incarnate and their impact on the present of the inhabitants, for whom the term heritage does not explicitly make sense, or introduces a shift in significations (Pumketkao-Lecourt and Peyronnie 2020). In addition, in a city where the majority of inhabitants come from the rural exodus, this relationship is still very much played out in the back-and-forth between the village of origin and the settlement area, while being enriched today by the experience of a new generation born in the city.

Our first field research studies in 2018 reveal the prevalence of a narrative of arrival in Yaoundé, whether for people who define themselves today as natives or for those who are presented as migrants and originate from other regions of Cameroon, the "allochtones" or "allogenic". The story depicts the arrival in the city of the individual or their ancestors, followed by the establishment of a place of residence, often in what was still "the heart of the bush", by obtaining or buying land. It is a process of taking possession of a piece of land associated with the act of clearing and marking out, followed by the construction of a house, that are often told. These narratives are aboutwhat has been built, as well as of what is now preserved and passed on: a plot of land, or even a house, which are the markers of a family's first attachment to the city (Roudart and Guénard 2019, p. 16).

> At the time, Mokolo was still the bush. He [my father] bought a small piece of land in Mokolo, like all the Bamilékés in fact. Most of the Bamilékés who arrived came after someone and that someone was towards Mokolo-Madagascar. So he bought a small piece of land, a little lower down, less than a kilometer from his uncle's house and there he built his first house (…) I was born there. It still exists. It is made of clay. It is still there (G., born in Yaoundé, migrant parents from the West, Yaoundé, January 16, 2018).

In the context of the need to subsist day after day (Simone 2004) for a majority of inhabitants, land property is perceived as an asset that can be passed on within the family for security purposes (housing, having tenants). This perpetuation of an urban and material resource also operates on a symbolic level. Some denounce the precariousness of their possessions due to the recurrent expropriations carried out by the colonial administration, then the State and the City. They also criticize the more or less legal resale of plots of land bequeathed by their parents in a recurrent context of land speculation and conflicts between heirs, even though they represent a family history (e.g. the graves in the courtyards of Ewondo concessions). Land does not only represent land assets, but also an attachment to a space (the house, the neighborhood or the city) and a membership to social networks. Obtaining land, developing it and perpetuating its ownership require relays within and outside the administrative procedures themselves. In so doing, we acquire a social status, consolidate and reify links of identity on an urban scale. Thus, land is implicated in relationships to places and people (Harrison 2013, p. 14), bridging material and immaterial dimensions.

These lands are therefore the object of a desire to perpetuate and transmit them. In this way, the leaders of family lines have a duty to manage the land affairs of the family, of the clan, within the neighborhoods of Yaoundé, as well as to pass on their place and their role to an heir. To carry out this type of task is to guarantee the transmission of a specific status and knowledge in the city. The challenge is not only to possess these material elements but to exist, collectively, through them (Fabre 2010).

These two case studies in Valparaiso and Yaoundé question the common definitions of heritage. The issue is to identify alternative heritage practices, even if they are not recognized or even named as such, both by the inhabitants and the public authorities. To do this, it is necessary to collect the narratives that individuals and groups make of their past, to identify the places, the objects, the ways (gestures, words, practices) through which this memory is embodied, potential channels of transmission and preservation, i.e. as many points of support to legitimize a presence in the city, to define and claim an urban identity. This dynamic is not only an invocation of the past that gives meaning to the present, it is also produced in the past, through practices of preservation or transmission, often linked to the instability of the urban condition.

In doing so, it is possible to identify "informal" heritage processes, beyond the word "heritage". In this, we can insist on the gap between a heritage field that has opened up to new actors, to alternative, even contesting, forms and uses of heritage, and the situations of domination and precariousness of city dwellers, forced to resort to informal, precarious and uncertain mediations to maintain access to resources in the city, both material and symbolic.

4.3.2. *An alter-patrimonialization to create commonality*

These heritage situations have a political dimension, linked to collectives and positioning in an urban future, in a conflictual way in Valparaiso or more implicitly in Yaoundé. In this perspective, J.L. Tornatore (2019b) emphasizes the importance of dissensus in thinking about heritage democracy, extending the work of J. Bondaz, C. Isnart, A. Leblon, devoted to "resistance and contesting uses of heritage" (2012). The heritage issue goes beyond the preservation of elements, and raises questions about urban mutations and the relationship between city dwellers and the city (Gervais-Lambony 1994). Finally, what these heritage situations or infra-heritage situations reveal are alternative ways of making the city, at variable scales.

Valparaiso and Yaoundé illustrate two different ways of relating to urban change (urban renewal, speculation, social change, etc.). In both cities, certain dynamics lead to a sense of danger and loss (eviction from working-class neighborhoods, sale of land for subsistence, gentrification, etc.), but without leading to the same practices of resistance nor to the same possibility of reading in heritage terms.

In Valparaíso, the irruption of heritage as a constituent of the city project had spillover effects (Tornatore 2017), insofar as new actors (resident collectives, investors in cultural tourism) have seized this notion to resist certain urban transformations. In doing so, they have not only challenged developments in the name of heritage, but have opposed an alternative heritage to hegemonic heritage narratives. Outside the UNESCO sector, Valparaíso is experiencing speculative dynamics on the coastal plain and on the hills, which result in building transformations (verticalization and densification), transforming the panorama and hiding the view for the neighbors.

This vision of the city as a landscape ensemble is opposed to a classical heritage reading, distinguishing monuments and periods. It operates through the politicization of the views on the city and towards the ocean (due to an urban topography in an amphitheater around the bay), by the city and heritage associations, by putting them on the agenda as well as by their status as emblematic objects of urban transformations. Indeed, the threats to the views symbolize a dynamic of real-estate speculation. Their preservation then becomes the main criterion for requests for heritage protection and modification of the urban regulations on building heights.

In this logic, the very possibility of views within the city, towards the ocean or towards another hill from houses, roof terraces or public spaces on balconies (*miradores*), becomes both the testimony of a certain relationship to the city and an aestheticization of the right to the city for all (as it is concretely manifested in the views from and to the city). For each citizen, the respect of the right to the view of the other requires the maintenance of the heights or the volumetry of their own house. The urban landscape is regarded as heritage because it expresses this relationship between city dwellers. It is an effect of the forms of urban production as well as a reminder of an ethic relation to the city. This heritage goes beyond UNESCO's categories and appears as the elaboration of a narrative legitimizing a popular and decentralized vision of the city.

Yaoundé, on the other hand, is marked by the absence of a public debate on heritage. In addition, participatory democracy processes are not generally encouraged and heritage proposals are often made by external actors, such as international institutions. However, heritage dynamics permeate daily relationships at the scales of concessions, neighborhoods or the entire city. Thus, understanding land as a heritage element in Yaoundé implies understanding the social relations that it mediates, expressing the desire to preserve a community, a clan, a family, in the face of various threats (of impoverishment, expropriation, loss of cultural values, etc.). This attachment is not turned exclusively towards the past of a family or clan in particular, but rather founds the relationship with the present and the future, in specific situations, such as precariousness (Tornatore 2017).

How to interpret this comparison? Is heritage a standard for bringing together and signifying multiple resistances to urban change? As a consequence, should we name "alternative heritage approach" only explicitly heritage movements, that appropriate this category in their opposition to dominant institutions, such as in Valparaiso? Doesn't this mean that its expression is strongly restricted to democratic regimes, and that its possibility is excluded in authoritarian regimes where memory is confiscated? Indeed, moments of "memorial mobilization" (Fouéré 2010, p. 6) are often linked to democratizations (Musset et al. 2014; Didier 2015). In Cameroon, the relationship to the past is played out in a situation of memorial denial, with fragmented and fragmentary reconstructions of the past. The non-recognition of certain forms of heritage, on the other hand, reinforces distinction and separation logics, which then weaken a shared experience of the city.

In Yaoundé, claims that can be interpretated as infra-heritage can be instrumentialized by a discourse with a hegemonic aim of one population at the expense of another, in support of autochthony and its ethnicization (Bayart et al. 2001; Ghattas 2019). The highlighting of certain forms of heritage may become an instrument for asserting affirmation of the primacy (and thus power) of certain groups.

For example, among the Ewondo, who have seen their village hamlets become the districts of a large metropolis since the 19th century, the sale of land is increasingly interpreted a posteriori as an eviction or invasion: "[We must not] sell the land, it is our heritage. (…) All our cousins have sold. It is our only family that has not sold. (...) We don't know what generation will follow. Those who sell go elsewhere. The village must not remain only with foreigners" (neighborhood chief and his wife speaking with one voice, Yaoundé, January 16, 2018).

Heritage practices respond to a feeling of dispossession, but at the cost of excluding the "others". In this way, "the land", as the Cameroonians call it, is the object of crystallization and the channel of differentiation for groups and collectives of inhabitants. More and more, the stories are silent about the practices of welcoming migrant populations, the mixing of languages, music and gastronomy, which are still inherent to the life of the neighborhoods. The interviews reveal forms of rejection and community withdrawal, while at the same time reconstructing a golden age in the capital where social climbing, land acquisition, house building and frequenting multicultural social places were commonplace. In this case, infra-heritage practices seem to be inscribed in private spaces, to the detriment of "an ethics of encounter" (Mbembé 2013).

4.4. Conclusion

The challenge of this chapter is first to question the logics of identification of urban heritage in the cities of the South. A new discussion of heritage categories has already been conducted on the basis of cities in the South. In the wake of this, and in echo to urban problematizations of political informality, by paying attention to the implicit, the invisible, the unrecognized, we propose to think of heritage logics that are deployed against, or even below, the dominant institutional logics.

In this perspective, our starting point concerns the identification of an infra-heritage relationship to the city, through its uses, either in resistance to dominant heritage logics and memorial occultations, or in apparently a-patrimonial logics. Infra-heritage refers to practices of preservation and transmission of what we are attached to and to which we attribute a value.

The cross-reading of the Valparaiso and Yaoundé cases reveals different modalities of urban relationship to heritage, according to the scales and collectives mobilized, and their political scope, questioning the conditions of possibility of a shared heritage-making. The identification of heritage objects reveals both the fractures and the common worlds that participate in the dynamics of urban societies.

Insofar as these heritage-type relationships are not necessarily stated or experienced as heritage, what happens to the data produced from these identification processes and the researcher's position? What is the significance of this data for the inhabitants in unequal and possibly authoritarian urban contexts? It is not a question of discovering heritage, which would pose the risk of a new essentialization of heritage, but to recognize affects, experiences, stories and practices in the city which aim towards the persistence of elements of the past. It is also a question of recognizing the city's as well as the people's skills in the production of memories and transmission.

In other words, this quest for heritage practices and situations in two cities of the South, on the margin of institutional arenas, invites a methodological decentering as well as an ethical reflection on the uses of the results of the research. The identification of an infra-heritage should not lead to a simple extension of the heritage field open to new valuations and instrumentalizations, for the benefit of elites or ethnicized and excluding readings. It is important not only to identify what is heritage, but also to recognize the memories of the inhabitants, the way in which they transmit them, and contribute to the construction of urban spaces. Faced with the discourse of withdrawal, the strength of which is matched only by the uncertainty and the spoliations lived for decades by the city dwellers, there are other words and other traces: of mobilities (forced or free) and of exchanges between individuals, of mediated amalgamations, notably by the diasporas. The collection of these narratives in all their diversity and manifestations would undoubtedly make it possible to reflect on the principles of a heritage policy that brings people together.

4.5. References

Aguilar, Y. (1982). La Chartreuse de Mirande, le Monument historique, produit d'un classement de classe. *Actes de la recherche en science sociales*, 42, 76–85.

Anatole-Gabriel, I. (2016). *La fabrique du patrimoine de l'humanité*. FMSH, Paris.

Anderson, B. (1996). *L'imaginaire national. Réflexions sur l'origine et l'essor du nationalisme*. La Découverte, Paris.

Auclair, E. and Hertzog, A. (2015). Grands ensembles, cités ouvrières, logement social : Patrimoines habités, patrimoines contestés. *EchoGéo*, 33 [Online]. Available at: http://journals.openedition.org/echogeo/14360 [Accessed 28 September 2020].

Bayart, J.-F., Geschiere, P., Nyamnjoh, F. (2001). Autochtonie, démocratie et citoyenneté en Afrique. *Critique internationale*, 10, 177–194.

Bayat, A. (2010). *Life as Politics. How Ordinary People Change the Middle East*. Stanford University Press, Stanford, CA.

Berry-Chikhaoui, I. (2009). Les notions de citadinité et d'urbanité dans l'analyse des villes du Monde arabe. *Les Cahiers d'EMAM*, 18, 9–20.

Blackburn, A.-M. (2011). *Early Preservation Efforts in Sri Lanka, William H. Gregory at Anuradhapura and Kandy, in Hall Melanie. Towards World Heritage, International Origins of the Preservation Movement, 1870–1930*. Ashgate, Surrey and Burlington, VT.

Bondaz, J., Isnart, C., Leblon, A. (2012). Au-delà du consensus patrimonial. Résistances et usages contestataires du patrimoine. *Civilisations*, 61(1), 9–22.

Bortolotto, C. (2011). *Le patrimoine culturel immatériel, enjeux d'une nouvelle catégorie.* Editions de la Maison des Sciences de l'Homme, Paris.

Bosredon, P. (2011). Recompositions spatiales et marginalisation sociale au centre. *Géographie et cultures*, 79, 47–65.

Bourdin, A. (1984). *Le patrimoine réinventé*. Presses Universitaires de France, Paris.

Bridonneau, M. (2011). Reconstructions paysagères autour des églises de Lalibela. *Géographie et cultures*, 79, 29–46.

Brinckerhoff Jackson, J. (2003). *À la redécouverte du paysage vernaculaire*. Actes Sud, Arles.

Chakrabarty, D. (2009). *Provincialiser l'Europe. La pensée postcoloniale et la différence historique.* Editions Amsterdam, Paris.

Chatterjee, P. (2009). *Politique des gouvernés. Réflexion sur la politique populaire dans la majeure partie du monde.* Editions Amsterdam, Paris.

Choay, F. (1992). *L'allégorie du patrimoine*. Le Seuil, Paris.

Connell, R. (2013). Using southern theory: Decolonizing social thought in theory, research and application. *Planning Theory*, 13(2), 210–223.

Coquery-Vidrovitch, C. (1993). *Histoire des villes d'Afrique noire. Des origines à la colonisation.* Albin Michel, Paris.

Coralli, M. and Houénoudé, D. (2013). La patrimonialisation à l'occidentale et ses conséquences sur un territoire africain : Porto-Novo au Bénin. *Espaces et sociétés*, 152–153(1), 85–101.

Didier, S. (2015). Temps et pouvoir dans la ville. Mémoire d'habilitation à diriger des recherches. Thesis, Université Paris Ouest Nanterre la Défense, Nanterre.

Esposito Andujar, A., Goldblum, C., Lancret, N. (2020). Le champ patrimonial et sa fabrique urbaine en Asie du Sud-Est. *Moussons*, 36 [Online]. Available at: https://journals.openedition.org/moussons/6337.

Fabre, D. (2010). Introduction. Habiter les monuments. In *Les monuments sont habités*, Fabre, D. and Luso, A. (eds). Editions de la Maison des Sciences de l'homme, Paris.

Fabre, D. (eds) (2013). *Emotions patrimoniales*. Editions de la Maison des Sciences de l'Homme, Paris.

Fabre, D. and Iuso, A. (eds) (2010). *Les monuments sont habités*. Editions de la Maison des Sciences de l'Homme, Paris.

Fairclough, G. (2009). *New heritage frontiers, in Council of Europe, Heritage and Beyond*. Council of Europe, Paris.

Fouda, J. (2014). *André Fouda, Premier Maire Noir de la ville de Yaoundé*. Editions Presse Monde, Yaoundé.

Fouéré, M.-A. (2010). La mémoire au prisme du politique. *Cahiers d'études africaines*, 197 [Online]. Available at: http:// journals.openedition.org/etudesafricaines/15768 [Accessed 24 April 2018].

Fournet-Guérin, C. (2005). Héritage reconnu, patrimoine menacé : La maison traditionnelle à Tananarive. *Autrepart*, 33(1), 51–69.

Gervais-Lombony, P. (1994). *De Lomé à Hararé : Le fait citadin. Images et pratiques des villes africaines*. Khartala, Paris/Nairobi.

Gfeller, A. (2015). Anthropologizing and indigenizing heritage: The origins of the UNESCO Global Strategy for a representative, balanced and credible World Heritage List. *Journal of Social Archaelogy*, 15(3), 366–386.

Ghattas, M. (2019). Enjeux de la patrimonialisation à Douala : Construction identitaire et aménagement urbain d'une ville d'Afrique subsaharienne. PhD Thesis, Université Paris 1 Panthéon Sorbonne, Paris.

Girard, M. (2006). Invention de la tradition et authenticité sous le Protectorat au Maroc. *Socio-anthropologie*, 19.

Gravari-Barbas, M. and Jacquot, S. (2014). Patrimoine mondial, tourisme et développement durable en Afrique : Discours, approches et défis. *Via*, 4–5 [Online]. Available at: http:// journals.openedition.org/viatourism/853 [Accessed 28 September 2020].

Harrison, R. (2013). *Heritage, Critical Approaches*. Routledge, London.

ICOMOS (1994). Document Nara sur l'authenticité [Online]. Available at: https://www.icomos. org/fr/notre-reseau/comites-scientifiques-internationaux/liste-des-comites-scientifiques-inter nationaux/179-articles-en-francais/ressources/charters-and-standards/186-document-de-nara-sur-lauthenticite [Accessed 4 March 2021].

Jacquot, S. (2015). Politiques de valorisation patrimoniale et figuration des habitants en banlieue parisienne (Plaine Commune). *EchoGeo*, 33 [Online]. Available at: https://doi. org/10.4000/echogeo.14317 [Accessed 17 January 2021].

Jacquot, S. and Morelle, M. (2018). Comment penser l'informalité dans les villes "du Nord", à partir des théories urbaines "du Sud" ? *Métropoles*, 22 [Online]. Available at: https:// journals.openedition.org/metropoles/5601 [Accessed 25 November 2019].

Labadie, S. (2007). Representations of the nation and cultural diversity in discourses on World Heritage. *Journal of Social Archaeology*, 7(2), 147–170.

Leitner, H. and Sheppard, E. (2016). Provincializing critical urban theory: Extending the ecosystem of possibilities. *International Journal of Urban and Regional Research*, 40(1), 228–235.

Logan, W. (2013). Australia, indigenous peoples and world heritage from Kakadu to Cape York: State party behaviour under the world heritage convention. *Journal of Social Archaelogy*, 13(2), 153–176.

Loumpet, G. (2003). Patrimoine culturel et stratégie identitaire au Cameroun, analyse d'un mécanisme intégratif transpose. *Enjeux*, 15, 7–11.

Martinez, P. (2016). Authenticity as a challenge in the transformation of Beijing's urban heritage: The commercial gentrification of the Guozijian historic area. *Cities*, 59, 48–56.

Mbembé, A. (1986). Pouvoir des morts et langage des vivants : Les errances de la mémoire nationaliste au Cameroun. *Politique Africaine*, 22, 37–72.

Mbembé, A. (2013). *Sortir de la grande nuit*. La Découverte, Paris.

Mitchell, N., Rossler, M., Tricaud, P.M. (2011). Paysages culturels du patrimoine mondial : Guide pratique de conservation et de gestion. In *Cahiers du patrimoine mondial*, Mitchell, N., Rössler, M., Tricaud, P.M. (eds). UNESCO, Paris.

Monnet, J. (1993). *La ville et son double. Images et usages du centre : La parabole de Mexico*. Nathan, Paris.

Monnet, J. (1999). *Ville et pouvoir en Amérique, les formes de l'autorité*. L'Harmattan, Paris.

Morange, M. and Spire, A. (2019). Le droit à la ville aux Suds. Appropriations et déclinaisons africaines. *Cybergéo*, 895 [Online]. Available at: https://journals.openedition.org/cybergeo/32166 [Accessed 5 July 2021].

Morelle, M. and Planel, S. (2018). Appréhender des "situations autoritaires". Lectures croisées à partir du Cameroun et de l'Ethiopie. *L'Espace politique*, 35(2) [Online]. Available at: https://journals.openedition.org/espacepolitique/4902 [Accessed 5 July 2021].

Musset, A., Gervais-Lambony, P., Guinard, P. (2014). La réparation des injustices du passé : Une approche territoriale. In *La justice spatiale et la ville. Regards du Sud*, Gervais-Lambony, P., Bénit-Gbaffou, C., Piermay, J.-L., Musset, A., Planel, S. (eds). Karthala, Paris.

Muzaini, H. and Minca, C. (2018). Rethinking heritage, but "from below". In *After Heritage, Critical Perspectives on Heritage from Below*, Muzaini, H. and Minca, C. (eds). Edward Elgard Publishing, London.

Orellana, L. (2006). Société civile, secteur privé : Les nouveaux acteurs de la concertation dans les centres historiques de l'Amérique Latine et des Caraïbes. *L'information géographique*, 2(70), 46–62.

Ouallet, A. (2009). Vulnérabilités et patrimonialisations dans les villes africaines : De la préservation à la marginalisation. *Cybergeo: European Journal of Geography*, 455 [Online]. Available at: http://www.cybergeo.eu/index22229.html [Accessed 28 September 2017].

Pumketkao-Lecourt, P. and Peyronnie, K. (2020). Extension de la notion de patrimoine et affirmation identitaire lanna à Chiang Mai : Mots et représentations. *Moussons*, 36, 191–219 [Online]. Available at: https://journals.openedition.org/moussons/6732 [Accessed 5 July 2021].

Ricœur, P. (2000). *La Mémoire, l'histoire, l'oubli*. Le Seuil, Paris.

Robertson, I.J. (2015). Hardscrabble heritage: The ruined blackhouse and crofting landscape as heritage from below. *Landscape Research*, 40(8), 993–1009.

Roudart, L. and Guénard, C. (2019). Introduction : Dépossessions foncières en milieu rural. Acteurs et processus entre pression et oppression. *Revue internationale des études du développement*, 2(238), 7–29.

Roy, A. (2009). Why India cannot plan its cities: Informality, insurgence and the idiom of urbanization. *Planning Theory*, 8(1), 76–87.

Roy, A. (2011). Slumdog cities: Rethinking subaltern urbanism. *International Journal of Urban and Regional Research*, 35(2), 223–238.

Roy, A. and AlSayyad, N. (eds) (2004). *Urban Informality. Transnational Perspectives from the Middle East, Latin America, and South Asia.* Lexington Books, Lanham, MD.

Roy, A. and Robinson, J. (2016). Debate on global urbanisms and the nature of urban theory. *International Journal of Urban and Regional Research*, 40(1), 181–186.

Samé Ekobo, M. (2015). Autour de l'exposition "La Bataille du Cameroun" : Mémoire, histoire et patrimoine". In *La nouveauté du patrimoine*, Mengue, M.-T., De Saulieu, G., Vidal, L. (eds). Ifrikiya, Yaoundé.

Samé Ekobo, M. and Morelle, M. (2016). *Yaoundé : promenades patrimoniales.* FPAE, Yaoundé.

Simone, A. (2004). *For the City Yet to Come: Changing African Life in Four Cities.* Duke University Press, Durham.

Sinou, A. (2005). Enjeux culturels et politiques de la mise en patrimoine des espaces coloniaux. *Autrepart*, 1(3), 13–31

Smith, L. (2006). *Uses of Heritage.* Routledge, London.

Smith, L. and Akagawa, N. (2009). *Intangible Heritage.* Routledge, London.

Stora, B. and Jenni, A. (2016). *Les mémoires dangereuses.* Albin Michel, Paris.

Tornatore, J.-L. (2017). Patrimoine vivant et contributions citoyennes. Penser le patrimoine "devant" l'Anthropocène. *In Situ, Revue des Patrimoines*, 33 [Online]. Available at: https://doi.org/10.4000/insitu.15606 [Accessed 5 July 2021].

Tornatore, J.-L. (2019a). *Le Patrimoine comme expérience. Implications anthropologiques.* FMSH, Paris.

Tornatore, J.-L. (2019b). Pour une anthropologie pragmatiste et plébéienne du patrimoine : Un scénario contre-hégémonique. *In Situ Revue des Patrimoines. Au regard des sciences sociales*, 1 [Online]. Available at: https://doi.org/10.4000/insituarss.449 [Accessed 5 July 2021].

Toulier, B. (2003). Saint-Louis du Sénégal, un enjeu pour le patrimoine mondial. *In Situ*, 3.

Veschambre, V. (2007). Patrimoine : Un objet révélateur des évolutions de la géographie et de sa place dans les sciences sociales. *Annales de géographie*, 2007/4(656), 361–381. doi: 10.3917/ag.656.0361 [Accessed 5 July 2021].

Veschambre, V. (2008). *Traces et mémoires urbaines, enjeux sociaux de la patrimonialisation et de la démolition*. Presses universitaires de Rennes, Rennes.

Winter, T. (2012). Beyond Eurocentrism? Heritage conservation and the politics of difference. *International Journal of Heritage Studies*, 20(2), 123–137.

Winter, T. (2013). Clarifying the critical in critical heritage studies. *International Journal of Heritage Studies*, 19(6), 532–545.

PART 2

Themes and Common Objects to Cross Global Changes and Territorial Dynamics

The European Union and the Energy Transition: Development, Environment and Regional Integration

5.1. Introduction

The notion of transition refers to "a transformation process during which a system moves from one equilibrium regime to another" (Grandjean et al. 2015) and goes back to the idea of reconfiguration or reorganization of the system. But this notion has weaknesses. It does not say anything precise about the modalities of this transition. For example, it assumes a linear conception of time, which oversimplifies the reality of the process. This process can be discontinuous, interrupted, slowed down or accelerated. This is particularly true when it comes to the construction of geographical space, whose temporal dynamics are not necessarily linear and regular, as the latter "functions by accumulating several rhythms and stages of change" (Coudroy de Lille et al. 2017). However, and perhaps precisely because of its imprecision, the notion of transition is widely used and declined in many fields: demographic transition, ecological transition, food transition, digital transition and health transition.

The "energy transition" refers to a change in the way energy is produced and consumed. It also refers to a process that tends towards practices with less environmental impact. The growing use of this notion is one of those conceptual fads that reflect a political and social concern. To speak of the energy transition is to raise the question of the compatibility between development in general and the preservation or even improvement of the environment. The European Union is seeking to define the basis for a new relationship between its recent environmental

Chapter written by Angélique PALLE and Yann RICHARD.

concerns, the methods of its economic growth and its future development, through the prism of the energy transition. This approach involves the European institutions (notably the Commission and the Parliament), the EU member countries and numerous actors of all types and levels. It is part of a general reflection on the challenges associated with "global change" (Arnaud de Sartre 2016) which refers to a set of changes observed in certain areas, such as the climate, the degradation and rarefaction of natural resources or the quality of the environment. These changes have such strong impacts on a planetary scale that they modify the functioning of the Earth system and call into question the very foundations and functioning of contemporary societies.

In a context where the energy transition is one of the societal responses to these changes, this chapter will question the conceptual and political frameworks that underpin the objective of energy transition as a priority for the EU in numerous speeches and official documents. These postulate that the transition objective is compatible with European energy integration, as it was conceived in the 1990s around the liberalization of energy markets. Finally, we seek to unveil the complex scalar issues of this policy. At what scales can the energy transition be implemented, how does it relate to the objective of integrating energy markets and networks in the European community space?

In section 5.2, based on the idea formulated by Laurence Raineau (2011), for whom "energy is not a simple variable feeding a technical system, but [...] engages institutions, political, economic and social systems", we show that the European energy transition lies at the crossroads of several fields of research that have given rise to an abundant scientific production over the past several decades: the social and political construction of spatial scales, governance, regional integration and the construction of Europe.

In section 5.3, we propose analyzing, by looking at the European legislative framework on energy and its progressive construction, the way in which the EU (as an institution) understands the notion of energy transition as a political positioning, an economic strategy and an instrument of power. This allows us to question the implementation of this desire to transition. On what and on whom does it rely? To answer this question, we will propose an analysis of the pillars of European energy policy and the close link that the EU makes between the transition dynamic and the regional integration dynamic which is at the heart of the European project.

In section 5.4, we describe the models of spatial construction which the ongoing regional integration is leading the European energy space towards. This description is based on fieldwork in geography initiated in 2012 and followed by successive periods until 2021 (the list of fields is exposed in the introductory paragraph of section 5.4). We will analyze the governance issues underlying the implementation of these models and we will show that the energy transition is an erratic and sometimes conflicting process, particularly with regard to the construction of the scales deemed relevant by the implicated actors, for the implementation of their strategies.

5.2. Integration, energy transition and space

5.2.1. *Defining regional integration*

For political science, integration is defined as a "process by which relations between states intensify in such a way that the closeness of interdependencies between them is led to question the principle of their sovereignty" (Grossman et al. 2001, p. 155). Several theories are mobilized by this discipline to describe and understand this process (Saurugger 2020, pp. 25–27). For neo-functionalism, political actors of several national communities reorient their aspirations and activities towards a new whole whose institutions acquire pre-eminence over the national states; the integration is carried out domain after domain with the aim of creating a federal state (Haas 1958, p. 451). In federalism, states remain essential actors and transfer only part of their sovereignty to higher-level institutions (Dosenrode 2010). Intergovernmentalism sees integration as the result of negotiation between states that create regional institutions so as to find compromises between their preferences (Moravcsik 1993, pp. 497–498). With a few exceptions, these works have a drawback: they give little room to geographical space as a social production and assume that the states involved in a regional agreement *form a region* from the outset. This is to forget that a region is a geographical space, a social construction (Paasi 2010), which can extend beyond the limits of a regional agreement. In this chapter, we will rely more on the work of researchers such as Hettne and Söderbaum (1998), who adopt a social-constructivist approach, while giving a central place to the idea of social production of space.

For geographers, regional integration goes hand in hand with spatial integration. At the most general level, spatial integration refers to the increasing interdependence between the constituent parts of a whole, or the inclusion of a spatial unit in an already existing system (Nonn and Martin 1980, pp. 34–35). The result is a new geographical reality that is more than the sum of its parts, freed from internal barrier effects (De Boe et al. 1999, p. 7). Spatial integration can be sectoral (one domain) or multisectoral. Integration occurs when finite spatial units form a system, a functional unit characterized by a spatial continuum.

5.2.2. *Energy transition and integration: a fluid theoretical articulation*

What constitutes European regional energy integration? There is little theoretical work on the definition of regional energy integration. Most of the available work is case studies of specific regions (Renner 2009; Palestini 2020).

If we refer to the objectives stated by the European Union in the various "energy packages" adopted since the 1990s, a European energy integration would include four to five components (Palle 2016, p. 321):

– technical integration of networks and functional exchange processes;

– integration of energy markets (gas and electricity) allowing exchanges, spatial and seasonal complementarities, as well as a competition between energy sources;

– integration of technical standards and operating processes of these markets and networks entrusted to a common regulatory authority (Agence de coopération des régulateurs européens de l'énergie, ACER);

– common policies regarding the supply and sources of energy used.

A fifth component would be the representations that EU citizens have of integration. Do they have a common representation in relation to a common project of society?

European energy integration and energy transition are produced by European institutions, member countries, energy companies, communities, individuals, etc. Each actor in this process has its own preferences and constraints. It can therefore be assumed that there are divergences between them. In theory, these divergences can be overcome. The best way to make them converge towards a common goal is to implement governance tools (Grossman 2001, p. 148), i.e. non-hierarchical mechanisms for making political decisions, involving actors of varying nature, not all of whom have constitutional legitimacy. These mechanisms play an important role in European regional integration, particularly in the context of so-called "multilevel" governance, which refers to a system of continuous negotiation between actors and authorities at different territorial levels, involving governmental and non-governmental actors in more or less formalized mixed political networks. According to Marks and Hooghe (2004), multilevel governance, clearly distinct from the model of the state monopoly of power, is more effective and includes non-state actors in decision-making.

Multi-level governance raises many questions and debates (Saurugger 2020, p. 235): should only public actors be included in this notion? Even theoretical criticisms: the notion of level is not always precisely defined (Stephenson 2013, p. 825). However, there is a consensus that, thanks to its fluid, inclusive and non-hierarchical character, it would allow tensions to be smoothed out by accommodating the diversity of expectations.

The European energy transition and integration are driven by actors who produce space by building and arranging facilities and infrastructures, at different scales according to their own objectives and contracts. Since the 1990s, geographic research has shown that spatial scales are no longer considered as a given. Scale is socially constructed, relevant to the development and implementation of strategies (Marston 2000), and contingent (Swyngedouw 2004, p. 130). For Mamadouh and Van der Wusten (2009, p. 295), the notion of multilevel governance underlies the notion of scale: the EU is not one more scale added to the others, but a type of scalar configuration where each scale can be in plural relation with the others. In this constitutive environment of regional integration, the relations between territories, actors and powers are reorganized in the production of spaces – and therefore scales – of governance.

We can therefore make two assumptions: multi-level governance allows all the actors and all the spaces they construct to work together in an integrated spatial device; on the contrary, the spaces constructed by the actors involved in the European integration and energy transition are incompatible, which can cause conflicts.

5.3. The energy transition as a lever for integration

The EU understands the notion of energy transition as a political position, an economic strategy and an instrument of power. The question of the implementation of the transition then arises. On what and on whom does it rely? To answer this question, we will propose an analysis of the pillars of European energy policy. We will also analyze the close link that the EU establishes between transition and integration; a link that the EU establishes empirically, without building a conceptual model beforehand.

The EU has made the energy transition one of its main battle horses. Energy has been at the heart of European integration since the Coal and Steel Community (founded in 1951) and the Euratom Treaty (founded in 1957). Marginalized for a time compared to other aspects of integration (currency or transport), energy returned to the top of the European agenda in the 1990s. The EU's energy policy was then based on the objective of integrating markets and networks with a view to liberalization, as evidenced by the legislative "packages" that were adopted.

The first directives on the gas and electricity markets in 1996 and 1998 paved the way for a policy of integration through liberalization and the construction of a single market. At the time, the EU did not have a specific legislative basis for implementing a common energy policy (Petit 2006). Energy was seen as an element in the construction of the single market or as an aspect of European environmental policy. After a second "energy package" in 2003, which reinforced the liberalization of markets, the Treaty of Lisbon[1] made energy a shared competence between the States and the EU and laid the foundations for a common policy in 2009. The third "energy package" (2009) establishes a total separation of production, supply and management of energy networks, reinforces the independence of the national regulator, establishes a European Energy Cooperation Agency bringing together national regulators, and creates two cooperation bodies for gas and electricity network operators (ENTSO-E and ENTSO-G), which are responsible for the development of the networks on a European scale and agree on common operating standards.

It is in this dynamic of integration through liberalization that European environmental concerns have been progressively introduced since 2000. The third "energy package", after the crisis of 2008, includes a first plan for recovery through "green" growth in the energy sector, associated with the development of renewable energies and low-carbon technologies. It was completed in 2016 by the Winter Package, which is intended to adapt the structure of the European market (market design) to developments in the energy sector (integration of networks, growth of renewable energies and decentralized production) and to strengthen the climate component of European energy policy. This policy, which is gradually being integrated into the construction of a common energy policy initially conceived as integration through liberalization, has culminated in the recent Green Deal or European Green Pact project, presented in 2019. This pact contains measures proposed by the European Commission to achieve "climate neutrality" by 2050.

European energy policy has gradually been built around three main pillars: competitiveness, security of supply and sustainability[2]. These three objectives are based on two cross-cutting dynamics, transition and integration, which the EU sees both as means to achieve them and as objectives in themselves.

The EU considers that the energy transition and integration serve the objective of competitiveness, because they would allow both a development of certain economic activities and energy savings that would be reflected in the price of goods or services produced in Europe (transition), and energy savings in both production and consumption (integration). The same logic is applied to the security of supply. The

1 Treaty of Lisbon, December 13, 2007, entered into force on December 1, 2009, art. 176 A.

2 Communication from the Commission to the European Council and the European Parliament of January 10, 2007 entitled "Une politique de l'énergie pour l'Europe" (COM(2007) 1 final – not published in the *Journal officiel*).

transition dynamic would contribute to this objective by allowing the development of energy production on European soil that would reduce European dependence on imports. The integration dynamic would also contribute to this objective by allowing mutual assistance between States in the event of supply disruption. Finally, transition and integration would serve a sustainability objective by increasing energy efficiency and energy savings, by developing renewable production sources and by allowing complementary relations between different production areas (e.g. between hydraulic production in the Alps, wind power in the North Sea and solar power in the Mediterranean basin)[3].

Apart from their usefulness for the implementation of a common energy policy, energy transition and integration are also promoted by the EU for their own sake. The energy transition is one of the components of a broader policy to combat climate change and reduce its impacts, led by the EU and the Member States. Energy integration is understood to be part of the essence of the EU project: by creating "de facto solidarities"[4], a market is created as well as a common space.

The energy transition is then envisaged by the EU in four ways. It is a political position based on an awareness of scientific realities by the political body and citizens, and which refers to a concern linked to the impacts of climate change and the idea of resource depletion[5]. In this, the EU joins a general movement that began in Germany at the end of the 1980s and is marked by a sensitivity to the impact of human activities on the environment. It has taken on board controversial concepts such as sustainable development and ecological transition (Hopkins 2008, p. 202), from which it draws its energy transition policy.

The energy transition is also an economic strategy for the EU. Energy is structurally the main source of deficit in the European trade balance (in the first half of 2017, a deficit of 139 billion euros for the EU[6]). The desire to position the EU as a world leader in transition is linked to a policy of post-crisis economic recovery through the search for competitiveness, the development of new sectors for European R&D, industry and employment, as well as an attempt to emancipate, at least partially, the European economy from the variation in fossil fuel prices.

---

3 See the results of the e-Highway 2050 project supported by the 7e EU Framework Program, *Europe's future secure and sustainable electricity infrastructure*, released in November 2015.

4 R. Schuman, French Minister of Foreign Affairs, declaration of May 9, 1950.

5 Eurobaromètre spécial 468, 2017; DG Communication, L'environnement pour les européens, October 2016. Read also the report of the MUSTEC research project (Horizon 2020), submitted to the European Commission in 2019: "Policy pathways for the energy transition in Europe and in selected European countries," deliverable 7.2. Read also the roadmap published by the European Union in 2012 (Energy Roadmap 2050).

6 Eurostat, euroindicators press release 141/2017 of September 15, 2017.

It is also a political strategy and an instrument of internal power. By establishing the primacy of integration as a means of this policy and the European scale as a reference scale, European energy policy legitimizes a transfer of power (and even sovereignty) from the member states to the EU. This is a neo-functionalist approach (Haas 1958, p. 457) to regional integration based on leverage effects. The construction of the Energy Union, launched in 2015, is based on the growing influence of the EU institutions: the creation of a European Commissioner for Energy in 2010 (DG Énergie), a European Agency for the Cooperation of Energy Regulators (ACER, created in 2009 and active since 2011) and two European networks of network operators (gas and electricity, ENTSO-E and ENTSO-G, created in 2008). This power strategy is made possible by the Lisbon Treaty, which lays the foundations for a European energy policy, while seeking a precarious balance (Bornard 2015, p. 69) between a common policy and the sovereignty of states over the energy mix and sources of supply.

The EU's energy transition policy can also be read through the prism of external geopolitics. Europe's dependence on external suppliers (Russia, Norway and Algeria) has grown: approximately 40% of the European Community's needs in the 1980s, 60% at the end of the 2010s. Some of these suppliers, such as Russia, are perceived as unstable, in particular because of their conflicting relations with certain transit countries, which affect European supplies. It may be recalled that gas supplies from Russia to the EU via Ukraine were interrupted from January 7–20, 2009, due to a serious crisis in relations between these two countries. In addition, since the beginning of the Russian invasion of Ukraine in February 2022, some EU member countries consider that their level of energy dependence on Russia, which can be transformed into a political dependence, is too high. It should be remembered that 55% of Germany's gas imports and 41% of its oil imports come from Russia. By promoting the electrification of uses and the production of energy directly on European Union soil, the energy transition must reduce European dependence and respond to this geopolitical uncertainty.

5.4. European energy transition and integration in practice: conflicts of actors and problems of scale

The energy strategies of the European institutions are based on a double postulate: integration policy and transition policy are compatible; the European scale is the most important for implementing transition policy. This double assumption calls for a questioning. The actors involved in the implementation of these policies, according to their preferences and constraints, construct multiple spaces and deploy their strategies at various scales, whose organizations are not necessarily compatible. This section analyzes these spaces based on a series of research missions conducted between 2012 and 2021 that identified several transition models.

– 2012 (April to June): European Parliament participant observation.

– 2013: European Commission, EU Joint Research Centre, Institute of Energy and Transport, French and UK regulators interviews.

– 2014 (February to July): participant observation of the European electricity and gas network operators, ENTSO-E and ENTSO-G.

– 2017: online survey of power system modelers.

– 2019: interviews with local actors of the energy transition in France who are members of the Positive Energy Territories movement, TEPOS.

– 2020–2021: participant observation, European Committee of the Regions Environment Commission.

Box 5.1. *List of research missions conducted in the field between 2012 and 2021 (Angélique Palle)*

5.4.1. *Imposition of a European scale by the EU*

European integration has developed since the end of World War II from a national model. Infrastructure, operations, standards, markets and energy policies are designed by states for which energy and security of supply are a matter of national sovereignty. Relationships (exchanges, regulatory arrangements or political consultations) do exist with neighbors, but they are mainly thought of bilaterally and as means of backup or local optimization of energy production.

Figure 5.1 illustrates this model built in the 19th century and in the first half of the 20th century.

Derived from this model is the European integrated model, which is one of the extremities on the scale of possible models for the evolution of the EU's energy space. This integrated model emerged after World War II and took off with the European regulations of 1996 and 1998 aimed at integrating electricity markets and networks. It takes the national model of total integration, on a single scale, and transposes it to the European scale. It aims to put in place the following:

– A homogeneous space with an integrated infrastructure network which the European network managers are responsible for setting up[7].

---

7 Regulation of the European Parliament and of the Council (EC) No. 714/2009 of July 13, 2009 on conditions for access to the network for cross-border exchanges in electricity; Regulation of the European Parliament and of the Council (EC) No. 715/2009 of July 13, 2009 on conditions for access to the natural gas natural gas transmission networks.

– A common normative architecture, allowing a single market to function as well as a European energy price[8].

– A common market based on the coupling of the European energy markets supported by the European Commission; this dynamic is supplemented by the strategies of the major European energy groups (mergers or acquisitions of stakes in the networks or producers of new entrants by groups inherited from the national monopolies of the first EU members).

– A common energy policy, based on the Treaty of Lisbon, on the action of the Commission, the Parliament and the Council, articulated around a more debated and concerted energy mix (renewable production targets, debates on a European position on the exploitation of shale gas and oil or the conditions for the use of civil nuclear power).

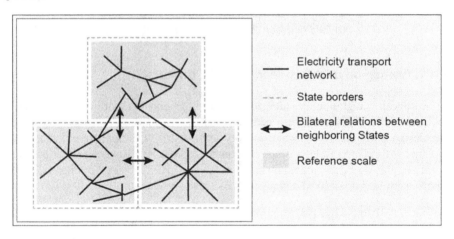

Figure 5.1. *Integration models: initial model (by A. Palle). For a color version of this figure, see www.iste.co.uk/peyroux/development.zip*

This total integration model is shown in Figure 5.2. It is a borderline case which the integration initiatives and projects observed at the European level are tending towards. During a study day at the Joint Research Center – Institute of Energy and Transport in Petten (Netherlands), one of the researchers from the team interviewed said: "The totally integrated, totally centralized, top-down system is utopian. It

8 Regulation of the Parliament and of the Council (EC) No. 713/2009 of July 13, 2009 establishing an Agency for the Cooperation of Energy Regulators.

resembles an engineer's or European civil servant's fantasy. It is politically impossible to achieve and technically complicated."[9]

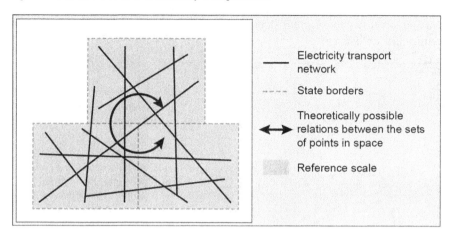

Figure 5.2. *Integration models: European extreme (by A. Palle). For a color version of this figure, see www.iste.co.uk/peyroux/development.zip*

5.4.2. The choice of integration and transition on a European scale: open and latent contestation

This predominant model in current dynamics is contested by actors who act at the other end of the spectrum of possible scales, promoting a model based on the predominance of the local, on the interconnection and interdependence of a multiplicity of small, independent spaces or those close to energy independence (Figure 5.3). It was structured from the end of the 2000s, defended by local actors (associations, local political bodies) and certain environmental NGOs that do not wish to associate energy transition with liberalization and infrastructure development[10]. The status of this model in relation to European policy is ambiguous. While European policies show an awareness of local games and the need to involve actors at this level in the implementation of these objectives, they nevertheless envisage governance between the EU and the Member States, when local actors wish to be involved (Palle and Richard 2021). European policies thus prevent local actors from defending a locally conceived transition in the European arena. These actors advocate a transition based on local dynamics and decentralized production. The growing use of renewable energies is reflected in a significant local component:

9 Interview, May 21, 2013, Joint Research Center – Institute of Energy and Transports, Security of Supply Unit, Petten, The Netherlands.
10 Greenpeace, 2014, "pow[ER] 2030 a European grid for ¾ renewable electricity by 2030".

individuals are becoming producers of all or part of the energy they consume. This dynamic makes it possible to envisage the emergence of "off-grid" spaces (Coutard and Rutherford 2013, p. 103), independent of the collective infrastructure. This is a paradigm shift, as the current dominant model mostly seeks to avoid electrical "peninsulas" or "islands".

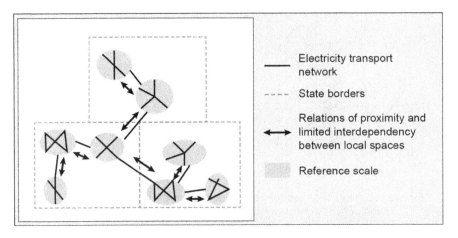

Figure 5.3. *Integration models: local extreme (realized by A. Palle). For a color version of this figure, see www.iste.co.uk/peyroux/development.zip*

This model of local evolution is still considered a marginal alternative by traditional energy actors (regulators, network managers, electricity producers). "It is a model that is being seriously debated in the German parliament, for example, but it is politically utopian and very expensive: it does not allow for any economies of scale."[11]

These developments at the local level have a profound impact on the governance of the energy provided and its management, particularly because local actors are entering the European energy "grand game". For economists Jean-Marie Chevalier and Olivier Pastré (Chevalier and Pastré 2015, p. 30): "the energy transition will be 'bottom-up' or it will not be. [...] A local dimension of governance must be mentioned. In numerous European countries, local authorities, municipalities are becoming increasingly involved in energy policy".

At the same time, the very principle of an energy policy of integration and transition on a European scale is being questioned. It is taking place on a

---

11 Researcher interview, May 21, 2013, Joint Research Center – Institute of Energy and Transports, Security of Supply Unit, Petten, The Netherlands.

macro-regional but infra-European scale and is bringing together groups of states to form "European sub-regions". This dynamic affects several areas of the European energy "millefeuille", which includes superimpositions of actors and initiatives concerning infrastructures, technical standards, the regulation and structure of markets, public policies at the local, national and European levels. At the infrastructural level, there are macro-European regional divisions that are paradoxically thought of by the institutions and actors acting at the European level. We see them in the development plans of electricity and gas infra-structures and in the choice of projects of common interest pressed by the Commission[12].

At the level of standards, the regional initiatives for gas and electricity created in 2006 provide a different division of the European space. Designed to be the first building blocks in the construction of an integrated European market, each "region" brings together regulators, industry and the member states concerned, as well as the European Commission and other affected parties, with the objective of developing and testing solutions to improve energy markets. The reference scale for these initiatives is ambiguous, as they were conceived on a regional scale to eventually serve the construction of a European scale.

At the market level, the target models of the future internal energy market envisage a partition of the market into "zones" (entry/exit zones or balancing zones for gas, separate zones or bidding zones for electricity) according to the possibilities of exchange and congestion of energy transmission networks. The geographic definition of these zones is a matter of debate. They constitute another regional division, which may change over time, depending on market conditions[13].

Finally, at the political level, bottom-up initiatives from groups of Member States have led to the creation of political consultation forums on a regional scale. The two main initiatives in this area are the Višegrad Group (Poland, Czech Republic, Slovakia and Hungary) and the Pentalateral Energy Forum (France, Germany, Belgium, Luxembourg, the Netherlands and Austria; Switzerland is only an observer). The aim of these structures is to enable joint operation, position-taking and action in the energy field on a regional scale (Figure 5.4).

Several scales of reference, European, macro-regional and local, driven by a diversity of actors, are thus in competition for the implementation of transitional energy policies, while national governments are trying to maintain control over these

---

12 European Commission, 2010, Communication to the European Parliament and the Council, "Priorités en matière d'infrastructures énergétiques pour 2020 et au-delà – Schéma directeur pour un réseau énergétique européen intégré" [COM(2010) 677 final].
13 ENTSO-E, 2014, Technical report bidding zones study; Ofgem FTA team, July 2014, Bidding zones literature review.

policies in the name of the energy sovereignty necessary for the independence of the State. Without a clear domination of one of these dynamics over the others, a phenomenon of hybridization is taking place.

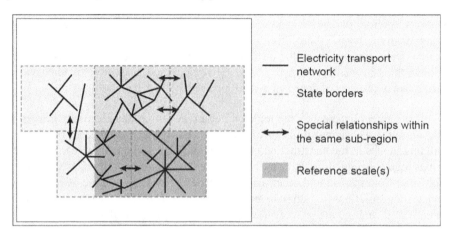

Figure 5.4. *Integration models: macro-regional model (by A. Palle). For a color version of this figure, see www.iste.co.uk/peyroux/development.zip*

5.4.3. *Hybrid energy space: spatial incompatibilities and conflicts of scales*

The three integration models (macro-regional, local and European) refer to three concurrent dynamics, which raises the question of their competition and compatibility. There is a hybridization of these models (Figure 5.5), which is perceived by European energy actors present at their intersections, notably the gas and electricity transmission system operators and the Institute of Energy and Transport of the European Union Joint Research Centre (IET-JRC). This prompts us to explore the issue of governance and interaction between actors. The number of actors involved or wishing to be involved in decisions is increasing. Incoherence and operational problems are appearing at all levels of integration, linked to the complexity of the structure put in place and to the problem of defining subsidiarity (what is the optimal scale for decision-making?).

At the infrastructure level and at the level of their operation, the interconnection of networks on a European scale, associated with the growth of decentralized renewable energy production at local scales (intermittent and uncontrollable) is a source of instability for the network. This is all the more the case when the managers and operators of these networks (who operate on a largely national or sub-European scale) do not have a global vision of the flows and tensions existing in the networks of neighboring countries to which they are connected. This mismatch between the network's deployment area and that of the management authority can lead, when coordination between the actors is not sufficient, to a lack of optimization or to disruptions aggravated by the cascade effects which exist in a network of this size[14].

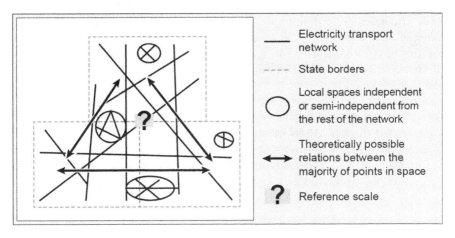

Figure 5.5. *Integration models: hybrid model (by A. Palle). For a color version of this figure, see www.iste.co.uk/peyroux/development.zip*

At the level of standards and the market, the dual authority of the European Union institutions and the Member States complicates the reading of the energy regulatory landscape in the EU. The harmonized European framework that the Commission wishes to put in place is opposed by certain uncoordinated state initiatives, for example, in the implementation of aid for the development of renewable energies. Germany's subsidies for renewable energies, in the context of European energy transition objectives, have been perceived as energy dumping by certain neighboring countries such as the Netherlands, which have become major importers of German electricity, which is considered artificially cheap.

At the political level, it is the differences between states in the choice of energy mix that are a source of tension. For example, with the interconnection of European electricity transmission networks in line with the European policy of energy integration, the German nuclear phase-out, carried out without consultation with its neighbors, has destabilized the Czech and Polish electricity networks (Palle 2017). This desire for independence in the choice of the energy mix can be seen at the local level, when some municipalities or citizen groups oppose renewable energy infrastructure projects supported by the EU but deemed exogenous to the territory

14 UCTE, 2007, Final Report, System Disturbance on November 4, 2006, Brussels.

concerned by local populations and contrary to their conception of an energy transition based on a local model (Oiry 2015).

At all levels of integration (infrastructure, standards, markets, policies), the hybrid nature of the spatial model towards which the EU is moving – a model in which dynamics from European, national and local models coexist, between European integration, sub-regional dynamics and local dynamics – translates into problems of governance and sharing of authority between actors. Virginie Schwarz, Director of Energy at the Directorate General for Energy and Climate, writes (Schwarz 2015, p. 92):

> The State remains legitimate to protect fundamental rights, to ensure security of supply, to set the major issues, but it can no longer decide and act alone […] it must work both with the European level and with local authorities. […] The ability to find new governance models and make them work will be decisive for the success of the energy transition.

5.5. Conclusion

Research on European integration gives an important place to the notion of multilevel governance (Saurugger 2020, p. 235). The available work on multilevel governance is based on several assumptions: states are not monolithic entities; they are not the only actors in the construction of Europe; the many actors involved in the construction of Europe share certain objectives in certain areas (Kohler-Koch and Eising 1999, p. 5). In a context of multi-level governance, all actors involved in a particular domain, including those without institutional legitimacy, build partnerships that facilitate compromise (Grossman 2001, p. 148). They implement non-hierarchical mechanisms for making policy decisions. In this sense, the notion of multilevel governance accounts for the complexity of community construction, by pointing to the existence of systems of continuous negotiation between actors and authorities placed at different territorial levels, in more or less formalized mixed political networks. In theory, these fluid networks are a means of smoothing out tensions and even conflicts between actors.

In the context of a confrontation with empirical reality, we may wonder whether this is not an excessively schematic perception of the European construction that somewhat neglects the weight and materiality, at times very constraining, of geographical space. The fluidity of governance mechanisms does not make it possible to overcome all the obstacles. This chapter shows that each actor constructs space in two ways, according to their expectations, preferences, and technical and economic imperatives. On the one hand, they produce spatial arrangements, particularly when it comes to deploying infrastructure. On the other hand, the spaces thus constructed are not all of the same size and are deployed at different scales. As it happens, these arrangements and scales are not necessarily superimposable and compatible. It can be difficult to articulate them and make them work together in an integrated whole. Tensions and blockages are thus observed here and there.

The road to European energy integration, in the service of transition, will be long and steep, both politically and environmentally, since the EU's stated objectives are very ambitious, notably in the Green Deal. There is certainly room for research on the effects of EU environmental policy in several major directions. Will European policy translate into tangible climate results in the medium term? Will it act as a powerful lever for integration? What spatial scales will be relevant to address major environmental issues? What model of energy integration will enable a significant reduction in greenhouse gas emissions (European, local, macro-regional, hybrid)?

5.6. References

Arnaud de Sartre, X. (2016). *Agriculture et changements globaux. Expertises globales et situations locales*. Peter Lang, Brussels.

Bornard, P. (2015). Politique énergétique européenne : Le codicille qui tue ! In *L'énergie en état de choc*, Chevallier, J.-M. and Pastré, O. (eds). Eyrolles, Paris.

Chevalier, J.-M. and Pastré, O. (eds) (2015). *L'énergie en état de choc*. Eyrolles, Paris.

Coudroy de Lille, L., Rivière-Honegger, A., Rolland, L., Volin, A. (2017). Notion à la une : Transition. *Géoconfluences* [Online]. Available at: http://geoconfluences.ens-lyon.fr/ informations-scientifiques/a-la-une/notion-a-la-une/notion-transition.

Coutard, O. and Rutherford, J. (2013). Vers l'essor de villes "post-réseaux" : Infrastructures, innovation sociotechnique et transition urbaine en Europe. In *L'innovation face aux défis environnementaux de la ville contemporaine*, Forest, J. and Hamdouch, A. (eds). Presses Polytechniques Universitaires Romandes, Lausanne.

De Boe, P., Grasland, C., Healy, A. (1999). Spatial integration. Report, Study Programme on European Spatial Planning, 14.

Dosenrode, S. (2010). Federalism theory and neo-functionalism: Elements for an analytical framework. *Perspectives on Federalism*, 2(3), 1–28.

Grandjean, A., Le Teno, H., Boulanger, P-M. (2015). Transition. In *Dictionnaire de la pensée écologique*, Bourg, D. and Papaux, A. (eds). PUF, Paris.

Grossman, E., Irondelle, B., Saurugger, S., Quermonne, J.-L. (eds) (2001). *Les mots de l'Europe. Lexique de l'intégration européenne*. Presses de Science Po, Paris.

Haas, E. (1958). The challenge of regionalism. *International Organization*, 12(4), 440–458.

Hettne, B. and Söderbaum, F. (1998). The new regionalism approach. *Politeia*, 17(3), 6–22.

Hopkins, R. (2008). *The Transition Handbook: From Oil Dependency to Local Resilience.* UIT Cambridge Ltd, VT.

Kohler-Koch, B. and Eising, R. (eds) (1999). *The Transformation of Governance in the European Union.* Routledge, London.

Mamadouh, V. and Van der Wusten, H. (2009). Echelles et territoires dans le système de gouvernance européen. In *Penser l'espace politique*, Rosière, S., Cox, K., Vacchiani-Marcuzzo, C., Dahlman, C. (eds). Ellipses, Paris.

Marks, G. and Hooghe, L. (2004). Contrasting visions of multi-level governance. In *Multi-level Governance*, Bache, I. and Flinders, M. (eds). Oxford University Press, Oxford.

Marston, S. (2000). The social construction of scale. *Progress in Human Geography*, 24(2), 219–242.

Moravcsik, A. (1993). Preferences and power in the European community: A liberal intergovernmentalist approach. *Journal of Common Market Studies*, 31, 473–524.

Nonn, H. and Martin, J.-P. (1980). La notion d'intégration régionale. *Travaux de l'Institut Géographique de Reims*, 41–42, 33–46.

Oiry, A. (2015). Conflits et stratégies d'acceptabilité sociale autour des énergies marines renouvelables sur le littoral français. *VertigO*, 15(3) [Online]. Available at: https://journals.openedition.org/vertigo/16724.

Paasi, A. (2010). Regions are social constructs, but who or what "constructs" them? Agency in question. *Environment and Planning A*, 42, 2296–2301.

Palestini, S. (2020). Orchestrating regionalism: The interamerican development bank and the central American electric system. *Review of Policy Research*, 22 June.

Palle, A. (2016). L'espace énergétique européen : Quelle(s) intégration(s) régionale(s)? : Réseaux, normes, marchés, politiques, des intégrations à plusieurs échelles ? PhD Thesis, Université Paris 1 Panthéon-Sorbonne, Paris.

Palle, A. (2017). Les flux électriques européens, de la mise en politique à la politisation. *Géocarrefour*, 91(3) [Online]. Available at: https://journals.openedition.org/geocarrefour/10229.

Palle, A. and Richard, Y. (2021). From multilevel governance to scalar clash, searching for the right scale for European energy policy. *Tijdschrift voor economische en sociale geografie*, 113(1), 1–18.

Petit, Y. (2006). À la recherche de la politique européenne de l'énergie. *Revue trimestrielle de droit européen*, 42, 593–620.

Raineau, L. (2011). Vers une transition énergétique ? *Nature Science Société*, 19(2), 133–143 [Online]. Available at: https://journals.openedition.org/rives/4918#:~:text=7Selon%20Laurence%20Raineau%20(2011,cela%20un%20choix%20de%20soci%C3%A9t%C3%A9%20%C2%BB.

Renner, S. (2009). The energy community of southeast Europe: A neo-functionalist project of regional integration. *European Integration Online Papers*, 13.

Saurugger, S. (2020). *Théories et concepts de l'intégration européenne*. Presses de Sciences Po, Paris.

Schwarz, V. (2015). Pas de politique énergétique sans démocratie participative ! In *L'énergie en état de choc*, Chevalier, J.-M. and Pastré, O. (eds). Eyrolles, Paris.

Stephenson, P. (2013). Twenty years of multi-level governance: Where does it come from? What is it? Where is it going? *Journal of European Public Policy*, 20(6), 817–837.

Swyngedouw, E. (2004). Scaled geographies. Nature, place, and the politics of scale. In *Scale and Geographic Inquiry: Nature, Society and Method*, McMaster, R. and Sheppard, E. (eds). Blackwell Publishers, Hoboken, NJ.

6

Transport in Africa: Between Global Influences and Local Know-how

6.1. African transport in search of modernity

"In the big league" was the headline in 2020 in *Jeune Afrique*[1] about the city of Cotonou, whose ambition is to "carve out a place of choice in the string of West African coastal cities". In the same release, the Beninese Minister of Living Environment and Sustainable Development added: "Cotonou must be an essential step on the Abidjan-Lagos corridor". These words could have been repeated for Dakar, Accra, Casablanca or Douala, so much so that the question of the place of each African capital and the role of transport in global competition is anchored in the agendas of political decision-makers and promoters of modernization and metropolization of the continent.

However, following the reflections that consider space as one of the fundamental dimensions of societies and individuals (Agnew 1994), it is necessary to take a critical look at these developments, the political orientations and societal choices that have guided them, as well as their effects on the different scales of territories. The concentration of transport infrastructure and services in metropolitan areas, particularly around port hubs that have become the gateways to the hinterland (Debrie 2010), has led to the strengthening of the main routes, rail corridors and mass transit systems, such as Bus Rapid Transit (BRT), but has not avoided the tunnel effects in the areas they cross. The consequences in terms of serving urban areas and opening up rural areas are detrimental to territorial integration. In the same way, the persistent isolation of entire parts of the territory (due to a lack of infrastructure or services) encourages regional irredentism, just as it hinders local

---

Chapter written by Jérôme LOMBARD, Nora MAREÏ and Olivier NINOT.

1 "Dans la cour des grands", *Jeune Afrique*, November 2020, no. 3094.

inter-regional and international relations, made difficult by the weakness of connections.

In this chapter, we will observe and analyze African circulations in all their diversity, both in territories and across scales and networks, "... mutually constitutive and relationally interrelated dimensions of socio-spatial relations" (Jessop et al. 2008, p. 389). The mobility of people, the displacement of goods must be understood through the practices of individuals (movements, places, activities) and their imaginations, as M. Sheller and J. Urry argued more than 15 years ago (2006), and not only through networks and intercontinental exchanges.

The radical transport transformations that are being undertaken in many African countries in the name of modernization either ignore or do not sufficiently take into account the daily reality of societies and territorial challenges. Turnkey solutions are based on the questionable assumption that the African continent is marginalized, but often ignore the specificities of each country or city. Characterized as informal, i.e. not subject to registration and/or not taxed, transport only offers (according to the latest report of the World Bank's Africa Transport Policy Program[2]) a few effective solutions[3].

The question of the much-desired modernity of African transport must be the result of a combination of solutions and their adaptation to geographical contexts. Governments, technical and financial partners (including international consulting firms) and global transport operators are not the only actors in reform on the continent. African transport systems are the result of arrangements that combine external experience and local approaches, as Mareï and Savy (2021) point out in relation to logistics in the cities of the South. The employees and the populations are also involved in the evolution of the sector, developing their own logistics and interacting with the institutional and infrastructural reforms carried out by the public authorities. More than 20 years ago, S. Latouche (1998) insisted on the importance of local know-how and its capacity for adaptation and innovation. Along with him, we emphasize the social function of the initiatives of individuals and neo-entrepreneurs in the transport sector, which translates into an increase in a variety of jobs, the provision of income to a number of individuals and families and the provision of unconventional services (such as mixed transport, which combines passengers and goods).

From this perspective, for more than 20 years, we have been developing an original methodology for approaching transport issues on the African continent, outlined in this

2 Sub-Saharan African Transport Program (SSATP) (2021): https://www.ssatp.org/publication/myths-and-realities-informal-public-transport-developing-countries-approaches-improving.
3 See also the general discussion of emerging and developing economies (Ohnsorge and Yu 2021).

chapter (Box 6.1). In section 6.2, we examine the ambivalence of these major transformations; then, in section 6.3, we focus on the prospects and risks of disconnection from the expectations and innovations of citizens and transport users.

The proposed reflection is the result of work shared between researchers using the same methodology, which gives priority to a qualitative approach and immersion in the field. In the African transport sector, the search for quantitative data is not always easy. In order to grasp the multiple facets of social transport practices and their effects in space, we have always combined different methods. Historical, with the study of the archives of major transport companies and the history of transport federations and unions, the monitoring of the evolution of regulations and texts and the reading of the press of the countries on which we focus our attention. Statistical, with the analysis of various files (lists of carriers, vehicles, driving licenses); data on the market share of each mode; origin/destination surveys of goods flows. Informative, through multiple questionnaire surveys, where possible, with transport managers, workers and users, and through interviews with heads of departments in the ministries and directors of infrastructure (ports, stations). Biographical, through repeated in-depth interviews with entrepreneurs, transporters, traders, emigrants and trade unionists. Participatory, by observing practices in garages, warehouses, markets or onboard vehicles; and by tracking changes in the location of key places, such as main markets, public or private company warehouses, bus stations and ports. The countries that have been particularly targeted and observed are mainly in West Africa (Senegal, Mali, Burkina Faso, Togo, and Ivory Coast) and the Maghreb (Mauritania, Morocco). The transformations underway along the coastal axis from Tangier to Abidjan are enlightening and put into perspective other examples from the rest of the continent.

Box 6.1. *Methodology for observing African mobility and transport in Africa*

6.2. Transport transformations: between dependencies, resistances and adaptations

In 2002, X. Godard, a specialist in African urban transport announced "the time of resourcefulness and inventive disorder" (Godard 2002), which came about with changes in national public policies[4]. In transport, as in other sectors, the time was ripe for the liberation of initiatives, the creation of businesses and the redirection of

---

4 This evolution has its origins in the Structural Adjustment Programs for Transport (*Programmes d'ajustement structurel des transports*, PAST), which became Sector Transport Programs (*Programmes sectoriels des transports*, PST) in the 1990s and were extended in the 2000s. The modernization of the sector required the duplication of formulas that had been tried elsewhere and the transformation of ways of doing business. Much of the responsibility of ministries was transferred to independent agencies; private operators were given responsibility for the most critical infrastructure and the most profitable markets; investment choices were guided by international standards.

the unemployed towards new activities that would generate wealth and employment (Lombard 2015). In reality, deregulation and liberalization policies have had ambivalent effects, which have resulted in the rise of informality. "[...] It is precisely with the economic and trade liberalization reforms that the informal sector has flourished the most to the detriment of the formal sector," recalls Daffé (2002, p. 77) in the case of Senegal.

6.2.1. *Reforms at the heart of the metropolization process*

The trend towards the primacy of economic and political capitals has increased in every African country, in direct relation to the internationalization of economies and the polarization of activities and jobs, as F. Ascher (2003) points out. The main characteristic of metropolization remains the concentration of the population in gigantic complexes of several million inhabitants spread over increasingly large areas: the hold of the capital city over "distended built-up areas" (Jaglin et al. 2018, p. 9) has only increased in recent decades. The need to serve expanding urban areas and millionaire city populations has been acute since the early 2000s. As states and local authorities embark on ambitious "urban renewal through transport" programs (Hervé et al. 2007), it is becoming a priority to have efficient transport systems that match the metropolitan ambitions of each city (Musil et al. 2014). Transport has thus become the primary focus of local governments in order to drive urban development projects, meet growing travel demands and dress up standard facilities with modernity.

Several major capital cities in sub-Saharan Africa have embarked on reforms of their transport systems (Infrastructure Consortium for Africa 2016), tackling congestion and the limitations of traditional service provision head on. Many cities are moving towards Bus Rapid Transit (BRT), a relatively inexpensive and adaptable system first tested in Bogotá and Curitiba. This is the case in Cape Town and Johannesburg in South Africa, which took advantage of the 2010 soccer World Cup to set up rapid bus systems running on reserved or separate lanes. Lagos since 2008 and, more recently, Dar es-Salaam and Accra have embarked on such projects. In addition or as an alternative, suburban rail transport is once again becoming a solution for the future, as in Cape Town with Metrorail, in Addis Ababa (since 2015), or in Dakar with the Transport Express Régional or TER (in service since 2021) and in Abidjan (metro line 1 is currently under construction). In these cities, logistics are undergoing multiple processes of reorganization and redeployment of the main freight activities outside the urban area, in order to respond to congestion and security problems. Dry ports and warehousing facilities are appearing on the outskirts of port cities; new bypasses and urban freeways are removing heavy transport from dense areas; new standards are being imposed on hazardous transport (containers, hydrocarbons).

Since the economic rebound of the 2000s, metropolises have become the bridgeheads of major infrastructure projects that define the fabric of the continental network (Mareï and Ninot 2018). Priority is given to national and international interconnections. These are presented as a political choice for development by international donors, governments, private operators, and also pan-African organizations, such as the Program for Infrastructure Development in Africa or PIDA (Banque africaine de développement et al. 2012; Nugent 2018). These programs have concrete effects in the territories, particularly in priority investment areas (ports), growth poles (cities),), and also on major road and rail routes. The role of Chinese companies is growing, as D. Bénazéraf (2014) reminds us. Various infrastructure projects have been launched in Angola (railroad, road, airport and pipeline), Nigeria (railroad), Djibouti (port, pipeline to Sudan, railroad to Ethiopia) and Kenya (railroad project between the port of Mombasa and neighboring Uganda). The diversification of financial and technical partners is accompanied by the import of foreign norms and standards that place national policies under influence (notably from China).[5]

The emergence of new port hubs (Tangier-Med, Lomé, Ngqura, Mombasa and Port Said) and airports (Casablanca, Dakar, Nairobi and Johannesburg) is indicative of the growing interest in Africa. These places are destined to become the continent's hubs thanks to reception and redistribution capacities that meet international standards and the investments of private companies (Mareï 2016). For example, the new container terminal in Lomé, managed by MSC and China Merchants, has the capacity to capture some of the traffic arriving directly from Asia and heading to West Africa. In another example, the international airport in the Dakar metropolitan area, which was surrounded by the urban fabric, has been moved 50 kilometers to the east (Dobruszkes et al. 2020). The relocation is expected to increase capacity to three million passengers per year and to accompany the emergence of the new economic hub of Diamniadio. These projects highlight the intertwining of the metropolization dynamics and the construction of a trans-African infrastructure network. This can be observed along the Gulf of Guinea, between Lagos, Cotonou, Lomé and Accra (Moriconi-Ebrard et al. 2016; Choplin 2019).

6.2.2. From the international network to local services: important links

The transformation of African political or economic capitals is the result of the dynamism of its populations. In the suburbs, the city is being built day by day. Transporters and drivers take the liberty of organizing the service to reach as many districts as they see fit. Many transport lines are created in this way, at the request of

---

5 See "Évaluer l'influence normative chinoise dans les projets d'infrastructure en Afrique, 2020" [Online]. EHESS, available at: https://webinaire3.ehess.fr/b/pai-u30-haj.

local residents and depending on the ability of drivers to understand the situation and to consider extending the line for which they are responsible. Where streets are not marked out, motorcycles are one way of getting around. According to A. Guézéré (2021), in the peri-urban area of Lomé (Togo), where the automobile is not dominant, the motorcycle is helping to overcome isolation and long distances more than ever. L. Diaz Olvera et al. (2007) consider the development of motorcycle taxis as a sign of the vitality of popular initiatives in the face of the economic crisis and unemployment. Their successful adoption can be observed in the neighborhoods of Abidjan (Kassi-Djodjo 2010) or Ouagadougou (Essone-Nkoghe 2012).

The figure of the transport corridor, emblematic of the policies of international donors on the continent since the 2000s (Holzbauer 2014; Steck 2015), has been diverted from its initial objective. Intended to transport bulky and/or heavy products quickly and at lower cost over long distances, the road and/or rail corridor serves the needs of the inhabitants of the areas it crosses in another manner. In Mauritania, for example, women traders import goods from Dubai through the local branch of the Maersk group. The products pass through the Tangier-Med hub (Mareï and Wippel 2020), arrive at the port of Nouakchott, and are then redirected inland to the border towns of Mali and Senegal via the Nouakchott–Bamako international road axis. The tunnel effect of the corridor, in this case, is not marked in the Mauritanian territory, which, on the contrary, is "fertilized", in the words of J. Lombard et al. (2014), by the connection between the international circulation of goods and local economic dynamics.

In the intercity transport segment, which uses the main roads, the principle of combining types of infrastructure and types of service is also found. These are characterized by the multiplication and improvement of services and, above all, by the diversification of the vehicles on the road. In the same trip, to go from a secondary road, such as a laterite track, to an asphalt road, a motorcycle or even a cart, can precede the use of a minibus at regular times, and sometimes that of a private sedan, as has been observed in the Mouhoun loop in Burkina Faso (Sirpé 2007). Local urban centers benefit from this. Also in Burkina Faso, the work of S. Néya (2020) highlights the strengthening of the role of the small town of Niangoloko during the Ivorian conflict of the 2000s. The town, located a few kilometers from the border on the Abidjan–Bouaké–Bobo Dioulasso–Ouagadougou axis, saw hundreds of people of Burkinabe origin settle there from Ivory Coast, giving it a new economic impetus, particularly in the transport sector.

It is the reactivity and adaptability of the transport actors that allow the populations and goods to benefit from the advantages of international services. A process of hybridization occurs of the logistics that underlie the operation of the corridors and the areas they cross.

6.2.3. *Alongside major projects, the negotiation of the transport territory*

On a daily basis, the initiatives developed by the populations question the action of national and local authorities. On the continent, more than anywhere else, "[...] subversion appears as rationality pushed to the limit [...]" and as a permanent process of "[...] temporary and conscious adaptation" (Retaillé 2005, p. 176). African transport is, in fact, subject to permanent change, which is due as much to the practices and itineraries of the actors who run it as to the policies implemented by the various authorities. In the cities, it is irrigated by imports of spare parts, shipments of second-hand vehicles and international financing, and is embedded in family strategies for finding employment and developing new resources. A few West African examples are illuminating. Since the 1960s, many emigrants have duplicated in their country of origin what they had developed during migration. As early as 1963, the repatriation of Dahomans from Ivory Coast who returned with their cabs, led to a change in the supply of transport in Cotonou (Agossou 2004). In 1990, in the aftermath of the Liberian civil war, many Liberian and Guinean refugees arrived in Conakry in the cabs or minibuses they had driven to Monrovia (Godard and Teurnier 1992). For their part, Burkinabes from Ivory Coast who returned in the 2000s, crossed the border with vehicles in good condition, previously used on Ivorian soil. Taking advantage of their capital and know-how, they set up rapid road links to Ivory Coast and a new way of offering services (Bredeloup and Kouraogo 2007).

A number of urban bus stations were created on the initiative of drivers. They have become focal points for transport lines and users, and have been recognized by the central authorities, despite having decried their informal and unorganized nature. According to Stasik and Cissokho (2018), in the case of railway stations, the relationship between the informal and formal spheres is characterized by a high degree of continuity. Unplanned implantations benefit local communities. In Abidjan, passenger loading and unloading sites are set up on sidewalks, sometimes in recessed spaces that open onto the roadways and are referred to as "shoulder stations" (Meite 2014). According to Zouhoula Bi (2018), transporters are strengthened by this quasi-recognition; as for the municipalities, they consolidate their legitimacy to organize local space, according to the principle of "governmentality" discharge (Hibou 1999). Some sidewalks and plazas in Abidjan, where cabs and minibuses are waiting, are under the control of young people from the surrounding neighborhoods who belong to what is known locally as a union, who organize the loading and unloading of passengers and the rotation of vehicles and who charge a fee for their services. The daily operation of the transport system becomes the subject of negotiation. Petty corruption organizes the relations of the police/transporter partnership, constituting a daily act of solidarity and survival (Doumbia 2010).

Arrangements between authorities and transporters or drivers reinforce the power of some and formalize the recognition of others within the transport systems of African cities. They allow the different actors to share control over the sources of financial revenue represented by bus stations and street stops, thereby consolidating the informality at the heart of state regulation systems (Jacquot et al. 2016).

6.3. Promises and risks in African transport

Despite the remarkable developments in African transport, many problems remain, such as rural isolation, the isolation of certain regions and urban congestion. Others are also emerging. Two major trends are perceptible: the increase in spatial differentiation, on the one hand, and the risk of a growing gap between the projects led by the States and the expectations and transformations carried by citizens/users, on the other hand.

6.3.1. *Accentuated social and spatial differentiation*

Road density, although increasing, barely exceeds 200 km/1,000 km² on the continent (compared to an average of nearly 950 km worldwide). More than elsewhere, the heavy investment required is a major obstacle to network densification (Chauvin et al. 2017). Locally, large mining or agricultural companies contribute, through the construction of roads and tracks, to the selective opening up of productive areas. However, transport costs remain high due to the price of fuel, difficult vehicle operating conditions, or legal and illegal levies mentioned by B. Steck (2021). The price of transport represents on average 12.6 percent of the value of exported products (6 percent on average worldwide), and even more than 50 percent for landlocked countries (Teravaninthorn and Raballand 2009). The weakest links in the transport chains are to be found mainly between cities and the countryside, as well as in rural areas. Passenger and freight services are more expensive than in the intercity segment and of lower quality. Because of the dispersal of demand over time and space, and the low level of practicability of the tracks, rural transport is often an alternative market for small-scale transporters operating old, unsafe and unreliable vehicles.

While the process of globalization gives the impression of multiplying the possibilities for each social category and for each individual, the policy of liberalization has, on the contrary, widened the gap between territories and people, generating a growing differentiation, and even opposition, between winning and losing spaces. While it has allowed many intermediaries to enter the sector and take advantage of the growing demand for travel by African urban dwellers, it has not always helped to improve the quality of service. In intercity transport, despite the growth in vehicle fleets, many rural areas remain isolated, with no roads or tracks, no motorized vehicles, and the only option is to use carts, or even to walk, to sell produce or to access markets. The little folk of the city, impoverished, deprived and dominated, seem far from being active social subjects, evoked by Fall (2008) in describing the suburbanites of the Dakar agglomeration. They manage as best they can with the hardships of transport.

The multiplication of the offer leads, in African cities, to fierce competition between operators, drivers, apprentices, touts and even clients (so as to get onboard minibuses or buses). The race for money has led to an increase in vehicle speed and the use of unscheduled stops and itinerary changes. It has led to increased road insecurity (Bonnet et al. 2018). The degradation of the services offered is pushed to its uttermost limit in the case of the process of monopolization of transport income by certain operators. In Senegal, the capsizing of the ship *Le Joola* in 2002, due to lack of maintenance and deficient operation and management, further accentuated the sense of isolation of the Casamance region (Lombard 2003). The Dakar–Bamako railway line, for example, was taken over by a private operator, but this did not result in any improvement in infrastructure or passenger service. The abandonment of the line and the failure to renew the equipment resulted in the derailment of a passenger train in 2009. In both cases, the carrier, which had been granted or sold the operation by the government, was negligent in withdrawing from service to the public in favor of more lucrative interests. In this case, the only objective of the operators appears to be to make a profit from the traffic activity, as can be seen on the Abidjan–Ouagadougou line (Dagnogo et al. 2012).

In contrast to these processes of disengagement, when mobility concerns wealthy social categories or privileged geographical areas, adequate investments in infrastructure are developed. The highway between Dakar and the new Ndiass airport in Senegal (Diop 2020), or the new HKB (Henri Konan Bédié) bridge in Abidjan, accentuates the tunnel effects on the areas crossed, which in turn suffer pollution, noise and health problems (Charlton and Vowles 2008). These projects illustrate not only the ambitions of the government to create a more efficient transport system but also the ambitions of national and local authorities to make the cities they are responsible for into metropolises that count on the international stage, at any price. The transport plan is therefore more a vehicle for inequalities than for territorial integration. Any investment that enters into metropolitan logic tends to reinforce the differences between the centers and the margins (MacKinnon et al. 2008, p. 28).

6.3.2. *Modernization for whom?*

The reforms carried out in African urban transport have been placed under the sign of modernization of services supposedly demanded by the population. However, a few studies on mobility demand and practices exist as reminded by Diaz Olvera et al. (2013), which point out the lack of knowledge of travel behavior on the part of both local authorities and governments. The latter seem more interested in building large infrastructure projects than in thinking about how to improve the services already in place. In Cape Town (Baffi 2016), the implementation of the BRT reveals the tensions and contradictions between metropolitan ambitions and the needs of city dwellers.

Drawing new lines, reserving parts of the roadway for the passage of public transport buses and minibuses, with the corollary of choosing precise locations for stopping the trains, accentuates the differentiation of spaces and their functions much more than was previously the case. Breaking with the existing interaction between roads and the spaces they cross, as evoked by Cissokho (2017), the key words are speed, fluidity and transport efficiency, forcing people to get closer to public transport stops by their own means, which are now spaced out, and for drivers and their assistants (especially in public transport) to respect these stops.

The question underlying these new operating methods is the future of the informal sector, which is considered to be out of step with the image that national or local authorities wish to give their country or their city. The leitmotiv of African administrations is the non-professionalism of private actors, and therefore, the need to rely on those who have the will to modernize themselves. In 2002, a senior official in the Senegalese Ministry of Transport said: "Work with the people who really live from transport." The redesign of urban transport lines and the renovation of vehicle fleets, the regrouping of the most dynamic operators and their integration into BRT schemes are essential means of transforming the transport offer. This makes it possible to attract new actors from outside the transport world, who are considered to be more efficient than the previous ones, as we have previously shown in Dakar and Abidjan (Bredeloup et al. 2008) and as can be seen in the case of Addis Ababa, Ethiopia (Hussen 2016). In the cities, as in intercity transport, there is a risk that small-scale entrepreneurs and the many people involved in related jobs, such as hawkers, mechanics and vehicle washers, who make a living from another way of doing transport, will be left out. As early as the 1990s and 2000s, plans to privatize the national companies responsible for operating the railroads linking the interior of the continent to the coast had greatly concerned employees and people living along the routes, as was the case in Tanzania with the Tazara Railway (Monson 2006). The consequences for the areas crossed were immediate, and the services were affected; a reduction in stopovers, or even their disappearance, as in Ivory Coast (Dagnogo 2014).

6.3.3. *In an era of transitions: changes and uncertainties*

The new challenges depend, in part, on the contexts and trajectories of African countries. They are related to global developments (reduction of fossil fuel consumption and greenhouse gas emissions), for which the responses provided locally will determine the place occupied by the countries of the continent in the world. These challenges represent both opportunities and uncertainties.

For transport systems, the challenge of demographic transition can be seen in two directions. The strong demographic growth experienced by most of the continent's countries is set to continue for several more decades, with a rapid doubling of the population (from 1.2 to 2.5 billion inhabitants by 2050) and its stabilization at 4 billion by 2100. The urbanization of the continent, which is already at or close to 50% according to sources, will increase, not only in the capitals, and also in small and medium sized cities. Transport systems, whether intra-urban or inter-urban, must respond to dispersed demand, which will make the mobility matrix more complex, especially between cities and the countryside (Cottyn et al. 2013; Ninot and Sakho 2021). One of the observable effects is the strong segmentation of transport markets, resulting in the diversification of service offers. On the one hand, this is synonymous with a variety of adaptations; on the other hand, it leads to growing inequalities (through fares, according to the areas serviced).

Another effect of population growth is the saturation of existing transport systems, which are dominated by road transport, with relatively small vehicle capacities and negative externalities (pollution, congestion, accidents). BRT and TER projects, in attempting to meet the challenge of demand, require, as in Cape Town, the reorganization of the entire urban transport system, involving massive investment in road infrastructure and the search for alternatives (rail, river or air). However, this is not the case everywhere. For the past two decades, despite annual support of between 25 and 40 billion dollars for the transport sector (according to the Infrastructure Consortium for Africa), there has been a significant infrastructure deficit on the continent. To be partially filled, these financial levels would have to be maintained for at least several decades. This prospect remains uncertain insofar as the investment capacity of African states and international donors depends on the global economic situation. This is no longer as favorable as it was in the first decade of the 21st century. The energy transition and its economic implications are slowing down the possibilities for transformation in African transport, which will increasingly depend on the adoption of new and costly technical and environmental standards (particularly with regard to energy consumption).

In every country on the continent, the question arises of how to transform transport systems and how to reconcile them with the imperatives of the transition. One of the solutions that is emerging is the introduction of digital technologies in the field of transport and mobility, mainly in cities (see the contribution of K. Tanikawa et al. in the same book). They are programmed to optimize transport services and reduce mobility by the principle of substitution. But, in reality, nothing is obvious. Although these tools are presented a priori as facilitators of access to transport, they do not have the expected effects on the overall level of demand. Other spatial organizations could also influence the cost of mobility, particularly in terms of energy and the environment. These are, for example, territories based on intense relations between cities and surrounding countryside which are densely populated (Losch et al. 2016), the promotion of economic complementarities within small territories, which favor short commercial movements, the regular distribution of goods and services on periodic rural markets (avoiding trips to distant urban centers) and the generalization of motorized two-wheelers and non-motorized modes of transport.

6.4. Conclusion

African countries are increasingly connected to the world by various networks, including transport (air and sea) and telecommunications. However, it is still difficult, if not impossible, to travel by road between certain parts of the national territory and in certain urban areas, particularly in the capital cities. This differentiation between geographical scales illustrates the growing disconnection between the need for spatial diffusion of development, from near to far, and the search for an exclusive relationship with the centre, whoever and wherever it may be, which is driven by metropolization and major infrastructure programs.

On the African continent, national and supranational public policies, as well as the programs of international donors, emphasize the transport corridor and the metropolitan region, to the detriment of non-hierarchical and looser networks located in less dense areas, and of spatial forms that promote inclusive development. These same policies also exacerbate the crystallization of private interests in situations of disguised monopoly, monopolization and income, at the expense of the general interest and the common good.

To consolidate the place of local territories in globalization (Alvergne 2007), to bring about the "global time of the local" (Chaléard and Sanjuan 2017, p. 115), it is necessary to rethink the articulation of scales within transport systems and the spatial forms that they carry. The evolution of transport systems is indeed indicative of local territorial functioning within larger groups. The growing importance of individual and collective initiatives – for example, by groups of residents, drivers or users – is an invitation for governments to review the organization of their cities and of space in general, i.e. investment programs, regulatory systems and redistribution methods, in order to maintain the fragile economic, social and spatial balance of territories.

Far from the inventiveness and resourcefulness of individuals, which do not sum up the transformations of transport systems in Africa, the transformations that are taking place are powerful indicators of the challenges of equitable, durable and alternative forms of development within the territories.

6.5. References

Agnew, J. (1994). The territorial trap: The geographical assumptions of international relations theory. *Review of International Political Economy*, 1(1), 53–80.

Agossou, N. (2004). Les taxis motos zemijan à Porto-Novo et à Cotonou. *Autrepart*, 32, 135–148 [Online]. Available at: https://www.cairn.info/journal-autrepart-2004-4-page-135.htm [Accessed 3 August 2021].

Alvergne, C. (2007). Quelles politiques territoriales pour inscrire l'Afrique dans la mondialisation ? *Les Cahiers d'Outre-Mer*, 238, 203–216 [Online]. Available at: https://journals.openedition.org/com/2374 [Accessed 3 August 2021].

Ascher, F. (2003). Métropolisation. In *Dictionnaire de la géographie et de l'espace des sociétés*, Lévy, J. and Lussault, M. (eds). Belin, Paris.

Baffi, S. (2016). Le chemin de fer et la ville dans les processus de territorialisation en Afrique du Sud : De la séparation à l'intégration territoriale ? PhD Thesis, Université Paris 1 Panthéon-Sorbonne, Paris.

Banque africaine de développement, NEPAD, Union africaine (2012). Programme pour le développement des infrastructures en Afrique. Interconnecter, intégrer et transformer un continent [Online]. Available at: https://www.afdb.org/fileadmin/uploads/afdb/Documents/Project-and-Operations/PIDA%20note%20French%20for%20web%200208.pdf [Accessed 16 June 2021].

Bénazéraf, D. (2014). Produire la ville avec les Chinois en Afrique : L'impact des pratiques chinoises d'urbanisme dans les trajectoires urbaines africaines. PhD Thesis, Université Paris 1 Panthéon-Sorbonne, Paris.

Bonnet, E., Lechat, L., Ridde, V. (2018). What interventions are required to reduce road traffic injuries in Africa? A scoping review of the literature. *PLOS One*, 13(11) [Online]. Available at: https://doi.org/10.1371/journal.pone.0208195 [Accessed 16 June 2021].

Bredeloup, S. and Kouraogo, O. (2007). Quand la crise ivoirienne stimule les trajectoires professionnelles des transporters Burkinabe émigrés. *Revue européenne des migrations internationales*, 23(3), 133–149 [Online]. Available at: https://journals.openedition.org/remi/4218#xd_co_f=MjEwNDQyYTItOWYwYi00MTE4LWE5MGQtNDc4NzkyOG I3MGFi~ [Accessed 3 August 2021].

Bredeloup, S., Bertoncello, B., Lombard, J. (eds) (2008). *Abidjan, Dakar : Des villes à vendre ? La privatisation "made in Africa" des services urbains*. L'Harmattan, Paris.

Chaléard, J.-L. and Sanjuan, T. (2017). *Géographie du développement. Territoires et mondialisation dans les Suds*. Armand Colin, Paris.

Charlton, C. and Vowles, T. (2008). Inter-urban and regional transport. In *Transport Geographies. Mobilities, Flows and Spaces*, Knowles, R., Shaw, J., Docherty, I. (eds). Blackwell Publishing, Oxford.

Chauvin, E., Mareï, N., Lombard, J. (2017). Les circulations mondialisées en Afrique : Promotion, adaptation et contournement. *Géocarrefour*, 91(3) [Online]. Available at: http://journals.openedition.org/geocarrefour/10313 [Accessed 16 June 2021].

Choplin, A. (2019). Cementing Africa. Cement flows and city-making along the West African corridor (Accra, Lomé, Cotonou, Lagos). *Urban Studies*, 57(9), 1977–1993 [Online]. Available at: https://journals.sagepub.com/doi/full/10.1177/004209801985194 [Accessed 3 August 2021].

Cissokho, S. (2017). Chronique bibliographique. L'asphalte, l'automobile et le chauffeur : La route en Afrique saisie par les sciences sociales. *Politique africaine*, 3(147), 159–170 [Online]. Available at: https://www.cairn.info/revue-politique-africaine-2017-3-page-159.htm [Accessed 3 August 2021].

Cottyn, I., Schapendonk, J., Van Lindert, O. (2013). Mobility in sub-saharan Africa: Patterns, processes, and policies [Online]. Available at: https://rurbanafrica.ku.dk/publications/briefings/2013/RurbanAfrica-Briefing-Paper2.pdf [Accessed 16 June 2021].

Daffé, G. (2002). La difficile réinsertion du Sénégal dans le commerce mondial. In *La société sénégalaise entre le local et le global*, Diop, M.C. (ed.). Karthala, Paris.

Dagnogo, F. (2014). Rail-route et dynamiques spatiales en Côte d'Ivoire. PhD Thesis, Université de Paris 1 Panthéon-Sorbonne, Paris.

Dagnogo, F., Ninot, O., Chaléard, J.-L. (2012). Le chemin de fer Abidjan-Niger : La vocation d'une infrastructure en question. *Echogéo*, 20 [Online]. Available at: https://journals.openedition.org/echogeo/13131 [Accessed 16 June 2021].

Debrie, J. (2010). From colonization to national territories in continental West Africa: The historical geography of a transport infrastructures network. *Journal of Transport Geography*, 18(2), 292–300.

Diaz Olvera, L., Plat, D., Pochet, P. (2007). Mobilité quotidienne en temps de crise. *Belgeo*, 2 [Online]. Available at: https://journals.openedition.org/belgeo/11255 [Accessed 16 June 2021].

Diaz Olvera, L., Plat, D., Pochet, P. (2013). The puzzle of mobility and access to the city in Sub-Saharan Africa. *Journal of Transport Geography*, 32, 56–64.

Diop, K. (2020). Nouvelle autoroute à péage Dakar-Diamniadio et mobilités périphériques : Opportunités et disparités. PhD Thesis, Université Gaston Berger, Saint-Louis du Sénégal.

Dobruszkes, F., Grippa, T., Tagne Foka, I.D., Tchouamounjoya, E. (2020). Inherited urban airports vs. new remote facilities: The issue of airport location in Africa. "Aviation in Africa". Report, G.A.R.S.

Doumbia, T. (2010). Corruption, culture et pauvreté dans le secteur du transport en Côte d'Ivoire [Online]. Available at: https://journals.openedition.org/sociologies/3133 [Accessed 25 November 2020].

EHESS (2020). Évaluer l'influence normative chinoise dans les projets d'infrastructure en Afrique [Online]. Available at: https://webinaire3.ehess.fr/b/pai-u30-haj [Accessed 16 June 2021].

Essone-Nkoghe, J.-P. (2012). Transports actifs et stratégies d'accès à l'emploi des populations des quartiers périphériques dans les villes africaines : Le cas de Ouagadougou. PhD Thesis, Université du Québec, Montreal.

Fall, A.S. (2008). *Bricoler pour survivre. Perceptions de la pauvreté dans l'agglomération urbaine de Dakar*. Karthala, Paris.

Godard, X. (ed.) (2002). *Les transports et la ville en Afrique au sud du Sahara : Le temps de la débrouille et du désordre inventif*. Karthala/INRETS, Paris.

Godard, X. and Teurnier, P. (1992). *Les transports urbains en Afrique à l'heure de l'ajustement structurel*. Karthala, Paris.

Guézéré, A. (2021). *Les taxis-motos dans les villes d'Afrique subsaharienne : L'informel en question à Lomé*. L'Harmattan, Paris.

Hervé, F., Chanut, A., Daunas, J., Guillaume, J. (2007). Bilbao ou le renouvellement urbain par les transports. Cours d'Organisation et management des transports urbains, IUP/ENPC, Paris.

Hibou, B. (1999). La décharge, nouvel interventionnisme. *Politique africaine*, 73, 6–13. [Online]. Available at: https://www.cairn.info/journal-politique-africaine-1999-1-page-6.htm [Accessed 3 August 2021].

Holzbauer, C. (2014). La Banque mondiale mise sur les corridors. *African Business*, 42–45.

Hussen, B.W. (2016). Sustaining sustainable mobility: The integration of multimodal public transportation in Addis Ababa. PhD Thesis, Université de Lyon II, Lyon.

Infrastructure Consortium for Africa (2016). Urban transport in sub-Saharan Africa. *Diagnostic Study & Project Development and Investment Pipeline* [Online]. Available at: https://www.icafrica.org/fileadmin/documents/Publications/ICA_Urban_Transport_Study_-_Summary_Oct16.pdf.

Jacquot, S., Sierra, A., Tadié, J. (2016). Informalité politique, pouvoirs et envers des espaces urbains. *L'Espace Politique*, 29(2) [Online]. Available at: http://journals.openedition.org/espacepolitique/3805 [Accessed 16 June 2021].

Jaglin, S., Didier, S., Dubresson, A. (2018). Métropolisations en Afrique subsaharienne : Au menu ou à la carte ? *Métropoles* [Online]. Available at: https://journals.openedition.org/metropoles/6065 [Accessed 16 June 2021].

Jessop, B., Brenner, N., Jones, M. (2008). Theorizing sociospatial relations. *Environment and Planning D: Society and Space*, 26, 389–401.

Kassi-Djodjo, I. (2010). Rôle des transports populaires dans le processus d'urbanisation à Abidjan. *Les Cahiers d'Outre-Mer*, 251, 391–402.

Latouche, S. (1998). *L'autre Afrique, entre don et marché*. Albin Michel, Paris.

Lombard, J. (2003). Des dérives du système des transports sénégalais à la catastrophe du *Joola*. *Afrique contemporaine*, 207(3), 165–184.

Lombard, J. (2015). *Le monde des transports sénégalais : Ancrage local et développement international*. Éditions IRD, Marseille.

Lombard, J., Ninot, O., Steck, B. (2014). Corridors de transport en Afrique et intégration territoriale en question. In *La régionalisation du monde, construction territoriale et articulation global/local*, Gana, A. and Richard, Y. (eds). IRMC-KARTHALA, Paris.

Losch, B., Pesche, D., Imbernon, J. (2016). *Une nouvelle ruralité émergente. Regards croisés sur les transformations rurales africaines*. CIRAD/NEPAD, Montpellier.

MacKinnon, D., Pirie, G., Gather, M. (2008). Transport and economic development. In *Transport Geographies*, Knowles, R., Shaw, J., Docherty, I. (eds). Blackwell Publishing, Oxford.

Mareï, N. (2016). Terminalisation, spécialisation et enjeux logistiques des ports africains. Note de Synthèse de l'ISEMAR, 179 [Online]. Available at: https://www.isemar.fr/wp-content/uploads/2016/04/note-de-synth%C3%A8se-isemar-179.pdf [Accessed 16 June 2021].

Mareï, N. and Ninot, O. (2018). Entre Afrique du Nord et de l'Ouest, les relations transsahariennes à un moment charnière. *BAGF*, 95(2) [Online]. Available at: https://journals.openedition.org/bagf/3189 [Accessed 17 June 2021].

Mareï, N. and Savy, M. (2021). Global South countries: The dark side of city logistics. Dualisation vs Bipolarisation. *Transport Policy*, 100, 150–160.

Mareï, N. and Wippel, S. (2020). Une perspective urbaine de la régionalisation du monde : Tanger, métropole (eur)africaine. *Belgeo*, 4, [Online]. Available at: https://journals.openedition.org/belgeo/43518 [Accessed 16 June 2021].

Meite, Y. (2014). Gouvernance du transport urbain et mobilité durable dans le district d'Abidjan (Côte d'Ivoire). PhD Thesis, Université de Strasbourg, Strasbourg.

Monson, J. (2006). Defending the people's railway in the Era of Liberalization: Tazara in Southern Tanzania. *Africa*, 76(1), 113–130.

Moriconi-Ebrard, F., Harre, D., Heinrigs, P. (2016). *L'urbanisation des pays de l'Afrique de l'Ouest 1950–2010: Africapolis I*. Éditions OCDE, Paris.

Musil, C., Ninot, O., Baffi, S., Drevelle, M. (2014). Évolutions des systèmes de transport urbains en périphérie du Cap et de Hanoi : Entre pragmatisme et ambitions métropolitaines. In *Métropoles* des *Suds. Le défi des périphéries ?* Chaléard, J.-L. (ed.). Karthala, Paris.

Néya, S. (2020). Burkina-Faso-Côte d'Ivoire, c'est chambre-salon. Retour au pays d'origine et reconfiguration d'un espace migratoire transnational. PhD Thesis, Université de Paris 1 Panthéon-Sorbonne, Paris.

Ninot, O. and Sakho, P. (2021). Évolution des relations villes-campagnes en Afrique de l'Ouest : Une lecture à partir des circulations des personnes et des biens. In *Crises des modèles ? Agricultures, recompositions territoriales et nouvelles relations villes-campagnes*, Berger, M., Chaléard, J.-L., Gana, A. (eds). Grafigéo-PRODIG, Paris.

Nugent, P. (2018). Africa's re-enchantment with big infrastructure: White elephants dancing in virtuous circles? In *Extractive Industries and Changing State Dynamics in Africa*, Schubert, J., Engel, U., Macamo, E. (eds). Routledge, London.

Ohnsorge, F. and Yu, S. (2021). The long shadow of informality, challenges and policies [Online]. Available at: https://www.worldbank.org/en/research/publication/informal-economy [Accessed 16 June 2021].

Retaillé, D. (2005). L'espace mobile. In *Le territoire est mort. Vive les territoires ! Une (re)fabrication au nom du développement*, Antheaume, B. and Giraut F. (eds). Éditions IRD, Marseille.

Sheller, M. and Urry, J. (2006). The new mobilities paradigm. *Environment and Planning A*, 38, 207–226.

Sirpé, G. (2007). Les services de transports ruraux au Burkina Faso : Le cas de la région de la Boucle du Mouhoun. Report Programme de politiques de transport en Afrique subsaharienne (SSATP), Washington.

SSATP (2021). Myths and Realities of "Informal" public transport in developing countries: Approaches for improving the sector [Online]. Available at: https://www.mobilise yourcity.net/sites/default/files/2021-05/SSATP_Informal_v_final_double.pdf [Accessed 16 June 2021].

Stasik, M. and Cissokho, S. (2018). Introduction to special issue: Bus stations in Africa [Online]. *Africa Today*, 65(2), 7–14 [Accessed 16 June 2021].

Steck, B. (2015). Introduction à l'Afrique des ports et des corridors : Comment formuler l'interaction entre logistique et développement. *Cahiers de géographie du Québec*, 59(168), 447–467.

Steck, B. (2021). Corruption in the corridors: Mapping abnormal practices in West Africa. *Journal of Transport Geography*, 92 [Online]. Available at: https://www.sciencedirect.com/science/article/pii/S0966692321000016 [Accessed 16 June 2021].

Teravaninthorn, S. and Raballand, G. (2009). Transport prices and costs in Africa: A review of the international corridors [Online]. Available at: https://openknowledge.worldbank.org/bitstream/handle/10986/6610/461810PUB0Box3101OFFICIAL0USE0ONLY1.pdf?sequence=1&isAllowed=y [Accessed 16 June 2021].

Zouhoula Bi, M.R. (2018). The Woro-Woro Gares Routières of Abidjan: Artisanal transport and local governance in Côte d'Ivoire's Largest City. *Africa Today*, 65(2), 23–34.

Digital Revolution in Urban Transportation of the Southern Cities Questioned

7.1. Introduction

In the large cities of the South, the emergence of ICT (information and communication technologies) and digital technology is taking place at a time when urban transport is being transformed by the effects of metropolization, with urban governments embarking on ambitious land-use planning and transport infrastructure modernization programs. This moment articulates the development of mass transport services such as Bus Rapid Transit (BRT) and individualized mobility platforms (taxi, on-demand transportation, micro-mobility), the role played by the dissemination of digital devices is being questioned, both by the urban transport regulatory authorities and by operators and users. Indeed, the deployment of new technologies and the widespread adoption of the smartphone are combined with reforms and systems integration projects aimed to promote "smart mobility" (Docherty et al. 2018). Cities in the South are thus questioning the developments and the place of digital technology in the implementation of flexible and optimized mobility.

In addition to the expected environmental impact of reduced road traffic, digital tools hold the promise of a form of accelerated development that allows for leapfrogging in infrastructure and technology development. These same tools, promoted by powerful international actors, convey an image of modernity (Capetown, Indore) that is both valuational and solutionist and that is likely to revolutionize traveler information, urban mobility practices and transport governance. However, under the impact of globalization, the convergence towards international models is being questioned.

Chapter written by Kei TANIKAWA OBREGÓN, Lisa COULAUD and Olivier NINOT.

This chapter analyzes the process of deploying digital tools in the transportation systems of Mexico City, Accra and Dakar[1].

The three cities, although contrasting in size, population and governance, share common transport characteristics, including the prevalence of the informal sector in the provision of individual and collective transport services.

The applied reading grid mobilizes the contributions of two main fields. The first is that of socio-technical systems (Akrich 1991; Geels 2004; Bacqué and Fol 2007; Moradi and Vagnoni 2018), which analyzes, through the appropriation of new technologies, the transformations brought about by the implementation of new technical systems in the various decision-making spheres. The aim is to understand the place of digital tools in access to services and the redefinition of urban governance, and also to question the forms of integration of innovations in traditionally atomized transport systems. The second field is that of the circulation of models (Robinson 2006; McCann and Ward 2013; McFarlane 2010; Peyroux and Sanjuan 2016), which focuses on the way in which they are constructed, imported, adapted and rethought in cities of the South. The objective here is to question the replicability of the "smart mobility" model in light of the three case studies. It is through the relationship between digital and paratransit that we address the issue of the integration of mobility systems and the discourse of smart mobility.

The first part of the chapter analyzes the rapid diffusion of digital technology and the ongoing transformations of the urban transport sector in the South. We then consider the role of digital technology in these transformations. Is it simply a companion or does it radically change the way transport systems evolve? Observation of the ways in which digital technology is deployed in the transportation systems of three cities in the South reveals contrasting local realities and also common features. Our work shows that the "digital revolution" is taking place in the form of an ad hoc and partly disorganized appearance of digital technology in the field of transport, through applications and the use of data that do not radically change the production of transport and its uses. Although digital technology seems to be favorable to the major logics guiding the new urban transport models (reduction of socio-spatial inequalities and of the environmental footprint), it is not, however, the main driving force behind their implementation. Finally, we will discuss the coexistence of digitalization with paratransit. Are we witnessing a reinforcement of existing configurations, i.e. an atomization of the

1 This collective work stems from the work of two ongoing geography theses (Tanikawa Obregón K. and Coulaud L.), focusing on the analysis of urban transport systems through the lens of digital technology. Data collection was conducted through semi-structured interviews, fieldwork, observations and questionnaires conducted since 2018. This data was recut with older empirical research (Ninot O.).

transport offer within the territories or is it a transition process that would integrate paratransit with the digitized offer? We defend the idea that, in the field of transport, a digital transition will not take place without the paratransit/informal sector.

7.2. Transformations in transport and the emergence of digital technology, a crucial "moment"[2] in the metropolization process in the South

Widespread digitization is presented as a process that sees the deployment of infrastructures, the multiplication of data and the evolution of ways of thinking about the city (Peyroux and Ninot 2019), for a digital accompaniment of all activities of daily life (Beckouche 2019). The rapid diffusion of tools transforms the ways of living, managing, governing, distributing and consuming services (Cheneau-Loquay 2008, 2010).

7.2.1. The adoption of digital technology by services and urban territories

In 2020, more than half of the world's inhabitants had access to the Internet (ITU 2020). In the South, digital technology is imposing itself at an unprecedented rate (Tcheng et al. 2008; Sylla 2009; Cariole 2018) and is accompanied by disruptions in the way knowledge is produced, shared and used. For example, the various forms of mobile payment (Mpesa in East Africa, Wari or Orange Money in West Africa) have revolutionized market exchanges and have become major components of social relations (Canzler and Knie 2016; Douay 2018). The medium for this digital revolution is the smartphone (Middleton et al. 2014; Napoli and Onar 2014). The decline in its price and that of mobile packages makes it easier to appropriate by the populations of cities in the South (Boutueil and Lesteven 2018).

Applications on smartphones or tablets are multiplying in essential service sectors. They are carried by a multitude of actors of different levels with various profiles and interests (Ninot and Peyroux 2018). On the one hand, civil society contributes to the process in different ways (e.g. the Open Street Maps community, transport user groups with WhatsApp[3]). On the other hand, large companies in the telecommunications sector, such as Orange in Africa, service companies (Wari) or start-ups, play a role in the development of digital innovations. Finally, public authorities, at national and local

---

2 A period of time during which several convergent transformations occur but whose duration and outcome cannot be defined, which may be a status quo (resilience) or an important bifurcation.

3 Instant messaging applications that work with an Internet connection.

levels, have an important role to play in supporting this process. Whether it is for the management of networks or the management of interfaces between services and users, they contribute to the adoption of new practices.

For example, in Mexico City, these applications are multiplying to facilitate access to administrative procedures (payment of water and energy bills), as well as the adoption of the QR code[4], which is becoming more widespread. The same logic applies in Dakar, where the massive use of Orange Money facilitates money transfers and the dematerialization of basic services.

At the urban level the processes of metropolization and the deployment of digital technology converge in the *smart city model*. Metropolization is understood here as both a process and a discourse, a desired horizon of urban policies[5]. In this sense, it is an envied status that seeks to reproduce a certain performance of urban management in a globalized market (Ghorra-Gobin 2020). Relying on a few slogans put forward timidly or awkwardly by both operators and public policies, the *smart city* is also presented as an enviable horizon for urban futures, or at least as a vaguely marked path for conducting urban reforms based on digital technology.

However, the transferability of this model to cities in the South is questionable (Ninot and Peyroux 2019). The notion of *smart* is vague and very culturally rooted, with each actor projecting their utopias onto it (Eveno 2018). Nevertheless, this model is asserting itself in the projects of metropolises in the South and is already partly reorienting the perspectives of governance and management of urban services towards a form of data-based urbanism (Kitchin 2014). In Mexico City, since the creation of the Centre for Command, Control, Computing, Communications and Citizen Contact (C5) in 2009, the command post has expanded its steering functions to urban services and to the production of data facilitating decision support and service management.

7.2.2. Urban transport in the midst of change

Paratransit remains the dominant offer in the cities of the South (Chapter 6), but the appropriation of mass transport models at the same time upsets the balance. The process of metropolization in Accra, Dakar and Mexico is characterized by rapid urban sprawl and a fragmented transport system. From the 1970s, but particularly since the 1990s, their transport systems have evolved alongside formal transport.

---

4 The QR (Quick Response) code, in the form of a barcode, allows data to be stored and accessed instantly.

5 Géoconfluences   about   metropolisation: http://geoconfluences.ens-lyon.fr/glossaire/metropolization.

This is characterized by the accelerated development of informal cabs and minibuses, as well as by an overabundance of vehicles and a lack of planning. However, paratransit transport is essential in contexts where public provision is largely inadequate (Figure 7.1). It serves the heart of neighborhoods and outlying areas and acts as an initiator of future lines that are recognized and perpetuated by the authorities. Since 2000–2010, the States have shown a desire to take over the transport sector once again. This is reflected in the implementation of major structural projects (BRT, regional express train, tramway) and the "migration" of certain paratransit modes. The development of mass transit is part of the global transition movement in cities. The latter responds both to environmental issues and to the need for governments to acquire control instruments. On the one hand, it is a lever for international standardization and a tool for financing infrastructure that is supported by banks for development. On the other hand, it enables cities to acquire digital tools (applications, paperless tickets, real-time passenger information). The process of metropolization thus seems to be exacerbated by the emergence of digital technology, which provides an innovative framework for urban transport projects.

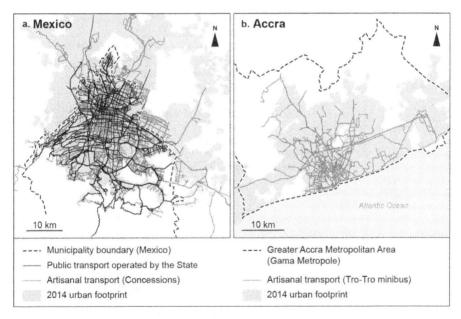

Figure 7.1. *Map of public and paratransit transport networks (Sources: NYU Urban Expansion Program, Lincoln Institute, UN Habitat, INEGI and Mexico City, OSM; authors: L. Coulaud and K. Tanikawa 2020). For a color version of this figure, see www.iste.co.uk/peyroux/development.zip*

Metropolitan area of the Valley of Mexico		Digital penetration (national scale)	
Number of inhabitants	21.8 million	Internet access (individual) 2018	65.8 %
Motorization rate	343 veh./1,000 inhab.	Internet access (household) 2018	52.9%
Governance	By State (State of Mexico: Secretaría de movilidad EDOMEX and City of Mexico: Secretaría de Movilidad SEMOVI Órgano Regulador del Transporte ORT)	Cell phone subscription (/100 hab) 2018	70.0%
		Population covered by 4G	71%
Modal split (source: INEGI 2017, 2020)	34 million daily trips: > 65% on 22.3% private vehicle 50.9% public transportation of which: 60% paratransit 40% public (metro, high service level buses, bus)	Government Services Online	81.8%
		Cost of SMS in USD (sources: Network readiness index 2020 and Measuring the Information Society Report ITU 2018)	$0.04
Agglomeration of Dakar		Digital penetration (national scale)	
Number of inhabitants	3.5 million	Internet access (individual) 2018	46%
Motorization rate	25 veh./1,000 inhab.	Internet access (household) 2018	24.3%
Governance	CETUD: executive council for urban transport of Dakar: metropolitan scale	Cell phone subscription (/100 hab) 2018	41.5%
		Population covered by 4G	62%
Modal split (sources: CETUD 2016, Olvera et al. 2005)	7 million daily trips: – 70% of daily trips: walking – 30% of daily trips: motorized > 88% by public transport – Public offering (DDD): 6%. – Urban cab: 10.5 – Paratransit supply: 37 – Private supply AFTU (renewed paratransit: 35%)	Government Services Online	47%
		Cost of SMS in USD (sources: Network readiness index 2020 and Measuring the Information Society Report ITU 2018)	$0.01

Table 7.1. *Urban transport characteristics data and penetration of digital devices in Mexico City and Dakar (authors: L. Coulaud and K. Tanikawa)*

7.2.3. *Digital technology and the transformation of urban transport: a new paradigm*

The adoption of the discourse based on the use of technology in transportation policies led, in the years 2000–2010, to the emergence of the concept of *smart mobility*. The underlying idea is that of optimizing urban transport through the capabilities of digital tools and actors (Pourbaix 2011; Courmont and Le Galès 2019).

This discourse is emerging in a particular context, that of environmental transition, transport being the second most important sector of activity in terms of GHG emissions (greenhouse gases). The fight against climate change has become a guideline for public action at all levels (Wachter 2003). The model thus articulates a dual ambition (Lyons 2018): that of optimization (economic and operational) and that of sustainability (Miroux and Lefèvre 2012). At the heart of the model are two essential processes. The first is the production of data useful for real-time management and planning (Surdonja et al. 2020). The second is the integration of different transport modes and operators into a unified metropolitan system. This is the case in Mexico City, where the "Integrated Mobility: One City, One System" program launched in 2019 by the Urban Transportation Authority UTA, the Secretaría de Movilidad (SEMOVI), announced a shift in the governance of urban transport in the direction of *smart mobility*.

This transport model is based on the principle of flexibility (intermodality, accesssibility, optimization, management). It is an integrated vision in which the modes of transport do not compete with each other but complement each other. In this sense, the technical skills of the public authorities and the articulation of the offer represent a fundamental lever (Cervero and Golub 2007; Godard 2008). Digital success in urban mobility is therefore based on the production and processing of abundant data. This data comes from devices capable of collecting, quantifying, storing, qualifying or establishing a mobility overview. The strategic objective of having a finer knowledge of travel is therefore a prerequisite for defining strategies and making tradeoffs (Peck and Theodore 2010; Ponelis and Holmner 2015; Kitchin et al. 2017).

Under the guise of a necessary regulation of the urban mobility sector, these changes herald a possible standardization of transport systems (Mirabel and Reymond 2019). Many international actors are positioning themselves in the mobility sector and offering diagnostic and decision support tools. In Latin America, we can cite the Center for digital urban transport, supported by the IDB (Inter-American Development Bank), Mastercard and the NGO WRI (World Resources Institute). In Africa, there is the Digital Transport 4 Africa program, supported by the World Bank and the AFD (Agence française de développement).

Some analyses suggest that this dynamic would benefit large international groups identified under the concept of Multinational Operators for Local Transport Services or MOLTS (Shibayama and Ieda 2011), with the aim of consolidating and opening up mobility markets (for companies such as Arriva, Transdev or Keolis).

This particular alignment of urban paradigms experienced by many metropolises in the South may be a tipping point in the evolutionary trajectory of their transport systems. The deployment of digital technology is bringing with it a wide range of local and international players, new ways of conceiving mobility and transport services and new instruments for steering and planning, the lifespan, evolution and transformation of which are still unknown.

7.3. The role of digital technology in the transformations currently underway

The deployment of digital technology in the metropolises of the South, the wave of reforms concerning urban mobility and the positive discourse (fueled by the figure of the smart city) on the effects of a potential digital revolution suggest an unprecedented turn (Lyons 2014). Digital technology would accelerate the transformations underway, and even determine their main directions. The observation of the modalities and effects of digital technology in the transport systems of the three metropolises studied invites us to examine the limits encountered in management and uses.

7.3.1. *Looking for greater efficiency, more complex governance*

The field of sectoral governance is perhaps the most invested by digital technology. At the level of metropolitan transport regulatory authorities and operators alike, the production of data for operations, planning and decision-making is at the heart of the process. Their use contributes to the construction of a discourse on the modernization of the sector, which motivates sectoral reform projects and justifies investments. This is particularly the case in projects to unify the transport system, as in Mexico City. The process under way aims to integrate, regulate and monitor urban transport through the creation of a data platform managed by the public authorities. With this data collection system, the public authorities are attempting to consolidate a new management mode based on the logic of "know, order, manage".

In the three cities studied, digital technology is deployed through a set of tools that appear to offer solutions and are identified by urban transport regulatory authorities as regulatory levers. This process is accompanied by the circulation of international actors, in particular experts promoting supposed "good practices". In Dakar, the partnership between AFTU (the professional association of transport operators), CETUD (the authority in charge of planning and regulation) and the start-up FireFly has led to the installation of Wi-Fi access in buses, as well as screens broadcasting advertising messages (and thus generating revenue). At the same time, the creation of a digital platform by transport actors AFTU and CETUD makes it possible to monitor buses and to digitize crew contracts. Here, the collection of information and the economic profitability of the system are combined. In Mexico City, the recent creation of data authorities, the Digital Agency for Public Innovation (ADIP) in 2019 and the Transport Regulatory Agency (ORT) in 2016, provides for a data management platform (geolocalization, ticketing validation, itinerary) of the different mobility services (informal, private and public).

With the multiplication of data and the devices to process them, the means of action of the public authorities are being expanded through integrated and unified management projects. New standards are being imposed, new skills are being mobilized, all of which is changing the power relationship within the sector. But this situation is not unanimous, especially in contexts where paratransit transport constitutes a strong political and economic power (Connolly 2014; Lombard and Steck 2015). Through the appropriation of data and the imposition of new tools used to organize and regulate the sector, the ability of actors to keep the power of negotiation is at stake. There are two opposing visions, one rooted in know-how and the other based on data presented as neutral and objective.

7.3.2. New tools for access to transport services

Digital technology is partly changing the way transport services are accessed, in particular by allowing the emergence of new forms of personalized services (Atchoua et al. 2020). In the cities that we are studying, the appropriation of digital technology in urban mobility is occurring at different rates and in multiple forms. It is accompanied by the strengthening and redefinition of socio-spatial inequalities.

In all three cities, the smartphone has become familiar to the majority of city dwellers (Table 7.1). In the context of daily mobility, it facilitates the production of and access to passenger information thanks to widespread real-time distribution. Smartphones provide access to online reservations, as in Dakar, with Senegal's Dem Dikk[6], or in Mexico City, for private minibus trips to the Central Business District with the URBVAN service. The extensive use of social networks, such as Facebook and Twitter, has led to the creation of web pages dedicated to sharing

---

6 Public company offering intercity travel between the main cities of the country.

transport-related experiences and information. This is the case in Accra with the Tro-Tro Diaries Facebook group. On these platforms, users have access to real-time information and can discuss traffic conditions.

At the same time, ride-hailing applications have been multiplying over the last 10 years. Numerous international companies are setting up in major cities. This is the case in Accra, where Uber has been present since 2017 as well as in Mexico City since 2013. Thanks to the smartphone, these applications offer on-demand transportation alternatives in the form of door-to-door service. These offerings are almost exclusively located in urban centers. The cost is relatively similar to that of local cabs, but is up to 10 times higher than a ride in a paratransit minibus (Tro-Tro, Car Rapide, Peseros). These applications are therefore not accessible to a large part of the population. The use of digital technology seems to fuel the process of individualization of motorized mobility, perpetuating the inequalities of access and the negative externalities (pollution, congestion) against which metropolises intend to fight.

Figure 7.2. *Informal "clandos" cabs in Keur Massar on the outskirts of Dakar (author: L. Coulaud 2018). For a color version of this figure, see www.iste.co.uk/peyroux/development.zip*

The added value of digital technology is not obvious in a context where cost remains the main determinant of modal choice. The phone is primarily a medium for communication and entertainment. Despite the rapid growth in the number of smartphones, knowledge of transport services is largely shared by word of mouth, particularly in those contexts where there is no official map of the networks. In Dakar, informal cabs, known as "clandos" (Figure 7.2), provide a local service in the heart of the peripheral districts. They offer an abundant, cheap and accessible service. Although they are not yet very concerned by the arrival of these new tools, they are historically and socially anchored in the habits of their users. In contrast, in Mexico City, on-demand transportation services have grown more widely with digital technology. Four out of ten people use an application to get around when it comes to a taxi-type trip, and 41% of cab users use Uber (Asociación de Internet MX 2018).

7.3.3. *A limited potential*

Without any major upheaval in the production of services or uses, the three case studies present contrasting situations in terms of the development and appropriation of digital devices, the deployment of which is still limited by numerous obstacles, including infrastructure, individual equipment and the emergence or consolidation of a digital economy. The disruptive aspect of digital technology must therefore be qualified, as its appropriation does not lead to a radical transformation of the transport operating model.

In the field of on-demand transport, local start-ups are experiencing real difficulties in developing: in Dakar, although no international ride hailing company is present, mobility entrepreneurs are struggling to find a sufficient mass of customers. The political strength of cabs, the financial limitations of city dwellers, the legal vacuum in Senegalese ride hailing legislation, the lack of access to data and socio-cultural practices related to mobility are all obstacles for nascent start-ups. The start-ups that manage to establish themselves mobilize telephone platforms to link clients and drivers, as the use of digital applications is still not widespread. This is not the case in Accra, where Uber and Txfy seem to be taking several Ghanaian apps with them. Mexico City, on the contrary, is experiencing spectacular success with cab apps, which are very much in use. Companies such as Uber, Txfy and Didi are competing with the traditional offer, which suffers from problems of insecurity. Here, the international companies trigger forms of mimicry among the other players and thus succeed in imposing their own business methods.

On the governance side, while digital technology is undoubtedly a part of the overall transport transformation process, it does not seem to be the main driver. The transport systems in Dakar, Accra and Mexico City have undergone several cycles of reforms, with significant changes in the relationship between operators and governments. The new cycle of transport transformation in these cities is, in fact, only partially dependent on digital technology to start and evolve, and is more a matter of major infrastructure and governance reforms in the sector. In Mexico City, the digital data production systems, deployed in a rather interventionist manner, are in fact at the service of a larger project that aims to reaffirm the government's control over transportation and to promote the formalization of the paratransit sector through its inclusion in a metropolitan transportation system. The production and use of data obviously play an important role, but in Mexico City, and even more so in Accra and Dakar, digital technology is above all an instrument for dressing up and enhancing the value of sectoral policies (Figure 7.3), and is used to renew the image of transport by offering more information to travelers as well as dematerialized payment methods.

This image of modernity brought by digital technology does not only serve the mass transportation projects carried by the public authorities. For example, in our three case studies, the middle class has largely embraced on-demand transportation services accessible by smartphone. They are looking for fast, safe and comfortable transportation, which has led to a strengthening of individual mobility practices. This is contributing to an increase in the number of private vehicles (even though car ownership remains low in Africa, see Table 7.1). It also strengthens the cab sector, which is divided between international companies and the so-called "traditional" paratransit sector.

Figure 7.3. *Sticker that emphasizes modernity "unit under video surveillance" on a 1990s bus in Mexico City (author: K. Tanikawa 2020). For a color version of this figure, see www.iste.co.uk/peyroux/development.zip*

It is perhaps in this field (that of paratransit) that digital technology can, in the long run, have the most tangible effects. Not only because it introduces efficient tools that are attractive (see the case of Mexico City for the security issue or the cashless payment issue), but also because the paratransit sector is a major challenge for the further development of digital transport.

7.4. Digital technology: a new front for negotiation in paratransit transport

If a transition must take place within the urban transport systems of the metropoles of the South, it will not happen without the paratransit sector. The issues related to the way in which transport actors appropriate digital technology are important. However, in this field, it seems unlikely that digital technology will take hold in the cities studied in the same way as elsewhere (particularly in the North). The international models are not as successful, and we can assume that specific forms of hybridization will emerge.

7.4.1. *Digital technology as a challenge for the transformation of the paratransit sector*

For public authorities at the local and national levels, the deployment of digital technology is a significant issue both for reasons of image and to pursue reform ambitions. The informal sector has also long been the object of targeted policies, either to encourage economic actors to move towards greater formality (the "professionalization" of the sector has been a leitmotif of sectoral policies, see Chapter 6 in this book), or to attempt to regulate its activities as it has done in the formal sector. The paratransit sector now appears as a resource for the regulatory authorities. The latter are seeking to ensure complementarity with mass-market models. In this context, the objectives of the public authorities with respect to digital and informal sectors are similar. The move to digital is an opportunity to include the informal sector, or to coax it into an integrated transport system, and to achieve goals that have been pursued for decades. Digital technology can be a means of ensuring continuity and efficient intermodality between various offers. Without radically disrupting the supply of transport services, digital technology is therefore a means of unifying systems.

In Mexico City, for example, the integrated mobility program is being implemented progressively through a fare system based on a single pass. The system involves public authority-owned transport (40 percent) and plans to integrate the remaining 60 percent of operators through a system that pays the (paratransit) operator according to the passengers carried (Table 7.1). The installation of GPS in every bus with a public concession allows data to be collected for the benefit of the regulatory authorities. Public powers' digital policy progressively and rather compulsorily includes the informal sector in the overall system.

More generally, in Dakar, Accra and Mexico City, international actors and governments are trying to negotiate with the paratransit sector to find compromises regarding its place in the metropolitan transport system. In Dakar, for example, the minibus fleet is being renewed and EIGs (economic interest groups) are being formed through negotiations between the paratransit sector and the public authorities. The aim is for the authorities to regain control of urban mobility through a public-private partnership process by retaining the crews already present and offering guarantees (insurance, low-interest loans, etc.). In Mexico City, the creation of seven BRT lines since 2005 has made it possible to reorganize the city's main corridors, to initiate negotiations with the paratransit sector, and above all to create an attractive public–private partnership model.

The smart mobility model, promoted from the North, emphasizes the flexible, universal and sustainable aspect of urban transport. In fact, the operational model of the informal paratransit system in the large cities of the South is already flexible and adaptable (Figure 7.1a and b). The informal sector is made up of a myriad of small-scale artisans and follows a liberal logic in which competition serves as regulation. The model itself leads to a form of optimization of the number of motorized vehicles, which rarely run empty, with drivers who adapt their routes, fares and stops as needed to optimize vehicle operation. According to this logic, transport systems, as they are generally presented in the South would already have been optimized. The informal sector does not appear to be an archaic sector with a low quality of service, but rather the bearer of specific know-how that allows flexibility to be introduced.

Another paradox is a limitation related to the costs of deploying digital infrastructures. Digital technologies remain costly, yet they will only be able to spread and become popular in societies and economies with limited resources if the infrastructures are adapted, the equipment is accessible and the data remains economically affordable. But in this field, there is still a lot to do in the cities we are studying and elsewhere (see the claims in South Africa on the price of communication in the context of the "data must fall" movement[7]). Standard digital solutions, based on technologies developed in the North (and promoted by large international groups), which are expensive to deploy and use, will probably adapt by taking the form of less expensive versions. On the contrary, locally produced solutions, economically and technologically more frugal, are likely to complement or even replace the previous ones.

7.4.2. *Towards forms of hybridization specific to the South*

Even though we observe forms of transition in the use of transport systems in Accra, Dakar and Mexico City, the diversity of forms and paces of appropriation in

---

7 Movement calling for lower Internet prices. BBC, 2016, "#DataMustFall: South Africans demand cheaper internet," Online: https://www.bbc.com/news/world-africa-37386428.

the urban transport sector rules out the hypothesis of a single model driven by digital technology. As it stands, innovations are scattered and poorly coordinated.

The integration of devices and the effort to produce digital data in the transport sector and the mobility of city dwellers vary according to contexts and do not follow a predefined pattern. Complex appropriation processes give rise to hybrid systems where digital devices are not strictly implemented or operated as might have been imagined. For example, in on-demand transport, the ways of doing things without applications are largely conserved, via SMS or inter-knowledge. Applications are adapted to local contexts (as with Uber, which allows cash payments in Africa). In this way, the reforms of transport systems do not lead to the disappearance of existing services, which are rooted in social habits and in the metropolitan areas, nor to the disappearance of the paratransit sector. Here again, hybrid systems are being set up, with mass transport (BRT, Trains), line services (buses, minibuses) and various individual transport services more or less rooted in formality. Should we see in these hybridizations a process eventually and inevitably leading to the alignment of transport in the metropolises of the South with a global model?

For their technical networks (urban services, water, electricity), African metropolises and those on other continents are already experiencing forms of hybridization that have long been described and analyzed (Jaglin 2014). The initial observation is an inadequacy of socio-technical systems for the existence of a conventional service. Urban contexts marked by strong growth (spatial and demographic), fragmentation (social and spatial), inherited infrastructural deficiencies and limited investment capacities do not allow for the rapid deployment of conventional services on a metropolitan scale (Bredeloup et al. 2008). The existence of alternative services, whether dominant or complementary to incomplete conventional services, creates a heterogeneity that allows for accessible services. This heterogeneity and "pragmatism" (Jaglin 2017) are found in the configurations of transport service provision that we observe, and produce analogical effects such as highly variable costs for users, the maintenance and upkeeep of forms of resistance to unifying or integrating reforms.

The prevailing model (or counter-model) therefore has its advantages and its limitations. Among these, from the point of view of public policy, there is, on the one hand, a persistent difficulty in regulating and guiding the metropolitan transport system and, on the other hand, the reinforcement of a context that is not conducive to engaging in the movement of a great transition defined at the global level as a process leading to more socially inclusive, environmentally friendly, and economically frugal modes of operation. The normative perspective of the countries of the North is difficult to circumvent for public authorities in the South, particularly because they are dependent on external support (financial, technical), which partly explains choices that are more oriented towards "showcase" objectives than towards pragmatic ones. Hybrid transport services are becoming more common at this particular time, when the emergence of digital technology coincides with major urban transport reforms. However, even though they do not have all the advantages, they do show that other models exist as there are solutions to meet the needs of city dwellers, the interest of operators and the objectives of public policy.

7.5. Conclusion

The processes of digitization, modernization and professionalization of the urban transport sector appear to be an essential element in the transition to the integration of multiple urban transport modes within integrated metropolitan systems for intelligent mobility.

However, the literature on the circulation of models invites us to question the relevance and transferability of models from the North to the South. Although some aspects point to attempts to standardize mobility services, the paratransit sector in the South questions the model promoted by the countries of the North. First, digital technology does not yet seem to create an environment of cooperation or complementarity between the institutional transport offer and the paratransit offer as observed in the North. However, it seems to us that it carries the narrative of a "utopian" (Ghorra-Gobin 2020) collaboration between the different actors of urban mobility. Second, the concept of *smart mobility*, as presented by international actors, tends to exclude the possible hybridizations that we have observed in our fieldwork. Finally, it is generally accepted that, under the guise of a necessary regulation, a transition to intelligent mobility in the South would be to the benefit of state control and also to the benefit of large international groups. This having been said, local digital solutions and adoptions are emerging. Nevertheless, if the model of paratransit transport is flexible, adaptable and profitable despite poor service conditions (comfort, safety, punctuality), it appears to be a sector that is difficult to include in the formal economic institutional framework inherent in the transport models that fuel the ambitions of Southern metropolises.

The analysis thus reveals the weak institutional capacity to transform urban mobility services. In 2021, digital technology had not yet led to a transformation of the business model. The operating model characteristic of the informal organization, based on a paratransit enterprise model, remains unchanged. This situation reveals the complexity and the institutional (normative) and economic limits of putting into practice an integral project driven by digital technology. It also confirms the political and negotiating weight of the informal sector.

Specific trajectories and models cultivating their own originality mark the future of informal/paratransit transport in the South. Hybridization, appropriation or circumvention of digital technology by the informal sector plays a fundamental role in the face of more or less digested global influences. Informal transport systems provide more than half of all urban travel. In this context, the transition to digitized mobility (if it occurs) will not take place without the inclusion of the dominant supply-side logics embedded in the organization of informal transport.

7.6. References

Akrich, M. (1991). L'analyse socio-technique. *La gestion de la recherche*. De Boek, Brussels, 339–353.

Asociación de internet MX (2018). Estudio de comercio electrónico en México. Report, Asociación de internet MX, Mexico.

Atchoua, J., Bogui, J.J., Diallo, S. (2020). *Digital Technologies and African Societies: Challenges and Opportunities*. ISTE Ltd, London, and John Wiley & Sons, New York.

Bacqué, M.H. and Fol, S. (2007). L'inégalité face à la mobilité : Du constat à l'injonction. *Revue suisse de sociologie*, 33, 89–104.

Beckouche, P. (2019). *Les nouveaux territoires du numérique. L'univers digital du sur-mesure de masse*. Sciences Humaines Éditions, Auxerre.

Boutueil, V. and Lesteven, G. (2018). The role of ICT-based innovations in transforming intermediate transport in African cities. The cases of cape town, Nairobi and Addis Ababa. Report, 7th Transport Research Arena, Vienna.

Bredeloup, S., Bertoncello, B., Lombard, J. (2008). *Abidjan, Dakar : Des villes à vendreIdubp25 !Napo : La privatisation made in Africa des services urbains*. L'Harmattan, Paris.

Canzler, W. and Knie, A. (2016). *Mobility in the Age of Digital Modernity: Why the Private Car is Losing its Significance, Intermodal Transport is Winning and Why Digitisation is the Key, Applied Mobilities*. Routledge, London.

Cariole, J. (2018). Boom de l'économie numérique en Afrique Subsaharienne : Quelles perspectives pour l'emploi ? FERDI Fondation pour les études et recherches sur le développement international, pp. 177.

Cervero, R. and Golub, A. (2007). Informal transport: A global perspective. *Transport Policy*, 14(6), 445–457.

CETUD (Conseil Exécutif des transports urbains de Dakar) (2016) Enquête de ménage sur la mobilité, le transport et l'accès aux services urbains dans l'agglomération de Dakar. Final report, CETUD partnered with CUREM and SITRASS.

Cheneau-Loquay, A. (2008). Rôle joué par l'économie informelle dans l'appropriation des TIC en milieu urbain en Afrique de l'Ouest. *Sociétés africaines de l'information*, 22(1/2), 109–126.

Cheneau-Loquay, A. (2010). La révolution des TIC : Du téléphone à Internet. *Bulletin de l'Association de géographes français, Association des géographes français*, 1–15.

Connolly, P. (2014). ¿Que se gobierna en materia de transporte y movilidad? El caso de la ciudad de México. In *Conference: What is Governed? Comparing Paris and Mexico governance. Conflict Solving, Governance Failures and Public Policies*, Mexico City.

Courmont, A. and Le Galès, P. (2019). *Gouverner la ville numérique*. PUF, Paris.

Diaz Olvera, L., Plat, D., Pochet, P. (2005). Marche à pied, pauvreté et ségrégation dans les villes d'Afrique de l'ouest. Le cas de Dakar. Post-Print halshs-00087917, HAL.

Docherty, I., Marsden, G., Anable, J. (2018). The governance of smart mobility. *Transportation Research, Part A: Policy and Practice*, 114–125.

Douay, N. (2018). *Urban Planning in the Digital Age*. ISTE Ltd, London, and John Wiley & Sons, New York.

Eveno, E. (2018). La Ville intelligente : Objet au cœur de nombreuses controverses. *Quaderni*, 29–41.

Geels, F.W. (2004). From sectoral systems of innovation to socio-technical systems. *Research Policy*, 33(6–7).

Ghorra-Gobin, C. (2020). La ville se métamorphose, elle se qualifie désormais de smart : Que révèlent ces "nouveaux" récits ? *Quaderni*, 27–37.

Godard, X. (2008). Transport artisanal, esquisse de bilan pour la mobilité durable. In *Conférence CODATU XIII*, Ho Chi Minh City.

INEGI (2017). Encuesta Origen – Destino en Hogares de la Zona Metropolitana del Valle de México (EOD). Instituto Nacional de Geografía y Estadística.

ITU (2020). *Measurinng Digital Development Facts and Figures*. International Telecommunication Union, Geneva.

Jaglin, S. (2014). Regulating service delivery in southern cities: Rethinking urban heterogeneity. In *A Routledge Handbook on Cities of the Global South*, Parnell, S. and Oldfield, S. (eds). Routledge, London.

Jaglin, S. (2017). Politiques d'infrastructures en Afrique subsaharienne. Le réseau est-il soluble dans la transition urbaine ? In *Les métamorphoses des infrastructures, entre béton et numérique*, Chatzis, C., Jeannot, G., November, V., Ughetto, P. (eds). Peter Lang, Brussels.

Kitchin, R. (2014). The real-time city? Big data and smart urbanism. *GeoJournal*, 79, 1–14.

Kitchin, R., Coletta, C., Evans, L., Heahphy, L., Mac Donncha, D. (2017). Smart cities, urban technocrats, epistemic communities and advocacy coalitions. *A New Technocracy Workshop*.

Lombard, J. and Steck, B. (2015). *Le monde des transports sénégalais, ancrage local et développement international*. IRD, Marseille.

Lyons, G. (2014). Viewpoint: Transport's digital age transition. *Journal of Transport and Land Use*, 8(2) [Online]. Available at: https://doi.org/10.5198/jtlu.2014.751/.

Lyons, G. (2018). Getting smart about urban mobility. Aligning the paradigms of smart and sustainable. *Transportation Research Part A: Policy and Practice*, 4–14.

McCann, E. and Ward, K. (2013). A multi-disciplinary approach to policy transfer research: Geographies, assemblages, mobilities and mutations. *Policy Studies*, 34(1), 2–18. https://doi.org/10.1080/01442872.2012.748563.

McFarlane, C. (2010). The comparative city: Knowledge, learning, urbanism. *International Journal of Urban and Regional Research*, 34(4), 725–742.

Middleton, C., Scheepers, R., Tuunainen, V.K. (2014). When mobile is the norm: Researching mobility information systems and mobility as post-adoption phenomena. *European Journal of Information Systems*, 23(5), 503–512.

Mirabel, F. and Reymond, M. (2019). Le numérique au service de la mobilité urbaine durable. *Annales des Mines, Enjeux numériques*, 7.

Miroux, F. and Lefevre, B. (2012). *Mobilité urbaine et technologies de l'information et de la communication (TIC), enjeux et perspectives pour le climat*. Institut du développement durable et des relations internationales, IDDRI, Paris.

Moradi, A. and Vagnoni, E. (2018). A multi-level perspective analysis of urban mobility system dynamics: What are the future transition pathways? *Technological Forecasting and Social Change*, 126, 231–243.

Napoli, P.M. and Onar, J.A. (2014). The emerging mobile internet underclass: A critique of mobile internet access. *The Information Society*, 30(5), 323–334.

Ninot, O. and Peyroux, É. (2018). Révolution numérique et développement en Afrique : Une trajectoire singulière, questions internationales. *Dossier La Nouvelle Afrique*, 90, 44–52.

Peck, J. and Theodore, N. (2010). Mobilizing policy: Models, methods, and mutations. *Geoforum*, 41(2), 169–174.

Peyroux, É. and Ninot O. (2019). De la "smart city" au numérique généralisé : La géographie urbaine au défi du tournant numérique. *L'information géographique*, 83, 40–57.

Peyroux, E. and Sanjuan, T. (2016). Stratégies de villes et "modèles" urbains : Approche économique et géopolitique des relations entre villes. *EchoGéo*, 36 [Online]. Available at: http://journals.openedition.org/echogeo/14642 and DOI: https://doi.org/10.4000/echogeo.14642.

Ponelis, S.R. and Holmer, M.A. (2015). ICT in Africa: Enabling a better life for all. *Information Technology for Development*, 21(1), 1–11.

Pourbaix, J. (2011). Towards a smart future for cities: Urban transport scenarios for 2025. *Public Transport International*, 60(3), 8–10.

Robinson, J. (2006). *Ordinary Cities: Between Modernity and Development*. Routledge, London.

Shibayama, T. and Ieda, H. (2011). MOLTS: Multinational operators for local transport services. *Asian Transport Studies*, 1, 234–249.

Surdonja, S., Giuffrè, T., Deluka-Tibljaš, A. (2020). Smart mobility solutions, necessary precondition for a well-functioning smart cit. *Transportation Research Procedia*, 45, 604–611.

Sylla, I. (2009). Les collectivités locales face au défi numérique : Le cas des communes d'arrondissement de Dakar. PhD Thesis, Université Cheikh Anta Diop, Dakar.

Tcheng, H., Huet, J.M., Viennois, I., Romdhane, M. (2008). Les télécoms, facteur de développement en Afrique. *L'Express – Roularta, L'expansion Management Review*, 129, 110–120

Wachter, S. (2003). *L'aménagement durable : Défis et politiques*. Éditions de l'Aube, Paris.

8

Artisanal and Small-scale Gold Mining and Territorial Development in Africa: A Difficult Equation

8.1. Introduction

Artisanal and small-scale gold mining (ASGM) has intensified considerably in many parts of Africa since the mid-2000s (Grätz 2004). This intensification is taking place in a context of multifaceted mutations linked to global changes, of which high population growth is a central dimension, against a backdrop of poverty, chronic underemployment and socio-political tensions. Gold occupies a prominent place within the African extractive boom (Magrin 2013). In many countries[1], its exploitation is the result of both industrial investments by Northern or emerging countries and the intensification or diffusion of artisanal mining, more or less mechanized (Dessertine 2016; Chevrillon-Guibert et al. 2019).

Chapter written by Anna DESSERTINE, Raphaëlle CHEVRILLON-GUIBERT, Laurent GAGNOL, Julie BETABELET, Lamine DIALLO, Robin PETIT-ROULET, Edith SAWADOGO, Tongnoma ZONGO and Géraud MAGRIN.

1 The materials used here come from our field research during relatively short but regular stays in Sudan, Niger, Chad, Burkina Faso and Mauritania over the past six years and longer stays in Guinea between 2011 and 2019. They also apply to other gold mining areas in Southern Africa (South Africa, Zimbabwe), Central Africa (DRC, CAR, Cameroon) and other West African countries (Ghana, Côte d'Ivoire).

ASGM[2] is re-emerging in the Sudanian and Nilotic space, where its existence is part of the long-term, and emerges in a relatively new way in the Saharan and North Sahelian space (Grégoire and Gagnol 2017; Chevrillon-Guibert et al. 2019; Gagnol et al. 2019). This is an activity that involves millions of people and a globalized activity, as the gold produced through the cross-border mobilization of funding, materials and humans is almost entirely exported. However, this historically artisanal activity often remains informal insofar as most states are reluctant, at least initially, to organize its formalization, even though it involves a very large number of actors. It is accompanied by social and political tensions, at different levels, over access to the resource and the sharing of the benefits and costs (particularly environmental) of exploitation. This is all the more true since the materiality of extraction and its pollution extends the extraction territory beyond the exploited sites. Conflicts arise between gold miners, indigenous people and "foreigners", gold miners and armed groups, gold miners and industrial companies, gold miners and the State, in a variety of configurations. How then can we explain the enthusiasm of miners for this activity, which is both hard and dangerous, the tolerance and even encouragement of certain states, and the support it receives from international donors?

ASGM is the driving force of territorial dynamics that question the relationship between development and the environment. If territory is a socio-political construction marked by an appropriation and delimitation of space, the territoriality of ASGM seems to be a nebulous topocentric space that reverses the territorial perspective by considering the center more structuring than the limits (Herbst 2000; Dessertine 2017). The sites organized in a network then draw a sort of labile, ephemeral pioneer front, built by the mobility of gold miners and undone by the play of states, sometimes under the influence of mining transnationals. The territoriality of ASGM is thus at first sight inscribed in the mobile African space (Retaillé 2005), confronted with the attempts at fixed divisions of the so-called "modern" states (Harvey 1982), of which the appropriation in the form of legalized permits, such as industrial mining concessions, constitutes an emblematic avatar.

The income derived from these activities concentrates the major negative effects of extractive activities in terms of development, which we consider here under the prism of redistribution issues: at the origin of a political economy centralized by the clientelist networks of State power, it escapes the majority of people and the inhabitants of the territories who nonetheless bear the deleterious effects (particularly on the environment) of industrial exploitation, leading to the famous "curse of natural resources" (Auty 2001). However, since the beginning of the

---

2 We use this term for convenience to designate all forms of artisanal gold mining, even mechanized ones, according to current usage in the countries studied.

2010s, some states tend to encourage or formalize ASGM. They are thus promoting forms of territorialization of this activity, proposing, for example, to secure it through the establishment of ASGM corridors, lands destined for artisanal miners whose fixed delimitation contradicts the mobility and temporary nature of historical ASGM sites.

We propose to shed light here on the ways in which these formalizations and territorializations of ASGM are put in place in order to question their socio-economic and environmental effects on development at the local level. We discuss the hypothesis that the current moment is characterized by a tension between the repression of ASGM in favor of industrial mines and the State's takeover of an artisanal sector in the process of mechanization, producing contrasted effects in terms of development and environmental impacts.

We will begin by describing the different forms of emergence, or re-emergence, of the exploitation of gold in various contexts. Then, we will question the power issues that govern its regulation. Finally, we will question the complex relationship between its exploitation and the development of territories. Starting from a territorial perspective, we will analyze the difficulties of formalizing a mobile activity such as ASGM: on the one hand, because formalization is based on logics of spatial fixation. In contradiction with this activity; on the other hand, it conveys a certain conception of development which, as we will see, struggles to include local development issues linked in particular to the local logics of the socio-spatial organization of these societies (reticularity of spaces, diversity of actors, etc.).

8.2. The (re)emergence of the gold resource

ASGM from the Gulf of Guinea to the Sahara is part of a diversity of historicities and relationships to space. While the resource is part of a complex socio-political construction (Raffestin 1980; Magrin et al. 2015), in some countries, ASGM is relatively recent, while in others it has been the basis of power building for several centuries. The socio-spatial issues at stake in ASGM are essentially related to the mechanization of activities and increasingly strict state control of mobility and the spaces associated with it. The gold resource is not limited to its materiality. It produces specific relationships in space that tend to form extractive territories.

8.2.1. ASGM: a centuries-old activity

The contemporary gold boom is based on contrasting legacies. In most Saharan regions, the recent gold rushes have emerged since the early 2000s in areas that had never known gold, or had lost the memory of it, as in the Nile Valley. Further south or east, ASGM is centuries old and has continued to the present day, particularly in the historical centers of Bambouk (Senegal-Mali), Bouré (Guinea-Mali), Lobi (Burkina-Faso) and Akan (Côte d'Ivoire and Ghana). Gold mining has played a fundamental role in the consolidation of political entities, whether it be the kingdom of Meroe or those of Nubia at the time of the Pharaohs, or later the empires of Ghana, Mali, Songhai and the Funj Sultanate of Sennar between the 4th and 19th centuries. It thus participated in the constitution of major regional poles for trade between the regions north of the Sahara and forested areas or central Africa, with the Sultanate of Darfur between the 17th and 20th centuries. This exploitation allowed the power of emblematic figures such as the Malian emperor Kankou Moussa, who is said to have spent between 10 and 13 tons of gold during his pilgrimage to Mecca between 1324 and 1325 (Mbodj 2011, p. 299), causing the price of gold in Cairo to fall for several years. Some gold territories such as Shaybun and Shawabna in the Nuba Mountains in Sudan became internationally renowned for centuries due to this exploitation.

During the colonial era (late 19th to early 20th century), industrial gold mining only took place in southern Africa, giving rise in particular to the urban and semi-urban region of Gauteng around Johannesburg. But attempts remained unsuccessful in the Sudano-Sahelian zone. During the 1990s, when the possession of natural resources was still widely considered to be one of the main factors of economic progress, the liberal policies initiated under the aegis of the World Bank favored the establishment of large new industrial mines (Sadiola in Mali; Siguiri in Guinea; Hassaï in Sudan). But far from promoting economic take-off, the exploitation of resources is, on the contrary, designated as a major factor in the weakening of states, the increase in inequalities, corruption and the multiplication of conflicts (Collier and Hoeffler 2000; Rosser 2006). To counter this "resource curse", the World Bank has encouraged African countries to reform their mining codes to better regulate these activities (Campbell 2010). This has led to the implementation of new schemes, with controversial effects (Magrin 2013), which highlight the heavy environmental and social impacts of unregulated artisanal mining (OECD 2018).

In a context marked by high mineral prices, particularly between 2008 and 2012 and since 2019, we are witnessing a boom in industrial investments, stimulated by new neo-liberal legislation in which the States, under the influence of the World Bank in the mining sector, are promoting a market (Campbell 2010), as well as a strong intensification of ASGM favored by the circulation of new techniques.

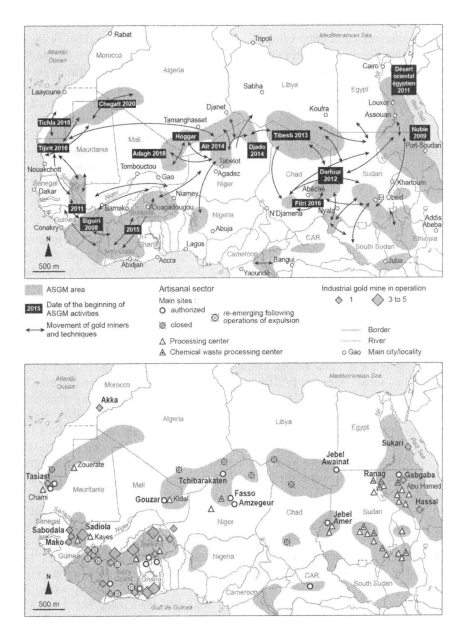

Figure 8.1. *Spatialities of ASGM in West Africa and the Sahel (source: Hérodote, 172; A. Afane, J. Betabelet, R. Chevrillon-Guibert, A. Dessertine, L. Diallo, L. Gagnol, G. Magrin, R. Petit-Roulet, E. Sawadogo, T. Zongo; portals of ministries of mines; EITI reports). For a color version of this figure, see www.iste.co.uk/peyroux/development.zip*

8.2.2. *Recent transformations in ASGM*

While the mining industry refers to a fixation of capital in space (Harvey 1982), of which the enclave constitutes the archetypal figure (Ferguson 2005), ASGM is a fundamentally mobile activity when it is weakly mechanized. It is based on the movement of gold miners – men and women, sometimes children – between sites that emerge, disappear and re-emerge as the vein is exploited. Its borders are thus often analyzed as flexible (Bryceson and Geenen 2016), temporary (Grätz 2004), approaching Kopytoff's (1987) internal boundaries. The aim here is to analyze the transformations of the mobile character of ASGM with regard to the mechanization of activities and the expansion of industrial permits, distinguishing contexts according to the age and continuity of activities.

8.2.2.1. *Towards the sedentarization of centuries-old ASGM*

Gold mining is seasonal and has been practiced for centuries. It is practiced during the dry season in a manner that complements rainy season agricultural activities, and is based on extraction techniques that are still found on certain current mining sites. In contrast to much of Sahelian and East Africa, in West Africa there is a high level of female involvement, estimated in some areas such as Mali at 50% of the workforce. The techniques have been described for the Bouré, Bambouk, Burkina-Faso and Benin regions (Grätz 2004; Panella 2007; Cros and Mégret 2009; Mbodj 2011; Dessertine 2016; Bolay 2017). Mining is carried out by mixed groups – men digging the pits and women hauling buckets of gravel with rope – authorized to work by a local customary (village or mine) chief. These sites generally take the form of temporary camps where gold miners who have come to try their luck cohabit for a time, alongside traders, small-scale gold buyers and the inhabitants of the villages who own the land. In this way, the ASGM sites are not chaotic, but rather structured and relatively autonomous spaces of financial opportunity with their own modes of local justice (tombolomanw in Guinea and Mali, for example), taxation rules, etc. They therefore more closely resemble moving and ephemeral points between which gold panners circulate, than fixed and delimited territories.

ASGM sites and the mobility associated with them have been reconfigured over the past decade as a result of the mechanization of activities, in particular the increasingly systematic use of metal detectors. This has led to at least two consequences: the masculinization of ASGM mobility and their increasingly itinerant character (Bolay 2017; Dessertine and Noûs 2021). First, while the participation of women in West African gold mining remains important, it is not so much mobile gold miners as women from the village near the mining site who are most often engaged in washing and processing the ore. In addition, the detectors give rise to more volatile mobility because they allow for more surface area to be covered in less time. The settlements of several weeks in temporary camps are then no longer necessary. This is especially true since these camps are increasingly the object of military missions known as "eviction" (e.g. Guinea, Mali) aimed at expelling gold miners, particularly when they are, as is increasingly the case on mining permit lands. In fact, the mobility of gold miners is increasingly constrained by the multiplication of mining industry permits, both for research and exploitation, testifying to processes of "spatial fixation" linked to global capitalism (Harvey 1982). In this case, this is expressed by the exclusion of gold miners from certain zones or by the delimitation of specific spaces which they are allowed to exploit, such as the gold mining corridors mentioned above. The formalization of ASGM, encouraged by the growing mechanization of artisanal activities and the attraction of states for the rent linked to them, thus takes on a categorically territorial form, enclosing this mobile activity in some way and bringing it closer to, but not corresponding to, the extractive territorialization of the mining industry.

8.2.2.2. *The Saharan "pioneer nebula"*

In Saharan areas where ASGM is relatively recent, the spatialization of these activities also appears initially diffuse and mobile. At first glance, it seems to take the form of a pioneer front (Chevrillon-Guibert et al. 2019). However, this phenomenon cannot be modeled by the figure of a linear and continuous advance. A metaphor could usefully be invoked: that of an extractive nebula made up of mining sites with changing contours, linked together by the mobility of the gold miners and the flows necessary for their functioning (food, inputs), these being more or less ephemeral. As is the case for the zones where ASGM is centuries-old, there is a continuous diffusion of activities in the form of nebula, in a rather pioneer form in this case[3]. These remain constrained, as in the West African regions, by processes of fixation linked to the territorial organization of the State (borders, industrial permits in particular).

Due to the absence of settlement and the lack of water, this Saharan pioneer nebula is characterized by the decoupling of mining, processing and urbanization (Gagnol and Afane 2021). The settlement of the mining sites resembles a shanty town made up of precarious habitats where any permanent construction is excluded. Women are not allowed there. It is the ore processing centers that polarize the mining area. Since they require a lot of water, they are generally located very far from the mining sites and in the immediate vicinity of large or small towns. This makes the latter more dynamic, but is not without local controversy; for example, the cyanide treatment center in Agadez was relocated in 2015 and only operates with a temporary permit from the town hall.

---

3 This notion of nebula makes it possible to account for the fact that the scale of observation is essential to understand the phenomenon. On a small scale, it is a single cluster in expansion; on a large scale, it is a multitude of particular phenomena in interaction.

Water, which is necessary to extract the ore from the rock, is a central factor in the mining chain. As a result, when mining sites are located near watercourses, as in humid regions, the mining stages (extraction, washing, crushing and amalgamation) are carried out in close proximity to each other, resulting in concentrated mining sites where extracting gold miners process the resource and reside for a time. In the Sahara, where the climate is more arid and water is scarce or saline, these activities are, conversely, separated, sometimes by several hundred kilometers.

In addition, in the Sahelo-Saharan zone, the mechanization of ASGM is reflected in the sedentarization of activities, unlike hyper-mobility in West African zones. The growing presence of machinery (crushers, backhoes, pickaxe hammers) and the mastery of techniques (explosives) make it possible to exploit lode gold in deep shafts or in quarries. The investments made at that time presupposed the spatial fixation of activities and encouraged their promoters to seek security from the State (Chevrillon-Guibert 2018).

In both the Sudanian and Sahelo-Saharan zones, the labile nature of ASGM does not appear to be compatible with models of development that are territorialized according to modern logics in the way that the spatial relationships of pastoralism and irrigated agriculture, for example, are opposed (Magrin 2013). The modes of governing the operation attempt to lead ASGM towards more fixed territorial logics (Dessertine and Noûs 2021). Indeed, as we will see, several states concerned by the increase in ASGM have chosen to authorize or even encourage the activity, favoring not only the fixation of ore extraction but also the constitution of marketplaces where gold is extracted from crushed rocks through various increasingly sophisticated mechanisms (Chevrillon-Guibert 2018).

8.3. Methods of governing the operation

The diversity of relationships to time and territory in ASGM is also found in the modes of government of the exploitation. How are access to the resource, its production and its sharing managed? We shall see that these modalities are expressed at different levels, which are sometimes juxtaposed, leading to ambiguities in the articulation of the prerogatives of the multiple authorities involved in ASGM, whether they are qualified as customary or more or less explicitly integrated into the central state.

8.3.1. *Customary rules for ASGM*

The place of customary authorities in the state systems concerned with gold mining varies greatly and is more or less integrated into the political-administrative system of the states. In West Africa, for example, customary chiefs form a parallel hierarchical system, which state authorities consider to be consultative, particularly with regard to access to land. This is the case in Benin, Burkina Faso, Ivory Coast, Mali and Guinea, where these arrangements are based on "tutelage" relationships (Chauveau 2007), in which the first arrivals install the newcomers. Here, precedence implies less land appropriation and spatial anchorage than the possibility of being inserted into a relational system in which the newcomer is the authority. The same is true for the modalities of access to ASGM, which are governed by customary land tenure norms. Important mining sites such as Kourémalé, on the Guinean-Malian border, are managed by a customary mining chief (*damanti* in Maninka) who heads self-defense groups, the *tombolomanw*. The *tombolomanw* have a role in monitoring and securing the sites where they exercise a form of moral justice. They are recognized as actors by the state security system (mainly the army and the police), but remain theoretically subordinate to state agents, reflecting a process of pluralization of security that can be found more widely in sub-Saharan Africa, also embodied, for example, by the presence of *dozo* hunters on mining sites in Mali or Ivory Coast.

These customary arrangements are based on forms of relational authority that are difficult to reconcile with national land legislation, and are based on the delimitation of areas and the issuance of titles. The rise of gold mining – ASGM or industrial exploitation – makes this reconciliation all the more complicated as it leads to increased land pressure. This is reflected in an increase in land conflicts (see Engels (2016) on Burkina Faso, for example). In addition to the latent conflict between a relational and reticular spatial organization, on the one hand, and a more territorial and national logic, on the other hand, there is also the potential stranglehold of armed groups over artisanal mines, whose members may be both discharged soldiers and *dozo* hunters. The local modes of governance of ASGM sites thus point to the fluidity of groups and the ambiguity of security practices.

8.3.2. The income races

The increase in ASGM activities has led to increased competition for control of the resulting income. In addition to the gold miners who extract the ore and share the profits from its sale according to the work and investments made, several other actors take a share of the resource. Initially, this was more at the local level of the state apparatus, whether it was the municipalities hosting the artisanal mines or the customary leaders. However, these actors are often overtaken by other actors, notably armed groups. The monopoly of income then participates in processes of militarization or milicianization by financing armed groups, as in western Central Africa (Betabelet Wouloungou 2018), in the South Kivu region of the Democratic

Republic of Congo (Geenen 2014), in the conflict regions of Darfur or the Libyan deep south (Tubiana and Gramizzi 2017; Chevrillon-Guibert et al. 2019), and also movements claiming to be global jihadists in the Sahelo-Saharan zone in northern Mauritania, Niger, Burkina Faso, Mali and Chad[4]. The often peripheral location of mining areas in their national territories as well as their difficult access and political instability favor the control of local armed actors over these lucrative activities in contexts of great poverty, while at the same time making accurate and reliable information about them rare.

The levies operated by armed groups can be only predatory, as with the informal checkpoints positioned on the roads used by gold miners or during violent raids on ASGM sites. They are more consensual, when collection is the counterpart of protection, and can also participate in more complex dynamics by articulating themselves in a system of local conflicts. The various configurations of these sometimes place the actors on the side of the central state and/or customary authorities, sometimes between these authorities and sometimes in more or less total opposition to them. The control of the large Jebel Amer mine in Darfur is a textbook case in this regard. It was controlled for a time by a customary chief of the area who became a militia leader for the Khartoum government during the early years of the war in Darfur, then declared a presidential advisor, then entered into opposition to that same government and was finally overthrown by one of his deputies. The latter has since become a military leader recognized by the government in Khartoum before participating in its overthrow and taking a leading role in the transitional government that has ruled over Sudan since the revolution of 2019 (Chevrillon-Guibert et al. 2020).

However, the (central) states are also playing an increasing role in the artisanal sector both to organize and control activities, and also to benefit from the income. First, states have encouraged the industrial sector with fiscally attractive legislation and geological mapping policies to identify and distribute the most promising concessions. Then, the slowness of industrial investment and the development of ASGM made them change. From an initially very hostile attitude (criminalization of activities, eviction of gold miners, active fight against what was considered illegal trafficking), most state policies have shown a certain tolerance, with attempts to organize the activity and sometimes to limit its negative environmental impacts. This is also the case for major international donors (World Bank, European Union, Deutsche Gesellschaft für Internationale Zusammenarbeit (GIZ), etc.) who, seeing the potential for economic growth associated with these activities, encourage their formalization. Nevertheless, like the states, they fear their development outside the

---

4 Lewis, Ryan McNeill, "Special Report: How jihadists struck gold in Africa's Sahel", Reuters, November 22, 2019: https://www.reuters.com/article/idUSKBN1XW11F.

formal circuits and favor a centralized organization. The installation of refineries[5] in the capitals or the largest cities appears to be a godsend for controlling the flow of artisanally mined ore, seeing as they can limit parallel transnational circuits[6].

These different attitudes vary from state to state and over time: while in countries like Guinea, governments tend to combat ASGM and struggle to enforce legislation (issuing permits), in others they have been quick to encourage the artisanal sector while continuing to promote the industry. For example, Sudan adopted an opportunistic attitude by promoting the artisanal sector (Calkins and Ille 2014) to compensate for possible industrialization due to the U.S. embargo, as the regime sought an alternative to the decline in oil revenues following South Sudan's independence. In Mauritania, the government, faced with the lack of new industrial investment and influenced by the Sudanese experience, encouraged the formalization of the sector into identified ASGM zones and processing centers (Gagnol et al. 2019). Some states (Sudan, Burkina Faso, etc.) have also created or strengthened gold buying companies. These companies play multiple roles: financing activities, as well as conflict management and security (Arnaldi di Balme and Lanzano 2013). They promote the control of commercial circuits and the establishment of monopolies.

State support for ASGM has not prevented tensions with the industrial sector when the same mining territories are coveted, even though some at times benefit from the work of others and vice versa. Indeed, it is not uncommon for industrial companies to benefit from the know-how of gold miners in order to identify the most favorable sites and, on the other hand, for gold miners to benefit from the activities of factories that reprocess their waste. Tensions frequently arise from the successive and brutal evictions of gold miners working on the concessions of mining companies (Bolay (2017) in Guinea), without them being consulted or even informed.

This formalization of extractive territories, whether artisanal or industrial, is not without clashes with the populations living near mining sites that are strongly affected by the negative impacts of the mine. The expectations of those responsible for the activity (companies, gold miners) and the central authorities that accompany them are multiple and fall under the registers of compensation for damages and claims to rights over the resource. In Burkina Faso and Niger, some mayors of

---

5 The proliferation of gold refineries in Africa – until 2012, there were only a handful; by 2021, 26 were in operation or under construction in more than 14 countries – reflecting the desire of states to benefit as much as possible from mining incomes, both industrial and small scale.

6 Lewis, Hobson, "Race to refine: the bid to clean up Africa's gold rush," Reuters (Business News section), January 15, 2020: https://www.reuters.com/article/idUSL4N28S33F.

mining communities have joined forces to influence the legislators of the mining code to ensure that a percentage of the industrial income is allocated to them. The degree of formalization of artisanal activities through the granting of permits remains low, however, particularly because of the mismatch between mining permits and the situation of gold miners (high cost of permits, very large areas involved, etc.; Ouédraogo 2019).

8.4. Questioning development from ASM activity

The forms and consequences of the gold mining boom on the territories vary according to the type of physical and geopolitical environment, as well as state choices. Beyond the diversity of legacies and contexts, the intensification of gold mining can be explained by its real and expected effects, at different levels (from the individual or household to the central state, via village customary authorities and local communities at the communal level), in terms of income redistribution, a prism that we adopt to think about development at the local level.

8.4.1. *The virtues of decentralized income sources*

The major difference in terms of monetary benefits between gold ASM and industrial mining lies in a wider redistribution of revenues to a large number of local and other actors, valuable in the context of population growth and employment shortages: in Burkina Faso, it is estimated in 2017 that 1.2–2 million people were living from the activity (Werthmann 2017), while at the same time, 11 industrial mines provided 9,651 jobs (Zongo and Some 2020). Of course, income from the activity is extremely unequal depending on the place of individuals in the artisanal production system and their success. In the most open contexts, a wide variety of actors (indigenous or non-indigenous, women, youth, elderly) may engage in the activity with capital (small or large urban traders) or with their labor power alone. In addition, gold mining is accompanied by the establishment of various services and businesses near the sites (hairdressers, restaurants, bars, prostitution, etc.), which represent employment and income opportunities.

In the places that the gold miners leave or in the villages near the sites, the profits from gold mining contribute to the economy of households and territories, as well as to urbanization from below. It provides complementary income to that of agriculture (Zongo 2019), in complex ways agricultural surpluses, which are not very likely to finance the search for gold, as well as ASGM successes, contribute to investment in farms through the purchase of inputs (plant protection products, fertilizers) (Ouédraogo 2019). Some gold miners practice a dual activity of ASGM and farming, which allows them to secure and increase their income (Hilson 2016);

ASGM also becomes a means of coping with youth unemployment (Hilson and Maconachie 2020).

The gains of ASGM can be seen in buildings and these feed vocations. They constitute one of the driving forces behind urbanization processes (Grégoire and Magrin 2018). In villages and small towns, many permanent buildings are attributed to successful gold miners. In Senegal, ASGM constitutes a vector of modernity in the rural areas of the southeast of the country: in addition to the modernization of the habitat and the change in the way of life, the villages of gold miners are connected to various networks on a national and international scale through the digital (Internet, installation of the canal network). According to mechanisms that are partly comparable to those of international migration, some gold miners finance collective infrastructures to affirm their success and also to make up for a social success that has been criticized due to the sulfurous nature of gold mining in some societies, due to its association with the world of supernatural genies (Cros and Mégret 2009).

While it distributes revenues to a large number of diverse actors, ASGM remains an economic sector like any other, where the accumulation of some people deepens inequalities. The search for gold appears to be relatively egalitarian during the first exploratory phase, when itinerant researchers work in an artisanal manner: qualities of observation, talent for handling the detector and a sense of where to look (based on village knowledge or participation as an employee in geological exploration campaigns) increase the chances of certain individuals. The gains are roughly proportional to the capital invested. *Success stories* are possible. However, the mechanization of activities is accompanied by a greater division between labor and capital and an unequal distribution of income from extraction to the benefit of equipment owners (Panella 2007). The more fixed and concentrated the exploitation is on deep vein mining, the more capital investment is a determining factor in the profitability of operations. In Sudan as in Guinea or Mauritania, the main processing locations reflect the growing inequalities linked to the rise in capital (Dessertine 2016; Chevrillon-Guibert 2018; Gagnol et al. 2019). The contribution to development can then be measured by the sector's capacity to foster accumulation that can be reinvested in productive economic activities (agricultural or otherwise).

8.4.2. *A new factor in the equation of local development*

The growth of artisanal gold mining has made it an important issue in local development. The revisions of the mining codes in the 2010s provide for a share of the mining income, whether industrial or artisanal, to be returned to local decentralized authorities. This is the case, for example, in Niger (2006), Guinea (2013) and Burkina Faso (2015). In practice, these provisions had only been marginally implemented by 2021 for the best-known incomes associated with industrial exploitation. Among these incomes, access to and sharing of taxes on mining activities are also sources of tension between local communities and the central state, and also between the different levels of decentralization (Mbodj 2011).

The fiscal mobilization of such resources from artisanal mining is hampered by the difficulties of formalizing and controlling the activity, which is located at various levels – even where central government control is strong, as in Sudan, a significant portion of artisanal production escapes it. Where states have opted to regulate artisanal production through control of processing (Sudan, Mauritania and planned in Chad), the question of the capture of the value of industrial treatment of artisanal mine tailings by powerful actors is a serious one (Gagnol et al. 2019; Chevrillon-Guibert et al. 2020).

Finally, in the same way that industrial corporate social responsibility (CSR) schemes appear to be a means of legitimizing their territorial anchorage, as well as a channel for planning and financing a form of infrastructural development (construction of roads, schools, hospitals, etc.) (Mbodj 2011; Magrin 2013; Denoël 2019), artisanal gold mining is also called upon to contribute to local development (Bazillier and Girard 2020). Here too, the demand for the provision of public goods is justified by the need to compensate for the impacts (notably environmental) of the activity on the territory. In the village of Koutouloyarce (Burkina Faso), for example, gold miners organized into an office engage in dialogue with village authorities to regulate the impacts of gold mining and contribute to development actions (school equipment, lighting, etc.) (Sawadogo 2018).

On a territorial level, the rise of artisanal gold mining has contributed to the integration of certain marginal territories into their national space, as many mining zones are located in these territories, in a manner that is ultimately comparable to the establishment of industrial mining sites (Grégoire and Magrin 2018). The circulation of people, the associated trade flows and also the representations fed by the national and other media have contributed to these processes. The result is often a reinforcement of the state's territorial control over these margins insofar as the state intends to benefit from the income that results from them, and to this end, it is reorganizing its modes of action on the local level. For example, in Sudan, the central state has set up a national agency responsible for managing artisanal activities in place of the municipalities, which initially did so.

8.4.3. *Environmental impacts and conflicting regulations*

While it contributes in a complex way to diffuse socio-economic processes of redistribution – from the domestic to the regional level – which we interpret in this chapter in terms of development, the intensification of contemporary ASGM has its environmental drawbacks. Their regulation suffers from multiple ambiguities.

The main environmental impacts are the loss of vegetation (land clearance, cutting of trees to support wells, consumption of wood for energy by gold miners), soil erosion, soil and water pollution, linked in particular to the increasing use of cyanide and mercury for the amalgamation of ore (Sawadogo 2021).

The regulation of these impacts is an important issue within the artisanal gold mining arena. Limiting the use of toxic products or switching to less polluting practices is at the heart of discussions between village authorities, civil society and gold miners' organizations. However, this regulation is not always perceived as essential by the gold miners themselves, who value the economic contribution of the activity and minimize its environmental impacts rate. This ambivalence is found at the level of the States, which in principle defend environmental protection while encouraging highly polluting activities. In Sudan, the international treaty prohibiting the use of mercury has been signed, although artisanal activities that use this product on a massive scale are authorized and even supported. Similarly, in Mauritania, one of the national ore processing centers has been set up on the outskirts of the town of Chami, which borders the Arguin Bank National Park Reserve, a UNESCO World Heritage Site, which now receives daily fumes from the mercury used in gold processing (Gagnol et al. 2019).

However, state condemnation of environmental impacts needs to be contextualized. In Sudan, artisanal activity has become so widespread in certain regions that any environmental degradation is now considered to be linked to this activity, forgetting the role of any other mechanism (desertification, climate change, etc.). The denunciation of gold washing is then used to mask other causes. In the same way, in Burkina Faso, ASGM is accused of being the driving force behind regressive environmental dynamics by local state officials as well as village authorities, even though in some cases agricultural clearing has been more important (Sawadogo 2021). The extent of landscape impacts attributed to ASGM thus depends not only on the scale of observation, and also on the positioning of actors with respect to this activity.

8.5. Conclusion

Gold mining is ambivalent. While being a centuries-old activity that was politically central at certain times in the past, in 2021 it fuels many of the tensions and armed conflicts from the Gulf of Guinea to the Sahara and the Red Sea. While its environmental impacts are significant, it constitutes a viable economic option for millions of people and is accessible to a large number of actors, at least in the short term. It regularly escapes the control of central States which, despite their efforts, remain more or less capable and inclined, depending on the context, by participating in development on a local scale to capture the linked income.

The multiplicity of scales and actors involved contributes to the complexity of the relationship between environment and development. The territorial perspective has made it possible to reveal the diversity of spatio-temporal forms of ASGM and its difficult formalization in extractive territories. The regulation of the impacts and benefits of exploitation constitutes the major political issue. In our view, the mobile and reticular nature of these activities plays an important role in their contribution to development at the local level by allowing a diffuse redistribution to a large number of actors. This dimension would benefit from being more fully included in discussions on the territorial development of the areas concerned. ASGM thus reveals fluid and localized development dynamics that allow for the consideration of actors and spatialities that are invisible to single territorial thinking, based on the grid, the delimitation and the production of exclusive spaces.

The complexity of the relationships that are built up through mining between the various actors thus testifies to the impossibility of concluding that a single development model would do only good at all the scales, where the activity is deployed. It therefore emphasizes the importance of leaving the fundamental choices concerning these models to those who will suffer the consequences. Finally, it invites reflection on the modalities for strengthening the power of action of actors at the local level, which is the most relevant for artisanal exploitation because of the number of people it involves, the extent of the spaces it covers and its reticular and shifting organization.

8.6. References

Arnaldi di Balme, L. and Lanzano, C. (2013). "Entrepreneurs de la frontière" : Le rôle des comptoirs privés dans les sites d'extraction artisanale de l'or au Burkina Faso. *Politique africaine*, 131(3), 27–49 [Online]. Available at: https://www.cairn.info/journal-politique-africaine-2013-3-page-27.htm [Accessed 26 July 2021].

Auty, R. (2001). *Resource Abundance and Economic Development*. Oxford University Press, Oxford.

Bazillier, R. and Girard, V. (2020). The gold digger and the machine: Evidence on the distributive effect of the artisanal and industrial Gold Rushes in Burkina Faso. *AFD Research Papers Series*, 77.

Betabelet Wouloungou, J.R. (2018). Ressources, territoires et conflits : Elevage bovin et exploitation minière dans l'Ouest centrafricain. PhD Thesis, Université Paris 1 Panthéon-Sorbonne, Paris.

Bolay, M. (2017). Gold journeys: Expulsion-induced mobility and the making of artisanal mining spaces in West Africa. PhD Thesis, Université de Neufchâtel, Neufchâtel.

Bryceson, D.F. and Geenen, S. (2016). Artisanal frontier mining of gold in Africa: Labour transformation in Tanzania and the democratic republic of Congo. *African Affairs*, 115(459), 296–317.

Calkins, S. and Ille, E. (2014). Territories of gold mining. International investment and artisanal extraction in Sudan. In *Disrupting Territories. Land, Commodification and Conflict in Sudan*, Gertel, J., Rottenburg, R., Calkins, S. (eds). James Currey, Woodbridge.

Campbell, B. (2010). *Ressources minières en Afrique. Quelle réglementation pour le développement ?* Presses de l''Université du Québec/CRDI/Nordic Africa Institute, Quebec/Ottawa/Uppsala.

Chauveau, J.-P. (2007). Transferts fonciers et relations de "tutorat" en Afrique de l'Ouest. Évolutions et enjeux actuels d'une institution agraire coutumière. *Le Journal des sciences sociales*, 4, 7–32.

Chevrillon-Guibert, R. (2018). Le gouvernement des mines au Soudan : Entre opportunisme et autoritarisme. *Égypte/Monde arabe*, 3(18) [Online]. Available at: http://journals. openedition.org/ema/4176.

Chevrillon-Guibert, R., Gagnol, L., Magrin, G. (2019). Les ruées vers l'or au Sahara et au nord du Sahel. Ferment de crise ou stabilisateur ? *Hérodote*, 172, 193–215.

Chevrillon-Guibert, R., Ille, E., Salah, M. (2020). Pratiques de pouvoir, conflits miniers et économie de l'or au Soudan durant le régime d'al-Inqaz. *Politique africaine*, 2020/2, 123–148.

Collier, P. and Hoeffler, A. (2000). On the incidence of civil war in Africa. *Journal of Conflict Resolution*, 46(1), 13–28.

Cros, M. and Mégret, Q. (2009). D'un idéal de virilité à l'autre ? Du vengeur de sang au chercheur d'or en pays lobi Burkinabé. *Autrepart*, 49, 137–154.

Denoël, M. (2019). Rapports de pouvoir dans l'activité minière : Entre modèle néo-extractiviste et variations territoriales. Le cas des provinces de Jujuy, San Juan et Mendoza en Argentine. PhD Thesis, Université Jean Jaurès, Toulouse.

Dessertine, A. (2016). From pickaxes to metal detectors: Gold mining mobility and space in Upper Guinea, Guinea Conakry. *The Extractive Industries and Societies*, 3(2), 435–441.

Dessertine, A. (2017). Du centre aux limites : La question de la fondation et de l'autorité en Haute-Guinée (Guinée). In *(Re)Fonder. Les modalités du (re)commencement dans le temps et dans l'espace*, Gervais-Lambony, P., Hurlet, F., Rivoal, I. (eds). Éditions de Boccard, Paris.

Dessertine, A. and Noûs, C. (2021). Hybrid territorialisation: A reconfiguration of rural spaces through gold mining in Upper Guinea. *Political Geography*, 86.

Engels, B. (2016). Not all glitter is gold: Mining conflicts in burkina faso. In *Contested Extractivism, Society and the State: Struggles over Mining and Land*, Engels, B. and Dietz, K. (eds). Palgrave Macmillan, London.

Ferguson, J. (2005). Seeing like an oil company. *American Anthropologist*, 107(3), 377–382.

Gagnol, L. and Afane, A. (2021). De sable et d'or. Note sur la production urbaine contrastée de la ruée vers l'or au Sahara. *Afrique contemporaine*, 269/270, 213–236.

Gagnol, L., Magrin, G., Chevrillon-Guibert, R. (2019). Chami, ville nouvelle et ville de l'or. Une trajectoire urbaine insolite en Mauritanie. *L'Espace Politique*, 38 [Online]. Available at: https://journals.openedition.org/espacepolitique/6562 [Accessed 26 July 2021].

Geenen, S. (2014). Qui cherche trouve. The political economy of access to gold mining and trade in South Kivu, DRC, IOB. PhD Thesis, University of Antwerp, Antwerp.

Grätz, T. (2004). Les frontières de l'orpaillage en Afrique occidentale. *Autrepart*, 30(2), 135–150.

Grégoire, E. and Gagnol, L. (2017). Ruées vers l'or au Sahara : L'orpaillage dans le désert du Ténéré et le massif de l'Aïr (Niger). *EchoGéo* [Online]. Available at: https://journals.openedition.org/echogeo/14933 [Accessed 26 July 2021].

Grégoire, E. and Magrin, G. (2018). Des mines entre villes et campagnes : Un autre regard sur le boom extractif ouest-africain (2000–2015). In *Tropiques, développement et mondialisation. Hommages à Jean-Louis Chaléard*, Sanjuan, T., Lesourd, M., Tallet, B. (eds). L'Harmattan, Paris.

Harvey, D. (1982). *The Limits to Capital*. Blackwell Publishers, Oxford.

Herbst, J. (2000). *States and Power in Africa. Comparative Lessons in Authority and Contro*. Princeton University Press, Princeton, NJ.

Hilson, G. (2016). Farming, small-scale mining and rural livelihoods in Sub-Saharan Africa: A critical overview. *The Extractive Industries and Society*, 3(2), 547–563.

Hilson, G. and Maconachie, R. (2020). Artisanal and small scale mining and the sustainable development goals: Opportunities and new directions for Sub-Saharan Africa. *Geoforum*, 111, 125–141.

Kopytoff, I. (1987). The internal African frontier: The making of African political culture. In *The African Frontier. The Reproduction of Traditional African Societies*, Kopytoff, I. (ed.). Indiana University Press, Bloomington, IN.

Magrin, G. (2013). *Voyage en Afrique rentière*. Publications de la Sorbonne, Paris.

Magrin, G., Chauvin, E., Lavie, E., Perrier-Bruslé, L., Redon, M. (2015). Introduction. Les ressources, enjeux géographiques d'un objet pluriel. In *Ressources mondialisées. Essais de géographie politique*, Redon, M., Magrin, G., Chauvin, E., Lavie, E., Perrier-Bruslé, L. (eds). Publication de la Sorbonne, Paris.

Mbodj, F.B. (2011). Boom aurifère à l'est du Sénégal, l'ouest du Mali et au nord-est de la Guinée : Mutations socio-économiques et spatiales d'anciennes marges géographiques et économiques. PhD Thesis, Université Panthéon-Sorbonne, Paris.

OECD (2018). *Illicit Financial Flows: The Economy of Illicit Trade in West Africa*. OECD Publishing, Paris.

Ouédraogo, L. (2019). Orpaillage artisanal et développement rural. PhD Thesis, Université de Laval, Quebec.

Panella, C. (2007). L'éthique sociale du damansen. *Cahiers d'études africaines*, 186, 345–370.

Raffestin, C. (1980). *Pour une géographie du pouvoir*. Librairies techniques, Paris.

Retaillé, D. (2005). L'espace mobile. In *Le territoire est mort. Vive les territoires ! Une (re)fabrication au nom du développement*, Antheaume, B. and Giraut, F. (eds). IRD, Paris.

Rosser, A. (2006). The political economy of the resource curse: A literature survey. Centre for the Future State, IDS Working Paper 268, Brighton.

Sawadogo, K. (2018). Régulation endogène de l'orpaillage à Koutouloyarcé (commune de Kaya, Burkina Faso). Master's Thesis, Université Al Asria, Nouakchott.

Sawadogo, E. (2021). Discours, pratiques et dynamiques environnementales autour de l'orpaillage dans la commune de Kampti (sud-ouest du Burkina Faso). PhD Thesis, Université Joseph Ki-Zerbo, Toma, and Université Paris 1 Panthéon-Sorbonne, Paris.

Tubiana, J. and Gramizzi, C. (2017). *Lost in Trans-Nation. Tubu and Other Armed Groups and Smugglers along Libya's Southern Border*. Small Arms Survey, Graduate Institute of International and Development Studies, Geneva.

Werthmann, K. (2017). The drawbacks of privatization: Artisanal gold mining in Burkina Faso 1986–2016. *Resource Policy*, 52, 41–426.

Zongo, T. (2019). Orpaillage et dynamiques territoriales dans la province du Sanmatenga "Le pays de l'or" au Burkina-Faso. PhD Thesis, Université Joseph Ki-Zerbo, Toma, and Université Panthéon-Sorbonne, Paris.

Zongo, T. and Some, A. (2020). Les travailleurs locaux de la mine de Bissa Gold au Burkina Faso : Précarité ou securité. *Baluki*.

9

New Approaches to City–Countryside Relations

9.1. Introduction

City–countryside relations have long been one of the key themes of geographers' research, both in the tradition of Vidal de la Blache, which emphasizes functional solidarities between territories, and in works of spatial analysis that focus on the search for regularities in the distribution of people and activities as well as on the identification of poles and gradients in the organization of space and its use.

For several decades, the accentuation of globalization and metropolization has seemed to call these approaches into question. For some authors (Lussault 2013; Brenner 2014; Brenner and Schmid 2014; Lussault 2016), generalized urbanization would erase the boundaries between town and country in terms of lifestyles and consumption patterns, and the location of jobs and services, rendering this classic dichotomy obsolete[1]. More and more rural dwellers regularly travel to the city for work and shopping, with the development of motorized mobility, in the North as in the South (Lombard and Ninot 2010, 2012; Ninot and Sakho 2021), allowing for income diversification strategies in the South (Tacoli 2002). Technological revolutions in the movement of people, goods and information are leading to a

Chapter written by Martine BERGER and Jean-Louis CHALÉARD.

1 The terms city and countryside designate socio-spatial combinations defined both by dominant land-use patterns (the respective shares of built-up areas and open spaces) and by levels of housing and employment density. It is also by these terms that people generally describe the places they live in or frequent. These concepts are therefore richer and more comprehensive than those of urban versus rural, which refer rather to statistical distinctions between types of space (which vary from state to state) or to differences in lifestyles (types of activities, distance to facilities and services).

widening of the scales of flows and exchanges, between territories, economies and societies that are increasingly connected to each other and to international networks driven by global cities whose growth is accelerating.

Of course, the debate on the relative erasure of differences and the emergence of new types of relations between cities and the countryside is not new. This is evidenced by the questions raised by sociologists and geographers during the colloquium "Cities and Countryside. Urban and Rural Civilization in France" organized in 1951 by the Centre d'études sociologiques (Friedmann 1953), in a context of accelerating rural exodus in France and in many European countries, or the debates on the urbanization of the countryside (Juillard 1961, 1973). From then onwards, misunderstandings often linked to different territories of reference depending on the authors, as well as frequent confusion between social, societal and spatial approaches contributed to obscure the debates and multiply the controversies (Mathieu 2017). But the recent evolution of global urbanization – signaling, for some authors, the passage to an "urban age" – and the growing concentration of powers, economic functions and populations in large urban regions, in the North as well as in the South, require us to reexamine the categories and theories, whether it is a question of interrogating the urban/rural dichotomy, or of the nature, frequency and scales of the relations between cities and the countryside.

Within the UMR Prodig, the diversity of fields and experiences of researchers and doctoral students has allowed for comparative approaches between countries of the North and South, mainly in the context of seminars and conferences organized with the support of the Labex DynamiTe or the GIS CIST, particularly during international conferences or seminars: "*Dynamiques des périphéries des métropoles des Suds*" (Dynamics of the Peripheries of the Metropolises of the South) (Paris 2012), "*Villes et campagnes en relations. Regards croisés Nords-Suds*" (Cities and Countryside in Symbiosis. North-South Perspectives) (Paris 2015), "*Crise des modèles? Agricultures, recompositions territoriales et nouvelles relations villes-campagnes*" (Model Crisis? Agriculture, Territorial Restructuring and New City–Countryside Relations) (Tunis 2017) and "*Des espaces ruraux face aux métropoles: l'apport de comparaisons Nords-Suds*" (Rural Spaces Facing Metropolises: the Contribution of North-South Comparisons) (Abidjan 2019)[2].

The reflections, nourished both by the work carried out within the UMR Prodig and by exchanges with researchers from other teams, have highlighted similarities

---

2 These meetings were the subject of publications: *Métropoles aux Suds, le défi des périphéries?* (Chaléard 2014); *Villes et campagnes en relations, regards croisés Nords-Suds* (Berger and Chaléard 2017); *Crise des modèles? Agricultures, recompositions territoriales et nouvelles relations villes-campagnes* (Berger et al. 2021); *Des espaces ruraux face aux métropoles. Actes du séminaire international d'Abidjan, 12-13-14 Novembre 2019* (Koffi-Didia et al. 2021).

and differences in the forms and processes observed in different territorial contexts and at different scales. They have contributed to new approaches to city–countryside contact, as well as to proximity relations through the analysis of peripheral urban sprawl and peri-urbanization, and finally to new food links between city and countryside with the rise of locavorism. They have shown the changes in the nature and scale of migratory exchanges, economic and monetary flows, service relationships and the effects of urban demand on agricultural production systems. They have also highlighted the effects of global changes in the representations of the city and the countryside, their respective functions and the emergence of sustainability concerns, questioning the links between development and the environment and the potential contradictions at different scales.

This chapter proposes a reflection based on a review of the state of the art of research, mainly based on French-speaking works. In the English language field, where the thematic segmentation of research is older and now well established, there are few works that tackle head-on, in an empirical manner, the recent evocation of relations between cities and the countryside. Few authors today position themselves at the interface between urban studies and rural studies, and even within these two fields, thematic specializations are strong. In Latin America, many works published in Spanish are not easily accessible and have not been used here. However, regardless of the language used, recurrent debates have emerged, showing important convergences between authors from different backgrounds and disciplines. Indeed, while we have mainly mobilized the work of geographers, we have taken into account the contributions of sociologists and anthropologists (on social change), economists (on monetary transfers, for example) and demographers (on migration, in particular), who have fed the debates on the relationship between cities and the countryside. Whether or not they have been carried out within multidisciplinary frameworks, this research, which sometimes compares the views of rural specialists with those of urban specialists, makes it possible to advance our understanding of interactions and solidarity between territories, by providing the empirical and theoretical insights needed on the relationships between the environment and development.

9.2. The city–countryside contact: front or transition zone, urban periphery and peri-urban spaces

For a long time, the question of contact between town and country was almost exclusively considered from the point of view of urban sprawl: the city consumes agricultural land or sterilizes it in waiting situations, urban metamorphism and the disappearance of agricultural land being considered as ineluctable and irreversible. The morphologies of the contact zones have now changed, the categories have been enriched and the view of the outskirts of the cities in the North as in the South puts forward processes of hybridization and new forms of transactions.

Peri-urban belts, organized in rings and sectors, have been created in developed countries with a long history of urbanization, where the growth of a large middle class has fueled a significant demand for suburban home ownership, likely to meet the desire for larger homes that are unaffordable in the city given the level of land and property prices. With the rise in power of these solvent middle classes in emerging countries, certain models are spreading, in particular that of closed suburban neighborhoods. But the spatial arrangements and social neighborhoods on the outskirts of cities refer to inherited rural patterns and to the conditions of urban production specific to each country or even to each region.

9.2.1. In the North, the emergence of a "third space": the peri-urban

The development of peri-urban rings around cities in the North has been made possible by automobile mobility, which allows residential de-densification, the distance between home and places of work, services and shopping. The explosion in household automobile ownership occurred at different times in different countries: France has had half a century of peri-urbanization, the United States nearly a century of loose suburbanization, while in England, the old model of rural residence for the upper class led to a rurbanization of the middle class when the metropolises surrounded themselves with green belts[3].

In France, where there is a tradition of dense urbanization of both suburbs and city centers, peri-urbanization, which began in the 1960s, has undergone successive inflections in its rhythms, clientele and representations of the contact between city and countryside (Poulot et al. 2016; Berger et al. 2017; Berger 2021). We can thus identify the passage from a first peri-urban age – in which the peri-urban rings are first considered as residential annexes of nearby urban centers, obscuring the place

---

3 The terms peri-urbanization, suburbanization and rurbanization, used to describe recent forms of urban sprawl linked to the spread of the automobile, refer to morphologies, distributions of population centres and administrative structures that differ from country to country. In France, the term peri-urbanization is the most commonly used: it has been statistically defined by INSEE and refers to a medium-density area combining village cores, housing estates and open spaces on the outskirts of urban areas. In the North American literature, the term *outer suburbs* or *postsuburbia* is used to describe the most recent and least dense clusters of suburban housing developments within large urban areas. In Great Britain, following the work of R.E. Pahl on the rural–urban continuum, the term *rurban* is the most widely used, the British *rurban belts* being similar to the *couronnes périurbaines* of the French terminology. On the difficulties of a term-by-term comparison between these different forms of urban sprawl (see Le Goix (2017)).

that open spaces hold there – to a strong valorization of rural landscapes and old village buildings in the vicinity of cities.

Thus, in the 1970s and 1980s, at the height of the wave of new construction in the inner suburbs, the households that moved there rarely put the search for a rural setting first, even though they appreciated a more airy local environment and lower density. The supply of peri-urban housing is perceived as opening up new possibilities, without there being a real desire to leave the city. From the 1990s onwards, there was a gradual promotion of the city-country, the city-nature (Poulot 2013): households moving to the peri-urban area increasingly favored its landscape qualities. In this evolution of the peri-urban model, part of it is due to a change in paradigms concerning the rural spaces and the urban spaces, with the rise of environmental issues; another part is due to the evolution of the origins of peri-urbanites and their practices. They have been living there for a longer period of time and have come to know and appreciate the rural environment, which plays an increasing role in their leisure activities. Recent movers are more likely to come from the fringes of urban areas, from the suburbs, or even from other peri-urban communes, rather than from the city centers.

While the media often broadcast a very negative image of "ugly" spaces (de Jarcy and Rémy 2010), of standardized constructions that can be reproduced ad infinitum (Billard and Brennetot 2009), of a crumbling model of urbanization highly consuming of land and energy, peri-urban spaces respond to aspirations for a less dense city that allows for the right distance to be maintained between neighbors (Jaillet 2004): their inhabitants appreciate being both outside the city, in a more natural space and close to the city, within reach of its jobs and services. Over time, the peri-urban area has become denser and has acquired a spatial and social complexity through the diversification of its populations. In the late 1990s, a hybrid category between rural and urban spaces was identified, a third space, according to M. Vanier (2000), or a *Zwischenstadt*, according to T. Sieverts (2001).

Peripheral open spaces are increasingly seen as necessary breathing space for the city. Peri-urban farms are no longer simply a means of protecting territories by closing them to urbanization, but are regaining a role in supplying nearby cities, justifying the implementation of agri-urban programs (Poulot 2014, 2021). The edges, interfaces that have long been considered as degraded boundaries between town and country, where abandoned spaces, wastelands and illegal dumping are multiplying, are the object of requalification operations to reconnect a territory perceived as fragmented (Aragau and Toublanc 2020). These developments reflect the maturation of peri-urban spaces where multiple initiatives from groups of residents and local authorities are emerging, giving rise to new planning practices and procedures. They mainly concern the first suburban rings, the most valued and closest to the cities, where the middle and upper classes are most present.

9.2.2. *In the South: the rapid growth of increasingly vast and socially diversified peripheries*

The explosion of urbanization is accompanied, in emerging and developing countries, by an often spectacular sprawl of the transition zone between town and country, which nevertheless retains its role as a reception area for recently immigrated populations, often of rural origin, waiting to integrate into the urban labor market and to find housing in the formal city. But at the same time as poor populations are being pushed out of city centers undergoing renovation and gentrification, the urban peripheries are welcoming new solvent middle classes in search of more comfortable housing, anxious to establish their social ascendancy on the back of home ownership (Yapi-Diahou et al. 2014). The phenomenon can spread far and wide, as in Mexico City (Martinez Borrego et al. 2015). Thus, in these peripheries, there remains a poor population, generally made up of recent migrants who live in precarious housing areas, contrasting with middle-class housing estates and well-to-do neighborhoods that are often gated. The extent of social inequalities, the rapidity of land use changes and the ups and downs of urban transition accentuate fragmentation and discontinuities (Dubresson 2014; Goldblum 2014; Prévôt-Schapira 2014).

The situations vary greatly from case to case. Latin American metropolises, notably Mexico City, are marked by the importance of population spillovers that shape extensive poor peripheries. In South and East Asia, population densities and forms of urban growth are leading to the emergence of specific configurations born of the rapid expansion of cities of all sizes. Thus, T. McGee (1991) analyzes what he calls *desakotas*, spaces where cities and densely populated countryside are closely intermingled around large metropolises, which are both vast urban peripheries and rural–urban regions.

In the South as in the North, the morphological and social diversity of the contact zones between town and country is increasing. If the cross-fertilization of views proves fruitful, can we go further in the comparisons? With regard to the cities of the South, it seems more justified today to speak of a vast transition zone, rather than a consolidated peri-urban space hosting a broad spectrum of households with the capacity to invest in housing – to build up savings to access property, to have formal income to take on debt over the long-term – and also to assume the costs of daily mobility. Large nuclei of solvent middle classes already exist in the metropolises of emerging countries, but even more than in the North (where they benefit from the social safety net), crises threaten their jobs, putting a brake on investment by developers (Yapi-Diahou et al. 2014). In the countries most dependent on raw material exports, price fluctuations reduce the capacity of governments to finance policies to support housing for the salaried middle classes, as well as to provide networks and to serve the peripheries (Musil et al. 2014).

The time lag also places the outskirts of cities in the South in a different energy context, with the search for denser morphologies to reduce motorized travel, to save land in a concern for food self-sufficiency, and to maintain agricultural activity as a source of employment (Mesclier et al. 2014). The New Urbanism model prevails more often in the new gated communities on the outskirts of Hanoi, Cape Town or Johannesburg, in the face of rising land costs and the concern of not consuming too much agricultural land: taller buildings (semi-collective), more often joined together, as well as few private or small gardens (Berger 2018). While the valorization of a city–countryside mix by the peri-urbanites of the North is based on the rediscovery of a largely mythologized countryside, nostalgia for the countryside has little to do with the city dwellers of the South, who have more recently come from a rural and agricultural world often equated with archaism and poverty. Agricultural work, which is still very present in the urban fringes, often mobilizes specific groups, from natives to migrants from further afield.

9.2.3. *Reviving or strengthening the agricultural belts around cities in the North and in the South*

In the countries of the North, after the quasi-disappearance of market gardening belts, cities of all sizes are taking a new look at the surrounding agricultural areas, not only as green spaces that are the lungs of the city, for which agricultural workers would be inexpensive managers, and also for their food production, in order to secure access for city dwellers to a high-quality supply. The success of the AMAPs, a movement in favor of locavorism that opposes the agro-industrial productivist model, attests to the value of local food networks. The desire to build new relationships between city dwellers and agriculture (Lardon and Loudiyi 2014; Le Caro et al. 2016) is expressed in numerous initiatives carried out at the local level by cities concerned with implementing territorial food strategies such as in the Île-de-France region (Poulot 2021) as well as in Lille and Nantes (Margetic et al. 2016) or intermediate cities such as Montpellier and Perpignan (Perrin et al. 2016) or Millau and Amiens (Baysse-Lainé et al. 2018). Supported by local government subsidies, these often very small, highly labor-intensive farms do not always provide remuneration to ensure their medium-term viability, and often mobilize a marginal workforce. Their integration into project territories does not make the traditional conflicts used in the peri-urban countryside disappear: protecting the environment by reducing the use of phytosanitary products, organizing the compatibility of rhythms and vehicle routes and having the owners of potentially buildable land accept a reduction in its value.

The conditions are more favorable a priori in the South: less expensive land, land ownership that is not always identified and registered, even though customary chiefs seek to take advantage of their role as managers of family assets, work that is often informal and poorly remunerated given underemployment and high demand, and a tradition of intra-urban agriculture (at least in Africa). In peri-urban areas where tenure is often poorly defined and land conflicts frequent, agricultural development can be a strategy for accessing land in different ways: in Yaoundé, it allows for long-term occupation of land before giving way to real-estate construction (Ndock Ndock 2020). In spite of the advancing urban sprawl, agriculture still occupies a large place on the periphery. It is shifting rather than shrinking, with farmers giving up their plots to developers so as to farm further away, as in Lima (Leloup 2021). It is also adapting, as in the North, by moving towards better quality and organic production to meet the demand of the wealthy classes (Moustier and Danso 2006). Some production is destined for the local market: market gardening almost everywhere, cassava as around Abidjan (Koffi 2007), rice near Ziguinchor (Diedhiou 2020), etc. But other productions have more distant destinations. Indeed, metropolises are ports or benefit from the presence of international airports, so that market gardening, fruit or flower crops are developed for the markets of the North. In addition, agriculture appears to be a means of urban integration for migrants in many cases, whether in Buenos Aires in Latin America (Le Gall 2011) or in Karthoum in Africa (Franck 2006), which contributes to its dynamism.

In the North as in the South, the agricultural belts can only cover a small part of the food needs of cities, whose supply areas are organized on regional, macro-regional and global scales.

9.3. New scales at play in the systems of relations between cities and the countryside

Migration and food supply systems have long been organized primarily in regional and national contexts. With the acceleration of globalization and metropolization, relations between cities and the countryside are becoming increasingly complex and interconnected, combining scales that range from local to international. The development of long-distance flows, both material and immaterial, does not always imply, however, a retreat from local relationships.

9.3.1. Agricultural countryside in the age of dominant urbanization

In the North, alongside a recent revival of interest in local food basins as a guarantee of quality, there is a growing disconnection between agricultural production systems, whose markets are increasingly globalized, and the economic dynamics of nearby cities. The knock-on effects within regional systems have been considerably reduced with the decline in the role of cities in the marketing of local agricultural production and the decline in urban land ownership in the countryside.

In the South, urban growth has allowed for the development of "market food crops" to feed the cities, which are grown in association or in competition with the export crops that previously provided most of the monetary income of farms (Chaléard 1996). This evolution has many consequences within rural societies, even modifying production and social relations (Guyer 1997). In addition, in a more general sense, the most dynamic countryside is often linked to cities that are themselves dynamic. Conversely, the crisis that affects certain rural regions marked by exodus is reflected by difficulties in local centers where activities are reduced. In active regions, such as the plantation regions (coffee or cocoa in particular) in sub-Saharan Africa, the cities, places of exchange and services, benefit from the growth of cash crops, while the countryside benefits in return from urban infrastructures (shops, administrations, banks, etc.) and from the needs of the cities for food, favoring the growth of production for urban markets (Chaléard and Dubresson 1999). In the context of globalization, however, these relationships are changing, with city–countryside dynamics increasingly becoming a part of both local and globalized relationships, with, for example, the weight of global markets on agriculture or industry, which can skip the intermediate urban levels or use them as relays (Agergaard et al. 2009).

The growing demand for agricultural commodities in the North makes export agriculture very profitable, within the framework of large agro-industrial operations. This is partly why, in many countries of the South, investments in land by city dwellers are developing, especially in regions where relative equality of land ownership prevailed. In Latin America, where agrarian reforms had led to a redistribution of land, we have seen, for example, in Peru since the 1990s, a liberalization that has allowed large companies and the urban bourgeoisie to acquire former cooperatives or land reclaimed from the desert (Chaléard and Marshall 2015). In West Africa, land acquisitions by urban dwellers are emerging, particularly in rubber plantation areas, such as in Côte d'Ivoire and Ghana (Ruf et al. 2014; Chaléard 2021). This new phenomenon in regions where small-scale indigenous or native village farming still dominates is leading to an increase in land tenure tensions.

9.3.2. *From rural exodus migrations to daily and circular mobility*

In the North, the often massive rural exodus triggered in the 19th century by the industrialization of cities has been followed by a short-range residential exurbanization movement from urban centers to their peri-urban cores. Even though agricultural and para-agricultural jobs, and, more broadly, rural employment, continue to decline, access to the urban labor market is becoming possible for motorized households (and more and more often two-motorized), new houses are built in villages, and old ones are renovated, keeping rural people in place. It is no longer necessary for them to move to work in the city, and it becomes natural for urban dwellers to move to the countryside to improve their housing conditions, especially since many jobs are moving to activity zones on the outskirts of cities. In times of economic or health crises, the attractiveness of rural areas can be reinforced: sometimes depopulated and landlocked countryside offers empty and inexpensive housing and employment opportunities, attracting a wide range of migrants, both regional and international (Tommasi 2017); sometimes the aspiration to a more natural environment and/or the soaring prices in the heart of metropolises pushes a greater number of households to the peri-urban fringes or to more distant rural areas. These gentrification processes have been extensively documented in the British countryside (Smith and Phillips 2001; Phillips 2005, 2007) and are now the subject of comparative research (Philipps 2010; Phillips and Smith 2018). In the face of increasing demand, rural supply is becoming more expensive, both for primary residences and for leisure and tourist accommodation (Tommasi et al. 2017).

Residential migration flows between cities and the countryside are being reversed and becoming more complex as a function of age and professional position. However, the balances of these movements are now very low, at a time when the vast majority of the population is urban. Thus, in metropolitan France, in 2014, 2/3 of inter-municipal migrations[4] were movements within urban areas or between urban units. In terms of population, the flows from cities to the countryside outweighed the departures from rural to urban areas (14 and 12.4 percent of migrants, respectively). In both directions, one-third of these movements take place within the same urban area, from the urban center to its peri-urban rings and vice versa, and also within peri-urban areas that include both rural communities and small or medium-sized cities[5]. While half of the new inhabitants of the peri-urban area come from urban centers, exchanges within the peri-urban belts, between rural communes and urban cores, are almost balanced. More than half of the residential mobility between rural communes is concentrated in the peri-urban cores of the major urban centers[6].

The ease and relatively low cost of travel leads to longer commutes and the concentration of jobs in the largest urban centers, to the detriment of small- and

---

4 Population one year or older who moved by changing municipalities in the year prior to the census (2012–2016, by municipality or neighborhood).

5 The peri-urban rings of an urban center (an urban unit with at least 1,500 jobs) are defined by INSEE as all the municipalities in which at least 40 percent of the resident population with jobs works in the center or in municipalities attracted by it. Small- or medium-sized urban units whose working population is strongly attracted by a large neighboring urban center (Rambouillet or Fontainebleau, for example, in the Île-de-France region) are thus considered peri-urban.

6 These are clusters with 10,000 or more jobs.

medium-sized cities, which often lose population, jobs and facilities: *shrinking cities* are not only former industrial cities or suburbs (Fol and Cunningham-Sabot 2010; Wolff et al. 2013). Their residents have lower living standards on average than neighboring rural residents (Floch 2014), who have often left these shrinking cities to become homeowners in the suburbs.

In the South, migration has not systematically emptied the countryside due to high natural growth rates and complex movements between metropolises, small towns and the countryside. Urbanization is progressing through natural growth and migration, but without the rural population decreasing, except in a few cases, such as in Brazil since the 1970s. In sub-Saharan Africa, the rural population even increased fourfold between 1950 and 2020. We are also witnessing the return of retired people or, in times of crisis, young unemployed people who return to the countryside where they can ensure subsistence. However, the return movements benefit large villages more as they have a certain level of equipment. The small villages are under-equipped.

The large scale of international migration leads us to also consider the links between rural spaces in the South and the metropolises of the North (Faret and Cortes 2019). Research on Senegalese or Malian migrants in Europe (Lima 2010) or on Ecuadorian migrants in the United States (Rebai 2013) and Bolivians in Argentina (Vassas Toral 2014) highlights complex strategies, between investments in local cities and the village of origin. At the same time, international migration contributes to social-spatial rearrangements: the metropolises of the North may have a greater influence on the destiny of rural spaces from which migrants originate than local cities; isolated countryside may be more transformed by migration than the countryside close to cities.

In the face of the rapidity and brutality of population transfers between cities and rural areas linked to urbanization in the South, rural migrants, whether nationals or immigrants, often remain underpaid neo-citizens, under-integrated into the cities. But in some rural areas, the relative enrichment of groups of farmers who better educate their children (especially in regions with small plantations) may allow for the gradual creation of a more educated generation that can integrate more easily into urban society (Chaléard and Dubresson 1999).

9.3.3. Inequalities and/or solidarities between cities and the countryside: "metropolises" versus "territories"

The theme of inequality of opportunity, of the abandonment of the countryside and rural people in favor of urban dwellers who are closer to the powers that be and have more and better facilities and services, is a leitmotif of political and media discourse that recent research by geographers and economists has largely helped to qualify.

In the North, many political actors, especially among rural elected officials, often invoke the work of Guilluy (2014) to highlight a territorial divide between metropolises polarizing large urban areas, where the economic elites are concentrated, and the countryside and small peri-urban towns, described as abandoned by a central state drastically reducing public services in the least dense areas. The expression of a feeling of downgrading and relegation, of inequality of opportunity in particular in terms of access to training and jobs, in France predates the yellow vest movement of winter 2018–2019, which reactivated debates around spatial justice and territorial equality. On the side of the central state, we observe the creation in 2014 of a General Commission for Territorial Equality, a Ministry of Territorial Cohesion in 2017 and a National Agency for Territorial Cohesion in 2019, which highlight the issue of accessibility to jobs and basic services, and its cost for the inhabitants of less dense territories.

For their part, most researchers reject the idea of a divide between "metropolises" and "territories" and insist on the existence of solidarities at different scales. Economists, such as Laurent Davezies and Magali Talandier (2014), insist on the importance of transfers and redistribution of income to the countryside, of the salaries of rural commuters working in cities or of the contribution of secondary residents and urban retirees living in the countryside. Geographers and planners are more interested in lifestyles and daily travel systems as indicators of urban–rural solidarity, through the notion of living areas that often reactivate countries. Pierre Veltz (2019) speaks of a "local turn" in reaction to the effects of globalization, with a strong demand for anchoring in proximity, and local initiatives valuing the complementarities between cities and the countryside. In France, the deconcentration of industrial jobs to the suburbs (which have taken in a quarter of the industrial jobs created over the last 10 years) strengthens the solidarity between small- and medium-sized urban centers and the surrounding rural areas. Each crisis brings its share of "reterritorialization" projects to bring about the emergence of "new ruralities".

In the South, until the 1980s, studies focused on the urban "bias" that translates into the exploitation of the countryside for the benefit of cities theorized by Lipton (Lipton 1977). Since then, authors have insisted on the complexity of the links between cities and the countryside (Chaléard and Dubresson 1989; Baker 1997; Chaléard and Dubresson 1999; Tacoli 2002, 2011; Chaléard 2017).

In Africa, we observe a tightening of the links between cities and the countryside (Ninot and Sakho 2021): with the opening up of the countryside, rural dwellers generally see their living conditions improve, but cities concentrate economic opportunities and services, resulting in a relationship of dependence. Households are seeking to diversify their sources of income through rural–urban complementarities, to take advantage of economic opportunities by having "one foot in, one foot out" (Chaléard and Dubresson 1989). An economist such as Philippe Hugon (2013) has shown the importance of public and private transfers from cities to the countryside in Africa. Urbanization takes place "from below", with large villages growing into small towns and retaining forms of rural life. New configurations are emerging (Losch et al. 2013). Cities and the countryside appear to be linked within territories, around small service centers, spreading out along the axes that connect them to the metropolises, giving rise to a new rurality and new city–countryside links. The role of small towns, places of proximity services for rural people, thus appears to be an essential element in the evolution of relations between cities and the countryside, as shown by the African case (Agergaard et al. 2019). In addition to the short-circuiting of certain proximity relations by the widespread diffusion of mobile telephone and virtual exchanges, we observe concentration effects in certain sectors where the densification of the population allows the development of services that meet a more regular demand from populations whose disenfranchisement has increased their monetary resources. The trajectories are, however, highly variable and the relationships of unequal intensity, depending on the location and the social situation of the individuals. And while an urban–rural continuum has been observed, in many cases, there are now breaks in this continuum (Charlery de la Masselière et al. 2020).

In the North as in the South, the question of inequality and spatial injustice cannot be limited to an opposition between cities that are well endowed by States and abandoned countrysides. The fact remains that different levels of population density are reflected in the distribution of public and private facilities and services, whether in terms of education or access to health care. Accessibility to services depends on the mobility possibilities linked to a transport offer that is itself unequal between cities and the countryside and in terms of the individual resources of households. Rural transport is less profitable, given the dispersion (and sometimes the lower solvency) of demand, and the individual forms of mobility that compensate for a deficient supply are all the more costly as the distances to be covered are greater, in a context of lower density. However, the explosion in mobility, which increases the frequency of contact between rural people and the urban world(s), contributes to transforming the representations and feelings of territorial belonging.

9.4. Conclusion

The analysis of city–countryside relations mobilizes a wide variety of thematic and disciplinary fields, relying on approaches whose different scales and methodologies make it difficult to construct a cumulative knowledge. The comparison between the North and the South, however, highlights similarities in the evolution of relations between cities and the countryside: the return or maintenance of agriculture and food preoccupations, the increasing complexity of flow systems, the growing perception of inequalities that are not only linked to different forms of distribution (concentrated/dispersed) of populations and activities, but also to the unequal powers of actors. Comparative approaches highlight very different regimes of urban–rural relations according to the context, and a diversity of processes, which refer to specific trajectories according to the country or even the region. They also highlight representations of the urban and rural environments that vary according to the experiences and life paths of individuals, who are increasingly "autonomous".

Faced with the acceleration of urbanization in recent decades, particularly in the South, of the globalization of trade and of metropolization, there is a need to revise the approach to relations between cities and the countryside, and to change and diversify the methods of analysis. But generalized urbanization does not erase the differences between urban and rural areas. Firstly, in the modes of occupation of space at the local level, where it can still be seen in the landscapes and persists in the representations of the inhabitants, even though the development of peri-urban rings complicates the nature of the contacts. Secondly, in the organization of space at the regional and supra-regional levels, with patterns combining short- and medium-term relationships with inter-regional and international exchanges. Relationships between rural areas and cities are less and less often based on simple regional solidarity, whether it be in terms of daily travel, of migration or in the flow of goods or information.

However, there is a tendency, accentuated by crises of various kinds, to revive or strengthen links of proximity, whether it is a question of forms of re-territorialization of agriculture to ensure better food security and/or quality, or a return, in terms of territorial planning, to a (re-)development of small- and medium-sized cities, so as to ensure a distribution of services more concerned with territorial equity. The growing recognition of environmental values, reinforced by the recent health crisis that questions the advantages of metropolitan areas, is leading to a revaluation of the rural environment, as a place of residence and leisure for city dwellers, and also of production, whether in terms of its nutritional functions or of new forms of integration into industrial value chains. The reflection on the necessary solidarities and the scope of exchanges between cities and the countryside is particularly necessary at a time when the growth of territorial inequalities and the need for systemic approaches to strengthen the links between the environment and development are being highlighted.

9.5. References

Agergaard, J., Fold, N., Gough, K. (eds) (2009). *Livelihoods, Mobility and Markets in African and Asian Frontiers*. Routledge, London.

Agergaard, J., Tacoli, C., Griet, S., Ørtenblad, S.B. (2019). Revisiting rural-urban transformations and small town development in sub-saharian Africa. *The European Journal of Development Research*, 31(1), 2–11 [Online]. Available at: https://doi.org/10. 1057/s41287-018-0182-z.

Aragau, C. and Toublanc, M. (2020). La lisière : Un outil de la fabrique agriurbaine. Lecture francilienne. *Territoire en mouvement. Revue de géographie et aménagement*, 44–45 [Online]. Available at: http://journals.openedition.org/tem/6334.

Baker, J. (eds) (1997). *Rural-Urban Dynamics in Francophone Africa*. Nordiska Afrikainstitutet, Uppsala.

Baysse-Lainé, A., Perrin, C., Delfosse, C. (2018). Le nouvel intérêt des villes intermédiaires pour les terres agricoles : Actions foncières et relocalisation alimentaire. *Géocarrefour*, 92(4) [Online]. Available at: http://journals.openedition.org/geocarrefour/10417.

Berger, M. (2017). Les relations villes-campagnes côté Nords. In *Villes et campagnes en relations. Regards croisés Nords-Suds*, Berger, M. and Chaléard, J.-L. (eds). Karthala, Paris.

Berger, M. (2018). Des marges aux périphéries et au périurbain. Regards croisés Nords-Suds. In *Tropiques, développement et mondialisation. Hommages à Jean-Louis Chaléard*, Sanjuan, T., Lesourd, M., Tallet, B. (eds). L'Harmattan, Paris.

Berger, M. (2021). Vers une "re-ruralisation" du périurbain ? L'exemple de l'ouest francilien. In *Crise des modèles ? Agricultures, recompositions territoriales et nouvelles relations villes-campagnes*, Berger, M., Chaléard, J.-L., Gana, A. (eds). Grafigéo, Publications de l'UMR Prodig, Paris.

Berger, M. and Chaléard, J.-L. (eds) (2017). *Villes et campagnes en relations. Regards croisés Nords-Suds*. Karthala, Paris.

Berger, M., Poulot, M., Rougé, L., Aragau, C. (2017). Réinterroger les contours et les contacts entre ville et campagne dans l'Ouest francilien. In *Villes et campagnes en relations. Regards croisés Nords-Suds*, Berger, M. and Chaléard, J.-L. (eds). Karthala, Paris.

Berger, M., Chaléard, J.-L., Gana, A. (eds) (2021). *Crise des modèles ? Agricultures, recompositions territoriales et nouvelles relations villes-campagnes*. Grafigéo, Publications de l'UMR Prodig, Paris.

Billard, G. and Brennetot, A. (2009). Le périurbain a-t-il mauvaise presse ? *Articulo, Journal of Urban Research* [Online]. Available at: https://doi.org/10.4000/articulo.1372.

Brenner, N. (ed.) (2014). *Implosions/Explosions. Towards a Study of Planetary Urbanization*. Jovis, Berlin.

Brenner, N. and Schmid, C. (2014). The "Urban Age" in question. *International Journal of Urban and Regional Research*, 38(3), 731–755.

Chaléard, J.-L. (1996). *Temps des villes, temps des vivres. L'essor du vivrier marchand en Côte d'Ivoire*. Karthala, Paris.

Chaléard, J.-L. (eds) (2014). *Métropoles aux Suds, le défi des périphéries ?* L'Harmattan, Paris.

Chaléard, J.-L. (2017). Les relations villes-campagnes côté Suds. In *Villes et campagnes en relations. Regards croisés Nords-Suds*, Berger, M. and Chaléard, J.-L. (eds). Karthala, Paris.

Chaléard, J.-L. (2021). Une nouvelle ruralité dans le sud-est de la Côte d'Ivoire ? In *Crise des modèles ? Agricultures, recompositions territoriales et nouvelles relations villes-campagnes*, Berger, M., Chaléard, J.-L., Gana, A. (eds). Grafigéo, Publications de l'UMR Prodig, Paris.

Chaléard, J.-L. and Dubresson, A. (1989). Un pied dedans, un pied dehors : A propos du rural et de l'urbain en Côte d'Ivoire. In *Tropiques : Lieux et liens. Florilège offert à Paul Pélissier et Gilles Sautter*, Antheaume, B., Blanc-Pamard, C., Chaléard, J.-L., Dubresson, A., Lassailly-Jacob, V., Marchal, J.-Y., Pillet-Schwartz, A.-M., Pourtier, R., Raison, J.-P., Sevin, O. et al. (eds). ORSTOM, Paris.

Chaléard, J.-L. and Dubresson, A. (eds) (1999). *Villes et campagnes dans les pays du Sud. Géographie des relations*. Karthala, Paris.

Chaléard, J.-L. and Marshall, A. (2015). Nouvelles vulnérabilités et implantation des entreprises agro-industrielles sur le piémont côtier péruvien. *L'Espace Géographique*, 44(3), 245–258.

Charlery de la Masselière, B., Bart, F., Thibaud, B., Benos, R. (2020). Revisiting the rural-urban linkages in East Africa: Continuity or breakdown in the spatial model of rural development? *Belgeo* [Online]. Available at: http://journals.openedition.org/belgeo/38669 and https://doi.org/10.4000/belgeo.38669.

Davezies, L. and Talandier, M. (2014). *L'émergence des systèmes productivo-résidentiels. Territoires productifs-territoires résidentiels : Quelles interactions ?* CGET, La Documentation française, Paris.

Diedhiou, S.O. (2020). Agriculture et sécurité alimentaire à Ziguinchor (Sénégal). PhD Thesis, Université de Nantes/Université Assane Seck, Nantes/Ziguinchor.

Dubresson, A. (2013). Fragmentation urbaine des métropoles africaines ? In *Métropoles aux Suds, le défi des périphéries ?* Chaléard, J.-L. (ed.). Karthala, Paris.

Faret, O. and Cortes, G. (2019). Les relations villes-campagnes au regard des migrations internationales. Un modèle en rupture ? In *Tropiques, développement et mondialisation. Hommages à Jean-Louis Chaléard*, Sanjuan, T., Lesourd, M., Tallet, B. (eds). L'Harmattan, Paris.

Floch, J.-M. (2014). Des revenus élevés et en plus forte hausse dans les couronnes des grandes aires urbaines. In *France, portrait social*, INSEE, Paris, 69–81.

Fol, S. and Cunningham-Sabot, E. (2010). Déclin urbain et Shrinking Cities : Une évaluation critique des approches de la décroissance urbaine. *Annales de Géographie*, 674, 359–383.

Franck, A. (2006). Maraîchers à Karthoum : Entre intégration et marginalisation. *Revue Tiers Monde*, 185(47), 39–55.

Friedmann, G. (1953). *Villes et campagnes. Civilisation urbaine et civilisation rurale en France*. Armand Colin, Paris.

Goldblum, C. (2014). Configurations périphériques de la métropolisation asiatique : Essai de synthèse. In *Métropoles aux Suds, le défi des périphéries ?* Chaléard, J.-L. (ed.). Karthala, Paris.

Guilly, C. (2014). *La France périphérique : Comment on a sacrifié les classes populaires*. Flammarion, Paris.

Guyer, J.I. (1997). *An African Niche Economy. Farming to Feed Ibadan 1968–88*. Edinburgh University Press, Edinburgh.

Hugon, P. (2013). *L'économie de l'Afrique*. La Découverte, Paris.

Jaillet, M.-C. (2004). L'espace périurbain : Un univers pour les classes moyennes. *Esprit*, 3–4, 40–60.

de Jarcy, X. and Rémy, V. (2010). Comment la France est devenue moche. *Télérama* [Online]. Available at: https://www.telerama.fr/monde/comment-la-france-est-devenue-moche,52457.php.

Juillard, É. (1961). L'urbanisation des campagnes en Europe occidentale. *Études rurales*, 1, 18–33.

Juillard, É. (1973). Urbanisation des campagnes. *Études rurales*, 49–50, 5–9.

Koffi, A.M. (2007) Mutations sociales et gestion de l'espace rural en pays ébrié (Sud-Est de la Côte d'Ivoire). PhD Thesis, Université Paris 1 Panthéon-Sorbonne, Paris.

Koffi-Didia, A.M., Yassi, G.A., Pistre, P., Aragau, C. (2021). Des espaces ruraux face aux métropoles. Actes du séminaire international d'Abidjan, 12,13,14 November 2019. *Géotrope*, Special issue, 1–224.

Lardon, S. and Loudiyi, S. (2014). Agriculture et alimentation urbaines : Entre politiques publiques et initiatives locales. *Géocarrefour*, 89(1–2) [Online]. Available at: http://geocarrefour.revues.org/9362.

Le Caro, Y., Jousseaume, V., Poulot, M., Rouget, N. (2016). Agriculture et ville : Des articulations renouvelées. *Annales de Géographie*, 712, 553–563.

Le Gall, J. (2011). Buenos Aires maraîchère : Une Buenos Aires bolivienne ? Le complexe maraîcher de la Région métropolitaine à l'épreuve de nouveaux acteurs. Geography PhD Thesis, Université Paris 1 Panthéon-Sorbonne, Paris.

Le Goix, R. (2017). Some reflections on comparing (post-) suburbs in the United States and France. In *What's in a Name? Talking about Suburbs*, Harris, R. and Vorms, C. (eds). Toronto University Press, Toronto.

Leloup, H. (2021). Renouvellement des relations entre agriculture et ville à Lima métropole : Quel avenir pour les espaces verts d'une ville grise ? In *Crise des modèles ? Agricultures, recompositions territoriales et nouvelles relations villes-campagnes*, Berger, M., Chaléard, J.-L., Gana, A. (eds). Grafigéo, Publications de l'UMR Prodig, Paris.

Lima, S. (2010). Migration, décentralisation, développement dans la région de Kayes (Mali). *Hommes et Migrations*, 1286–1287, 258–267.

Lipton, M. (1977). *Why Poor People Stay Poor: Urban Bias in Developing Countries*. Temple Smith, London.

Lombard, J. and Ninot, O. (2010). Mobiles des Suds, mobiles au Sud. *Espace, populations, sociétés*, 2(3), 155–165.

Lombard, J. and Ninot, O. (2012). Des mobilités aux transports. Regards croisés en Afrique de l'Ouest. *EchoGéo*, 20 [Online]. Available at: http://journals.openedition.org/echogeo/13127.

Losch, B., Magrin, G., Imbernon, J. (eds) (2013). *Une nouvelle ruralité émergente. Regards croisés sur les transformations rurales africaines*. CIRAD, Montpellier.

Lussault, M. (2013). L'urbain s'étale. *Esprit*, 2013/3, 131–143.

Lussault, M. (2016). Le rural : De l'urbain qui s'ignore. *Tous urbains*, 14, 36–43.

Magrin, G. and Poulot, M. (2017). Les relations villes-campagnes : Un prisme d'analyse toujours efficace pour une géographie en renouvellement. In *Villes et campagnes en relations. Regards croisés Nords-Suds*, Berger, M. and Chaléard, J.-L. (eds). Karthala, Paris.

Margetic, C., Rouget, N., Schmitt, G. (2016). Le foncier agricole à l'épreuve de la multifonctionnalité : Desseins environnementaux et alimentaires dans les métropoles lilloise et nantaise. *Norois*, 241 [Online]. Available at: http://journals.openedition.org/norois/6012.

Martinez Borrego, E., Lorenzen Martiny, M., Salas Stevanato, A. (2015). *Reorganizacion del territorio y transformacion socioespacial rural-urban*. IISS and Bonilla Artigas Editores, Mexico.

Mathieu, N. (2017). *Les relations villes/campagnes. Histoire d'une question politique et scientifique*. L'Harmattan, Paris.

McGee, T.G. (1991). The emergence of desakota regions in Asia: Expanding a hypothesis. In *The Extended Metropolis – Settlement Transition in Asia*, Ginsburg, N., Koppel, B., McGee, T.G. (eds). University of Hawaii Press, Honolulu.

Mesclier, É., Chaléard, J.-L., Anh, D.T., Fanchette, S., Henriot, C., Hurtado, J.-R., Monin, É., Moustier, P., Yapi-Diahou, A. (2014). Les formes actuelles du recul des terres agricoles : Quels modèles pour quels enjeux ? Comparaison à partir de quatre métropoles. In *Métropoles aux Suds, le défi des périphéries ?*, Chaléard, J.-L. (ed.). Karthala, Paris.

Moustier, P. and Danso, G. (2006). Local economic development and marketing of urban produced food. In *Cities Farming for the Future: Urban Agriculture for Green and Productive Cities*, van Veenhuizen, R. (ed.). IIRR, Cavite.

Musil, C., Ninot, O., Baffi, S., Drevelle, M. (2014). Évolutions des systèmes de transport urbain en périphérie du Cap et de Hanoi. In *Métropoles aux Suds, le défi des périphéries ?* Chaléard, J.-L. (ed.). Karthala, Paris.

Ndock Ndock (2020). Cultiver d'abord et habiter après : L'agriculture périurbaine comme stratégie d'appropriation foncière dans l'arrière-pays de Yaoundé. *Territoire en mouvement. Revue de géographie et aménagement*, 44–45 [Online]. Available at: http://journals.openedition.org/tem/6257.

Ninot, O. and Sakho, P. (2021). Évolution des relations villes-campagnes en Afrique de l'Ouest : Une lecture à partir des circulations des personnes et des biens. In *Crise des modèles ? Agricultures, recompositions territoriales et nouvelles relations villes-campagnes*, Berger, M., Chaléard, J.-L., Gana, A. (eds). Grafigéo, Publications de l'UMR Prodig, Paris.

Perrin, C., Soulard, C., Chias, E. (2016). La gouvernance du foncier agricole périurbain : Entre planification urbaine et projets de développement. *Revue d'Économie Régionale & Urbaine*, 713–736 [Online]. Available at: http://www.cairn.info/revue-d-economie-regionale-et-urbaine-2016-4-page-713.htm.

Phillips, M. (2005). Differential productions of rural gentrification. *Geoforum*, 36(4), 477–494.

Phillips, M. (2007). Changing class complexions in and on the British countryside. *Journal of Rural Studies*, 23(3), 283–304.

Phillips, M. (2010). Counterurbanisation and rural gentrification: An exploration of the terms. *Population, Space and Place*, 16(6), 539–558.

Phillips, M. and Smith, D.P. (2018). Comparative approaches to gentrification. *Dialogues in Human Geography*, 8, 5–27.

Poulot, M. (2013). Du vert dans le périurbain. *Espacestemps.net* [Online]. Available at: http://www.espacestemps.net/articles/du-vert-dans-le-périurbain-les-espaces-ouverts-une-hybridation-de-lespace-public-2/.

Poulot, M. (2014). L'invention de l'agri-urbain en Île-de-France. Quand la ville se repense autour de l'agriculture. *Géocarrefour*, 89(1–2), 11–19.

Poulot, M. (2021). Les territoires agriurbains en Île-de-France. Modèle agricole ? Modèle urbain ? Nouveau modèle ? In *Crise des modèles ? Agricultures, recompositions territoriales et nouvelles relations villes-campagnes*, Berger, M., Chaléard, J.-L., Gana, A. (eds). Grafigéo, Publications de l'UMR Prodig, Paris.

Poulot, M., Aragau, C., Rougé, L. (2016). Les espaces ouverts dans le périurbain ouest francilien : Entre appropriations habitantes et constructions territoriales. *Géographie Économie Société*, 18, 81–104.

Prévot-Shapira, M.-F. (2014). Les villes du Sud dans la mondialisation. Des villes du "Tiers-monde" aux métropoles en émergence ? In *Métropoles aux Suds, le défi des périphéries ?* Chaléard, J.-L. (ed.). Karthala, Paris.

Rebaï, N. (2013). Quand l'argent de la migration change la donne : Développement agricole et dynamique foncière dans une localité de la province andine de l'Azuay (Équateur). *Autrepart*, 68, 193–212.

Ruf, F., Bini, S., Cursio, M. (2014). The rubber boom in Ghana; Success and impact of a diversification project. AFD report, UMR Innovation, Montpellier.

Sieverts, T. (2001). *Zwischenstadt, zwischen Ort und Welt, Raum und Zeit, Stadt und Land.* Birkhaüser Verlag, Basel.

Sieverts, T. (2004). *Entre-ville, une lecture de la Zwischenstadt.* Parenthèses, Marseille.

Smith, D.P. and Phillips, D.A. (2001). Socio-cultural representations of greentrified Pennine rurality. *Journal of Rural Studies*, 17(4), 457–469.

Tacoli, C. (2002). *Changing Rural-Urban Interactions in Sub-Saharan Africa and their Impact on Livelihood: A Summary.* IIED, London.

Tacoli, C. (2011). Links between rural and urban development in Africa and Asia. Paper, Population Distribution, Urbanization, Internal Migration and Development: An International Perspective. UNDESA, New York, 110–122.

Tommasi, G. (2017). Quelle ville, quelle campagne ? Pratiques et représentations des nouveaux habitants dans la Sierra de Albarracín. In *Villes et campagnes en relations. Regards croisés Nords-Suds*, Berger, M. and Chaléard, J.-L. (eds). Karthala, Paris.

Tommasi, G., Richard, F., Saumon, G. (2017). Le capital environnemental, nouvelle clé d'interprétation de la gentrification rurale ? *Norois*, 243, 89–110.

Vanier, M. (2000). Qu'est-ce que le tiers-espace ? *Revue de géographie alpine*, 88(1), 104–113.

Vassas Toral, A. (2014). *Partir et cultiver. Essor de la quinoa, mobilités et recompositions rurales en Bolivie.* IRD éditions, Paris.

Veltz, P. (2019). *La France des territoires, défis et promesses.* Éditions de L'Aube, La Tour-d'Aigues.

Wolff, M., Fol, S., Roth, H., Cunningham-Sabot, E. (2013). Shrinking Cities, villes en décroissance : Une mesure du phénomène en France. *Cybergeo: European Journal of Geography* [Online]. Available at: http://cybergeo.revues.org/26136.

Yapi-Diahou, A., Assi Yassi, G., Do Bi Tchan, A. (2014). Les classes moyennes dans les périphéries d'Abidjan. La clientèle des promoteurs dans des espaces en recomposition. In *Métropoles aux Suds, le défi des périphéries ?* Chaléard, J.-L. (ed.). Karthala, Paris.

10

Using Scientific Modeling for Adaptation of Agriculture to Climate Change: A Political and Organizational Challenge

10.1. Introduction

As the scientific community's work has progressed, it has become possible to model climate change on increasingly finer scales, which makes it possible to envisage adaptation policies adjusted to local situations, particularly in agriculture. Agriculture is based on localized production factors and is therefore particularly difficult to relocate. It is also considered to be a key sector for bringing about the necessary changes in response to the environmental degradation. Peasant societies in particular, because of their local presence and social cohesion, and because they "maintain direct relations with the living and with the territory […] seem, by their very nature, to be key actors in sustainable development" (Aubertin and Pinton 2006, p. 15). Indigenous and peasant knowledge is "called upon as a lever for saving the planet from famine and pollution and for confronting climate change" in numerous international agreements (Kleiche-Dray 2017, p. 5).

However, in practice, the adaptation of agriculture to climate change is mobilizing more diverse actors with more varied scales of action than just the peasantry: these include international bodies, agribusiness entrepreneurs, producers' unions, heads of state and ministers of the environment and agriculture, as well as mayors of rural municipalities and regional presidents. All of them, in the South and

---

Chapter written by Malika MADELIN and Évelyne MESCLIER.
Gérard Beltrando (1956–2016) participated in the Prodig Lab Seminar and contributed to the reflections in this chapter.

in the North, in the tropical rainforests as well as in the desert, express their willingness to act regarding climate change, providing an example of the awareness of the "global environment" that contributes to the unity of the "Global Space" (Dollfus 1994, p. 41). Behind this apparent consensus, however, lies the difficulty of articulating divergent interests, power relationships and social, geographical and environmental representations built over time, and very different levels of access to information. Thus, the scientific representation of climate change is linked to its local translation, to its social meaning, to human experience (Jasanoff 2010), not through a single path but through multiple channels.

To understand how a dynamic, both global and localized, is created, based on climate simulations provided by scientists and also on the perceptions, interests and organizational modes of other actors, we focus on the case of two countries: France, considered a "North" country, and Peru, which belongs to the "South". Both have participated for decades in international negotiations on climate change and have had an active role: Peru organized the COP20 (or 20th Conference of the Parties) in Lima in 2014, during which the Lima Call for Climate Action was approved, which paved the way for the signing of the Paris Agreement developed in France in 2015 at COP21 (MINAM 2015, p. 17). Agriculture is important to both, but with agricultural worlds with very different structures and very diverse places in society. Finally, while the issue of reducing the impacts of human activities on the climate concerns both countries very differently, the issue of adaptation is indeed part of their common concerns. The comparison is used here for heuristic purposes, in "a state of mind intended to shift the researcher's gaze" (Vigour 2005, p. 18), facilitating the identification of discrepancies and particularities. We use the fieldwork carried out with farmers, by other researchers and ourselves, as well as the documents drawn up by the States in the context of the dynamics of international meetings and the work of climatologists that serve as a basis for them.

In section 10.2, we show that models simulating climate change are becoming increasingly accurate, but not in the same way in Peru as in France, which has implications for their use. In section 10.3, we will see that States program adaptation policies also, and perhaps mainly, according to their perceptions of vulnerability, on the one hand, and their pre-existing modes of organization, on the other hand. In section 10.4, we will finally examine the channels through which scientific knowledge and its translation by public policies can be used by farmers who are themselves very diversely situated in societies and also diversely dependent on the State and other actors.

10.2. Unequal countries facing regionalized modeling

10.2.1. *The global evolution towards models with a greater spatial resolution*

The appropriation by societies of simulations of future climates depends in part on their characteristics and their presentation. In general, these simulations are based on models of the climate system, made from different scenarios of evolution of greenhouse gas (GHG) emissions/concentrations according to socio-economic projections, from the global scale to more regional scales and gathered by the IPCC (Intergovernmental Panel on Climate Change; see Chapter 13).

The predominance of a physicalist perspective and global scale in early IPCC reports (Aykut and Dahan 2015) has often been criticized as being distant from sensitive, local experiences and societal responses. The purpose of using global temperature as a reference indicator of climate change was, among other things, to "move policies along" around key figures (as expressed by H. Le Treut, at the International Geography Festival 2020). This having been said, this indicator does not necessarily allow decision-makers and farmers to imagine concrete strategies. Moreover, in 1990, the IPCC presented "the problem of climate change as a global one, i.e. a problem of global environmental limits, whereas most countries in the South already look at it as a problem of overconsumption in the North" (Aykut and Dahan 2015, p. 73). Gradually, however, the divergent interests between these groups of countries will lead to differentiation of expected commitments in terms of mitigation and to integrate adaptation into policy.

In order for societies to take measures to adapt, they need to predict changes on a scale that corresponds to their activities, often local in the case of agriculture. So-called "regional" simulations, which differentiate probable developments for each of the continents and also for zones within them, respond in part to this concern. They are based on dynamic climate modeling over limited geographical areas and/or on statistical modeling based on climate data (see Chapter 13). However, even though simulations have improved, the spatial resolution of current models remains too broad for impact studies, let alone adaptation studies (Beltrando 2010, 2015). For example, the maps of projected temperatures in South America proposed in the 5th IPCC report (IPCC 2013) are based on simulations with a resolution from 2.5° (~ 275 km at the equator) for the CMIP models (see Chapter 13) to 60 km for the Meteorological Research Institute (Japan) model.

10.2.2. *Inequalities with significant consequences in the production of local information*

While the IPCC coordinates continental-scale modeling projects (South America-Cordex, Euro-Cordex, etc.), simulations on national or finer scales are proposed by national organizations or research groups. In France, the "DRIAS, the future of climate" portal, hosted on the website of the Ministry of Ecological Transition, is supported by Météo France, The Institute Pierre Simon Laplace and the European Centre for Research and Advanced Training in Scientific Computing. It offers access to regionalized climate projections made by these same French climate modeling laboratories, in the form of maps in discovery mode, for the general public, or access to data, for experts/scientists. This portal is one of the "climate services[1]" offered at the national level. The DRIAS-2020 gathers simulations on a grid of 8 km resolution, after a statistical adaptation based on the outputs of several regional models (over Europe). The latter are forced at the lateral boundaries by several global climate models and according to different GHG concentration scenarios.

Similarly, Peru's National Meteorological and Hydrological Service (SENAMHI) develops climate projections at the sub-national level. It has produced temperature and precipitation projections for 2030 and 2050 for two of the 24 departments of the country, located in the Andes, Apurímac and Cusco, using "dynamic regionalization techniques with spatial resolution of 20 km and statistics of local resolution" (MINAM 2016, p. 145). Other projections, again using dynamic and statistical regionalization techniques, were made at various time horizons over several watersheds (MINAM 2016, p. 149). However, for other departments, projections to 2030 are based solely on the evaluation of the latest global models of the fifth phase of simulations (CMIP5) of 50 km horizontal resolution, without regionalization, and the authors of the report consider that the results for this last study "must be considered as an approximation, basically of trends, rather than of numerical values [...]" (MINAM 2016, p. 146). Furthermore, a map locating information at the sub-national scale clearly shows that for much of the national territory, no projections are available (MINAM 2016, p. 138).

In fact, while the regionalization techniques used in Peru and France seem very similar, the number of meteorological stations that produce the historical series is clearly less in Peru, which drastically limits the possibilities of developing regionalized simulations. Indeed, these long series are essential to calibrate and

---

1 "Climate services" are defined as "all information and services that make it possible to evaluate and qualify the past, present or future climate, to assess the vulnerability of economic activities, of environment and society to climate change and to provide elements for undertaking mitigation and adaptation measures" (AllEnvi 2014).

validate this spatial downscaling. In Peru, these simulations are based (SENAMHI 2014, p. 6) on 265 meteorological stations with regard to precipitation (out of 366 stations providing daily data) and on about 100 with regard to temperatures (out of 171 stations). In comparison, for metropolitan France, over a territory half the size of Peru, the statistical regionalizations of DRIAS-2020 are based on more than 1,000 stations for temperature and nearly 3,700 for precipitation (Quintana-Seguí et al. 2008).

10.2.3. *From the production of information to its integration into adaptation strategies*

The organization of public policy responses to the need to adapt to climate change is also globalized in its form. As the Conferences of the Parties take place, the States must produce the same types of documents, establishing strategies and plans. France, for example, produced its National Strategy for Adaptation to Climate Change in 2007, from the Interministerial Committee for Sustainable Development, based on the work of the National Observatory on the Effects of Climate Change (ONERC 2007); followed by the French National Adaptation Plan for Climate Change (PNACC), developed by the Ministry of Ecology, Sustainable Development, Transport and Housing, in 2011 (MEDDTL 2011), updated for 2018-2022 with the PNACC-2 (ONERC 2017). Peru has proposed a National Climate Change Strategy (ENCC), the first version of which, developed in 2003 as recounted by Calvo (2010), was updated in 2015 (MINAM 2015); and the Climate Change Adaptation and Mitigation Action Plan published by the Ministry of the Environment in 2010 (MINAM 2010). The other stakeholder states have also produced similar documents in parallel.

However, its weak capacity to produce regionalized models does not allow Peru to conceive the future of its climate with a greater precision than the information provided by the IPCC. Peruvian documents developed to implement climate change plans rely explicitly on IPCC reports. The ENCC (MINAM 2015) presents two national-scale scenario maps, showing the change in annual minimum temperature and the percentage change in precipitation, respectively, both for the 2030 horizon. These maps are taken from a SENAMHI (2009) study simulating regional-scale climate under the A2 scenario with the Regional Atmospheric Modeling System (RAMS) model forced at the boundaries by the global NCAR model (National Center for Atmospheric Research, USA). As with the sub-national scale projections, the authors point out that these are only approximations and that more climate information is urgently needed (SENAMHI 2009, p. 15). By the way, some of the extreme values in the legend do not correspond to any of the projected increases or decreases at the national scale; however, SENAMHI's warning no longer appears in the 2015 NCS (MINAM 2015).

In the case of France, the first two adaptation plans, the national strategy (ONERC 2007) and the PNACC-1 (MEDDTL 2011) explicitly refer to the IPCC reports, so as to contextualize in the introduction and recall the objectives of the planning. Conversely, PNACC-2 (ONERC 2017) mentions the IPCC at the margin and is much more in the context of the Paris Agreement (COP21). Unlike the case of Peru, maps or figures extracted from IPCC reports are rarely used. Simulations from French laboratories, in this case the CNRM Météo-France (National Centre for Meteorological Research) and the LMD (Laboratoire de météorologie dynamique) of the IPSL (Institute Pierre-Simon Laplace), are preferred. These laboratories have developed global models (respectively ARPEGE-Climat and LMDz) and regional models for Météo-France (ALADIN-Climat).

In addition to the accuracy of the available models, the territorial translation of adaptation strategies to climate change is also embedded in social, political and cultural contexts specific to each country.

10.3. Strategies embedded in pre-existing modes of organization

10.3.1. *Different framings of vulnerability*

Faced with hazards, i.e. phenomena considered as physical in the adaptation scheme, States are called upon in strategic documents and plans to determine "vulnerabilities". The introduction of this notion in the management of risk represented an advance over a view "[... confusing] risk with a threatening and external agent" (Gilbert 2013, p. 66). It is the combination of hazards generated by climate change and vulnerabilities that makes it possible to identify concrete situations of risk.

The French plans, organized around ecosystems (water, soil, etc.) and economic sectors (tourism, fisheries and aquaculture, etc.), are based on a fair common framework for adaptation (for example the work of the IPCC Group II, IPCC 2014). Specific environments are the subject of files, such as mountains, but no specific population is designated as vulnerable as such. This position is held without avoiding certain ambiguities. Thus, there is mention of "raising awareness amongst and educating mountain populations" (MEDDTL 2011, p. 64), as if this were a relatively homogeneous human group that is less informed about climate change than others. For the Overseas Territories, the PNACC-1 simultaneously and contradictorily states that "the consultation organized in the Overseas Territories in mid-2010 showed that most of the recommendations put forward in the report of the national working groups could meet the challenges of adaptation in the Overseas Territories" and that "many relevant adaptation proposals will require, for their implementation in the Overseas Territories, a prior technical development phase (particularly in the case of knowledge of future climate scenarios, hydrological functioning, etc.)" (MEDDTL 2011, p. 19).

This approach to vulnerability through environments and sectors also avoids placing the responsibility for adapting to climate change on a single type of agriculture: corn producers or wine growers, fishermen or stockbreeders, in metropolitan France or in the French Overseas Territories, whatever the size and nature of their farms, are concerned by adaptation plans, through environments and economic sectors. These choices reflect the fundamental principles of the French Republic, which limit the consideration of ethnic origins, standards of living or places of residence in policies, at the risk of denying the difficulties specific to populations facing particular economic or geographical situations.

In the Peruvian plans, by contrast, adaptation is envisaged in the National Strategy (MINAM 2016) as a response to the "impacts" that climate change would cause for environments, and also specific populations, that would be vulnerable to it. Another document, Peru's "Intended Contribution" of September 2015 (INDC Intended Nationally Determined Contributions, República del Perú 2015), identifies at the national level, with regard to adaptation, five items: water, agriculture, fisheries, forests, health; and vulnerable populations. The latter are referred to in different ways: indigenous populations, poor populations and cordillera populations. In this case, living in the mountains is considered a determinant of poverty, and also of rurality, in the dominant national representations (Mesclier 2002). Although many of the country's main cities are located at high altitudes (like Arequipa, 2nd city of the country, some 2,300 m above sea level, or Cusco, ancient political center of the Incas and which counts today a half-million inhabitants, at 3,500 m of altitude), one of the National Strategy's diagrams depicts an urbanized coastline, with a conurbation composed of modern buildings and lush green spaces, versus a mountainous slope where tiny tin-roofed houses sit alongside sparse vegetation (MINAM 2015, p. 13). In the context of risk management documents, written by the Lima-based government, this is translated into the concept of "vulnerability". This construction of perceptions of vulnerability refers not only to real socio-economic inequalities, especially between cities and the countryside, but also to strong structures of geographical representations in Peru: around the opposition between a Pacific piedmont inhabited by populations descended from the Spanish conquerors or "acculturated", and an Andean cordillera populated by "indigenous", descendants of the first Amerindians, considered as backward or, on the contrary, as the custodians of Andean traditions (Mesclier 2002).

The national contexts thus lead to a significant gap between the French and Peruvian plans. In the latter, reference is systematically made to the existence of "ancestral practices" (MINAM 2010) and "ancestral knowledge" (MINAM 2015), which must be safeguarded and revalued. The chosen approach is also qualified in terms of "gender" and "interculturality" (MINAM 2015; República del Perú 2015). Peru is, in fact, part of a group of countries that have signed Convention 169 of the International Labor Organization (unlike France) and recognizes interculturality in its territory. In these strategies, the indigenous and peasant populations appear both as particularly vulnerable and as holders of traditional knowledge capable of balancing the natural forces at work. In contrast, export-oriented agriculture, both the second source of foreign exchange in Peru (Mesclier et al. 2013) and a major user of natural resources (Marshall 2014; Oré and Muñoz 2018), does not appear with regard to the vulnerability nor to the means that should be developed in order to combat climate change, in a pattern similar to that of sustainable development: "on the one hand, we will find spaces dedicated to the productivist model, on the other, spaces dedicated to the management of natural objects" with farmers, perceived as peasants, in charge of the latter (Aubertin and Pinton 2006, p. 27).

10.3.2. Territorial strategies determined by criteria other than climate change simulations

In order to implement the strategies defined in the plans, Peru and France have resorted to arrangements involving collaboration between various institutions. These are organized according to various territorial approaches, without any apparent link with the simulations of future climates.

Since the beginning of the 2000s, Peru has begun a process of decentralization which makes the governors and regional assemblies a predominant element of the country's politics and management. These elected authorities, whose jurisdiction corresponds broadly to the departments, are required to develop their own "Regional Climate Change Strategies". However, decentralization is still a work in progress, with difficulties such as the complexity of the distribution of competencies, the failure of the geographical and institutional resizing of territories, the tensions between the central and regional governments, these having already been evident 10 years ago (Bey 2010). At the time of the Paris Agreement, 20 out of 25 regional governments had already drafted their Regional Climate Change Strategy, but only 10 had plans to implement this strategy (Morales Saravia 2016).

At the central government level, the Ministry of the Environment (created in 2008) has developed a Climate Change Adaptation and Mitigation Action Plan, which refers to the objective of developing land-use planning and an ecological and economic zoning that incorporate "variables of natural threats and climate change" (MINAM 2010, p. 28). For its part, the Ministry of Agriculture has produced a Plan for Risk Management and Adaptation to Climate Change in the Agrarian Sector 2012–2021 (PLANGRACC-A, (MINAGRI 2012)), whose proposals have been agreed with the regions and which contain national maps of areas at risk of frost, drought, *friaje* (low temperatures out of season) and flooding, and finally maps at the level of local municipalities of the same risks and of the vulnerability of farmers and livestock breeders. The sources used are data from SENAMHI and INEI (Instituto Nacional de Estadística e Informática), but these maps do not seem to have incorporated the information from the climate change simulations.

In the direction of greater collaboration, a temporary multi-sectoral working group created in 2016 brings together representatives of ministries under the leadership of MINAM. A National Commission on Climate Change was created by supreme resolution in 2009, with five working groups, one of which focuses on "Science, Technology and Institutional Strengthening" and two others on "Climate Risks" and "Ecosystems and Climate Change" (Morales Saravia 2016). A large quantity of actors is called upon to participate: ministries, NGOs, the private sector, indigenous peoples' organizations, representatives of regional and local governments, whose scales of action are quite different from each other.

In France, the governance system appears at first glance to be less complex and more centralized. ONERC has an essential coordinating role in national planning, and coordinated the work of the working groups and consultation groups for PNACC-1 and 2. Created by the State in 2001, it has three main missions: to gather and disseminate information on the impacts, in particular on the risks related to global warming, to recommend adaptation measures and to liaise with the IPCC. The actions are then mainly managed by the central administration, for example, the Directorate General for Energy and Climate, the Agency for the Environment and Energy Management (Agence de l'environnement et de la maîtrise de l'énergie), the Ministry of Higher Education and Research or, if necessary, a national institute such as IRSTEA (National Research Institute of Science and Technology for Agriculture and Environment, now part of INRAE, French National Research Institute for Agriculture, Food and Environment), with also very diverse partners, such as universities, technical study centers, the hydrographic and oceanographic services of the Navy, and so on.

One of the six "action areas" that structure the priorities of the PNACC-2 (ONERC 2017), called "Governance and steering", deals with the implementation of adaptation in the territories by involving society, the articulation of adaptation and mitigation policies, as well as the legal framework and monitoring and evaluation. In the PNACC-1 (MEDDTL 2011), a "Governance" sheet already mentioned the following:

– The need for articulation with the territories: "the National Strategy for Sustainable Development has shown that the success of a national approach depends on its appropriation and implementation in the territories, within the framework of broader governance".

– Mechanisms to put it in place: "concerning adaptation to climate change, the 'Grenelle 2' law has planned the development of regional climate, air and energy plans (SRCAE) and territorial climate-energy plans (PCET) which must include an adaptation component".

– Doubts about the possibility of this declination: the sheet mentions, among other things, the desirable reinforcement of "interregional coherence" and emphasizes that "the preparation of these documents requires methodological assistance, in particular for the SRCAEs" (MEDDTL 2011, p. 67 and following).

As in Peru, the Ministry of Agriculture appears to be both an indispensable element of climate change adaptation and quite detached from its particular challenges. It is co-responsible for specific actions around "water resources", "forest", "natural risks" and "mountains". Its Directorate General for Agricultural, Agri-food and Regional Policies is also (obviously) in charge of the main actions of the theme of "agriculture" and, in particular, the promotion of "water-efficient agriculture". However, the "National Agricultural and Rural Development Program", in its presentation on the institution's website[2], does not mention climate change as such, even though it associates words such as autonomy and competitiveness with public health, the environment and anticipation capacity.

In total, Peruvian and French public policies seem to be based on rather complex assemblies, whose own vulnerability is not subject to much evaluation: it seems that, as in other areas, "the focus on human vulnerabilities has been to the detriment of organizational vulnerabilities" (Gilbert 2013, p. 71). There is also little coherence between the "regionalization" of modeling climate change – for example, that proposed by SENAMHI at the level of watersheds – and the territorial organization of the human and organizational means put in place. These follow the usual political and administrative demarcations, such as regions, which are often quite heterogeneous in terms of physical characteristics and agricultural production. In other documents, reference is made, on the contrary, to natural groupings that do not correspond to a single type of climate projection: thus, the Andean cordillera or the French mountains, without corresponding to a single trend in temperature or rainfall, appear as a category for part of public adaptation policies.

Nevertheless, it is within this general framework that the actions envisaged are articulated with the needs of farmers, on the basis of specific projects, through which they have unequal access to the technical tools developed by scientists.

---

2 http://agriculture.gouv.fr/le-programme-national-developpement-agricole-et-rural-pndar [Accessed May 2021].

10.4. Concrete progress through projects on different scales of action

10.4.1. *Climate change read at the plot level*

In France as in Peru, farmers are aware of climate change from the already present evolutions, which have immediate consequences for production results. The medium-term agricultural calender is modified by water availability and the temperatures, as foreseen by simulations. However, they also perceive a multiplication and intensification of extreme events and a greater irregularity of meteorological phenomena, aspects that the simulations have more difficulty in transcribing.

Viticulture is widely cited as an example of an agrosystem sensitive to climate, its interannual variations (at the origin of vintages) and its future evolution, as shown by the numerous scientific works of very varied disciplines and methodological approaches (Madelin et al. 2010; IPCC 2014; Mosedale et al. 2016). In 2002, Battaglini et al. (2009) asked winegrowers in three European countries (Germany, France, Italy) about their perception of climate change and their preparation for adaptation: 80% noted an increase in autumn and winter temperatures and hotter summers; they mentioned an advance in phenological stages and impacts on yields, strong variability in the quality of the wines produced, and an increase in pests and diseases. For some vineyards, at the northern limit of potential, conditions are clearly improving, maturity is reached every year and it is, for example, no longer necessary to add sugar to the grape juice produced. For others, located further south, the management of water stress or wines that have become too alcoholic call into question the sustainability of the crop.

In Peru, farmers report changes in rainfall and temperature in a large number of surveys. In addition to increases or decreases, there is a greater irregularity, which can challenge their production systems. For example, in response to a survey focused on changes in their farming practices, farmers in Conchucos, a town located 3,200 m above sea level in the Andes in the north of the country, report that they have stopped growing old varieties of potatoes because of increased disease and unusual frosts. This having been said, they can now grow wheat, barley and corn thanks to the availability of new varieties and increased temperatures (Vergara Rodríguez 2012, p. 115ff). In Tambo Real, northwest of Cusco, also around 3,200 m above sea level but in the south of the country, in a high plain surrounded by reliefs, the irregularity of rainfall and frosts today practically prevents crops, according to farmers, which pushes them to turn increasingly to the breeding of dairy cows, even though it means having to buy their feed (Mesclier 2015). On the Altiplano, in the Puno region, farmers in Santa María, a locality located at about 3,800 m above sea level, report that frosts are stronger, the heat is more intense, and there is less rain, and also that it no longer rains at the right time, resulting in a loss of production (Rivera Vela 2010, p. 379).

10.4.2. *The difficulties and contradictions of local adaptations*

The climate changes of the last two decades imply immediate adaptations that can effectively rely on peasant knowledge, as seen, for example, in the case of Santa María, with the use of more resistant seeds (Rivera Vela 2010, p. 380). This context has also drawn the attention of policymakers, social scientists and the media to ancient practices that allow for adaptation to climate variability, such as *amunas*, systems for infiltrating rainwater upstream for its later use in the downstream part of a collectively managed territory (Alencastre 2015). However, although these multifaceted local knowledge and practices are considered important by farmers, they also feel they require the knowledge produced by universities or research centers (Rivera Vela 2010), or the support of the municipality and regional government, in addition to the local communal institution (Vergara Rodríguez 2012, p. 119). In Conchucos, producers now purchase potato seeds produced in agronomic research centers. Some of the adaptations to the new conditions are also related to markets. Farmers in Tambo Real are moving from a crop-livestock system to specialization in dairy farming, also in response to offers from the food industry. However, this type of conversion to livestock farming, which has become common in the Andes, runs counter to climate change mitigation measures, insofar as the gases produced by the cows are one of the factors that increase GHGs in the atmosphere.

For viticulture, while the average annual climate conditions largely define the potential of a region, its variability on a finer scale leads to a diversity of cultivation practices, of grape varieties and of winemaking techniques, in other words, to a multitude of local adaptations which sometimes compensate for extreme conditions. Based on several examples of vineyards around the world, the ANR-Terviclim and GICC-Teradclim research programs have shown that climate variability on a local scale can be greater than on larger scales (Madelin et al. 2010; Quénol 2014), especially when it comes to cold extremes (Madelin and Beltrando 2005). Winegrowers play on these local differences to express the typicality of the wines produced or even to organize agricultural work. This knowledge of local climates is then considered as one of the levers for adapting to climate change (Quénol 2014).

According to Petit et al. (2020):

> An examination of knowledge on climate and the way it is constructed leads us to believe that the crux of adaptation is not only in the regionalization of global models to switch from a global to a local scale [...] but rather in what we can say and do from the local level, that is, a

form of 'territorialization of of climate action' (Bertrand and Richard 2014).

Even in Peru, however, the so-called "inclusive" perspective, which emphasizes local knowledge, also calls for a pooling of contributions from different "cultural matrixes" (Bernex and Castro 2015, p. 20), desired by the farmers themselves. The specific projects that aim to improve adaptation call, in varying proportions, on technological knowledge produced by scientists, such as improved varieties or climate simulations, as well as the so-called ancestral knowledge and farmers' thinking.

10.4.3. *Projects of varying scope and size*

Farmers access scientific information most often through concrete action research projects which are part of the general framework of adaptation plans through various funding mechanisms. These projects, as such, have variable contours and dimensions and integrate farmers differently in the definition, participation and decision processes.

In France, research projects on agriculture and climate change are often multidisciplinary, with INRAE playing a central role, and are organized in particular around the agricultural sectors, which determine the scope of action in spatial and social terms. The research focus was initially on simulations of the impacts of climate change on the main crops, following the example of the CLIMATOR research project (Brisson and Levrault 2010). Currently, research is focusing more on adaptation, with a stronger integration of the agricultural world. The LACCAVE (Long-term Adaptation to Climate Change in Viticulture and Enology) project for wine-growing considered as a "model system to study adaptation" (Aigrain et al. 2019), is a good example. Based on a median IPCC scenario, the project researchers, in collaboration with experts from the INAO (Institut national de l'origine et de la qualité) and FranceAgriMer (Établissement national des produits de l'agriculture et de la mer), proposed four adaptation strategies over a period of 30 years, depending on the extent of innovations and the displacement of vineyards: a "conservative" strategy, i.e. without major changes in practices and without relocation, which would lead to a retraction of vineyards and a more random production; a "nomadic" strategy with a relocation of vineyards; an "innovative" strategy where the adaptation would be based on the integration of innovations without relocation; a "liberal" strategy which would lead to an industrialization of wine (Aigrain et al. 2019). These scenarios were discussed at participatory forums in seven wine regions, bringing together between 50 and 100 stakeholders in the industry (Touzard et al. 2020), and a national adaptation strategy taking into account these discussions is being developed by INAO, FranceAgriMer, IFV (Institut de la Vigne et du Vin) and INRAE.

In Peru, agribusiness often holds the keys to power at the regional level, which allows it to propose ambitious projects, as shown by the process of creating a scientific water institute in the Ica region. In this region of the Pacific piedmont of the Andes, south of Lima, the decrease in the level of groundwater now used mainly by large plantations is not so much due to climate change but rather to overexploitation of resources (Marshall 2014; Oré and Muñoz 2018). However, projections predict likely decreases in precipitation in both the piedmont and the Andes. For the creation in 2018 of this institute, the regional governor, himself a landowner and entrepreneur, solicited the Trusteeship Council of Science in Peru, CONCYTEC, which has chosen the main university of the country, the Pontificia Universidad Católica del Perú (PUCP) as project leader, with the participation of other national institutions, as well as the French National Research Institute for Sustainable Development (IRD) and two North American universities. The objective is primarily to increase the volume of water available for agri-export, although the project is also expected to benefit neighboring regions, particularly in the Cordillera[3].

Regarding the peasantry and small farmers, they are integrated into projects initiated by actors other than themselves, such as international donors or NGOs, in consortium with the central or decentralized state, the private sector and universities, which determine their scope of action according to their means and priorities. For example, the Andean Community of Nations launched, at the end of the 2000s, a regional Andean adaptation project that involved two watersheds in Peru located at the foot of glaciers. Risk and vulnerability studies, climate projections for these watersheds for the period 2015–2039, and also reforestation, construction of small reservoirs, improvement of irrigation canals, among others, should allow local populations to better cope with the gradual disappearance of glaciers, which initially generates an excess of water but will then make them lose an important natural storage. The partnerships involved the Ministry of Agriculture and SENAMHI, regional and local governments, CARE Peru and IRD (Calvo 2010, pp. 230–231).

Large NGOs such as ITDG (Intermediate Technology Development Group) are also involved in disseminating information related to climate change and its projections during experiences of technological adaptation in rural areas. For example, various models are used in a document accompanying an action undertaken in seven localities, alongside information on El Niño events and the retreat of the Andean glaciers. Local knowledge is also involved in the process (Torres and Gómez 2008).

----

3 http://investigacion.pucp.edu.pe/investigacion/instituto-cientifico-del-agua-ica-beneficiara-ica-huancavelica-ayacucho-apurimac-junin/ [Accessed May 2021].

These various experiences paint a picture of piecemeal progress, without an overall vision of the agriculture "of tomorrow" necessarily articulating the proposals, and without erasing the inequalities of access of different types of agriculture to decision-making and science, but with the effective perspective of a coordinated use of different types of knowledge on a local scale.

10.5. Conclusion

The concept of climate change is now widely shared, from the Global Space to the villages of the Andes. The need to adapt is also widely recognized. Information apparently circulates fairly well between scientists who propose increasingly precise simulations, international institutions, the States that are responsible for mitigation and adaptation policies, decentralized entities, civil society, and even, at least in part, farmers. The scientific information contained in the models is used beyond what has been described in this short contribution, for multiple applications, and funding is proposed for applied research. Moreover, farmers' knowledge is also taken into account and valued, at least in speeches and during specific actions.

However, the comparison carried out here between France and Peru has allowed us to identify the importance of the gaps in this circulation, due to the conceptions of the actors, the inequalities in conditions, means and information, as well as the particular interests and the power relations that structure societies. The observation of the circulation of models, from their production to the final users, within the sole framework of the adaptation of agriculture to climate change, has allowed us to observe the historical scarcity of meteorological stations in a country like Peru, the propensity of both the French and Peruvian States to think of the world in terms of existing political demarcations, the weight of representations of space and social groups, which lead Peru to organize adaptation in terms of ethnic origins and regional particularities, and France to minimize these aspects. There is also a latent conflict, within the institutions themselves, between opposing conceptions of what agriculture should be, between "competitiveness" and access to world markets or, conversely, the illusion of the capacity of the most vulnerable to resolve the new problems posed by rapid climate change by means of their "ancestral knowledge" alone, without taking into consideration the other constraints they are subject to. Nevertheless, at the same time, projects of varying scale are using, developing and disseminating scientific information useful for adaptation and proposing specific solutions, taking into account indigenous knowledge and encouraging the participation of farmers in reflection and decision-making.

Thus, if the States formulate technical recommendations that are rarely territorialized and if there are general solutions to climate change proposed by experts without taking agrosystems into account (Cochet et al. 2020; Chapter 13), the comparison between France and Peru makes it possible to identify inequalities of means, representations and power relationships rooted in national histories that invite us to consider the adaptation of agriculture as a political and organizational challenge with multiple dimensions and involving numerous actors.

10.6. References

Aigrain, P., Bois, B., Brugiere, F., Duchene, E., Garcia de Cortazar-Atauri, I., Gautier, J., Giraud-Heraud, E., Hammond, R., Hannin, H., Ollat, N. et al. (2019). L'utilisation par la viticulture française d'un exercice de prospective pour l'élaboration d'une stratégie d'adaptation au changement climatique. *BIO Web of Conferences*, 12, 03020.

Alencastre, A. (2015). Las Amunas de Tupicocha y la construcción del territorio. In *Río+20. Desafíos y perspectivas*, Bernex, N. and Castro, A. (eds). Fondo editorial de la Pontificia Universidad Católica del Perú, Lima.

AllEnvi (2014). Mise en œuvre de la stratégie scientifique de développement des services climatiques. *Alliance nationale de recherche pour l'environnement*, 3(10).

Aubertin, C. and Pinton, F. (2006). Les paysans : Figure emblématique du développement durable. In *Le retour des paysans ? A l'heure du développement durable*, Auclair, L., Aspe, C., Baudot, P. (eds). IRD Éditions/Édisud, Aix-en-Provence/Paris.

Aykut, S.C. and Dahan, A. (2015). *Gouverner le climat ? 20 ans de négociations internationales*. Presses de Sciences Po, Paris.

Battaglini, A., Barbeau, G., Bindi, M., Badeck, F.W. (2009). European winegrowers' perceptions of climate change impact and options for adaptation. *Regional Environmental Change*, 9, 61–73.

Beltrando, G. (2010). Les géographes-climatologues français et le changement climatique aux échelles régionales. *EchoGéo*, 21 [Online].

Beltrando, G. (2015). Dans un contexte de changement climatique, quels sont les futurs possibles dans le domaine agricole ? Seminar, Central Prodig.

Bernex, N. and Castro, A. (2015). Introducción. In *Río+20. Desafíos y perspectivas*, Bernex, N. and Castro, A. (eds). Fondo editorial de la Pontificia Universidad Católica del Perú, Lima.

Bertrand, F. and Richard, E. (2014). L'action des collectivités territoriales face au "problème climat" en France : Une caractérisation par les politiques environnementales. *Natures Sciences Sociétés*, 22(3), 195–203.

Bey, M. (2010). Réformes néolibérales et tensions sur les ressources dans la décentralisation au Pérou et au Mexique. *Revue internationale de politique comparée*, 3(17), 127–142.

Brisson, N. and Levrault, F. (eds) (2010). *Changement climatique, agriculture et forêt en France : Simulations d'impacts sur les principales espèces. Le Livre Vert du projet CLIMATOR (2007–2010)*. ADEME, Paris.

Calvo, E. (2010). Cambio climático y sistemas productivos rurales con énfasis en la gestión del agua y el manejo de los recursos naturales. In *Sepia XIII. Perú: El problema agrario en debate*, Ames, P. and Caballero, V. (eds). SEPIA, Lima.

Cochet, H., Ducourtieux, O., Garambois, N. (2020). *Systèmes agraires et changement climatique au Sud. Les chemins de l'adaptation*. Editions Quae, Paris.

Dollfus, O. (1994). *L'Espace Monde*. Economica, Paris.

Gilbert, C. (2013). De l'affrontement des risques à la résilience. Une approche politique de la prévention. *Communication & Langages*, 2(176), 65–78 [Online]. Available at: https://www.cairn.info/journal-communication-et-langages1-2013-2-page-65.htm [Accessed 16 July 2021].

IPCC (2013). Climate Change 2013: The Physical Science Basis. Contribution of WG I to the Fifth Assessment Report of the IPCC. Cambridge University Press, Cambridge.

IPCC (2014). Climate Change 2014: Impacts, Adaptation et Vulnerability. WG II Contribution to the Fifth Assessment Report of the IPCC. Cambridge University Press, Cambridge.

Jasanoff, S. (2010). A new climate for society. *Theory, Culture & Society*, 27(2–3), 233–253.

Kleiche-Dray, M. (2017). Les savoirs autochtones au service du développement durable. *Autrepart*, 81, 3–20.

Madelin, M. and Beltrando, G. (2005). Spatial interpolation based mapping of spring frosts hazard in the Champagne vineyard. *Meteorological Applications*, 12(1), 51–56.

Madelin, M., Bois, B., Chabin, J.-P. (2010). Modification des conditions de maturation du raisin en Bourgogne viticole liée au réchauffement climatique. *EchoGéo*, 14 [Online]. Available at: https://journals.openedition.org/echogeo/12176.

Marshall, A. (2014). *Apropiarse del desierto. Agricultura globalizada y dinámicas socioambientales en la costa peruana. El caso de los oasis de Virú e Ica-Villacurí.* IFEA-IRD, Lima.

MEDDTL (2011). Plan national d'adaptation au changement climatique PNACC 2011-2015. MEDDTL, Paris.

Mesclier, É. (2002). De la complementariedad a la voluntad de "aplanar los Andes" : Representaciones de la naturaleza y pensamiento económico y político en el Perú del siglo XX. *Bulletin de l'Institut Français d'Études Andines*, 30(3), 541–562.

Mesclier, É. (2015). "L'adaptation au changement climatique", rouage (involontaire) de l'affirmation du modèle de développement agricole néolibéral ? Seminar, Central Prodig.

Mesclier, É., Marshall, A., Chaléard, J.-L., Auquier, C. (2013). L'agriculture entreprenariale d'exportation : Un choix politique aux enjeux complexes. Dossier Pérou : Emergence économique et zones d'ombre. *Problèmes d'Amérique latine*, 88, 55–76.

MINAGRI (2012). PLANGRACC-A : Plan de gestión de riesgos y adaptaciónal cambio climático en el sector agrario. Período 2012–2021. Ministerio de Agricultura, Lima.

MINAM (2010). Plan de Acción de Adaptación y Mitigación frente al Cambio Climático. MINAM, Lima.

MINAM (2015). Estrategia Nacional ante el Cambio Climático. Ministerio del Ambiente, Lima.

MINAM (2016). El Perú y el Cambio Climático. Tercera Comunicación Nacional del Perú a la Convención Marco de las Naciones Unidades sobre Cambio Climático. Ministerio del Ambiente, Lima.

Morales Saravia, R. (2016). Balance de la implementación de la Estrategia Nacional ante el Cambio Climático y de los compromisos climáticos asumidos. MINAM, Conference, Acuerdo de Paris e implementación nacional.

Mosedale, J.R., Abernethy, K.E., Smart, R.E., Wilson, R.J., Maclean, I.M. (2016). Climate change impacts and adaptive strategies: Lessons from the grapevine. *Global Change Biology*, 22(11), 3814–3828.

ONERC (2007). Stratégie nationale d'adaptation au changement climatique. La Documentation française, Paris.

ONERC (2017). Vers un 2e plan d'adaptation au changement climatique pour la France: Enjeux et recommandations. La Documentation française, Paris.

Oré, M.T. and Muñoz, I. (eds) (2018). *Aguas en disputa. Ica y Huancavelica, entre el entrampamiento y el diálogo*. PUCP – Fondo editorial, Lima.

Petit, S., Vergote, M.-H., Castel, T., Richard, Y. (2020). Le climat "par procuration". De l'usage des proxys pour relier les savoirs. *Natures Sciences Sociétés*, 28(1), 12–23.

Quénol, H. (ed.) (2014). *Changement climatique et terroirs viticoles*. Lavoisier Tec et Doc, Paris.

Quintana-Segui, P., Le Moigne, P., Durand, Y., Martin, E., Habets, F., Baillon, M., Canellas, C., Franchisteguy, L., Morel, S. (2008). Analysis of near-surface atmospheric variables: Validation of the SAFRAN analysis over France. *Journal of Applied Meteorology and Climatology*, 47, 92–107.

República del Perú (2015). Contribución prevista y determinada a nivel nacional (INDC) de la República del Perú.

Rivera Vela, E. (2010). Cambio climático en comunidades aimaras: percepciones y efectos en la producción agropecuaria en Santa María y Apopata, Puno. In *Sepia XIII. Perú: El problema agrario en debate*, Ames, P. and Caballero, V. (eds). SEPIA, Lima.

SENAMHI (2009). Escenarios Climáticos en el Perú para el año 2030. Segunda Comunicación Nacional de Cambio Climático. Resumen Técnico. MINAM, SENAMHI, Lima.

SENAMHI (2014). Regionalización Estadística de Escenarios Climáticos en el Perú. SENAMHI, FAO, Lima.

Torres, J. and Gómez, A. (eds) (2008). *Adaptación al cambio climático: De los fríos y los calores en los Andes. Experiencias de adaptación tecnológica en siete zonas rurales del Perú*. Soluciones Prácticas-ITDG, Lima.

Touzard, J., Ollat, N., Aigrain, P., Bois, B., Brugiere, F., Duchêne, E., Garcia de Cortazar-Atauri, I., Gautier, J., Hammond, R., Hannin, H. (2020). La filière Vigne et Vin face au changement climatique : Enseignements d'un forum de prospective pour le Val de Loire. *Norois*, 255, 83–89.

Vergara Rodríguez, K. (2012). *Variabilidad climática, percepción ambiental y estrategias de adaptación de la Comunidad Campesina, de Conchucos*. Sociedad Geográfica de Lima, Lima.

Vigour, C. (2005). *La comparaison dans les sciences sociales. Pratiques et méthodes*. La Découverte, Paris.

Hydrogeography: Towards a Systemic Analysis in the Context of Global Changes, from Watershed to Spillway Basin

11.1. Introduction

At a time when environmental policies have become more integrated in terms of resources management, risks and biodiversity, understanding the functioning of watersheds and the watercourses that drain them is of paramount interest. In physical and environmental geography, this question has been a major field of research for several decades. The studies carried out in this framework generally focus on understanding the flows of water, materials and nutrients through the physical (geology, climatology, geomorphology, hydrology, biogeography, pedology) and human processes taking place in the watershed (Schumm 1977; Amoros and Petts 1993). The rise of hydrogeography or the development of critical approaches to the relationships between environment and societies, such as political ecology (Chartier and Rodary 2016) or critical physical geography (Dufour and Lespez 2020), demonstrates, however, that watersheds are complex and constantly changing objects. The bio-physical processes that drive them are in fact largely hybridized by social, political and economic processes, making watersheds complex systems that can be affected by a diversity of trajectories linked to global changes such as climate change, peri-urbanization, the intensification of agricultural production systems and agricultural abandonment. These changes result in changes

Chapter written by Vincent VIEL, Émilie LAVIE, Guillaume BROUSSE, Benoît CARLIER, Luc MICHLER, Mathilde RESCH, Gashin SHAHSAVARI and Gilles ARNAUD-FASSETTA.

in land use, landscape characteristics, management practices and development, which in turn lead to changes in the functioning of the system (Viel et al. 2020).

Geographers that work on watersheds and the flows that drive them, are debating on more and more complex objects (e.g. the multiplication of the factors of control of the processes because of the global changes and their uncertainties). Hence, we propose in this chapter to discuss some ways these highly anthropized objects can be studied. To do this, we will make three assumptions:

– The concept of hydrosystem has allowed hydrogeographers to analyze hybrid objects in an integrated way, and this evolution of approaches has taken place in an epistemological context that favors critical approaches.

– This renewal of hydrogeography has benefited from methodological developments, particularly in the field of modeling, allowing a better understanding of processes at intermediate scales.

– Such a scientific framework leads to a new discussion of the management modalities of watersheds and of water resources.

We propose here to illustrate these hypotheses through a series of studies carried out within the UMR Prodig on different anthropized objects at different spatial and temporal scales.

We will first specify the way in which the questions in the field of geography of water have evolved over the last century. We will then explain why understanding the dynamics associated with the functioning of watersheds also means analyzing complex processes at the interface between humans and the physics of the environment. There, socio-economic and political practices play an essential role, which raises original questionings and requires the mobilization of new tools. Finally, we will discuss the way the co-constructed and systemic character of the processes in the watersheds is taken into account today in the management modalities of water-related environmental resources.

11.2. Epistemology of water issues in geography

11.2.1. *Emergence of systemic approaches: towards the rise of the hydrosystem concept*

Geographers gradually took up hydrology (the physical science of water) between the 1920s and 1980s, giving rise to hydroclimatology and hydrogeomorphology (Pardé 1964). Although Maurice Pardé was interested in the effects of rainfall stimulus on the Rhone floods, he has influenced the emergence of studies on fluvial dynamics in a context where geomorphology was a major field of geography. His students continued the institutionalization of hydrology as the core of the geographic discipline within a series of doctoral studies defended between 1960 and 1977. These contributed to a growing body of knowledge about (sub)surface flow processes in watersheds.

At the same time, the linking of the water cycle with other environmental variables such as climate and geomorphology has increased the complexity of the water cycle. This complexification is linked to the multiplicity of factors controlling water or material flows in the watersheds and to the diversity of temporalities, thresholds and spatial scales on which they act. The watershed object becomes a complex system whose analysis requires a systemic approach (Chorley and Kennedy 1971), materialized in the 1970s by the emergence of the concept of fluvial system (Schumm 1977). This concept allowed the consideration of upstream–downstream dynamics in water and sediment transfers. It also integrates stocks and flows over longer time scales than those proposed by the Pardes approach.

The implementation during the *"Trente Glorieuses"*[1] of numerous hydraulic infrastructures by "engineering" policies in the watersheds (Laganier and Arnaud-Fassetta 2009) then broadened the hitherto naturalistic reflections to several other themes such as risk management, river restoration (Scarwell and Laganier 2004; Pigeon 2005; Dufour and Piégay 2009; Morandi et al. 2014; Brousse 2020), the political management of resources (Blanchon and Maupin 2009) or the making of the city by the networks in urban geography (Jaglin 2008). The time of hydrogeography then emerges in which geographers are not only interested in water flows within watersheds, but also in their uses and the political, social and economic issues associated with them (Blanchon and Graefe 2012). The latter are based on the concept of hydrosystem, which brings together all the branches of the water and nature sciences. Based on the close systemic approach to the fluvial system (Amoros and Petts 1993), it was born from discussions in the framework of the Interdisciplinary Environmental Research Programs (Programmes interdisciplinaires de recherche sur l'environnement, PIREN) Rhône and then Seine. This conceptual model has been adopted by hydrogeomorphologists who see the value of adding transverse (slope/channel), vertical (water table/stream) and temporal dynamics to the Stanley A. Schumm's fluvial system (1977). It is also used by geographers working on questions of resource or risk management, the construction of territories and the associated power games.

---

1 30 years following the end of World War II in France.

11.2.2. *Conceptualizing the role of societies in the water cycle: the hydrosocial cycle and the hydrosocial territories*

The hydrological cycle of water as conceptualized by Robert H. Horton (1933) is modified to varying degrees by and for anthropogenic activities. The term hydrosocial cycle emerged (Linton 2008), which better emphasizes the effect of water practices and uses on the natural cycle. It is composed of three components of water, which is considered to be a hybrid object: physical water (H_2O), power issues and social structures (notably historical and cultural contexts) and technical infrastructures.

The hydrosocial cycle adds two essential elements to the hydrological cycle, on the one hand the role of politics (Walker 2006) and policies (Walker 2007) and on the other hand the role of technical elements, which involve the way engineers and managers intervene in the hydrological cycle. While it allows for a discussion of the dialectical relations between water and societies, the hydrosocial cycle remains conceptual and only partially takes into account the way in which socio-physical and historical constructions are manifested in the territories (Damonte and Boelens 2019). In order to overcome these limitations the notion of hydrosocial territories has been developed. It is interested in the behavior of stakeholders and spaces, taking into account technical, physical, social and natural variables in the construction of water territories which are conceptualized, planned or even imagined by societies. The question of the "natural" and "social" limits of the spaces studied is central to this (Boelens et al. 2016). The notion of hydrosocial territories thus appears to be better suited to social sciences and spaces, in particular by its multidimensional analysis of the interactions between social and territorial transformations (Damonte and Boelens 2019).

11.2.3. *The processes in hydrogeography*

The development of the concept of hydrosystem, and later of hydrogeography and the hydrosocial cycle, underlines the desire to take greater account of the role of societies in the functioning of watersheds. However, this desire masks numerous discussions seeking to define the place to be given to physical processes and societies in the functioning of watersheds. In hydrogeography, this is illustrated by two critical approaches that go beyond the simple disciplinary aspect: political ecology in the social sciences and critical physical geography in the environmental sciences.

Political ecology emerged from long debates in the social sciences in the 1960s and 1970s. It became a movement of thought in the 1980s, as "a way of conceptualizing political ecology and nature in the context of environmental movements" (Gautier and Benjaminsen 2012). It now dominates scientific production, particularly in the English-speaking world, not only in geography but also in economics, anthropology and sociology, on issues of relations between societies and their environment. It is considered a scientific approach that analyzes power relations on several scales or from a more militant angle. In the field of hydrogeography, research in the field of political ecology was initially interested in resource management, within the framework of hydraulic developments, for example (Béthemont 1977), emphasizing the growing impact of anthropization on the functioning of physical processes in watersheds. The contribution of the social sciences, particularly sociology, then favored research on water that was less focused on the physical object than on the social and constructed object (Graefe 2011). Water landscapes, whether "natural", anthropized or artificial, were thus born of the combination of the powers of nature and the powers of social class struggle. Anthropology has finally favorized the integration of culture in these social approaches to natural objects (Baviskar 2007).

Far from an approach centered on the management of water resources based on the volumes to be distributed, French hydrogeography has developed since the 1990s the idea that political questions constitute an essential entry of the management of hydrosystems. It is part of a remarkable duality, confronting the disciplinary character of hydrogeography, linked to the natural sciences (including hydrology), with its multidisciplinary opening in the wake of political ecology. Thus, like political ecology as a whole, a part of geographic studies on water has progressively branched out towards a so-called post-structuralist approach rejecting biological, physical and chemical processes in studies of hydrosystems (Dufour and Lespez 2020). In this context of evolution of *political ecology*, a critical approach to physical geography emerged in the 2010s entitled *critical physical geography*. The objective then was to reinforce the initial link of *political ecology* between nature and culture. *Critical physical geography* develops its research through skills in measuring processes. There is no question of opposing quantitative and qualitative approaches in the analysis of relations between nature and culture, but going beyond the simple consideration of societies as black boxes in environmental issues (Tadaki et al. 2015; Lave et al. 2018; Dufour and Lespez 2020). The aim is to demonstrate that the processes driving watersheds are in essence hybrids and that it makes no sense to either obscure them or to oppose them from research conducted with a social input.

11.3. The study of complex anthropized hydrosystems

11.3.1. *Better understanding the complexity of the processes in watersheds*

Understanding the processes affecting a watershed generally consists of investigating how water or material flows in space and time between the source areas and the watershed outlet. These analyses require taking into account a plurality of controlling factors, which act at various spatial and temporal scales and which are both physical (e.g. gravity, topography, geology) and social in nature. The objective here is then to underline the complexity of the transfers and processes that animate them, in a context of global changes. This leads physical geographers to take up new scientific questions requiring the mobilization of original methods and tools. Two examples illustrate this idea, that of the Peynin watershed (Queyras, Southern French Alps), which embodies the spatio-temporal complexity of internal sedimentary flows in a watershed with little anthropization, and that of the Wadi Leuben watershed (central Tunisia), which highlights the way in which the development of rural territories, and agricultural practices in particular, disrupts the sedimentary transit.

The Peynin there is a torrent of the Haut-Queyras particularly sensitive to rapid flooding (1957, 2000, 2008 and 2011) and gravity hazards (avalanches, landslides, debris flows), which makes people and property from the municipality of Aiguille (Hautes-Alpes) located on its alluvial fan, particularly vulnerable. Studies conducted as part of Benoît Carlier's PhD thesis in geography (2019) and the ANR *"Adaptation de la société aux risques en montagne dans un contexte de changement global"* (SAMCO; 2013–2017) have led to a better understanding of the mechanisms interacting between hazards and vulnerability with the objective of mitigating flood risk. The results show that the origin of the sediments exported to the outlet is limited to a very small part of the watershed corresponding to two small mountain torrents on the left bank of the Peynin: the Peyronnelle and the Trois arbres (Figure 11.1a). This very heterogeneous sedimentary contribution from one sub-watershed area to another demonstrates the variability of the sedimentary production of the rock faces. It also illustrates different levels of sedimentary cascade efficiency. The spatial organization of the torrential drains assuring the transfer of alluvium shows a significant variability in drainage density, higher on the north slope (against the dip) than on the south slope (in accordance with the dip; Figure 11.1b), thus allowing a more efficient transfer of sediments to the watershed outlet.

At the same time, the efficiency of the process relays (i.e. the capacity of the processes involved in the sedimentary cascade to link up in time and space), which intervene between the source zones of the Peyronnelle and Trois Arbres watershed, and the significant availability of sediments likely to be mobilized by floods favor a particularly important contribution of these sub-watersheds. The efficiency of sediments transfers from upstream to downstream is thus the result of a combination of factors that facilitate, or on the contrary constrain, the migration of sediments downstream, a combination that is likely to evolve at a time when the Queyras Regional Natural Park is questioning the perspectives of economic development (agricultural and tourist) of its territory, and in the context of a probable increase in rainfall in the medium and long-term. The role of the development of the watersheds, which is well illustrated by Wadi Leuben, can be added to the complexity of the internal dynamics of the watersheds observed in Peynin.

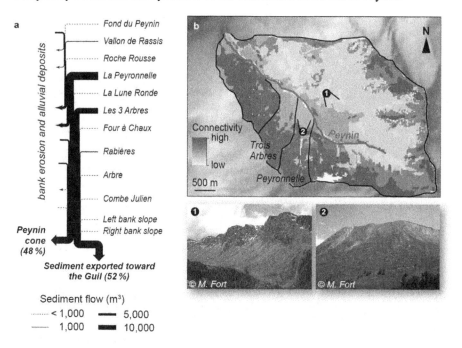

Figure 11.1. *Sediment dynamics of the Peynin watershed (Queyras, French Southern Alps). a) Watershed-scale sediment budget (2000–2020); b) mapping of sediment connectivity in the watershed. Source: Viel et al. (2018). For a color version of this figure, see www.iste.co.uk/peyroux/development.zip*

In the heart of the main olive growing region of Tunisia, the watershed of the Wadi Leuben, located south of the town of Sfax (Figure 11.2), sees its agricultural land subjected to strong pressures materialized both by a progressive extension of olive groves and a massive intensification of production systems. In order to increase the cultivable areas, farmers have set up hydraulic equipment making regular agriculture possible in areas where rainfall and soils do not usually allow it. Called *jessour* and *tabia*, these works, known as water and soil conservation, are made up of sediment levees taken from the slopes or valley bottoms. They are positioned perpendicular to the slope, in the talwegs for the former or on the slopes for the latter (Figure 11.2). The objective is to trap fine sediments upstream of the structures, thus allowing agricultural development, and then to promote the infiltration of rainwater in order to guarantee a sufficiently abundant rainwater resource for the crops while limiting the processes of runoff and therefore of soil erosion. These facilities are sometimes accompanied by works designed to divert part of the wadi's flood waters, allowing an increased supply of water and sediment to the agricultural plots.

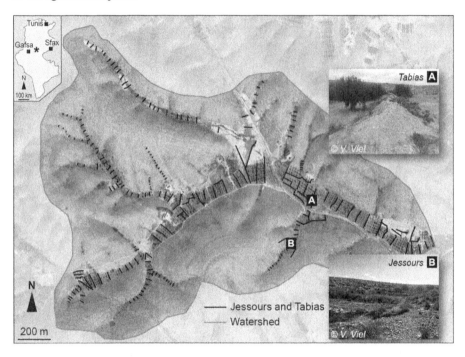

Figure 11.2. *Hydraulic equipment (jessours and tabias) introduced in the in the Wadi Leuben watershed (central Tunisia). Source: (CNES 2020). For a color version of this figure, see www.iste.co.uk/peyroux/development.zip*

By promoting water infiltration and sedimentation upstream, these hydraulic equipments partition the talwegs and almost completely interrupt sediment transit further downstream. The studies carried out within the framework of the SARDYN project (financed by the LABEX Dynamite[2]) entitled "*L'hydrosystème des îles Kneiss et du bassin Leuben (Tunisie), interactions socio-environnementales et valorisation d'un territoire protégé*" (The Kneiss islands hydrosystem and the Leuben basin (Tunisia), socio-environmental interactions and valorization of a protected area, 2019–2022) have shown that the high density of structures today constrains the sedimentary cascade, disconnecting the erosion zone of the fluvial system from the rest of the watershed (Figure 11.2). This creates a deficit in

2 Laboratory of excellence in territorial and spatial dynamics.

sediments which raises the question of maintaining the geomorphological balance of the lagoon and the Kneiss Islands, located at the outlet of the watershed, which are home to an internationally recognized nature reserve, classified as an IBA (1990) and Ramsar (2007).

These two examples illustrate the complexity of sediment transfers in watersheds, which are largely influenced by landscape structures such as hedges, embankments, ditches or the road network. They also demonstrate the possibility for the scientific community to go beyond the simple approach of balances (e.g. hydrological, sedimentary) usually carried out at the outlets of the main watersheds. Indeed, to understand the geomorphological behavior of a watershed, it is necessary to question its dynamics observed at intermediate space and time scales, by integrating from the beginning of the reflection the role of anthropical structures collecting or inhibiting sediment transfers and the way in which their spatial organization allows or does not allow a downstream transfer of sediments in the watershed. The challenge here is therefore to open the black boxes that watersheds often still constitute in order to better understand the complexity of the processes that occur within them. The difficulty of the task generally increases with the size of the watershed. To do this, it is necessary to mobilize concepts from spatial analysis (coupling, connectivity, connectedness) that allow us to understand how the structure and functionality of energy and material flows influence the efficiency of transfers in the entire watershed system (Viel et al. 2020).

The emergence of these scientific questions is made possible by the improvement or the mobilization of new tools and methods that more finely take into account the processes, which are at times complex to apprehend because of the multiplicity of the physical, social, economic and political controlling factors that affect them. The development of sensors that quantify processes at high frequency and the increase in the number of measurement networks in river basins have made it possible, for example, to considerably increase the spatial and temporal resolution of measures. This expansion is favored in France by the implementation of the European Water Framework Directive (WFD 2000), which implies a quantitative monitoring of the state of watercourses. At the same time, the development of tools from GIS and remote sensing allows us to better take into account the characteristics of the watersheds (topography, land use, landscape structure) with tightened time steps and spatial resolutions. Finally, the development of modeling and simulation tools (cellular automata, multi-agent systems, artificial intelligence, hydraulic or stock-and-flow modeling) makes it possible to consider a wide range of interrelated factors that are difficult to understand using a classical empirical approach. In the context of global changes which require the consideration of a larger number of general variables, these tools make it possible to better understand the complexity of the internal functioning of anthropized watersheds as well as the way in which the global response of hydrosystems gradually emerges.

11.3.2. *A better apprehension of the effect of practices on the construction and functioning of hydrosocial territories*

If the biophysical aspects constitute the support of all the processes within the watersheds, societies act today in a more preponderant way on the trajectories of evolution and their modalities, sometimes going as far as modifying the topographic limits of watersheds. This is the case in particular when inter-basin transfers take place for drinking water supply, energy production, irrigation (Figure 11.3) or when hydrogeological conditions are favorable for the transfer of water from one basin to another. The term "spillway basin" (Ghiotti 2006) is often used to emphasize this area of both hydrological and hydraulic influence. In basins whose physical characteristics have been profoundly modified, members of the Prodig team have sought, based on the scientific production on the hydrosocial territories (Boelens et al. 2016), to better understand the effects of domestic and agricultural water uses on the functioning of the latter. We develop three examples here that deal with policies and their territorial consequences on two hydraulic spaces: the small water cycle in Paris and the irrigation networks in the Minervois region.

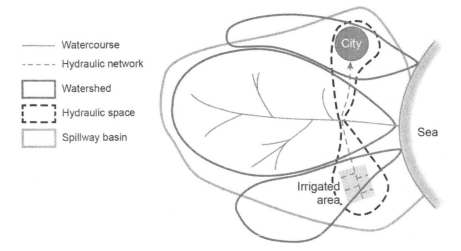

Figure 11.3. *The spillway basin, integrator of the watershed and hydraulic spaces. For a color version of this figure, see www.iste.co.uk/peyroux/development.zip*

The City of Paris imports half of the water it distributes to Parisians from rural areas located at a distance from the place of consumption. Mathilde Resch's doctoral research in geography (2020) discussed the construction of the Parisian hydrosocial territory and its interactions with other territorialities in the Voulzie watershed (Seine-et-Marne), where the capital city operates several drinking water catchments.

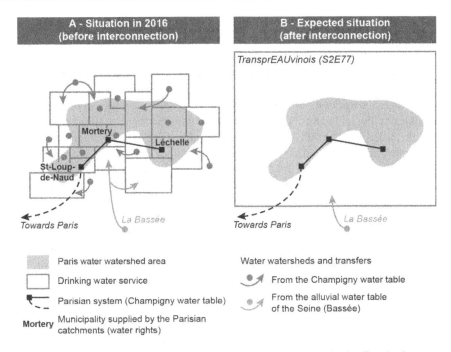

Figure 11.4. *Territorial evolution of water management in the Provinois, Seine basin, France. Source: modified from Resch (2020). For a color version of this figure, see www.iste.co.uk/peyroux/development.zip*

This work was carried out on two temporal scales. A geo-historical approach on the project to divert the sources of the Voulzie and its tributaries (1885–1929) allowed us to consider the construction of the Parisian territory as a contested process, favored by the hydro-hegemony of the capital. The protests of the riparians have contributed to the shaping of this hydraulic space, which has led to important landscape, economic and social transformations in the Voulzie watershed. Today, the issues related to the degradation of the quality of water resources lead to the emergence of two new hydrosocial territories. While the Parisian municipality aims to secure its water supply through policies of prevention of diffuse agricultural pollution, local authorities have opted for the interconnection of drinking water networks of the Provinois (Figure 11.4). The superimposition of these two distinct logics in the same area raises questions about the possibility of integrated water resource management. This work makes a real contribution to research on the hydrosocial territories of drinking water by showing that they are shaped not only by issues of water volumes, as certain bibliographical references tend to suggest (see summary in Damonte and Boelens 2019), but also by issues of the quality of the water distributed. This case study on the drinking water supply for the city of Paris allows us to analyze the relationships between the production territory and the consumption territory.

Downstream of the small domestic water cycle in Paris, the network of wastewater collectors requires monitoring by the City of Paris. The intra- and inter-annual management of the combined sewerage system is confronted with various cascading problems. The overdimensioning and the low slope of the initial network lead to a recurrent sedimentation that the City of Paris manages through human interventions. It appears that the life expectancy of Parisian sewage workers is 15 years lower than the national average. The City of Paris, the PROLOG Ingénierie engineering firm and the University Paris Cité/Prodig Lab have been asked to experiment with the effect of hydraulic flushing in the Parisian combined sewer system, which should eventually lead to the elimination of human intervention to clean the sewers. The doctoral thesis in geography by Gashin Shahsavari (2018) demonstrated the effectiveness of these flushes, notably through the development of two models of sediment transport (uniform and non-uniform) that are now internationally recognized and can be used in other large urban areas.

A second example of the construction of a hydrosocial territory is developed with the case of irrigation in the Minervois (Southern France). In the early 2010s, the Languedoc-Roussillon region, then Occitanie, launched the construction of a huge hydraulic area called Aqua Domitia via its regional development company Bas-Rhône-Languedoc (BRL). The objective was threefold: to meet the challenge of supplying drinking water, particularly in the tourist sectors of the coast; to extend the irrigated areas (mainly vineyards) while securing long-term water needs; and to meet environmental challenges by replacing in situ withdrawals in order to comply with the WFD. It is in this context that the construction of a new hydraulic space in the Minervois (11) was studied. The Jouarres system is being extended in the lower valley of the Argent Double (Lavie et al. 2018). Water from the Aude River, diverted upstream and transported via the Canal du Midi to the Jouarres reserve, will serve as a resource for a future hydraulic system. Today, the irrigators are putting pressure on subsoil water by taking water from a deeper aquifer, used as drinking water supply in the same sector, which is experiencing a drop in piezometric level. In addition, the prefect, applying the WFD, imposed a halt to in situ withdrawals in 2021. The extension of the Jouarres system in the context of the implementation of the regional Aqua Domitia network therefore seems to gain consensus in this study sector, despite the slow progress in financing and implementing the project.

The current study of the creation of a new hydraulic space has already revealed the transformation of the hydrosocial territory: with regard to technical and management levels on the one hand, since the passage from individual "island" irrigation by an "archipelagic" network automatically implies a collective management that takes time to build; and via the power games on the other hand, since the agricultural/viticultural sector is gradually losing its power over the use of resources to the benefit of the urban sectors. This is materialized, for example, by the reinforcement of inter-municipality through the NOTRe [3]law of 2013, with Carcassonne-Agglo having the competence for drinking water distribution as well as participating in the BRL's Board of Directors.

Depending on the local problems and issues, or even on the researchers' interests, the study of complex hydrosystems can therefore be oriented towards a better understanding of the functioning of physical processes in an anthropized watershed and/or towards a more in-depth apprehension of the practices (agricultural, domestic, industrial, energy, etc.), which can have effects on this functioning. The role of public policies, whether they concern the environment (WFD) or land use planning (NOTRe law), is therefore dominant.

11.4. How can the hybrid nature of hydrosystems be taken into account in the management of water-related resources?

Whether it is the implementation of large-scale water strategies for the management of water resources or the simple development of agricultural areas, anthropogenic action is nowadays inherent to the functioning of hydrosystems. It is therefore interesting to examine the way in which human activities are perceived and taken into account in the management of water-related environmental resources. We propose here to take as an example the application of the WFD (2000).

11.4.1. *Reference states inherited from ancient agricultural practices*

The expected objective of the WFD is to achieve "good status" or "good potential" in terms of ecology and chemistry. For its evaluation, it relies on biological, physico-chemical and hydromorphological criteria that must be close to a reference state defined as not (or only very slightly) modified by companies (Roche et al. 2005). In order to comply with these regulatory obligations, the managers have been led to implement ecological restoration projects which are based on the reestablishment of ecological, hydrological and sedimentary continuity. These operations aim not only to remove or develop the transverse structures at the origin of upstream/downstream discontinuities but also to restore the dynamic processes at work in the decompartmentalized river beds (passive physical restoration (Adam et al. 2007)). These operations are therefore based on the resilience capacity of

---

3 *Nouvelle Organisation Territoriale de la République* (New Territorial Organization of the Republic).

hydrosystems in the face of disturbance, allowing for self-restoration of a bed degraded by anthropization through processes internal to the system.

The question of the reference state is central in the application of the WFD since it leads to establishing a diagnosis of the degradations undergone by a watercourse and constitutes a state towards which the remainder of the hydrographic network, considered as altered, must tend. This status of undisturbed (or very slightly) state, by the companies of the reference sites (i.e. before works), can however be discussed with regard to the long haul evolution of the valley bottom landscapes and of the processes at play. For the rivers of northwestern France, the reference state takes the form of a meandering channel in a silty alluvial plain. The work of Laurent Lespez et al. (2015), carried out in collaboration between the UMR LETG, LGP and Prodig, questions the "natural" aspect of these landscapes. Through the example of the Seulles watershed (Normandy), they demonstrate the major effect of anthropization since the end of the Bronze Age on the current landscapes of the valley bottoms. They underline the direct link between the development of agriculture, which promotes the activation of erosive processes on the slopes and the sudden landing on the valley bottoms, multiplied by a factor of 20 in the space of 2,500 years (Viel 2012). This remarkable sedimentary influx is at the origin of a significant and definitive evolution of the valley bottom landscapes, and is reflected in the fossilization of deposits inherited from the last cold period and the channelization of the river. The hydraulic control favored by the development of artisanal and industrial activities starting in the Middle Ages finally stabilized the entire river system (Beauchamps 2017; Viel et al. 2020). The reference state retained by the managers, as well as the functionalities it harbors, thus constitutes a legacy of human activities over the long-term (Lespez et al. 2015) and a watercourse whose dynamics would never have existed in the absence of the hydraulic facilities that we now wish to see disappear. It is therefore surprising to note the discrepancy between the role attributed to human activities, considered within the framework of the WFD as altering the hydrosystems, and the essential role played by these activities on the establishment of the reference states that we wish to safeguard today for the richness of its functionalities.

11.4.2. Hydrosystem resilience versus active restoration

The implementation of the WFD raises the question of the capacity of rivers, once decompartmentalized, to recover an "undisturbed" reference state (passive restoration), by themselves. This question of the resilience of hydrosystems, as well as those of the costs and the durability of the restoration operations implemented, are discussed in the geography doctoral theses of Luc Michler (2018) and Guillaume Brousse (2020), who studied low- and high-energy French rivers, respectively.

Luc Michler (2018) worked on the Yerres watershed (Essonne) whose main course is affected by a strong artificialization of the bed which results in a deep modification of the morphological characteristics of the channel and a significant longitudinal segmentation, i.e. a structure every two kilometers on the main branch. In a context of WFD application, the objective of the work was to identify and quantify the consequences of the removal of the structures on the bed in order to predict the potential evolutions of the decompartmentalized sections (incision of the channel, erosion of the banks, evolution of the piezometry of the alluvial water table). The question was to know if the weak capacity of self-adjustment of this low-energy river would be sufficient to allow it to recover a dynamic close to the sought-after reference state (fluvial style with free meanders). The results obtained show that the low specific stream power observed on the Yerres in a decompartmentalized context favors the great stability of the silty banks, including during the exceptional flood of June 2016. It seems illusory to want to recreate a channel with active morphological dynamics for this type of watercourse and a passive restoration is difficult to envisage. The restoration operations should rather result in the implementation of a so-called "active" restoration consisting of artificially rebuilding the river morphologies expected in the framework of the WFD. The density of the structures to be removed makes the scale of the active restoration work to be carried out titanic, which raises the question of the cost/benefit ratio of such operations.

The work carried out by Guillaume Brousse (2020) on the effectiveness of restoration work and the resilience of altered torrential rivers confirms the strong influence of anthropogenic activities in the functioning of high-energy watersheds. In order to evaluate the effectiveness of three restoration operations carried out on representative sites of alterations (diking, dam and extraction), the study confirms the difficulty of the hydrosystem to recover a stable hydro-sedimentary equilibrium over time. The results indicate that on the Argent Double (tributary of the Aude, Minervois), the restoration of the freedom space (i.e. the removal of lateral constraints) allows the restoration of the channel dynamics and the diversification of ecological habitats while allowing the regulation of liquid and solid flows. However, the expected flood control function is much less effective since the 50-year flood of October 2018, since only one of the three expansion zones remains functional. In the Buëch watershed (tributary of the Durance, Alps), sediment reinjection downstream of the Saint-Sauveur dam is an effective but unsustainable solution to reduce the sediment deficit. The morphological efficacy is better with embankments placed parallel to the main channel during the hydraulic transparencies, but the ecological function of this operation does not appear significant. The return to a sediment deficit in the short-term requires further consideration of the alluvial management strategy. Finally, on the Drac (tributary of the Isère, Alps), marked by significant incision of its channel due to the sediment deficit caused by gravel extraction upstream of the watershed, the reconstitution of the alluvial mattress at

Saint-Bonnet-en-Champsaur has made it possible to stop the incision and to initiate a return to braiding. The restored section is thus successfully adjusted to the reference section. The morphological adjustments have allowed an intensification of the braiding, a diversification of the habitats and considerable hydrobiological gains. The bet of a self-recovery of the braiding seems to have been won, but the temporal hindsight remains insufficient to conclude that the watershed is completely and durably resilient, notably because of the absence of follow-up after a truly morphogenic flood. The work once again emphasizes the intrinsically anthropized nature of the functioning of watersheds whose hydromorphological or ecological functions can only be maintained through heavy restoration operations whose sustainability remains poorly assured. The restoration operations carried out only deal with local disturbances which only attenuate the forcing linked to the global changes, without truly treating them.

All these examples reposition the question of the place of human activities in the functioning of hydrosystems. The latter depend at present and since a long time ago, on anthropic practices, which interfere with natural forcing (Arnaud-Fassetta 2007). A return to an unaltered state, in the sense of a "natural" state, is therefore unthinkable. It appears equally difficult to seek a historical state that is often difficult to maintain. The hydrosystems are in fact in a state of dynamic equilibrium, constantly adjusting to the changes observed in the watershed (intensification of agricultural production systems, agricultural abandonment, sediment extraction, installation of flood control structures). Artificially maintaining this balance requires heavy "restoration" operations that are not always sustainable in terms of cost/benefit ratio. It would undoubtedly be preferable to look for functionalities that allow the various environmental amenities desired by societies to be met (Dufour and Piégay 2009), such as the maintenance of biological functions, heritage safeguarding, risk management and bottomland development or even to the practice of hobbies associated with these spaces. The aim is to present it as such and not as a return to a supposedly natural or initial state.

11.5. Conclusion

At present, watersheds are complex systems whose function results from the combination of physical, social, political and economic processes. They are therefore objects that change in space and time, which leads researchers involved in water-related issues to constantly redefine the framework, the questions and the methods and tools used.

The plurality of control factors to be taken into account, which act on different spatial and temporal scales, makes the problems singularly complex and raises new questions. It is indeed necessary to consider the combined effects of each of these factors on the functioning of the processes and their evolution. The development of slopes by societies can thus lead to a significant modification of water and sediment transfers in the watersheds, sometimes disconnecting large areas from their outlets or, on the contrary, making the sedimentary cascade more efficient. This observation allows us to question the functioning of watersheds at intermediate scales. It mobilizes new tools associated with spatial analysis and benefits from data whose spatial and temporal resolution has greatly improved in recent years.

The fact remains that human activities, often considered as disruptors of physical environments, are still not easily perceived as an inherent component of the functioning of hydrosystems in the management policies of water-related environmental resources, such as the WFD. The research currently conducted on the complexity of the functioning of hydrosystems will undoubtedly make it possible to gradually change this perception. In particular, it should show that it is preferable to look for a state of equilibrium that will enable us to respond to the issues that are considered crucial today, such as the sustainable development of societies, through the safeguarding of biodiversity, patrimonialization and the development of recreational spaces, or even the management of risks.

In a global context of climate change and globalization of land use practices, particularly by agriculture, research on hydrosystems has made it possible to diversify registers of knowledge (e.g. vernacular, expert/non-expert) and their articulation. Research in hydrogeography has long taken into account the prospective and simulation stakes, in particular via modeling; these are now being pursued in the theological contexts of global change and of the Anthropocene (under debate). The studies carried out in the Prodig laboratory with regard to these issues are opening up new fields of research on the interactions between science and society, especially *Big Data* which have increased the potential to access quantitative research material.

11.6. References

Adam, P., Debiais, N., Malavoi, J.R. (2007). *Manuel de restauration hydromorphologique des cours d'eau.* Agence de l'Eau Seine-Normandie, Nanterre.

Amoros, C. and Petts, G.E. (1993). *Hydrosystèmes fluviaux.* Masson, Paris.

Arnaud-Fassetta, G. (2007). L'hydrogéomorphologie fluviale, des hauts bassins montagnards aux plaines côtières : Entre géographie des risques, géarchéologie et géosciences. HDR, Université Paris-Diderot/PRODIG, Paris.

Baviskar, A. (2007). *Waterscapes: The Cultural Politics of a Natural Resource.* Permanent Black, Delhi.

Beauchamps, A., Lespez, L., Rollet, A.J., Germain-Vallée, C., Delahaye, D. (2017). Les transformations anthropiques d'un cours d'eau de faible énergie et leurs conséquences, approche géomorphologique et géoarchéologique dans la moyenne vallée de la Seulles, Normandie. *Géomorphologie : Relief, processus, environnement*, 23(2), 121–132 [Online]. Available at: https://journals.openedition.org/geomorphologie/11702 [Accessed 30 August 2021].

Béthemont, J. (1977). *De l'eau et des hommes, essai géographique sur l'utilisation des eaux continentales*. Bordas, Paris.

Blanchon, D. and Graefe, O. (2012). La radical political ecology de l'eau à Khartoum. Une approche théorique au-delà de l'étude de cas. *L'Espace geographique*, 41(1), 35–50.

Blanchon, D. and Maupin, A. (2009). Géopolitique de l'eau en Afrique australe. *Sécurité Globale*, 3, 79–96.

Boelens, R., Hoogesteger, J., Swyngedouw, E., Vos, J., Wester, P. (2016). Hydrosocial territories: A political ecology perspective. *Water International*, 41(1) 1–14 [Online]. Available at: https://www.tandfonline.com/doi/full/10.1080/02508060.2016.1134898 [Accessed 30 August 2021].

Brousse, G. (2020). Éfficacité des travaux de restauration et résilience des rivières torrentielles altérées. Geography PhD Thesis, Université de Paris/PRODIG, Paris.

Carlier, B. (2019). Les risques d'origine torrentielle et gravitaire dans la haute vallée du Guil (Queyras, Alpes du Sud, France). PhD Thesis, Université Paris-Diderot/PRODIG, Paris.

Chartier, D. and Rodary, E. (2016). *Manifeste pour une géographie environnementale. Géographie, écologie et politique*. Les Presses de Sciences Po, Paris.

Chorley, B.A. and Kennedy, R. (1971). *Physical Geography: A System Approach*. Prentice-Hall, London.

Damonte, G. and Boelens, R. (2019). Hydrosocial territories, agro-export and water scarcity: Capitalistic territorial transformations and water governance in Peru's coastal valleys. *Water International*, 44(2), 206–223.

Dufour, S. and Lespez, L. (2020). *Géographie de l'Environnement. La nature au temps de l'Anthropocène*. Armand Colin, Paris.

Dufour, S. and Piégay, H. (2009). From the myth of a lost paradise to targeted river restoration: Natural references to focus on human benefits. *River Research and Applications*, 25, 568–581.

Gautier, D. and Benjaminsen, T.A. (2012). *Environnement, discours et pouvoir. L'approche Political ecology*. Editions Quae, Paris.

Ghiotti, S. (2006). Les Territoires de l'eau et la décentralisation. La gouvernance de bassin ou les limites d'une évidence. *Développement durable et territoires*, 6.

Graefe, O. (2011). Eau et société : Rapports, théories et concepts. *Séminaire hydrosystèmes et hydropolitique*. Université Paris-Ouest, Nanterre.

Horton, R.E. (1933). The role of infiltration in the hydrological cycle. *American Geophysical Union Transactions*, 14(1), 446–460.

Jaglin, S. (2008). Differentiating networked services in Cape Town: Echoes of splintering urbanism? *Geoforum*, 39(6), 1897–1906.

Laganier, R. and Arnaud-Fassetta, G. (2009). *Les géographies de l'eau. Processus, dynamique et gestion de l'hydrosystème*. L'Harmattan, Paris.

Lave, R., Biermann, C., Lane, S.N. (2018). *The Palgrave Handbook of Critical Physical Geography*. Palgrave Macmillan, London.

Lavie, E., Guillemot, M., Mangeret, C. (2018). Le futur espace hydraulique minervois. Mutations de l'irrigation dans le contexte de la mise en place du projet Aqua Domitia Méditerranée [Online]. Available at: http://journals.openedition.org/mediterranee/8656 [Accessed 7 July 2021].

Lespez, L., Viel, V., Rollet, A.J., Delahaye, D. (2015). The anthropogenic nature of present-day low energy rivers in western France and implications for current restoration projects. *Geomorphology*, 251, 64–76.

Linton, J. (2008). Is the hydrologic cycle sustainable? A historical–geographical critique of a modern concept. *Annals of the Association of American Geographers*, 98(3), 630–649.

Michler, L. (2018). Impacts hydromorphologiques et sédimentaires du décloisonnement de l'Yerres. Identification, quantification, spatialisation. PhD Thesis, Université Paris-Diderot/ PRODIG, Paris.

Morandi, B., Piégay, H., Lamouroux, N., Vaudor, L. (2014). How is success or failure in river restoration projects evaluated? Feedback from French restoration projects. *Journal of Environmental Management*, 137, 178–188.

Pardé, M. (1964). *Études potamologiques sur la Loire et ses affluents*. Sfil, Poitiers.

Pigeon, P. (2005). *Géographie critique des risques*. Economica, Paris.

Resch, M. (2020). Les territoires d'approvisionnement en eau potable de Paris. Du transfert à la préservation des ressources. PhD Thesis, Université de Paris/PRODIG, Paris.

Roche, P.A., Billen, G., Bravard, J.P., Décamps, H., Rennequin, D., Vindimian, E., Wasson, J.G. (2005). Les enjeux de recherche liés à la directive-cadre européenne sur l'eau. *C.R. Geoscience*, 337, 243–267.

Scarwell, H.J. and Laganier, R. (2004). *Risque d'inondation et aménagement durable du territoire*. Presses Universitaires du Septentrion, Lille.

Schumm, S.A. (1977). *The Fluvial System*. Wiley, New York.

Shahsavari, G. (2018). Experimental and numerical investigations of flushing in combined sewer networks. Study case of a Parisian trunk sewer. PhD Thesis, Université Paris-Diderot/PRODIG, Paris.

Tadaki, M., Brierley, G., Dickson, M., Le Heron, R., Salmond, J. (2015). Cultivating critical practices in physical geography. *The Geographical Journal*, 181, 160–1714.

Viel, V. (2012). Analyse spatiale et temporelle des transferts sédimentaires dans les hydrosystèmes normands. PhD Thesis, Université de Caen-Normandie, Caen.

Viel, V., Fort, M., Lissak, C., Graff, K., Carlier, B., Arnaud-Fassetta, G., Cossart, E., Madelin, M. (2018). Debris-flow functioning and their contribution to sedimentary budgets: The Peynin subcatchment of the Guil River (Upper Queyras, Southern French Alps). *Landform Analysis*, 36, 71–84.

Viel, V., Reulier, R., Lespez, L., Rollet, A.-J., Lissak, C. (2020). Comprendre le fonctionnement des bassins versants anthropisés. In *Géographie de l'Environnement. La nature au temps de l'Anthropocène*, Dufour, S. and Lespez, L. (eds). Armand Colin, Paris.

Walker, P.A. (2006). Political ecology: Where is the policy? *Progress in Human Geography*, 30(3), 382–395.

Walker, P.A. (2007). Political ecology: Where is the politics? *Progress in Human Geography*, 31(3), 363–369, 59–76.

PART 3

Knowledge Production and Knowledge through the Relationship between Science and Society

12

The Ecological Transition
of the Coastline in France

12.1. Introduction

Designating "any process of transformation of the economy aimed at maintaining its resources and regulations below critical thresholds for the viability of our societies" (Dron and Franq 2013), the notion of ecological transition (ET)[1] aims to complete and clarify the concept of sustainable development by considering different levels of commitment – low, medium and high – of society to enable it to ensure its sustainability (Bourg 2012). It has become not only a priority of the French state, but also an obligatory frame of reference for public action and research. Energy, agri-food or industrial transitions have thus become priority projects in France, requiring the implementation of new modes of consumption, production and exchange in line with the objectives of sustainable development as well as a reflection on how to manage this transition (Rumpala 2010).

In terms of territorial public action in favor of the sea and the coast, this reflection has developed in connection with the establishment in 2005 of a policy of integrated coastal zone management (*gestion intégrée de zones côtières*, GIZC) (Drobenko 2012) for territorial planning, set by the LOADDT law[2] of 1999. Without questioning the principle of sustainability, the implementation of the ecological transition through an "interactive process aiming to build a common representation

Chapter written by Frédéric BERTRAND and Brice ANSELME.

1 The ecological transition is originally a permaculture concept made up of a set of principles and practices derived from experiments on local autonomy in a context of oil dependency and global warming (Hopkins 2008).

2 Law of orientation for the planning and the sustainable development of the territory no. 99–355 of June 25, 1999, also known as "Voynet law".

of the coastal reality" has raised numerous questions about the declination of sustainable development for coastal areas and its efficiency on territorial governance (Meur-Ferec 2009). Feedback from experiences and the inclusion of GIZC territory projects in a kind of "stimulating utopia" (Meur-Ferec 2009) lead to the hypothesis that the development of French coasts is in the context of a "new" paradigm. French coasts are in a position of average sustainability, expressing their involvement in the ecological transition to varying degrees, between two poles – weak and strong – of sustainability (Neumaye 2003) (Table 12.1).

Sustainability Source of ambiguity	Low	Average (open sustainability)	High (closed sustainability)
Model (epistemic)	Acceptance of the total ecological substitution by human.	Acceptance of the partial ecological substitution by human ("hybridization").	Defense of naturalness. Refusal of the ecological substitution by human.
Rules (ethical)	Restoration of market regulation.	Reform of the system through "ecological modernization" (Rudolf 2013).	Radical transformation of the socio-economic system.
Value (axiological)	Anthropo-centric. Instrumental value of coastal nature. Commodification of nature.	Geo-centric. Variability of protection levels and statuses according to territorial issues.	Eco-centric. Intrinsic value of nature. Homogeneity of the statuses of protection.
Objectives, goals (teleological)	Maintaining a level of welfare. Sustainable growth.	–	Integration of the responsibility of human activity in the biosphere. Degrowth.

Table 12.1. *Sustainable development issues bounded by the positionings between economy and development according to sources of ambiguity*

The objective of this chapter is to show how, based on a variety of approaches to environmental change, the research actions conducted at the UMR Prodig during the 2010s have been put at the service of a change of paradigm in the way of managing the coasts by placing their development in a transitional space, open to the expression of intermediate positions between economy (weak sustainability) and environment (strong sustainability) (Arias-Maldonado 2013).

This paradigm shift in coastal management accompanies the overall dynamic of stakeholder mobilization initiated by the new national strategy for sustainable development (*stratégie nationale de développement durable*, SNDD) 2010–2013 and reaffirmed by the national strategy for transition to sustainable development (*stratégie nationale de transition vers le développement durable*, SNTEDD) 2015–2020. The latter is "intended to reconcile long and short time frames and to promote the progressive and long-term appropriation of the ecological transition by stakeholders" (MEEM 2017). The 2012–2015 National Coastline Management Strategy (*stratégie nationale de gestion du trait de côte*, SNGTC), whose primary objective was the ecological transition for the sea and coastline, already placed public and private actors at the heart of strategy development to "prepare actors for the implementation of the long-term relocation of exposed activities and assets" (MEDDE 2012). The message is clear: the evolution towards a recomposition of the territory is subordinated to the coordination of the multiple potential actors of the transition and to citizen participation approaches within a coherent and stable socio-technical system. This injunction from the public authorities responds to a lack of federative organization of goodwill and expertise highlighted on a national scale by sociologists (Jollivet 2015) as much as to the prolonged absence of a real state doctrine on the coast (Whiteside et al. 2010).

The finalized research program LITEAU in support of sustainable development of the sea and coastline (Baron 2017) had already supported, as early as 1998, the development of knowledge, methods and scientific practices useful for the definition and implementation of collective actions and public policies on the coastline. However, it was not until the following decade that the public process of reflection and negotiation between the State, elected officials, economic actors and civil society, which led to the "*Grenelle de l'environnement*" in 2007, led coastal territories into a "reflexive moment pertaining to the development of the adaptive governance of socio-technical systems" (Chaffin et al. 2014).

Through a renewed methodological approach to coastal risks, the BARCASUB[3] research project, led by UMR Prodig, on the issue of depoldering as a possible solution to the management of the risk of marine submersion around the Arcachon basin, has sought to highlight the ambiguities in the positions expressed by territorial actors concerning the contours and content of the notion of sustainable development. Placed in the context of complex systems (multiplicity of rationalities and representations, interdependence between the dimensions at work in the coastal system, dynamic and random nature of the system) and open to a transdisciplinary

---

3 Marine submersion and its environmental and social impacts in the Arcachon basin. Institutional partners: Prodig, LGP, EPOC, Conservatoire du littoral, SIBA, Aquitaine region, CG Gironde. Funding (2009–2012): Liteau III program (MEDDE). Co-leaders: Lydie Goeldner-Gianella and Frédéric Bertrand (UMR Prodig).

vision (Horlinck-Jones and Sime 2004), these ambiguities have subsequently occupied a prominent place in the methodological approach to risks developed by the coastal geographers of the UMR Prodig. They have also been mobilized according to the precepts of cindynics[4] (Kervern 1999) in a research field abroad (Bertrand et al. 2014a), where the identification and characterization of these ambiguities were proposed as a key to reading and understanding the ecological transition on French coastlines. Following the typology proposed by Kervern (1999), the postulate is that the positioning of coastal actors between economy (weak sustainability) and environment (strong sustainability) varies depending on the actors but also over time – according to four forms of ambiguity (Table 12.1):

– Epistemic ambiguities in relation to the hypotheses of substitution between technical capital and natural capital based on more or less proven facts (renewal rate of resources, carrying capacity of coastlines, efficiency of natural defenses versus protection works).

– Axiological ambiguities about the value system attributed to coastal nature oscillating between instrumental and intrinsic value (Hess 2013).

– Ambiguities on the rules of deontology framing the functioning of the regional planning system capable of putting sustainable development into action at the local level (Bertrand et al. 2014a).

– Teleological ambiguities on the objectives pursued by each actor involved in the planning and development of coastal territories.

Because they originate from and are justified by teleological ambiguities about the objectives pursued by coastal actors, the research projects on the coastline involving teacher–researchers from UMR Prodig (CRISSIS[5]/Aude, LITAQ[6]/Médoc, DIGUES[7]/Authie, ARESMA[8]/Mayotte, LittoSIM[9]/Oléron, BARCASUB/Arcachon)

---

4 Cindynics or the science of danger, theorized by Georges-Yves Kervern, is a systemic approach that focuses on sources of danger that are not directly perceptible, because they are subject to ambiguities about data, models, objectives, norms and values.

5 "Caractérisation des risques submersion sur des sites sensibles (CRISSIS)". CSFRS project (Conseil supérieur de la formation et de la recherche stratégiques) 2015-2017. Institutional partners: LGP, Gred, BRGM. Leader: B. Anselme (UMR Prodig).

6 "Du Pléistocène à l'Anthropocène : connaître les mécanismes passés d'évolution des populations (végétales, animales, humaines) et des milieux pour prédire les réponses futures. L'exemple du littoral aquitain (LITAQ)". INTERLABEX project COTE/LaScArBx 2015-2017. Institutional partners: UMR Ausonius, UMR Biogeco, UMR EPOC, UMR Pacea, UMR Prodig. Co-leaders: F. Verdin (Ausonius) and F. Eynaud (EPOC).

7 "Digues, interactions, gestion, usages, environnement, scénarios (DIGUES)". ANR project 2019-2021. Institutional partners: LGP, LAREP, CRH-UMR8558 Centre de recherches historiques, LADYSS, Prodig, LIENSs. Leader: L. Goeldner-Gianella (LGP).

fall into the categories of action research approaches (Thietard 1999) that we will first identify (section 12.2). We will then see that the will to reduce these ambiguities is at the heart of the research devices of projects forced to adapt to the contingencies of the field (section 12.3). In light of the results of these programs, some elements of appreciation of the efficiency of ecological transition (section 12.4) before concluding by questioning the reality of the ecological transition on the coasts and the operational scope of this concept applied to an object that is by its very nature moving.

12.2. Categorization of action research projects on the coasts

These research projects can be distinguished according to whether they aim first and foremost to produce knowledge on environmental change with a view to changing reality ("to know in order to change", section 12.2.1) or whether they give priority to accompanying environmental change ("to change in order to know", section 12.2.2). But whatever the purpose of the projects, the knowledge/change articulation often appears to be a source of tension between researchers and field actors directly linked to political networks (section 12.2.3).

12.2.1. Projects focusing on the development of scientific knowledge

We distinguish here a set of approaches that allow us:

– to produce knowledge on the territorial system and its functioning as a prerequisite or support for the definition of public policies such as the LITAQ and ESTRAN projects;

– to develop knowledge that is both scientifically rigorous and "actionable", with a general scope (generic property) and that can be used by the actors within situations, according to the aims of the research (BARCASUB and CRISSIS projects);

– to evaluate the effectiveness of the models and management tools such as the management of aquatic environments and flood prevention (GEMAPI), which has

---

8 "Agir pour la résilience des systèmes socio-écologiques de mangroves de Mayotte afin de favoriser leur préservation (ARESMA)". Fondation de France (FdF) project. Institutional partners: CUFR, Prodig. Leader: C. Golléty (CUFR Mayotte).

9 "Simulation participative pour la sensibilisation des acteurs de l'aménagement du littoral face au risque de submersion marine (LittoSIM)". CNRS Coastal Challenge Project. Institutional partners: LIENSs, UMMISCO, Prodig, CITERES, PACTE, Géolab. Leader: N. Bécu (LIENSs).

been entrusted to the intercommunalities since January 1, 2018, and whose implementation by territorial actors is monitored by the DIGUES project from a research-intervention perspective (David 2000).

12.2.2. *Projects focusing on socio-environmental change*

The production of knowledge, seen as the result of mutual learning between researchers and field actors, is considered to be the best way to promote socio-environmental change. Thus, beyond achieving the objectives of the BARCASUB project, the researchers' concern was to analyze the effects of their intervention in inter-municipal territory projects in the Arcachon basin. The project aimed to help the actors define possible evolution trajectories, choose the coastal protection options best adapted to the local context to carry them out and even to evaluate the outcome (Bertrand and Goeldner-Gianella 2013; Goeldner-Gianella and Bertrand 2014). Following the BARCASUB project, the ANR DIGUES has set itself the objective of determining the evolution trajectories of coastal diking systems on the Channel-Atlantic coast, no longer as sets of independent protective structures but as real diking systems.

It will be observed that the nature and purpose of this knowledge and, consequently, the socio-environmental change targeted, vary. The objective of the research may be:

– to reveal the mechanisms of attachment to the place of the populations living in the areas undergoing depoldering (BARCASUB project[10]);

– to co-construct conceptual models combining societal and ecological dimensions in order to determine key variables influencing the resilience of mangroves to guide their sustainable management (ARESMA project);

– to create, in a more "activist" participative approach, knowledge on the local apprehension of the stakes – with the help of landscape mediation – and on the applicability of the operating rules – with the help of agent-based role-playing games – in order to emancipate oneself from visions of territorial management that are too technocratic or too conformist (LittoSIM, DIGUES).

Here, action and intervention go beyond their status as a means of elaborating on knowledge which they benefit from in the first type of project, in favor of the participation of the actors of the social systems to which they are applied.

---

10 See the program presentation on the website: https://www.lgp.cnrs.fr/digues/.

12.2.3. *The dynamic tension between knowledge production and change*

The CRISSIS program illustrates how coastal risk studies are often initially misunderstood by stakeholders who see an antagonism between economic development, through land use planning and tourism, and natural risks. Considered as a factor causing panic for the local populations, which could dissipate the financial windfall represented by tourist activity, this risk study could not be carried out in the zone foreseen at the time of the assembly of the project, because of a development project giving rise to many controversies but defended by the regional elected officials. On the contrary, the desire to articulate knowledge and change was able to generate a real collective appetite in the development and implementation of the LittoSIM project (Bécu et al. 2017). The stated objective here was to develop a pedagogical tool to raise awareness among land-use planners of prevention and planning measures related to the risk of marine submersion. Stimulated by an operational objective defined in partnership with the community of municipalities, the exchanges between researchers and field actors conducted in the framework of participatory simulation workshops made it possible to continue the research by extending it to new partners specializing in risk prevention and planning (Direction générale de la prévention des risques (DGPR), Centre d'études et d'expertise sur les risques, l'environnement, la mobilité et l'aménagement (CEREMA) and the Conseil départemental).

These two research experiences raise the question of whether or not a coastal research project should be linked to a territorial project. The ARESMA project conducted in Mayotte is rich in lessons from this point of view. The relationships and collaboration between researchers (ecologists, geographers, linguists) and field actors (Conservatoire du littoral, Parc naturel marin de Mayotte, ONF, DEAL, UICN, Association des naturalistes de Mayotte) around the confrontation and the production of new knowledge are taking place in the following territories – Dembéni, Bandrélé – which are well targeted. However, they are not accompanied by a territorial development project despite the many social and environmental issues at stake in the coastal areas of Mayotte Island. This approach to coastal space indirectly targeted on spatial planning issues may seem to limit the operational scope of the research project. However, in coastal areas on the margins, this approach can just as easily promote the construction of new territories through the development of internal links between researchers and field actors, as well as external links between program participants and territorial operators, in the coastal territory. One of the functions of the steering committees is to contribute, through an approach that is decoupled from the issues in the field, to the progressive transformation of the mangrove study object analyzed from the point of view of their functioning and the impacts of climate change into a territorial object with a view to its appropriation by all local actors.

12.3. Research systems with variable geometry

12.3.1. *The importance given to the construction of the research object*

The research-action projects conducted at UMR Prodig are based on the desire to solve problems of risk management and coastal development. The transformation of these problems into research objects, understood as "questions that articulate theoretical, methodological and/or empirical objects that crystallize the researcher's knowledge project" (Allard-Poesi and Perret 2003) and possibly here, the participants, can take different paths. The transformation of the problem can proceed, as in the DIGUES project, from a translation of the problem expressed by the actor managers through the researcher's considerations and/or theoretical concerns. Thus, the initial problem of the assumption by local authorities of the GEMAPI competence of flood protection was transformed into a problematic on the future of dikes through that of diking systems, a newly consecrated notion to designate the dike and the diked territory it protects (decree no. 2015-526 of 12 May 2015). Based on the shared observation that the paradigms of dike management have now changed and the general assumption that the question of dikes must be reexamined independently of the technique, ANR DIGUES intends to answer the question of the future of dikes in the form of a series of specific hypotheses submitted to the test of consultation. In the absence of a duly expressed social demand, the initial problem can be formulated through a socio-political or socio-ecological theoretical perspective aimed at unveiling the territorial actors. The socio-ecological analysis developed by the ARESMA project based on the concept of socio-ecosystem thus aims to determine how and when to involve the residents of the mangroves in management actions before acting on the resilience of mangroves in the study sites through several informative and participatory actions (Golléty 2020). One working hypothesis is that one of the obstacles to mangrove protection resides in the scientific and societal uncertainties associated with the ecosystemic services provided by the mangrove. The project consists of translating the findings of the study into action, in order to improve the quality of the mangrove's ecosystems. The project consists of translating the observation of the decline of the mangrove into a mission of "revelation" to the actors and populations of the conditions allowing them to envisage a sustainable use of the environment. If the object of research is the product of a construction with the participants, it is part of the framework of knowledge which the researcher coming from metropolitan France or abroad initially controls the acquisition and capitalization of, thus recalling the gap between the concerns of researchers and non-researchers in the South (Anadon 2013).

The more resolutely participative approaches of the BARCASUB, DIGUES, ESTRAN and LittoSIM projects are different from this logic of "translation" and the "suffered" model of participation that underlies it. The research object here proceeds from a construction process aiming either at mutual learning and change (pragmatist and cooperative approaches of the BARCASUB, DIGUES or LittoSIM projects) or at the production of actionable knowledge (engineering and research-intervention approaches of the CRISSIS project). The forms and paths taken by this construction will vary according to the approach.

12.3.2. A range of methods varying according to the participation of the actors

	Data collection, analysis and processing tools	Qualitative and quantitative methods for survey research	Stakeholder group discussions	Modeling (conceptual, physical, multi-agent, role-playing)
"Knowing to change"				
FdF ARESMA	XXX	XX	X	
interLABEX LITAQ	XXX		XX	
Région ESTRAN	XXX		XX	
CSFRS CRISSIS	XX	XX	XX	XXX
"Changing to know"				
Liteau BARCASUB	XX	XXX	X	XX
ANR DIGUES	XX	XX	XXX	XX
CNRS/FdF LITTOSIM	XX	X	XXX	XXX

Table 12.2. Methods and tools of action research projects involving UMR Prodig (number of crosses proportional to the relative importance of the methods and tools used in the different projects)

Two groups of projects can be distinguished according to the combination of investigation, diagnosis and reflection methods used (Table 12.2). The first group mobilizes to varying degrees all the methods and tools (BARCASUB, CRISSIS, DIGUES and LittoSIM), while a second group of projects uses a more limited range of methods (ARESMA, ESTRAN, LITAQ). This second group of projects is free of modeling tools and focuses instead on data collection, analysis and processing tools. This dichotomy covers the distinction between projects that prioritize the accompaniment of territorial changes and projects that prioritize the acquisition of knowledge. It reflects the importance of the epistemic (use of models) and deontological dimensions (definition of rules) in collaborative approaches compared to the statistical dimension (production of data) prevailing in environmental engineering and research-intervention approaches.

In the latter, the collection and processing of biophysical and human data also give rise to group discussions within the framework of steering committees facilitating the practice of interdisciplinarity (ARESMA, LittoSIM). This having been said, the territorial facilitation to bring together actors and untie the complexity in the implementation of projects is not a guarantee of efficiency, as demonstrated by the difficulties of the CRISSIS project due to prior political differences between territorial actors (Anselme et al. 2011).

12.3.3. More or less reflective investigation strategies

Whether their primary aim is the development of scientific knowledge or the production of environmental change, action research generally proceeds in distinct phases that follow a description of the system (structure of the group and its context, relative position of the entities that make it up and their structuring dimensions), intervention on the system (actions), observation of the changes induced by the actions and a final phase of interpretation of the results of the project. While the architecture of the projects more or less follows this system, the status accorded to it varies from one approach to another. In the CRISSIS and LITAQ projects, compliance with the established program guarantees the inferences produced, whereas in the DIGUES, LittoSIM, ARESMA and ESTRAN projects, the program is conceived more as a framework that makes it possible to articulate the different elements of a research in accordance with collective learning and modifications that may lead to its evolution.

In the participatory approaches of the ARESMA and LittoSIM projects, meetings between researchers and stakeholders-managers on the one hand, and the setting up of surveys on the other have allowed the development of a subjective and critical reflexivity. However, the research process including a survey does not guarantee participation or collective learning. Indeed, when the time lag between the acquisition of social data and environmental data is too great, the commitment of the populations surveyed in the process of co-construction of knowledge is limited, particularly with regard to strategic questions concerning the evaluation of the risk of submersion (Bertrand and Goeldner-Gianella 2013). Overcoming these organizational constraints seems only possible through the coordination of a participatory simulation device to produce learning among local government representatives in charge of risk prevention strategies (LittoSIM).

All in all, if the projects mentioned have the same objective of inciting participation of actors, not all of them are supposed to lead to the empowerment of the group of actors in which the research takes place, as the project framework was not conceived at the outset as a framework that could be malleable by the actors themselves. The LittoSIM project stands out, once again, with the setting up of a project axis dedicated to the transfer of the LittoSIM system to local authorities.

12.3.4. *The flexibility of research systems in the field*

Action-research projects on the coastline take place during periods in which the concerns of actors under the influence of coastal events linked to natural hazards (storms, marine submersions) or anthropic actions (protection works, infrastructure construction), which will necessarily change. Without mentioning here a major disturbance such as the pandemic crisis linked to Covid-19 whose scope and impact go far beyond the scope of these projects, it is appropriate to consider the role and place of exceptional meteorological and marine events, such as the storms of February 2010 (Xynthia), the winter of 2013–2014, on the Atlantic coast of France, or January 2018 (Eléanor) in the Channel, in the development of the action research.

These events occupy an important place in reflection on the nature of the danger of the BARCASUB, CRISSIS and DIGUES projects related to the theme of natural risks. Their occurrence offers the opportunity to observe and analyze in real time, as if in "full scale", phenomena that are at the center of the research system, justifying the human and financial commitment of the programs. In projects that aim to characterize adaptation trajectories to ancient (LITAQ) or current (ARESMA) environmental changes, these extreme events have less of an impact on the understanding of the research object than on the development of field and preventive archaeology protocols.

In projects that focus on accompanying coastal territorial changes (BARCASUB, DIGUES), extreme events sometimes suddenly reveal the potential for damage of the whole or a fraction of the coastal territories. But the collaboration expected by the researchers with the actors on the ground and the managers of damaged sites, or those likely to be damaged, is often postponed or even hindered by the appearance or the unveiling of territorial issues that were previously hidden. The evolution of the positioning of territorial operators directly concerned by these issues (Conservatoire du littoral) can lead to a modification of the initial mechanism in the direction of an autonomization of its parts instead of the integration of the expected scientific and management approaches.

In projects whose priority is the production of knowledge, "external" events, linked to natural or societal processes unrelated to the fundamental question of the project, can serve as a pretext for bringing together different forms of local and scientific knowledge. These may be simple opportunities that arise during the course of the project, such as the addition of an in situ crisis simulation "marine submersion" exercise in Leucate which reinforced the operational approach of the CRISSIS project compared to the analytical approach of the risk situation and widened the panel of actor–managers (Anselme et al. 2019). But the relationship between researchers and managerial participants extends beyond a one-time action to reveal a community of interest around, for example, the diversity of heritage issues of the Medoc coastline (archaeological remains, Belle Époque villas, back-dune natural habitats) highlighted by erosion and coastline recession (Bertrand et al. 2019a). The rapprochement between the researchers of the LITAQ project and the local authorities (community of municipalities of Médoc, Nouvelle-Aquitaine region) concerned with the management of the coastline has thus enabled geoarchaeological investigations to be continued through the regional ESTRAN project, around a problematic extended to the adaptation of several coastal territories to past and present environmental changes. In the ARESMA project, exchanges with institutional partners have allowed the consolidation of a common linguistic fund around the constitution of a problematic intended to popularize and raise awareness on the island's mangroves with a dual heritage, with both natural and cultural dimensions (Rasoamanana 2019). In a politico-administrative context in the process of consolidation, the regular consultation with the representatives of the institutional managers (ONF, PNMM, CELRL, DEAL, Conseil départemental) facilitated the appropriation of the deliverables of the project according to the respective progress of the management actions and the research actions relating to the representations and the uses of the mangroves[11].

The modifications of the initial system reflect in all the projects mentioned, according to the intrinsic property of action research, the issue of the system's adjustment to the reflection processes of constituted research groups. The dynamic tension between knowledge production and territorial change can lead to conflict situations (Port-la-Nouvelle for the CRISSIS project, Baie d'Authie for the DIGUES project) to a transformation of the object during the process. This transformation refers, at a more general level, to the ambivalence and diversity of the actors' representations, the analysis of which only can lead to a deep understanding of risk situations (Kervern 1999). It confirms the role and responsibility of researchers and stakeholder-managers in the transition of coastal areas towards sustainable development, which the projects conducted at UMR Prodig allow us to specify the scope of.

11 Thesis in progress by Anliati Ahmed Abdallah, Sorbonne University/Centre universitaire de formation et de recherche de Mayotte, under the direction of F. Bertrand: "Dynamique, savoirs écologiques et usages des mangroves de Mayotte".

12.4. The commitment of the French coastline in the ecological transition: elements of discussion

As an object of reflection, enunciation and government, can the ecological transition also be an object of evaluation? Yes, provided that the transition is placed in relation to the objective of perpetuating coastal societies (sustainability) and in the overall perspective of the mode of development to achieve this (sustainable development). Considering with Rotmans and Kemp (2003) that "sustainability represents a challenge involving the management transitional problems of adaptation costs, resistance from vested interests and of special interests and uncertainty these three variables can be used as criteria for judging, estimating and defining the degree of commitment of coastal territories in the transition towards sustainable development".

12.4.1. *An evaluation biased by the institutional reflexivity of ET*

One of the difficulties of transition evaluation is linked to the importance of reflexive contributions in the transition process initiated at the institutional level through the implementation of public action strategies. Indeed, the normative and performative logics of these strategies, where the selection and valorization of "good projects" and "good practices" constitute factors of legitimization and structuring of public action (Rocle 2017), lead public institutions to be both judge and a part of transition processes. Thus, the approval on April 23, 2019, of the 10 plans for the prevention of the risk of flooding by marine submersion (*prévention du risque d'inondation par submersion marine*, PPRSM) of the Arcachon basin in line with the national strategy for the management of flood and marine submersion risks (MEED 2014) was presented by the Prefecture of the Gironde and the General Directorate for Risk Prevention (*Direction générale de prévention des risques*, DGPR) as a success since "these plans have been the subject of extensive consultation with many working meetings that have allowed elected officials, unions, associations and local stakeholders to actively participate in their development". The legitimacy of the strategy deployed by the State in the Arcachon Basin should not obscure the late start of this consultation, six years after the prescription of the PPRSM (Goeldner-Gianella et al. 2013), whilst a provisional mapping of the marine submersion hazard had been sketched out since the publication of the circular of 27/07/11 relating to the consideration of the risk of submersion in prevention plans (Bertrand et al. 2014b). The time lag between the implementation of the PPRSM in April 2019 and a devastating natural event such as the Xynthia storm in February 2010 cannot be considered as the mark of a very successful ecological transition in terms of coastal risk management. The geographical issue of the ecological transition is not so much the efficiency of public action through the reflexive returns of projects (Rocle 2017) as the measurement of territorial changes to assess the effectiveness of actions taken on the ground.

12.4.2. General criteria for evaluating mastery of ET

Encouraged by the recommendations of the Eurosion project (2004), the use of cost–benefit analysis in the evaluation of coastal development projects only became truly important with the relocation of highly exposed assets, recommended by the State after the Grenelle de la Mer in 2007 (MEDDE 2012). As major development projects come up against the acceptability constraints of the populations concerned, their economic legitimacy implies calculating future avoided costs as well as the benefits resulting from the maintenance of environmental amenities, in particular recreational ones. The long sandy coasts of the Gulf of Lion and the Bay of Biscay, which were made vulnerable to erosion and marine submersion by the massification of tourism practices orchestrated by the regional planning missions of the 1960s, have thus become privileged areas for experimenting with methods of economic evaluation of relocation and studying the feasibility of this strategy on a regional scale. The performance of a cost–benefit analysis, to justify the adoption of a strategic retreat rather than maintaining and reinforcing the artificialization of the coastline, tends to be imposed on all development projects of sites subject to coastal risks. This can be a national project of relocation experimentation (MEDDE 2012) or a flood prevention action program (*programme d'actions de prévention des inondations*, PAPI) involving local public establishments of inter-communal cooperation.

While the evaluation of coastal developments marks for many institutional actors a commitment to the transition to sustainable development, it does not address the control of adaptation costs linked to the recomposition of coastal and retro-coastal spaces, nor of the potential attractiveness of the territories redeveloped after relocation (Mineo-Kleiner 2017). Displaying the cost of the transition towards a more sustainable model of coastal development does not allow us to prejudge the acceptability of climate change adaptation measures either. Perceptions and views on relocation reflect among many residents and managers an evolutionary approach to adaptation measures where relocalization occurs in the medium term after a phase of protection and transition to this type of operation consisting of a validation of the hypothesis of long-term benefits of relocation (Rey-Valette et al. 2019). Indeed, the doubts expressed about the institutional mechanisms, organizational modes and financing conditions of a relocation operation favor the resistance of particular interests in the name of attachment to place, including in regions strongly committed to these procedures such as the Arcachon basin. Around the basin, the project to relocate tourist activities in the town of La Teste-de-Buch and the projects of depolderization reinforce the Promethean dimension of the project to fix the tip of Cap Ferret pursued relentlessly since 1985 (Goeldner-Gianella et al. 2015)[12] .

The feedback from experiences in relocation and strategic retreat show the difficulty of making a change of "culture" and a "transition" (semantic, organizational, administrative) to move from "sea defense" to "integrated coastline management" (Rocle 2017). Even when consultation and communication with the stakeholders and populations concerned benefit from the support of a public policy facilitator, such as the Aquitaine Coastal Public Interest Group, reflection on coastal issues remains dependent on the urgency of risk situations likely to catch the project owners unaware and to reinforce the divergence of views on the order of strategies.

Despite the improved predictability of hazardous weather events, the damage caused remains random, thus maintaining uncertainty in terms of the best option for reducing the vulnerability of the territories that are most obviously at risk. The reduction of the uncertainties of the forecasting models thus represents a high-priority scientific challenge supported both by institutional actors and by municipally elected officials, anxious to be able to justify to their populations the taking into account of the constraints fixed in the PPRSM. This persistent uncertainty plays into the hands of "developers", encouraging, in a context of depleted backshore land reserves, as in the commune of Le Teich, the declassification of wooded areas for the creation of ecotourism facilities (Bertrand and Magri 2019). Isn't the least of the paradoxes of the actions undertaken in the name of the ecological transition to want to deal with the uncertainties and changing conditions of the natural and institutional environment while being limited by local event-based constraints?

12.5. Conclusion: scope and limitations of the ET concept on the coasts

The very mixed results of the ecological transition belatedly initiated by the State in the early 2010s raise questions about the operational scope of the concept of transition and its meaning. Have the French coasts had the time to find a middle way between two models of sustainability – weak and strong – that are considered antinomic? Are coastal territories moving, beyond regional specificities, from a situation of "non-sustainability" to "sustainable" development, thereby validating the hypothesis that they are in a transition phase? The reading and appreciation grid of transition problems, which are the costs of adaptation, the resistance of particular

---

12 The "defensive" positions of the instigator and builder of the dike of Cap Ferret, Benoit Bartherotte, were reinforced in 2018 by the report commissioned by the Direction régionale de l'environnement (Dreal) to Cerema and to a reversal of positions of elected officials.

interests and uncertainty about the best possible option, provides some elements of an answer.

If we consider that the concertation actions undertaken on the coast have made it possible to more directly question the principles and practices of governance in the face of complexity and uncertainty of situations, we will admit that the results of these actions are positive. The territorial projects initiated around relocation and ecological innovation have enabled the "mobilization of territories", the "articulation and crossing of scales" and the development of "synergies", according to the global referential of public policies.

The overall effectiveness of the guidelines for the use of coastal areas as a function of the importance of erosion or flooding phenomena is more debatable, insofar as it includes the effectiveness of the choice of methods in relation to the processes of coastal dynamics and the efficiency of public action in terms of risk reduction. However, the joint assessment of these two variables is made difficult by the fact that they are related to disjointed temporalities that can give rise to contradictory injunctions from public authorities in terms of coastal protection. The scientific and societal uncertainties associated with the notion of ecosystem service lead in particular to doubts about the immediate effectiveness of "soft" solutions intended to protect the coast and the appropriateness of integrating them into long-term strategies for reducing natural coastal risks.

In general, the interweaving of territorial governance and risk prevention issues on the French coastline places all territorial actors and coastal populations on an equal footing in the absence of a sustainable development situation to which to refer. France probably still lacks a planning project that achieves a balance between national integration and territorial differentiation through a true articulation between short- and long-term actions as well as between administrative efficiency and democratic imperative. Such a project would undoubtedly give a directional sense to the current reflective moment and strengthen the still fragile links between planning and sustainable development in coastal territories.

The strategic documents for the maritime façade, which aim to take into account local specificities, could also contribute to increasing the overall effectiveness of guidelines for the use of coastal areas. They will complete a decade of institutional framing of coastline management that will have restored a form of verticality to the governance of coastal territories after a period focused on prevention (Rocle 2017). However, the failure of several attempts to accelerate the adaptation of coastal territories to climate change since the Xynthia storm shows that the paths to transition are strewn with pitfalls. The appropriation of transition issues remains subject to the contradictions between the interventionist and planning tradition of the State and the attachment of a large part of the population to the choice of living by the sea, complicating the application of Marcus Aurelius' maxim "Always walk by the shortest route; and the shortest way is that which is according to nature; that is to say, we must conform to the soundest reason, in all our words and in all our actions" (Marcus Aurelius, *Thoughts*, Book IV, L1). The development of support modeling tools to implement participatory approaches in coastal territories and to allow the appropriation of the approach by the various stakeholders is certainly one of the most promising ways to overcome these contradictions.

12.6. References

Allard-Poesi, F. and Perret, V. (2003). La recherche-action. In *Conduire un projet de recherche, une perspective qualitative*, Giordano, Y. (ed.). EMS, Caen.

Anadon, M. (2013). Recherche participative. In *Dictionnaire critique et interdisciplinaire de la participation*, Casillo, I., Fourniau, J.M., Neveu, C., Lefebvre, R., Barbier, R., Blondiaux, L., Chateauraynaud, F., Salles, D. (ed.). GIS Démocratie et Participation, Paris.

Anselme, B., Durand, P., Thomas, Y.-F., Nicolae-Lerma, A. (2011). Storm extreme levels and coastal flood hazards. A parametric approach on the French coast of Languedoc (district of Leucate). *Comptes Rendus Géosciences*, 343(10), 677–690.

Anselme, B., Durand, P., Nicolae-Lerma, A. (2019). Coastal flooding and storm surges: An example of the CRISSIS research program on the French coast of Languedoc. *Facing Hydrometeorological Extreme Events: A Governance Issue*, 413–431.

Arias-Maldonado, M. (2013). Rethinking sustainability in the Anthropocene. *Environmental Politics*, 22(3), 428–446.

Baron, N. (2017). Politique publique du littoral et recherche finalisée : Des pratiques et concepts en co-évolution. *Nat. Sci. Soc.*, 25, S36–S41.

Becu, N., Amalric, M., Anselme, B., Beck, E., Bertin, X., Delay, E., Long, N., Marilleau, N., Pignon-Mussaud, C., Rousseaux, F. (2017). Participatory simulation to foster social learning on coastal flooding prevention. *Environmental Modelling and Software*, 98, 1–11.

Bertrand, F. and Goeldner-Gianella, L. (2013). BARCASUB : La submersion marine et ses impacts environnementaux et sociaux dans le Bassin d'Arcachon (France) : Est-il possible, acceptable et avantageux de gérer ce risque par la dépoldérisation? Report, LITEAU, Ministère de l'Écologie, du Développement Durable et de l'Énergie.

Bertrand, F. and Magri, S. (2019). Le Teich. In *Villes et rivières de France*, Carcaud, N., Arnaud-Fassetta, G., Evain, C. (eds). CNRS, Paris.

Bertrand, F., Becu, N., Anselme, B. (2014a). Analyse et gestion du risque d'envasement autour de la baie d'Antonina, Brésil : L'apport d'une démarche d'accompagnement. *Bulletin de l'Association de géographes français*, 91(3), 289–308.

Bertrand, F., Goeldner-Gianella, L., Anselme, B., Durand, P., Thomas, Y.-F. (2014b). L'aléa submersion marine sur la rive interne du Bassin dArcachon : Exposition actuelle, cartographie prévisionnelle et capacité d'atténuation par la restauration des marais salés. *Colloque Connaissances et compréhension des risques côtiers*, Brest, 124–134.

Bertrand, F., Verdin, F., Eynaud, F., Arnaud-Fassetta, G., Stéphan, P., Costa, S., Suanez, S. (2019). Settlement potential and constraints on the lower Médoc coastline: Results of the Litaq project and considerations on coastal palaeo-risks in the protohistoric periods. *Quaternaire*, 30(1), 97–111.

Bourg, D. (2012). Transition écologique, plutôt que développement durable. *Vraiment durable*, 1(1), 77–96.

Chaffin, B.C., Gosnel, H., Cosens, B.A. (2014). A decade of adaptive governance scholarship: Synthesis and future directions. *Ecology and Society*, 19(3), 56 [Online]. Available at: http://www.ecologyandsociety.org/vol19/iss3/art56/.

David, A. (2000). La recherche-intervention, cadre général pour la recherche en management. In *Les nouvelles fondations des sciences de gestion*, David, A., Hatchuel, A., Laufer, R. (eds). Vuibert, Paris.

Drobenko, B. (2012). De la gestion intégrée des zones côtières (GIZC) a la politique maritime intégrée (PMI) : Un nouveau droit pour le littoral ? *Revue juridique de l'environnement*, 225–246.

Dron, D. and Franq, T. (2013). Livre blanc sur le financement de la transition écologique. Mobiliser les financements privés vers la transition écologique. Report, Direction générale du Trésor/Commissariat général au développement durable.

Goeldner-Gianella, L. and Bertrand, F. (2014). Gérer le risque de submersion marine par la dépoldérisation : Représentations locales et application des politiques publiques dans le bassin d'Arcachon. *Natures Sciences Sociétés*, 22(3), 219–230.

Goeldner-Gianella, L., Bertrand, F., Pratlong, F., Gauthier-Gaillard, S. (2013). Submersion marine et dépoldérisation : Le poids des représentations sociales et des pratiques locales dans la gestion du risque littoral. *Espace populations sociétés*, 1–2, 193–209.

Goeldner-Gianella, L., Bertrand, F., Oiry, A., Grancher, D. (2015). Depolderisation policy against coastal flooding and social acceptability on the French Atlantic coast. *Ocean & Coastal Management*, 116, 98–107.

Golllety, C. (2013). ARESMA: Act on the resilience of the socio-ecological mangrove systems of Mayotte in order to improve their conservation [Online]. Available at: https://www.researchgate.net/project/ARESMA.

Hess, G. (2013). *Éthiques de la nature*. Presses Universitaires de France, Paris.

Hopkins, R. (2008). *The Transition Handbook. From Oil Dependency to Local Resilience*. Green Books, Totnes.

Horlick-Jones, T. and Sime, J. (2004). Living on the border: Knowledge, risk and transdisciplinarity. *Futures*, 36(4), 441–456.

Jollivet, M. (2015). *Pour une transition écologique citoyenne*. Editions Charles Léopold Mayer, Paris.

Kervern, G. (1999). *Éléments fondamentaux des cindyniques*. Economica, Paris.

Meur-Férec, C. (2009). La GIZC à l'épreuve du terrain : Premiers enseignements d'une expérience française. *VertigO – La revue électronique en sciences de l'environnement*, 5.

Mineo-Kleiner, L. (2017). L'option de la relocalisation des activités et des biens face aux risques côtiers : Stratégies et enjeux territoriaux en France et au Québec. Thesis, Université de Bretagne, Brest.

Ministère de l'Écologie, du Développement Durable et de l'Énergie (2012). Stratégie nationale de gestion intégrée du trait de côte. Vers la relocalisation des activités et des biens. Report, MEDDE.

Ministère de l'Écologie, du Développement Durable et de l'Énergie and DGPR (2014). Stratégie nationale de gestion des risques d'inondation [Online]. Available at: http://www.side.developpement-durable.gouv.fr/EXPLOITATION/DEFAULT/doc/IFD/IFD_REFDOC_0526091/strategie-nationale-de-gestion-des-risques-d-inondation.

Ministère de l'Environnement, de l'Énergie et de la Mer (2017). Stratégie nationale de transition écologique vers un développement durable. Report, MEDDE.

Neumayer, E. (2003). *Weak Versus Strong Sustainability: Exploring the Limits of Two Opposing Paradigms*. Edvard Elgar, Cheltenham.

Rasomanana, L. (2019). Les représentations des mangroves de Mayotte dans la littérature francophone : Approche géocritique dans le cadre du projet interdisciplinaire ARESMA. *Voix Plurielles*, 16(2), 88–105.

Rey-Valette, H., Rocle, N., Mineo-Kleiner, L., Longépée, E., Bazart, C., Lautredou-Audouy, N. (2019). Acceptabilité sociale des mesures d'adaptation au changement climatique en zones côtières : Une revue de dix enquêtes menées en France métropolitaine. *VertigO*, 19(2), 1–29.

Rocle, N. (2017). L'adaptation des littoraux au changement climatique : Une gouvernance performative par expérimentations et stratégies d'action publique. PhD Thesis, Université de Bordeaux, Bordeaux.

Rotmans, I. and Kemp, R. (2003). Managing societal transitions: Dilemmas and uncertainties: The Dutch energy case-study. Report, OECD workshop on the benefits of climate policy.

Rudolf, F. (2013). De la modernisation écologique à la résilience : Un réformisme de plus ? *VertigO*, 13(3).

Rumpala, Y. (2010). Recherche de voies de passage au "développement durable" et réflexivité institutionnelle. Retour sur les prétentions à la gestion d'une transition générale. *Revue française de socio-économie*, 6, 47–63.

Thiétart, A. (1999). *Méthodes de recherche en management*. Dunod, Paris.

Whiteside, K.H., Boy, D., Bourg, D. (2010). France's "Grenelle de l'environnement": Openings and closures in ecological democracy. *Environmental Politics*, 19(3), 449–467.

13

IPCC Reports and their Implementation into Policy: Between Science and Strategy

13.1. Introduction

The history and functioning of the IPCC (Intergovernmental Panel on Climate Change), as well as the use that is made of its results and publications can be considered as a singular object of study. We will approach this subject from very different disciplinary horizons and therefore from contrasting points of view: atmospheric sciences on the one hand, and agricultural development economics on the other. This crossing of approaches around a common object, the environment/development issue, is the fruit of the unlikely meeting of two researchers belonging to the same research unit (Prodig).

In this chapter, we will try to retrace this history and its outcome in the modalities of functioning and publications of this unique collective. We will try to highlight the gap between the richness of the database collected and synthesized by the IPCC experts and their recommendations, on the one hand; and the sometimes rather simplistic use made of it by certain scientific teams for political promotion purposes, on the other.

After recalling the context of the creation of the IPCC, as a federator of a large scientific community involved in the study of climate change, its history and mode of operation, we will briefly analyze its publication strategy and the different types of documents produced. The nuanced nature of the positions put forward by the IPCC, particularly in the second volume *Impacts, adaptation and vulnerability* of the 5th report will then be highlighted. We will then see how these nuanced positions differ profoundly from those supported by certain donors and international

Chapter written by Jean-Claude Bergès and Hubert Cochet.

organizations that, paradoxically enough, base their conclusions on the IPCC results. An example of this notable distortion will then be presented based on the analysis of an article devoted to the adaptation of Tanzanian agriculture to climate change.

13.2. The context of the creation of the IPCC

The questions about the possible influence of carbon dioxide as a greenhouse gas are old. The first World Climate Conference (WMO 1979) held in Geneva in February 1979 mentioned the hypothesis of climate change induced by CO_2 among other mechanisms of climate change induced by human activities, such as intensive agriculture, nuclear explosions and deforestation. The conference recommended developing the climate observation system and supporting research in this area. However, this document did not make any recommendations in terms of public policies, as knowledge of physical processes was not yet sufficiently advanced. In the synthesis of the above-mentioned document, Fedorov underlines the still conjectural character of the theories on the impact of greenhouse gases. Since then two factors mainly contributed to make this theme dominant: the success of the action to ban chlorofluorocarbon gases (CFCs or Freon) and a dramatic change in the atmospheric sciences.

13.2.1. The Montreal Protocol and the CFC ban

The international effort to control CFC production was both early and effective. In 1928, when T. Midgley, then working for Frigidaire, patented CFC, his invention marked a significant advance for American industry. Refrigerating devices could be produced from gas without danger to human health or detonating power. It is estimated that in 1980, Dupont de Nemours alone CFC sales were about 600 million dollars (Maxwell and Briscoe 1997). While conducting atmospheric surveys in Antarctica, J. Lovelock discovered abnormally high CFC levels in 1971 (Christie 2001), but this observation was not alarming based on the knowledge available at the time. However, after Molina and Rowland (1974) published their article on the role of stratospheric CFCs in a photochemical process of ozone destruction, the reactions in economic and political circles were strong. Indeed, referring to experimental data and to a summary evaluation of the quantities of CFCs in the upper atmosphere, the authors had highlighted the consequences of a worrisome photochemical reaction: the disappearance of a layer protecting the planet from excess ultraviolet radiation. First, Dupont de Nemours tried to invalidate these conclusions. This controversy induced NASA to develop the TOMS (Total Ozone Mapping Spectrometer) sensor in order to measure stratospheric ozone. This sensor has been integrated in the Nimbus-7 satellite launched in 1978 and very quickly the observations confirmed the Molina and Rowland's hypothesis. These results prompted a rapid reaction and, in October 1978, the United States banned the use of CFCs as aerosol propellants. At the same time, Dupont de Nemours, adapting its industrial strategy, filed a patent for a CFC substitute and supported actions to limit the use of this gas. This favorable climate made it possible to quickly conclude international agreements and a treaty, the Montreal Protocol, was ratified in 1987. This treaty, which prohibits almost all use and production of CFCs, is the first binding international initiative to protect the environment (Levy 1997).

13.2.2. *The epistemological disruption of the atmospheric sciences*

In the 1980s, atmospheric sciences evolved so rapidly that it lead to an epistemological disruption, the investigative approaches and evaluation criteria becoming radically different. From this evolution, new players appeared, and this scientific field has been reorganized (Pagney 2012). The principle of numerical weather prediction and its basic equations were described very early on by W. Bjerknes (1904), but this publication remained without immediate follow-up due to a lack of calculation and measurement resources. In 1917, the same author formulated the theory of fronts, which could be used in an operational context of meteorological forecasting. These new procedures were based on graphical representations and empirical knowledge of the forecaster who intervenes in the spatialization of point observations and the dynamics of the structures generated. It is only 70 years later that Bjerknes' first theory could find a field of application. This evolution was made possible by two technical changes: the increase in computing resources and the development of a space observation system. Whilst the first computers appeared in 1945, their capacity remained for a long time very insufficient for the numerical prediction of the states of the atmosphere. In 1975, the ECMWF (European Center for Medium-range Weather Forecast) was created, federating the capacities of European meteorological services. For its part, Météo-France integrated numerical models into its forecasting system from 1985 onwards, after 10 years of experimentation (Rousseau et al. 1995). These first applications opened the way to the modeling of atmospheric phenomena and made it possible to quantify what had been conjectural approaches. Although previously the results were based on the coherence of functional schemes, the effective capacity to compute numerical models leads to a deeply different approach. Another factor that contributes to this mutation of the 1980s is the appearance of spatial observation sensors (Hamon 1995). While for many disciplines, spatial remote sensing was a continuation of aerial photography, it was radically new in meteorology insofar as the flight altitude of airplanes did not allow the phenomena follow up on a relevant scale. Although images of atmospheric phenomena could be transmitted as early as 1960, the use of these data requires continuity of observations, stability of sensors and transmission capacities which were only obtained very gradually. In Europe, the first geostationary satellite capable of providing continuous coverage was

Meteosat-2, launched in 1981, and, initiated by the World Meteorological Organization (WMO), a coordination of meteorological satellites was established in 1975. It was therefore possible to understand meteorological phenomena in their spatial and temporal continuity. These decisive innovations have profoundly modified the atmospheric sciences. Wiscombe and Ramanathan (1985) have evaluated the impact of these innovations on the training system of the American meteorological units, focusing on the necessary integration of fluid mechanics concepts in the training of meteorologists.

13.3. The IPCC, history and organization

13.3.1. *James Hansen's intervention*

The creation of the IPCC was facilitated by institutional support. It was preceded by WMO and UNEP creation of a working group on greenhouse gases in 1985. However, the key event was the hearing of J. Hansen, then a member of a NASA research center, before the United States Congress where he presented results published that same year (Hansen et al. 1988). This publication displays a particular interest presenting a methodology still used today in the works on climate change. The authors' argument is organized as follows:

– surface and upper air observations show a global increase in temperature;

– an increase in carbon dioxide content is also observed;

– a numerical model simulates the last hundred years of climate change by introducing various greenhouse gas emission scenarios;

– it is found that only the model corresponding to the observed emissions can account for the warming;

– based on the same model a warming amplification is expected if the emission rate is maintained.

This approach may seem similar to the one described above with regard to the impact of CFC emissions on stratospheric ozone, but they are deeply different.

On the one hand, since greenhouse gases exist in the atmosphere without any human intervention, the basis of this hypothesis is quantitative and supposes a capacity to model energy flows on a global scale. Carrying out such a model requires the coordination of various scientific disciplines dealing with the Earth's fluid envelope (biosphere, atmosphere and hydrosphere). Furthermore, as the sources of emissions are diverse and multiform, it is much more complex to design reduction or substitution policies. Climate models play a key role here, as the causality scheme depends entirely on them. Thus, without a numerical model, it would not be possible to determine whether the increase in CO_2 is a cause or a consequence of the increase in temperature. Indeed, since the solubility of this gas in water decreases with temperature (Wiebe and Gaddy 1940), cold seas have stronger absorption capacities than warm seas.

As the scientific communication is often carried out in a disciplinary framework, such a diversity of disciplines, in the only part of the study of the global warming physical sciences basis, could induce an illegibility of the results obtained. To enable political action to be taken in front of the presumed urgency of these environmental phenomena, the need to create a specialized institution, the IPCC, has emerged. This institution is an intergovernmental group of experts where each of the 195 member states of the WMO or the UN mandates a delegate. The objective of this group of experts is to realize summaries of scientific results. It is complementary to international climate study programs such as GEWEX (Global Energy and Water cycle Experiment), and its terms of reference exclude it from carrying out its own research activities or contributing to the collection of environmental data.

The IPCC is supported by a Bureau, currently composed of 34 members, which acts as the Executive Secretariat. This Bureau is elected in plenary session by all the participating States for the duration of the preparation of an assessment report (AR), which is the IPCC's main publication. The Bureau is composed with respect to the balance between the different WMO regions as well as the ratio of men to women. As the members of the Bureau remain attached to their home institutions, the IPCC has very few permanent staff and its annual budget of around €5 million (IPCC 2019) covers only coordination and publication costs. Following the creation of the IPCC, the United Nations Framework Convention on Climate Change (UNFCCC) was adopted at the Rio Earth Summit in 1992 and helps translate the IPCC's synthesis work into environmental policies. Within the framework of this convention, conferences of the parties (COPs) are organized annually to monitor and coordinate these policies.

13.3.2. *Some significant events*

Because of its reference terms, the IPCC has an intermediary position between the worlds of science and politics, which explains why debates, constituting the heart of scientific activity, can appear as controversies. The Climatigate affair, which cast suspicion on the CRU (Climate Research Unit – East Anglia University – Great Britain) – a research center strongly involved in the IPCC activities – is representative of the ambiguity of this position. Specialized in climatology, this research center provided historical series of records of meteorological parameters. This work was important and sensitive because, although the meteorological observation system is currently dense and coherent, its historical depth is short in relation to the problem of climate change, and the use of old data requires control and correction procedures. In 2009, following a malicious intrusion into their computer system, messages exchanged with other researchers were intercepted and disseminated shortly before the Copenhagen COP. Some of these messages, referring to unsystematic data processing procedures, weakened the credibility of the IPCC's conclusions insofar as the basic data had been modified to conform to the report's conclusions. Several commissions of inquiry have been established to assess the scientific integrity of the CRU. In its report (Russell et al. 2010), the commission appointed by the University will present a contrasting analysis. On the one hand, it found no clear evidence of intentional falsification of data and stressed that the distortions generated were not such as to profoundly alter the conclusions of the IPCC Fourth Report. On the other hand, it expressed reservations about the scientific practices of the CRU: lack of rigor in the processing procedures, failure to comply with the Open Science principles of data communication and excessively partisan positions. Despite these reservations, the commission felt that the CRU team had not violated scientific ethics, but their results were inaccurate and their procedures should be improved. In this context, the controversy arose from a misunderstanding of the nature of expertise and the scientist's neutrality. This same controversy highlights the difficulty of the IPCC communication strategy.

The entire scientific community does not agree with the IPCC's conclusions. Thus, among other initiatives, a group defending positions opposed to those of the IPCC, the NIPCC (Non-Intergovernmental Panel on Climate Change) was created in 2003 (Plehwe 2014). However, one of the successes of the IPCC is that it has created a space for debate that integrates diverse environmental concerns and public actions and has given it a central place in development policy. And, to some extent, controversies such as the one generated by the NIPCC contribute to advancing studies on climate change and its impacts.

The Nobel Prize awarded to the IPCC in 2007 marks the international recognition of this institution. Since then, public policies have explicitly relied on its analyses and the Conferences of the Parties are events that are widely covered by the media. The COP 24 organized in 2018 in Katowice brought together more than 20,000 participants. This expansion was accompanied by an extensive interpretation of the institution's terms of reference. Thus, it is significant that the IPCC refers to the concept of the Anthropocene in its interim report published in 2018 (IPCC 2018). This very encompassing concept, which tends to designate all anthropogenic actions on the environment, is explicitly discussed in the aforementioned document (IPCC 2018, p. 54). As a matter of fact, it federates the fields of intervention of the three conventions that emerged from the Rio Earth Summit: UNFCCC, CBD (Convention on Biological Diversity) and UNCCD (United Nations Convention to Combat Desertification).

13.4. IPCC reports and their interpretations

13.4.1. *The IPCC publication strategy*

The IPCC produces two types of publications: on the one hand, documents which are mainly *Assessment Reports* and, on the other hand, databases that support the conclusions of these reports. Among these databases, the CMIPx (*Coordinated Model Intercomparison Project Phase x*) contains the results of general atmospheric circulation models. These models are calculated from different greenhouse gas emission scenarios, the RCPy (Representative Concentration Pathway) where *y* designates an emission level. The most pessimistic scenario, RCP8.5, is commonly used to assess the impacts of climate change.

The main IPCC reports are organized in a way that reflects the organization of this institution. The Bureau is appointed for the duration of the preparation of an assessment report and coordinates the work of drafting the report. It includes subgroups specialized on the three volumes that make up the assessment reports: physical science basis, impacts and mitigation policies as well as a working group on greenhouse gases. This tree-structured organization is replicated in each volume layout. The organization of the volumes is determined by the Bureau and validated by the IPCC Plenary Assembly; coordinators and lead authors are chosen for each chapter by the Bureau members in charge of the volume. They are responsible for the chapter and may, if they wish, integrate contributions from external authors. These documents are validated through a process controlled by a board of experts, which is also appointed by the Bureau. The review process is open to the entire scientific community by a simple registration on the website. The comments contribute to the factual accuracy of the reports, but the effective consideration of the feedback from this community depends on these reviewers. Each volume is accompanied by two synthesis texts: a technical summary highlighting the key points and an even more compact policy summary. This policy summary (*Summary for Policy Maker*) is subject to a special review process that reports directly to the IPCC plenary. Through this complex process, the IPCC does not obtain a consensus, which is obviously impossible, from the entire scientific community, but guarantees the broadest possible consultation of all stakeholders while maintaining its editorial line. Because of the constraints of publication, this mode of writing is nevertheless likely to introduce discrepancies between the different levels of writing, from the basic text to the most synthetic summary, since the detailed parts of the document present a more nuanced view of the phenomena than the different levels of summaries. This discrepancy is part of the mission of the IPCC, whose mandate is to propose explicit recommendations to policy makers. The objectivity of the approach lies, not in the absence of bias, but in the explicitness of the sources on which its conclusions are based. A similar point can be made about the confusion of interests.

Following the plenary meeting held in Kampala (IPCC, 2011), it was decided that the key stakeholders in the writing of the report should fill in a questionnaire specifying their degree of personal involvement. This is not to exclude any participant with potential conflicts of interest associated with IPCC themes, which would prevent the appointment of any expert, but to specify the nature of these interests.

13.4.2. *The nuanced positions of the IPCC*

The IPCC assessment reports (*supra*) are characterized by an often cautious and nuanced approach. For example, in their fifth report, published in 2014, and in particular in Chapter 7 "Food Security and Food Production Systems" of the *Impacts, Adaptation, and Vulnerability* (Porter et al. 2014), the experts of Working Group 2 highlight the complexity of the processes at play. The actors rightly emphasize the adaptive capacity of farmers, particularly in developing countries, and their past experience of taking climate change into account in their farming practices. They note the multiple adjustments made by farmers to adapt to climate change and their impact on reducing vulnerability. Based on a review of the scientific literature, they provide multiple examples of these adaptive practices: changes in sowing dates, changes in varieties, development of new crops, adjustments in the organization of work, etc. Porter et al. 2014, pp. 514–515), examples that are widely illustrated in other chapters of this report[1].

They also insist on the need to take into account local knowledge in the search for adaptive solutions, especially in regions where farmers have only difficult and uncertain access to scientific information. For example, in Chapter 22 on Africa, they write:

> Recent literature has confirmed the positive role of local and traditional knowledge in building resilience and adaptive capacity, and shaping responses to climatic variability and change in Africa (...). The recent report on extreme events and disasters (IPCC 2012) supports this view, finding robust evidence and high agreement of the

---

1 They refer to all of these practices as incremental adaptations and define them as follows: "Autonomous adaptations are incremental changes in the existing system including through the ongoing implementation of extant knowledge and technology in response to the changes in climate experienced. They include coping responses and are reactive in nature" (Porter et al. 2014, p. 513). These practices are opposed to "Planned adaptations", adaptations planned on a larger scale, generally by actors outside the rural world (authorities, public, projects, agricultural entrepreneurs) and likely to provoke, it is said, a real change of system in the direction of greater adaptation.

positive impacts of integrating indigenous and scientific knowledge for adaptation (Niang et al. 2014, p. 1,232).

On the other hand, the interrelationship between adaptation to climate change and adaptation to other changes faced by farmers is repeatedly highlighted (IPCC 2012, p. 519); the impact of climate change on food security is then put into perspective in relation to other global changes: "It is likely that socioeconomic and technological trends, including changes in institutions and policies, will remain a relatively stronger driver of food security over the next few decades than climate change" (IPCC 2012, p. 513).

Finally, the experts emphasize the socio-economic dimension of vulnerability and the need to move beyond purely technological approaches to adaptation in favor of resilience-building approaches. They write, in Chapter 22 devoted to Africa, and drawing on a large body of scientific literature that:

> In recognition of the socio-economic dimensions of vulnerability (…), the previous focus on technological solutions (…) is now evolving toward a broader view that highlights the importance of building resilience, through social, institutional, policy, knowledge and informational approaches (…), as well as on linking the diverse range of adaptation options to the multiple livelihood-vulnerability risks faced by many people in Africa (Niang et al. 2014, p. 1,226).

The second volume of the 5th IPCC report therefore invites decision-makers to a close application that is not limited to "technical" recommendations but integrates socio-economical and political aspects, while insisting on the need to value "indigenous knowledge", and to strive to strengthen the resilience of the most vulnerable groups.

13.4.3. *Forecasting models based on a very selective reading of the work of the IPCC*

However, it is clear that the directives formulated by the financial backers, international institutions and governments are sometimes quite different from the IPCC's nuanced analyses. Far from relying on the remarkable body of social sciences mobilized in the second volume of the IPCC's 5th report, they rely rather on modeling work that relies more, if not exclusively, on the results presented in Volume 1 of the IPCC's "Physical Bases" (IPCC 2013).

Indeed, the work of this first working group provides a timely basis for many scientific works that go far beyond the disciplines and analytical frameworks of this first volume. By combining the scenarios for the evolution of greenhouse gas concentrations for the 21st century (RCP: RCP 2.6, RCP 4.5, etc.) and different socio-economic scenarios or "common profiles of socio-economic evolution" (SSP)[2], it is indeed possible, from a formal point of view, to construct scenarios of the effect of climate change on income, cultivated areas, production, prices or poverty, etc, which is something that the IPCC experts are careful not to do.

This is how the models proposed by the work of IPCC Working Group 1 are widely used in the work carried out by an institution such as IFPRI (International Food Policy Research Institute), notably in its IMPACT (*International Model for Policy Analysis of Agricultural Commodities and Trade*) model. This model, in its third version presented in 2015 by S. Robinson et al. (2015) is described as "An integrated modeling system that links information from climate models (*Earth System Models*), crop simulation models (e.g. *Decision Support System for Agrotechnology Transfer*) and water models to a core global, partial equilibrium, multimarket model focused on the agriculture sector"[3]. It aims to "provide researchers and policymakers with a flexible tool to assess and compare the potential effects of changes in biophysical systems, socio-economic trends, technologies, and policies"; and more specifically to promote technology transfer in agriculture as explicitly stated: "to simulate the effects of large-scale adoption of agricultural technologies consistent with sustainable intensification. (...) the adoption of no-till, integrated soil fertility management; drought- and heat-tolerant crop varieties; and several improved irrigation technologies" (Robinson et al. 2015, p. 8).

13.5. The example of the adaptation policy of Tanzanian agriculture to climate change

One of these models was presented in an article published in 2011 in *Global Environmental Change* by a team of researchers from the World Bank and several American and Canadian universities (Ahmed et al. 2011)[4]. This article seems to us

2 The common socio-economic evolution profiles (SSPs 1-5) describe different plausible hypotheses of future societal and ecosystem evolution during the 21st century. They are used in conjunction with RCPs to analyze the feedback between climate change and factors such as global population growth, economic development and technological progress. They are based on scenarios describing possible developments that pose different adaptation and mitigation challenges.

3 For version 3 of the IMPACT model, the climate data are taken from the 5th IPCC report (AR5).

4 Another example of this type of modeling, published by IFPRI, is given by Jalloh et al. (2013), for the case of West Africa. See also the a-critical literature review proposed by Rhodes et al. (2014) in which numerous studies of this nature are cited. See also the other references proposed by Leichenko and Silva (2014).

to provide a particularly illuminating example of a form of instrumentalization of the IPCC report (Volume 1 *Physical Basis*) for the purpose of promoting technology transfer in agriculture.

13.5.1. *From forecasting yields to promoting the Green Revolution model*

The stated objective of the paper is to examine, for the case of Tanzania, the link between climate change maize yield change and poverty, using a quantitative and modeling approach, based on both past and future trends over a time span of 60 years, from 1971 to 2031. To do this, the authors of the article highlight the following:

– Monthly averages of temperature and precipitation for the maize growing season, January through June, based on data from CMIP3 (Meehl et al. 2005), and considering the SRES A2 emissions scenario (Ahmed et al. 2011, p. 48). To extract these two parameters, the authors consider, in addition to the average of the 22 models constituting CMIP3, three models considered as representing extremes in terms of variability. Beyond the difficulties generated by the dispersion of estimates between models, the use of products developed from a global perspective for an analysis of regional phenomena requires a downscaling procedure. In CMIP3, the models produced by the CCCMA (Canadian Center for Climate Modelling and Analysis), the GFLD (Geophysical Fluid Dynamics Laboratory) and the GISS (Goddard Institute for Space Studies) have very coarse spatial resolutions (3°75', 1°25' and 2° in longitude, respectively). Therefore, after interpolation to a finer grid, the data were simply averaged over Tanzania.

– A link, via multiple linear regression models, between climate change and maize yield based on national production statistics for the 17 regions of the country, data available for the period 1992–2005: "The temperature coefficients are negative, while the coefficients for precipitation are positive. (…) An increase in average growing season precipitation by 1 mm/month is enough to increase maize and rice yields by 0.005 tonnes per hectare" (Ahmed et al. 2011, p. 49)[5].

– To link the evolution of corn yields to the evolution of prices, the authors refer to a general equilibrium model. They therefore stick to the well-known assumption of "free and perfect" competition, although they recognize the lack of scientific basis

---

5 "Furthermore, the authors do not hesitate to write: "The estimated statistical model, by being based on ex-post data, has the added advantage of endogenizing some adaptive farmer behavior. (…). The historical yields thus reflect some adaptability, as do the estimated parameters in the statistical mode" (Ahmed et al. 2011, p. 49).

for this assumption regarding Tanzania[6]. They even write, in relation to the factor market: "We assume a constant combination of land, labor, and capital reflecting the belief that this combination of factors – land capital and work – is unaffected by climate change" (Ahmed et al. 2011, p. 50) "a closed market of production factors (...) in which land, capital, and natural resources are immobile between sectors" not taking into account the frequent migrations between sectors of activity (rural/urban) or the pluriactivity of rural households.

– Finally, in order to deduce the possible consequences in terms of poverty, they decide to attribute the evolution of poverty to that of rainfed agricultural yields, explicitly excluding other possible causes of poverty growth[7]. It is also understood, without question, that only free markets (open trade regimes) have the power to reduce price volatility (Ahmed et al. 2011, p. 54)[8].

Thus, by relying on the various climate models available, on national production statistics and on the economic model of general equilibrium, the authors try to demonstrate that:

– it is climate change which, through the decline in cereal yields, explains poverty;

– only policies aimed at increasing maize yields – in particular through Green Revolution-type technical packages (including high-yielding seeds, mineral fertilizers, pesticides) – and in a context of free competition, are likely to allow for a virtuous "adaptation" to climate change.

13.5.2. *Far from the IPCC recommendations*

The fact that the development and popularization of these modeling techniques by researchers from the World Bank and an international institution (IFPRI) attached to the international agricultural research centers[9] that have promoted the Green Revolution lead to technical recommendations from these same institutions is

---

6 "Since a review of the literature does not offer strong evidence on the nature of competition in the Tanzanian food sector, we opt for the empirically robust assumptions of constant returns to scale and perfect competition here as well. Clearly, this assumption could be altered as more evidence becomes available on the nature of market structures in the food sector" (Ahmed et al. 2011, p. 49).

7 "We resolve this complication ... allowing us to attribute poverty changes solely to climate-based agricultural productivity changes, and not any other event that may cause vulnerability" (Ahmed et al. 2011, p. 51).

8 "Open trade regimes have the potential to reduce domestic price volatility" (Ahmed et al. 2011, p. 54).

9 Grouped within the CGIAR.

of course no coincidence, as Lise Cornilleau (2016) points out: "Developed in 1995, it [the IMPACT model developed by IFPRI] was first used to evaluate different technological scenarios internally at the CGIAR (*Consultative Group on International Agricultural Research*), before becoming indispensable in international expert assessments formed on the Intergovernmental Panel on Climate Change (IPCC) model" (Cornilleau 2016, p. 174).

This attraction for simple, standard and applicable models, regardless of the conditions, seems irresistible. The simplifications imposed by mathematical modeling – working with a single crop, grown in pure culture, often under "average" conditions and applying a "standard" technical package – and the fact that the more general the model claims to be, the more it must be based on increasingly simple, even simplistic, hypotheses, do not faze decision-makers. For example, the 2016 FAO report, largely devoted to adaptation, states that simulations based on IFPRI's IMPACT model indicate that "the number of people at risk of undernourishment in developing countries would be reduced in 2050 by 12% (or nearly 124 million people) if nitrogen-efficient crop varieties were widely used, by 9% (or 91 million people) if zero tillage (planting directly without first tilling the land) were more widely adopted, and by 8% (or 80 million people) if heat-tolerant crop varieties or precision agriculture were adopted" (FAO 2016, pp. 62–64).

The recommendations made by the United Nations Food and Agriculture Organization (FAO), those made by the *Global Alliance for Climate-Smart Agriculture* (GACSA) launched in September 2014 at the World Climate Summit and also those of the AAA Initiative (Adaptation of African Agriculture to Climate Change (2016), an initiative launched in the run-up to COP 22 in July 2016)[10] reveal a shared vision of adaptation: an essentially technically oriented approach that is in line with the Green Revolution. It is not surprising therefore that the various agricultural policy documents (in terms of adaptation) drafted by the States are in the same vein, whether they are NAPAs (National Adaptation Programs of Action, drafted in 2006–2007), NAPs (National Adaptation Plans, drafted from 2010 onwards) or CPDNs (voluntary contributions) drafted by the States in connection with COP 21 (contribution determined at the national level, CPDN-INDC).

Thus, this modeling work which, based on the work of IPCC Working Group 1 (Volume 1: *Physical Basis*), explores the link between climate change evolution of yields and poverty, and are partly responsible for the non-contextualized prescriptions that result in standard technical packages with devastating effects. The local specificities of each agrosystem are not taken into account, and even less so are

---

10 This includes the Soil Fertility Initiative (WB/FAO), the Green Revolution in Africa (AGRA), the Bill Melinda Gates Foundation, the Africa Fertilizer and Agro-Business Partnership (fertilizer industry), etc.

the inequalities of access of farmers and breeders to resources, means of production and the market. Local know-how and the past experience of farmers are forgotten. The gap between these unilateral prescriptions and the much more nuanced – and diverse – recommendations of the IPCC expert group that drafted the adaptation volume (No. 2) appears to be considerable, and out of step with the principles and procedures that governed the emergence of the IPCC.

13.6. Conclusion

The emergence of the IPCC appears to be a unique historical process of gathering and making available a large number of scientific works from various disciplines and fields. The main products of this considerable body of work reflect this diversity: Volume 1 of the successive IPCC reports deals with the "Physical Basis" of the problem, with approaches based in particular on the atmospheric sciences; Volume 2 deals with questions related to "Impacts, Adaptation and Vulnerability", drawing on the social sciences; Volume 3 deals with the question of mitigation, also with a diversity of approaches and disciplines. But as rich, diverse and nuanced as they are, these works are not always mobilized by the scientific community itself – not to mention the decision-makers to whom the operational summaries are addressed – with the same tact and caution. We have shown an example dealing with the issue of poverty alleviation and the necessary adaptation of Tanzanian farmers to climate change where, far from relying on approaches inspired by the one put forward in Volume 2 of the 5th IPCC report devoted to this issue, the researchers only supported their modeling on the "physical bases" presented in Volume 1 and the hypotheses of neoclassical economic theory. The result is, unsurprisingly, the promotion of policies aimed at increasing maize yields – in particular through Green Revolution-type technical packages – in a context of free competition. This conclusion is the antithesis of those advocated by many experts who participated in the drafting of Volume 2 of the IPCC's 5th Report, or those put forward by other communities of researchers working on these issues (Cochet et al. 2018). Reflecting on the modalities for implementing real climate change adaptation policies in a context of strong demographic growth, scarcity of certain resources and a marked increase in inequalities, and taking into account the necessary reduction in the contribution of agriculture to climate change (mitigation) leads to a complete rethinking of agricultural development policies and to turning the page on the development of agriculture based on a small number of technical packages or "adaptation techniques" designed at the top and unsuited to the diversity of ecosystems and to the conditions in which farmers work (Cochet et al. 2018).

13.7. References

Adaptation de l'Agriculture Africaine (2016). Initiative pour l'adaptation de l'agriculture africaine (AAA) aux changements climatiques : Faire face aux défis du changement climatique et de l'insécurité alimentaire. White paper, AAA.

Ahmed, S.A., Noah, S., Diffenbaugh, N.S., Thomas, W., Hertel, T.W., David, B., Lobell, D.B., Ramankutty, N., Rios, A.R., Rowhani, P. (2011). Climate volatility and poverty vulnerability in Tanzania. *Global Environmental Change*, 21, 46–55.

Bjerknes, W. (1904). Das Problem der Wettervorhersage, betrachtet vom Standpunkt der Mechanik und der Physik. *La météorologie*, 9, 57–62.

Christie, M. (2001). *The Ozone Layer, a Philosophy of Science Perspective*. Cambridge University Press, Cambridge.

Cochet, H., Ducourtieux, O., Garambois, N. (2018). Quelles politiques pour l'adaptation ? Leçons du passé et possibilités à venir. In *Systèmes agraires et changement climatique au sud. Les chemins de l'adaptation*, Cochet, H., Ducourtieux, O., Garambois, N. (eds). Editions QUAE, Versailles.

Cornilleau, L. (2016). La modélisation économique mondiale, une technologie de gouvernement à distance ? Généalogie, circulations et traductions d'un modèle de la sécurité alimentaire globale de l'IFPRI. Dossier "Mesurer et standardiser : Les technologies politiques du gouvernement de l'Afrique". *Revue d'anthropologie des connaissances*, 10(2), 171–196 [Online]. Available at: https://www.cairn.info/revue-anthropologie-des-connaissances-2016-2-page-171.htm.

FAO (2016). *La situation mondiale de l'alimentation et de l'agriculture : Changement climatique, agriculture et sécurité alimentaire*. FAO, Rome.

Hamon, J. (1995). Trente années de météorologie spatiale. *La Météorologie*, 8, 101–106.

Hansen, J., Fung, I., Lacis, A., Rind, D., Lebedeff, S., Russell, G., Stone, P. (1988). Global climate changes as forecast by Goddard Institute for Space Studies three-dimensional model. *Journal of Geophysical Research – Atmosphere*, 93(D8), 9341–9364.

IPCC (2011). Thirty fourth session of the IPCC. Progress report, Task Group on Data and Scenario Support for Impact and Climate Analysis (TGICA). IPCC-XXXIV/Doc., 13.

IPCC (2012). Managing the risks of extreme events and disasters to advance climate change adaptation. A special report of Working Groups I and II of the Intergovernmental Panel on Climate Change. Cambridge University Press, Cambridge.

IPCC (2013). Climate Change 2013: The physical science basis. Contribution of Working Group I to the Fifth Assessment Report of the Intergovernmental Panel on Climate Change. Cambridge University Press, Cambridge.

IPCC (2018). Global warming of 1.5°C. An IPCC special report on the impacts of global warming of 1.5°C above pre-industrial levels and related global greenhouse gas emission pathways, in the context of strengthening the global response to the threat of climate change, sustainable development, and efforts to eradicate poverty. Cambridge University Press, Cambridge.

IPCC (2019). IPCC trust fund program and budget. Report, IPCC-LII/Doc., 2.

Jalloh, A., Nelson, G.C., Thomas, T.S., Zougmoure, R., Roy-Macauley, H. (2013). *West African Agriculture and Climate Change*. IFPRI, Washington, DC.

Leichenko, R. and Silva, J.A. (2014). Climate change and poverty: Vulnerability, impacts, and alleviation strategies. *WIREs Climate Change*, 5, 539–556 [Online]. Available at: https://wires.onlinelibrary.wiley.com/doi/full/10.1002/wcc.287.

Levy, D. (1997). Business and environmental treaties: Ozone depletion and climate change. *California Management Review*, 39(3), 54–71.

Maxwell, J. and Briscoe, F. (1997). There's money in the air: The CFC ban and DuPont's regulatory strategy. *Business Strategy and the Environment*, 6(5), 276–286.

Meehl, G.A., Covey, C., McAvaney, B., Latif, M.M., Souffer, R.J. (2005). Overview of the coupled model Intercomparison project. *Bulletin of the American Meteorological Society*, 86, 89–93.

Molina, M. and Rowland, F. (1974). Stratospheric sink for clhorofluoromethane, chlorine atom catalysed destruction of ozone. *Nature*, 249, 810–812.

Niang, I., Ruppel, O.C., Abdrabo, M.A., Essel, A., Lennard, C., Padgham J., Urquhart, P. (2014). Africa. In IPCC, Climate change 2014: Impacts, adaptation, and vulnerability. Part B: Regional aspects. Contribution of Working Group II to the Fifth Assessment Report of the Intergovernmental Panel on Climate Change. Cambridge University Press, Cambridge.

Pagney, P. (2012). La climatologie française, la modélisation des climats et le réchauffement climatique : La climatologie en question. *Echogéo*, 22, 1–22 [Online]. Available at: https://journals.openedition.org/echogeo/13273.

Plehwe, D. (2014). Think tank network and the knowledge-interest nexus: The case of climate change. *Critical Policy Studies*, 8(1), 101–115.

Porter, J.R., Xie, L., Challinor, A.J., Cochrane, K., Howden, S.M., Iqbal, M.M., Lobell, D.B., Travasso, M.I. (2014). Food security and food production systems. In IPCC, 2014. Climate change 2014: Impacts, adaptation, and vulnerability. Part A: Global and sectoral aspects. Contribution of Working Group II to the Fifth Assessment Report of the Intergovernmental Panel on Climate Change. Cambridge University Press, Cambridge.

Rhodes, E.R., Jalloh, A., Diouf, A. (2014). Revue de la recherche et des politiques en matière d'adaptation au changement climatique dans le secteur de l'agriculture en Afrique de l'Ouest. Working document 090, IDRC/CRDI, Future Agricultures.

Robinson, S., Mason-D'Croz, D., Islam, S., Sulser, T.B., Robertson, R., Zhu, T., Gueneau A., Pitois, G., Rosegrant, M. (2015). The international model for policy analysis of agricultural commodities and trade (IMPACT): Model description for version 3. Working document, IFPRI Discussion Paper 01483, Washington.

Rousseau, D., Pham, H.I., Juvanon, R. (1995). Vingt-cinq ans de prévisions numériques à échelles fines (1968–1993) de l'adaptation dynamique à maille fine au modèle Péridot. *La météorologie*, 8, 129–134.

Russell, M., Boulton, G., Clarke, P., Eyton, D., Norton, J. (2010). The independent climate change [Online]. Available at: http://www.cce-review.org/ [Accessed 10 April 2021].

Wiebe, R. and Gaddy, L. (1940). The solubility of carbon dioxide in water at various temperatures from 12 to 40° and at pressures to 500 atmospheres. Contribution from the Bureau of Agricultural Chemistry and Engineering, US Department of Agriculture, Washington.

Wiscombe, W.J. and Ramanathan, V. (1985). The role of radiation and other renascent subfields in atmospheric sciences. *Bulletin of the American Meteorological Society*, 66(10), 1278–1287.

WMO (1979). Declaration of the world climate conference [Online]. Available at: https://unesdoc.unesco.org/ark:/48223/pf0000037648 [Accessed 10 April 2021].

14

Research, Expert Assessment and Development: The Difficult Dialogue Between Social Sciences and Public Policies Around Lake Chad

14.1. Introduction

The Lake Chad Basin belongs to those margins of globalization that have little concern for international investments, but are very affected by global changes: while record population growth in a context of great poverty feeds socio-political tensions and recurrent geopolitical crises, climate change threatens the fragile balance between societies and the environment (Lemoalle and Magrin 2014). Since the early 2010s, Nigerian Borno has been the epicenter of a geopolitical crisis due to the action of armed Islamist groups, known as Boko Haram. Affecting the Lake Chad region, this crisis has caused the displacement of more than 2 million people and is disrupting the economy and cross-border trade (Magrin and Pérouse de Montclos 2018).

Since the early 2000s, Official Development Assistance (ODA) has been mobilized by multilateral organizations and Northern states concerned with maintaining regional disorders at an "acceptable" level from an international point of view. ODA has been reconfigured, attempting to establish modes of co-production of public policies that are less asymmetrical than during the decades of structural adjustment (1980–1990). However, the weak presence of civil society (international and national) in the region does not favor such changes. Since 2010, the

Chapter written by Géraud MAGRIN, Charline RANGÉ, Audrey KOUMRAÏT MBAGOGO, Abdourahamani MAHAMADOU, Jacques LEMOALLE and Christine RAIMOND.

environmental urgency of climate change has been giving way to a security crisis as a central development issue identified by public action actors. The regional situation, which was already difficult to understand (fragmentation of local situations, violence, information fog), is becoming more complex with the deployment of an international humanitarian system and the increasing interweaving of the 3Ds approach (development–diplomacy–defense) in North/South relations. It is in this context that the mobilization of social science research is reinforced by the world of international aid.

We will show here that the knowledge and the messages that we produce through expert assessment as researchers from a Northern institution (united around the UMR Prodig joint research unit) mainly affect our sponsors, international financial backers, but that ideas also circulate beyond to national decision-makers or society, according to complex processes of infusion. Networks of research/experts/ investigators/donors are structured, until the emergence of a hybrid complex where research and expert assessment are embedded. This in turn feeds research, in contexts where it becomes almost impossible in the usual ways, with a North/South asymmetry that deepens and sets limits in terms of the legitimacy of the ideas put into circulation.

After presenting the expert reports to which we have contributed and our motives for doing so, we will show the hiatus in the formulation of problems between decision-makers and researchers; then, we will question the way in which our messages as expert–researchers are received by public actors.

14.2. Researchers enlisted as experts: materials and motivations

14.2.1. *Materials*

From a scientific point of view, the Lake Chad region is an ancient terrain whose richness lies in its nature as an ecological and human crossroads[1]. However, due to insecurity, this area has been progressively closed to foreign and national field research since 2010. At the same time, members of UMR Prodig have been involved in several expert appraisals corresponding to their fields of expertise, which reflect central issues for public policies (Box 14.1): the links between the agricultural economy and natural resources, cross-border movements and the governance of territories.

---

1 For example, since 1987, 17 volumes have been published based on the symposiums of the Mega-Chad network: https://www.cepam.cnrs.fr/megatchad/index-fr.html.

2010. Global Forum on Sustainable Development "Safeguarding Lake Chad". Passages, N'Djaména, October 2010. Financing Chad, MAE France (Ministry of Foreign Affairs). Participation in the Scientific Committee (G. Magrin).

2012-2013. Collegial expert assessment "Preservation of Lake Chad: contribution to a sustainable development strategy of the lake", carried out by IRD for CBLT-FFEM-AIRD. Coordination (J. Lemoalle and G. Magrin) and participation (C. Raimond, C. Rangé, A. Mbagogo, A. Maha madou) (Lemoalle and Magrin 2014).

2015. The Lake Chad Development and Climate Resilience Action Plan. World Bank, LCBC. Presented at COP 21 in December 2015. Coordination of the study (G. Magrin).

2017. Baseline study on the Lake Chad region, AFD. Co-coordination (G. Magrin) and participation (C. Raimond, C. Rangé, E. Chauvin) (Magrin and Pérouse de Montclos 2018).

2018. *Policy brief* Insecurities in the Lake Chad region: where does pastoralism stand and how should we think about its development? FAO, CIRAD. Coordination (C. Rangé).

2020. Study "Contrasting Impacts of the security crisis on land tenure situations in the Lake Chad region", RESILAC, October 2020. Coordination (C. Raimond).

Box 14.1. *Corpus: contributions of Prodig researchers to expert assessments in the Lake Chad Basin (2010–2020)*

Prodig's researchers are also solicited because of their legitimacy based on networks of long-standing partners in the South. The knowledge and approaches cover a wide range (regional or local approaches, integration of scales; study of territorial dynamics and city–community and city–country links; circulations and mobilities; political dimensions of access to resources). Our ability to construct interdisciplinary questions, notably on the interactions between the environment and development, is also sought after.

14.2.2. Expert assessment as a form of the researcher's commitment

For the social science researchers that we are, agreeing to participate in expert reports is a form of commitment. While our research is focused on the analysis of power relations and exclusion, it is a question of promoting the framing of problems that take better into account the interests of local actors, and in particular the most marginalized. Fueling dialogue processes favorable to fairer models of society requires the recognition of production systems or forms of socio-spatial organization that are unfairly misunderstood and more effective, despite appearances, than classical development paths based on large developments allowing technical control of the environment. However, the normative dimension of expert assessment (the proposed framing of problems, even solutions) raises the question of the legitimacy of the researcher in accomplishing this "transgression" (Lavigne-Delville and Le Meur 2016). When such an adventure towards the field of action is made from a position of researchers from the North in countries of the South, this transgression is twofold.

In parallel with the desire to make committed research come to life, our motivations to try expert assessment also stem from the conviction that this mode of knowledge production can constitute a fruitful experience for our research practices, even if the short time of expert assessment – which is also that of politics – and its questioning oriented on a pre-defined "problem" seem contradictory with the principles of an autonomous research field anchored in the long-term of societies.

14.2.3. *Accessing field research and developing intuitions*

Expert assessment is first and foremost a means of accessing actors (administrations, silent partners, companies), documents and negotiation processes that are often beyond the researcher's reach, outside the circumscribed framework of the interview (Lavigne-Delville 2016). To be able to observe public action in the making from the inside is to see "from above" the modalities of international circulation of ideas and norms, the transnationalization and fragmentation of modes of governance to which they give rise (Copans 2011; Fresia and Lavigne-Delville 2018). These observations should be put into perspective with the "bottom" processes that are more familiar to our research fields, in order to produce a geography of development integrating the different levels of analysis.

In this sense, the practice of expert assessment could well paradoxically nourish a *political ecology* approach by facilitating the study of power relations concerning access to and control of natural resources, conflicts of representation to which they give rise and the links between the production of knowledge and public policies. Paradoxically, because the critical posture inherent to *political ecology* disqualifies from the outset the position of the expert. However, on the condition that a critical distance is maintained by alternating the posture of expert and researcher, expert assessment allows for a closer understanding of the interplay of alliances between national and transnational actors and of the systems that are at work. It thus allows for an empirically more solid – and more nuanced – analysis of the power relationships that structure globalization processes (Fresia and Lavigne-Delville 2018).

Designed to inform public action, expert assessment often invites interdisciplinarity. It can give rise to original interactions between disciplines and the literature, in which translations take place all the more easily since addressing non-academics obliges us to make the concepts accessible. Expert assessment can lead researchers to leave the "path of dependence" of their disciplinary questioning to take a new look at the interactions between development, environment and territories.

Expert assessment, constrained by the short time available, requires efficiency in the production of analytical frameworks, questions, hypotheses and even empirical knowledge. Its approach hardly allows for rigorous scientific production or theoretical elaboration, but it brings about original intuitions in a short time that can be useful for research (Lavigne-Delville 2016). To exploit them, leeway is required to build a solid methodology (testing survey grids, for example), which can collide with very constrained schedules. Time must then be taken to identify and exploit the empirical and theoretical opportunities that arise from these imposed framings.

14.2.4. *An opportunity to rethink the relationship with field research in insecure zones*

The current context is not favorable to long fieldwork in Africa. Increasing insecurity and decreasing research funds are reducing the presence of researchers in the field. The question arises as to how to renew social science fieldwork practices, which until now have been largely based on observations and interviews conducted by the researchers themselves (Ayimpam et al. 2014). Faced with insecurity, researchers are often led to abandon "their" fields, due to the impossibility of working with the required scientific rigor. The researcher then deprives themselves of understanding what is at stake in situations of violence (Kovats-Bernat 2002; Bouju 2015). This position is tantamount to nourishing the illusion of a compartmentalization between (exceptional) times of war and (normal) times of peace – the latter being the only ones suitable for research. However, the need to analyze situations of violence from a continuum perspective, taking into account the intertwining of temporalities and history, is widely accepted in the social sciences (Chauveau et al. 2020). The challenge of research in situations of violence "lies perhaps less in the reiteration of the very act of observing on the spot, at every moment, than in the desire to resolve, by any means available, a new question posed to an object of research that is already partly known" (Bouju 2015, p. 161). Expert assessment leads us to rethink our research methods and our relationship with the field when the latter seems to escape us.

14.3. Different narratives, divergent framings: decision-makers and researchers facing the future of Lake Chad

The difference in narratives between public actors (governments and donors) and researchers on the subject of the "future of Lake Chad" implies a review of the processes of public debate in which the expert assessment is positioned.

14.3.1. *Saving Lake Chad*

Lake Chad has been the subject of a crisis narrative since the late 2000s by states in the region and international organizations such as the Lake Chad Basin Commission (LCBC) and the FAO (Magrin 2015a, 2016). The latter postulates that this lake, which was one of the largest freshwater reserves in Africa, would be threatened with disappearance under the effect of anthropogenic withdrawals and climate change. This story has its origins in an ancient fear of the disappearance of Lake Chad, dating back to the first European explorations that noted its high variability. These fears were reactivated by the Sahelian droughts of the 1970–1980s. This crisis discourse insists on the reduction of the surface area of Lake Chad, which is said to have gone from a large single lake of 25,000 km² before 1973 to a relict pocket of water of 1,500 km² in 1984. This trend is illustrated by a set of NASA maps suggesting the gradual and inexorable nature of dewatering (Figure 14.1). This discourse leads to an alarm: a population of 30 million people would be threatened in its means of existence (agriculture, fishing and livestock), which would lead to the risk of emigration and conflicts.

This formulation of the problem is associated with a solution: a major project to transfer water from the Congo basin to the Chad basin would be the only way to save the lake. The idea was formulated by an Italian consulting firm in the 1980s and then taken up by the heads of state in 1990. At the end of the 2000s, the project was taken up by Chadian President Idriss Déby, who is asserting himself in Central Africa thanks to oil revenues and is seeking to legitimize himself, despite strong internal opposition, through a developmentalist stance which is attentive to environmental issues. The contribution to the Great Green Wall project in combatting desertification and the safeguarding of Lake Chad are the most emblematic (Magrin and Mugelé 2020).

I. Déby is supported by other heads of state in the region, such as Colonel Gaddafi before being overthrown in 2011 and successive Nigerian presidents. A summit was being held in Abuja in February 2018 so as to mobilize international support for the inter-basin water transfer. The African Development Bank and the

FAO relayed these positions. The international media echoed them. Leading political figures, such as the former President of the European Commission Romano Prodi, or the then French Minister for the Environment, Ségolène Royal, adhered to the crisis discourse and its implications for public policy (Magrin 2016).

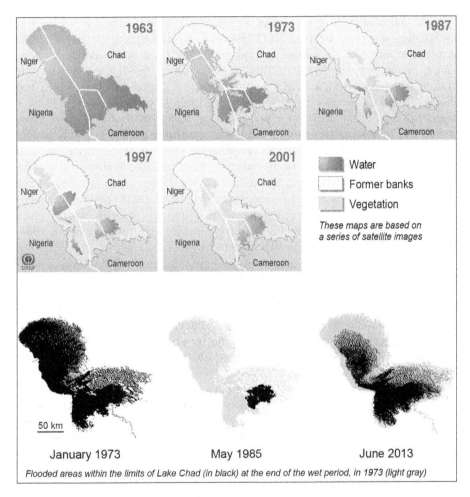

Figure 14.1. *Two opposing representations of the dynamics of Lake Chad. Top: Lake Chad as seen by the institutional and media sphere: the thesis of progressive drying up (source: UNEP, 2004). This collection of maps has been sourced from a series of satellite images provided by NASA Goddard Space Flight Center. https://www. earthobservatory.nasa.gov/images/1240/africas-disappearing-lake-chad. Bottom: an alternative image of the researchers: the natural variability of the lake (Magrin and Lemoalle 2015) (source: NASA - Landsat data). For a color version of this figure, see www.iste.co.uk/peyroux/development.zip*

14.3.2. *Defending successful endogenous systems*

Researchers approach the problems of the Lake Chad region differently. In the expert assessments with which they are associated, they formulate another diagnosis, leading to alternative orientations in terms of public policies. Our analysis adopted a systemic perspective from the outset, articulating hydrological and environmental knowledge, and knowledge in social sciences. By considering the scale of the century, we insist on the natural variability of Lake Chad due to its shallowness, strong evaporation and the variability of the contributions of the Chari Logone system. Although Lake Chad has gone from being one single-pieced Big Lake Chad during the humid decades of 1950–1960 to a Little Lake Chad since 1973, it is composed of a fairly stable open water zone of 2,000 km^2 in the southern basin surrounded by a wide crown of swamps. The variability and vulnerability mainly concern the northern basin. This was completely dried up on several occasions until 1994, causing the scarcity of livelihoods (recession agriculture, fishing, livestock) and triggering mobility towards the southern basin. Our analysis is based on the production of counter-messages that are intended to be simple to speak to politicians and deconstruct the thesis of a progressive drying up, such as a card game illustrating three lake moments (Great Lake Chad in 1973; Small Lake in 1984; return to an intermediate level in 2013; Figure 14.1).

We also put into perspective the consequences for societies of the variability of the lake: national censuses and territorialized analyses of mobility systems (seasonal agricultural migrations, pastoral mobility) and exchanges of agricultural products show that in 2014, only 2 million people lived directly from the resources of Lake Chad, while 13 million people, within a radius of around 250 km, lived indirectly from these resources (Lemoalle and Magrin 2014) (Figure 14.2). Above all, we replace the discourse of crisis (drying up–poverty–migration–conflicts) with a narrative emphasizing the productive potential and the effectiveness of the modes of exploitation of the environment by societies, requiring the deployment of public services and infrastructures (security, health, accessibility, market regulation) and the commitment of the States to the renegotiation of more equitable and less conflictual local modes of governance. We show that the societies bordering the lake have developed productive systems adapted to the variability of the environment based on the 3Ms: a formula likely to make an impression designating practices of mobility, multiactivity and multifunctionality. Without much state support, these rural societies have been capable of innovation and agricultural intensification, providing employment for many young people and generating precious food surpluses in a context of regional population and urban growth (Lemoalle and Magrin 2014; Rangé 2016). We deduce the following recommendation: it would be dangerous to wipe the slate clean of these endogenous production systems by a costly and random attempt at complete control of the environment, as assumed by the inter-basin water transfer.

In terms of water governance, we highlight the inconsistency of trying to achieve a very complex mega-transfer of water when the simple application of the Water Charter of the LCBC, which came into force in 2014 to promote a concerted basin-wide management of water resources among different countries, is very difficult. Finally, we challenge the propensity of the inter-basin water transfer debate, which we consider a utopia, to occupy the entire horizon of forward thinking on regional development, to the detriment of analyses that take into account the real problems and potentials of societies.

14.4. Production and circulation of messages from researchers remobilized in public action

Public policy is a matter of institutions, ideas, interests (Palier and Surel 2005) but also of actors, alliances, conflicts, and misunderstandings (Sabatier and Weible 2007; Lavigne-Delville and Ayimpam 2018). In this constellation of politics, expert assessment responds to a demand from certain actors that allows researchers to disseminate messages that can influence decisions. Ideas circulate through the expert assessment in this complex and eventually contribute to reconfiguring it.

14.4.1. *The political work of research*

The origin of the expert assessment mentioned here is a donor. More precisely, individuals who are sensitive to research analyses, due to their own training or a particular sensitivity to society–environment interactions, and who try to orient their institutions towards alternatives to the dominant readings that tend to "naturalize" climate change or insecurity. In the Sahel, since 2010, the prestige of research institutions has provided the necessary guarantee to maintain activities in areas or on subjects that are considered deadlocked from the point of view of public action. Coalitions are being formed to direct the demand for expert assessment.

The IRD's collegial expert assessment relies on a college of specialized researchers from different institutions to answer a question formulated by the sponsor. In practice, the subjects are selected by a committee according to their scientific and societal interest and the associated funding. It is therefore necessary to have a fourfold concordance – scientific interest, pool of experts, sponsors and funding – to engage collegial expert assessment (IRD's 2006–2009 contract of objectives).

In the case of IRD/LCBC expert assessment, a convergence of interests was observed between, on the one hand, research actors wishing to disseminate ideas that run counter to the report on the disappearance of Lake Chad and, on the other hand, donors seeking to argue their opposition to the inter-basin transfer project strongly supported by the states of the region. Some IRD researchers took advantage of their institution's policy in favor of expert assessment to "stimulate a demand" from the LCBC, with the support of a donor specialized in the environment (the French Global Environment Facility (*Fonds français sur l'environnement mondial*, FFEM)). Researchers thus had considerable leeway to define the central question, formulated in terms of a blurred image of the situation of Lake Chad. They relied on the capitalization of research results in hydrology, geography, ecology and agronomy, reinforced by research programs underway in 2013–2014, including several doctoral students (E. Chauvin, H. Kiari Fougou, A. Koumraït Mbagogo, A. Mahamadou, C. Rangé).

This request came at a time when the LCBC had commissioned a feasibility study of the inter-basin transfer project. Although it signed the letter of order and participated indirectly in the work of the college of experts, it did not really adhere to the proposal to re-evaluate the statement of the disappearance of the lake and finally did not retain the conclusions of the expert assessment[2]. However, the latter provides a very detailed baseline, just before the region was plunged into a security crisis.

AFD expert assessment intervened only three years after the IRD/LCBC collegial expert assessment. However, everything has changed in the region, which has been partially deserted due to the violence and the state of emergency measures that prohibit access to the lake in order to "dry up" the resources of the armed insurgent groups that have taken refuge there. Donors no longer know how to intervene in a field they know little about, on the margins of the countries they already help, in environments where the deployment of infrastructures and services is structurally difficult and temporarily impossible, due to insecurity. For a donor like AFD, maintaining funding is essential in crisis areas in the context of very strong political pressure around the 3D nexus (diplomacy, defense, development). Researchers are then asked to clarify the origins of the crisis and its consequences... a bit like in the colonial era so as to govern "poorly known" territories (Geschiere 1987). Their solicitation also responds to the sincere concern of better understanding the situation in order to redefine a positioning.

The panel of convened disciplines evolves. Less importance is given to environmental issues in favor of political science and a focus on Nigeria, the epicenter of the geopolitical crisis. The researchers redefine the regional and chronological framework of the crisis to clarify its foundations and protagonists. A

---

2 While CBLT technical staff in contact with the researchers may have appeared convinced individually, the institution's position, expressed by its executive secretary, has not changed (Magrin 2015b).

"Lake Chad region" centered on Borno, the epicenter of the political and humanitarian crisis, replaces the attention paid to variations in lake surface and its causes and consequences interpreted at the scale of the hydrological basin. They play with scales to assess the consequences of the crisis on societies and the management of natural resources. and provide knowledge that can be used by aid actors (Figure 14.2). As with the IRD/LCBC collegial expert assessment, the researchers rely on their network of academic partners in the countries concerned, and have full latitude to orient their analyses, which are validated by a peer-review committee. It is important to recognize that there is a greater convergence of views and interests between the researchers and their sponsors from different AFD departments than with the governments of the countries concerned. The focus on Lake Chad as the central pole of the regional system may have overshadowed analyses that focused more on the relations between Borno and the rest of Nigeria, which were little addressed in the AFD expert assessment. This may explain why its messages did not seem very appropriate to experts in that country, despite an effort to translate and disseminate the study in Nigeria.

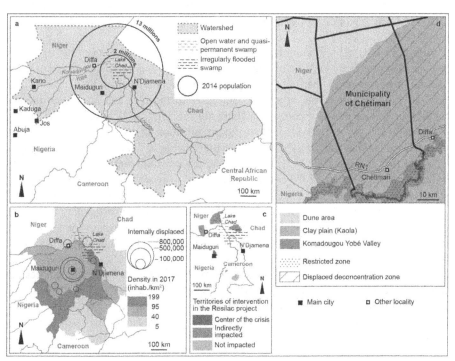

Figure 14.2. *From one form of expert assessment to the other. Framing and scales of analysis that evolve. For a color version of this figure, see www.iste.co.uk/peyroux/development.zip*

COMMENTARY ON FIGURE 14.2. – *a) An initial focus on the hydrological dynamics of Lake Chad and the population that depends on it, at the watershed scale (source: J. Lemoalle and G. Magrin, 2014). b) Then a narrowing of the study framework to a transboundary "Lake Chad region" defined through the impacts of the Boko Haram crisis (source: G. Magrin and M.-A. Pérouse de Monclos, 2018). c) and d) The need to operationalize knowledge in the service of emergency aid projects leads to varying scales of analysis, by country and at the local level (source: C. Raimond and V. Basserie, 2020).*

14.4.2. *Bounce-back of messages between researcher–experts*

An expert assessment has no impact in itself. It depends on the networks of actors ready to mobilize it in the power relations in which they are involved (Lavigne-Delville and Le Meur 2016). Thus, the messages disseminated circulate according to rhythms and processes that are difficult to anticipate and evaluate. While researchers in the North interrogate the networks of actors they can reach, the concerned actors work to select and reappropriate or even divert these messages.

In the Lake Chad region, donors and aid actors influence the definition of public policies. Among these, outside of Nigeria, the AFD has a significant influence. If we use the metaphor of the bark and the core (van Vliet and Magrin 2010) to describe how organizations function, how they legitimize themselves and how they interact with other actors, then the core researchers are referring to "the bark of the bark". The core refers to "the component of the organization in charge of protecting the essential production functions", in this case the security and mobilization of funding. The bark has the function of legitimizing the organization and its actions and acts mainly at the beginning of the cycle. Researchers, who are mainly solicited in these start-up phases to give meaning to new orientations, are even on the periphery of this bark represented by the NGOs and the interdisciplinary departments of donors[3]. They are not destined to accompany the process in the long-term, nor to directly influence the core (the public policies implemented by the State/ODA system).

The circulation of original messages that are different from the dominant ideas is obviously dependent on the networks of partners (academics, students), the connivances that may have been established among donors or the executives of public institutions (LCBC and others). The vitality of international collaborations between researchers is established over the long-term, with joint research projects,

---

3 For example, at AFD, the Innovation, Research and Knowledge (*Innovation, recherches et savoirs*, IRS), or the Fragility, Crisis and Conflict Division (*Fragilité, crises et conflits*) are opposed to the operational departments (financing, infrastructure) coming from the core, the first favoring regional and holistic approaches, and the others favoring more sectoral approaches.

exchanges of researchers and the training of students who are later integrated into both public and research institutions. However, the conditions of access to the field, restricted by insecurity (and recently by the Covid-19 pandemic), weaken these networks and the capacity of researchers, from the North as well as the South, to formulate original and convincing results.

From one expert report to the next, despite the different coalitions of researchers, ideas are taken up, deepened or, on the contrary, criticized and abandoned in favor of new hypotheses and avenues of reflection. Thus, the AFD expert assessment is based on the baseline provided by the IRD/LCBC expert assessment, and the expert assessment on land (Raimond and Basserie 2020) on the latter, introducing an analysis at two scales, regional and local. The researchers thus ensure a post-study follow-up and access to field actors where they cannot go directly.

It also often happens that we lose track. The knowledge platform concerning the Lake Chad region that was supposed to be the result of AFD's expert assessment in order to capitalize on research results, monitor developments in the region and formulate new research avenues has not been created. AFD's internal restructuring, which has made the Innovation, Research and Knowledge strategy autonomous from the Fragility, Crisis and Conflict Division and then created a new Sahel department, drowned out the intentions of the agents who were carrying this project. It was reformulated into a call for tenders on the scale of the Sahel, where the security issues of the "three borders" region (Mali, Burkina Faso, Niger) predominate. Despite a humanitarian crisis affecting nearly 10 million people (IOM 2019), the Lake Chad region is relegated to the background of the PASAS platform (Platform for Analysis, Monitoring and Learning in the Sahel) implemented by the IRD and financed by the AFD.

The promises of the inter-basin canal project – a multi-billion dollar investment that was supposed to solve all the problems of the region – rendered the results of the expert appraisal unheard in the countries concerned, and the LCBC never appropriated the results of the peer review, nor of the subsequent ones.

The COP 21 held in Paris in 2015, when the IRD/LCBC expert assessment had just been published (Lemoalle and Magrin 2014), could have been an opportunity to raise awareness among a variety of actors. The "Lake Chad" session organized by civil society, which had invited the IRD/Prodig team, could have provided an opportune moment, its political significance ensured by the participation of the French Minister of the Environment, Ségolène Royal. Two unexpected events, however, silenced the researchers. Congolese deputies, who were very well informed about the inter-basin transfer project, invited themselves into the arena and focused the debate on the environmental consequences in the withdrawal areas. The Minister, who arrived very late, imposed her intervention, without regard for the debate that was taking place. Stating that she was going to ask French researchers to "stop saying that Lake Chad is not disappearing", she adopted a diplomatic posture similar to that of the Chadian President (Figure 14.3).

Highlighting the exactions of African armies, the impacts of state of emergency measures and the misappropriation of aid is difficult for riparian states to appropriate, as shown by the ignorance of the results of the AFD expert assessment at the Abuja summit in 2018.

These arguments are more acceptable in aid circles, but difficult to translate into concrete actions when donors work with the armed forces of the countries involved. Donors will thus "pick and choose" the messages they can implement from our results without defending an overall vision that could legitimize an alternative intervention. The report written for the World Bank for COP 21 was hardly disseminated, whereas the AFD's expert assessment has been much more widely disseminated. The Hague Summit in February 2019 was to build on these findings to formulate a new direction for Dutch aid in the Lake Chad region, but the renewed insecurity on the ground has frozen the implementation of its recommendations. Some of the results are taken up by other projects, which draw their legitimacy from our diagnosis and proposals, and formulate new calls for proposals (with some shortcuts), such as the study on land tenure in the Resilac project (EU/AFD).

Figure 14.3. *Two irreconcilable visions at COP 21 (in pink, Minister of the Environment Ségolène Royal; on the right, researchers Hadiza Kiari Fougou, Jacques Lemoalle and Géraud Magrin) © C. Raimond. For a color version of this figure, see www.iste.co.uk/peyroux/development.zip*

Occasionally, some of the results do not always convey what we felt was essential. The LCBC's communication has used some of our messages to support its arguments about the lake-dependent population or the regional dimension of the problems. The Adelphi think tank used some of the illustrations in its report (Nagarajan et al. 2018). The choremes developed for the IRD/LCBC foresight analysis were adapted for a study on the impacts of the Boko Haram crisis on pastoral mobilities between Cameroon and Chad (Sutter 2016) and in various high-level meetings on security (Boko Haram Panel CAAS 2019, at UQAM (Canada), CNESS[4], July 2020). These are all signs that these expert reports are being read, and that certain ideas are circulating, which gives us hope that they will reach a greater diversity of actors.

14.5. Conclusion

In a high-stakes region that is a rich and ancient terrain for research, and while the Boko Haram crisis promises to reshuffle many cards in terms of access to land, local governance and productive systems, we must remain present in order to defend, in accordance with the results of the research, a conception of the development of territories based on the recognition of local know-how adapting to the variability of the environment, as well as on equity, local citizenship and dialogue. This has a deep meaning for us as researchers.

However, venturing into expert assessment from a research position raises many questions. On the one hand, if we claim to exert an influence that goes beyond the production of reports, it requires considerable effort. To influence the networks of actors that produce public policies in contexts such as those of the Lake Chad region, requires a long-term presence that is increasingly beyond the reach of our status as researchers, particularly in the North.

On the other hand, once we have noted our difficulty in forming new narratives inspired by our research in the hope of transforming the posture of States, the real nature of our influence raises questions. Is it reduced to framing the fields of action of donors and feeding the narrative of the international media? This would be problematic, implying that development is reduced to policies decided by donors and a rational public decision. However, this myth has long since been shattered, which leads us to question the legitimacy of the expert to inform public action (Lascoumes 2002). This questioning is all the more important in countries where expert assessment is financed and largely conceived by institutions in the North,

---

4 The National Center for Strategic and Security Studies in Niamey, a security center attached to the Presidency of the Republic of Niger, during a seminar on understanding Niger's security environment for senior officials of Niger's defense and security forces.

maintaining extraverted forms of governance. This raises the question of our role in the asymmetrical interplay of actors that produces these public policies, and of the ethical principles on which we base our decision to collaborate with States whose operations are biased in many ways, but which are sovereign. Expert assessment is finally presented as one of the instruments of the political work of researchers to influence the power relations at the heart of the process of the selection of ideas that precedes and/or justifies action.

In fact, in order for this system of relations that governs public policies in aid regimes to evolve, researchers in the countries concerned must be able to develop in-depth, non-dependent and critical knowledge about their realities (Barbedette 2000; Olivier de Sardan 2011). At the same time, our research colleagues in these countries are subject to strong constraints, between internal political pressure, the weight of a degraded socio-professional context, and alignment with the norms of national inter-cooperation, which forces them to carry out expert assessments in a non-selective manner, at the risk of losing sight of the requirements of scientific rigor (Olivier de Sardan 2011). North/South scientific partnerships are essential (Droz and Mayor 2009), provided that they allow for the affirmation of truly autonomous research, which cannot be taken for granted. The legitimacy of researchers/experts from the North in the public debate is based on their knowledge of the field and their networks. However, if the ground is lost under the weight of insecurity, their networks risk withering away. In contexts where only expert assessment still allows access to the field, it is essential to keep these research networks alive, through expert assessment itself, by mobilizing a research reference framework and negotiating with donors in relation to the margins of freedom in the framing of problems as well as the dissemination of results that are our raison d'être.

14.6. References

Ayimpam, S., Chelpi-den Hamer, M., Bouju, J. (2014). Défis éthiques et risques pratiques du terrain en situation de développement ou d'urgence humanitaire. *Anthropologie & développement*, 40–41.

Barbedette, L. (2000). Sciences sociales et coopération en Afrique : Les rendez-vous manqués, Jacob. *Nouveaux Cahiers de l'IUED, 10*. IUED/Presses Universitaires de France, Paris.

Bouju, J. (2015). Une ethnographie à distance ? *Civilisations* [Online]. Available at: https://journals.openedition.org/civilisations/3933.

Chauveau, J.P., Grajales, J., Léonard, É. (2020). Introduction : Foncier et violences politiques en Afrique : Pour une approche continuiste et processuelle. *Revue internationale des études du développement*, 3(3), 7–35. doi.org/10.3917/ried.243.0007.

Copans, J. (2011). Le développement et la mondialisation dans les sciences sociales françaises. *Journal des anthropologues*, 126–127.

Droz, Y. and Mayor, A. (eds) (2009). *Partenariats scientifiques avec l'Afrique. Réflexions critiques de Suisse et d'ailleurs*. Karthala, Paris.

Fresia, M. and Lavigne Delville, P. (2018). Les institutions de l'aide et leurs pratiques. Regards ethnographiques sur des fragments d'une gouvernance globalisée. In *Au cœur des mondes de l'aide internationale. Regards et postures ethnographiques*, Fresia, M. and Lavigne Delville, P. (eds). Karthala/IRD/APAD, Paris/Marseille/Montpellier.

Geschiere, P. (1987). Introduction. In *Terrains et perspectives*, Geschiere, P. and Schlemmer, B. (eds). Éditions de l'ORSTOM, Leyde.

IOM (2019). Regional displacement and human mobility analysis. *Displacement Tracking Matrix*, 43.

Kovats Bernat, J.C. (2002). Negotiating dangerous fields: Pragmatic strategies for fieldwork amid violence and terror. *American Anthropologist*, 104, 208–222.

Lascoumes, P. (2002). L'expertise, de la recherche d'une action rationnelle à la démocratisation des connaissances et des choix. *Revue française d'administration publique*, 103(3), 369–377.

Lavigne Delville, P. (2016). Pour une socio-anthropologie de l'action publique dans les pays sous régime d'aide. *Anthropologie & développement*, 45, 33–64.

Lavigne Delville, P. and Ayimpam, S. (2018). L'action publique en Afrique, entre normes pratiques, dynamiques politiques et influences externes [Online]. Available at: https://journals.openedition.org/anthropodev/660.

Lavigne Delville P. and Le Meur P.Y. (2016). Expertise anthropologique et politiques foncières au Sud. *Économie Rurale*, 353–354, 81–94.

Lemoalle, J. and Magrin, G. (eds) (2014). *Le développement du lac Tchad : Situation actuelle et futurs possibles*. IRD Editions, Marseille.

Magrin, G. (2015a). Double alchimie au lac Tchad : Ou comment transformer la ressource en pénurie et la pénurie en ressources. In *Ressources mondialisées. Essais de géographie politique*, Redon, M., Magrin, G., Chauvin, E., Lavie, E., Perrier-Bruslé, L. (eds). Publications de la Sorbonne, Paris.

Magrin, G. (2015b). Des liaisons dangereuses ? Géographie, coopération et développement au lac Tchad. In *Esplorazioni per la cooperazione allo sviluppo : il contributo del sapere geografico*, Bignante, E., Dansero, E., Loda, M. (eds). Geotema.

Magrin, G. (2016). The disappearance of Lake Chad: History of a myth. *Journal of Political Ecology*, 23, 204–222 [Online]. Available at: http://jpe.library.arizona.edu/volume_23/ Magrin.pdf.

Magrin, G. and Lemoalle, J. (2015). Lake Chad: Present situation and possible future management. In *Conference: Our Common Future Under Climate Change*, UNESCO, Paris [Online]. Available at: http://www.slideshare.net/CFCC15/poster-p2222-05lemoalle-magrin.

Magrin, G. and Mugelé, R. (2020). La boucle de l'Anthropocène au Sahel : Nature et sociétés face aux grands projets environnementaux (Grande Muraille Verte, Sauvegarde du lac Tchad). *Belgeo*, 3 [Online]. Available at: http://journals.openedition.org/belgeo/42872.

Magrin, G. and Pérouse de Montclos, M.A. (2018). *Crise et développement. La région du lac Tchad à l'épreuve de Boko Haram*. AFD, Paris.

Nagarajan, C., Pohl, B., Ruttinge, L., Sylvestre, F., Vivekananda, J., Wall, M., Wolmaier, S. (2018). Climate-fragility profile: Lake Chad Basin. *Adelphi* [Online]. Available at: https://www.adelphi.de/en/publication/climate-fragility-profile-lake-chad-basin.

Olivier de Sardan, J.P. (2011). Promouvoir la recherche face à la consultance. *Cahiers d'études africaines*, 202–203.

Palier, B. and Surel, Y. (2005). Les "trois I" et l'analyse de l'État en action. *Revue française de science politique*, 55, 7–32.

Raimond, C. and Basserie, V. (2020). Étude régionale de recherche. Impacts contrastés de la crise sécuritaire sur les situations foncières dans la région du lac Tchad. *Resilac*, 210.

Rangé, C. (2016). Gouvernance foncière et intensification du multi-usage de l'espace : Le cas de la fenêtre camerounaise du lac Tchad. *Économie rurale*, 3(3–4), 45–63 [Online]. Available at: https://doi.org/10.4000/economierurale.4919.

Sabatier, P.A. and Weible, C.M. (2007). The advocacy coalition framework: Innovations and clarifications. In *Theories of the Policy Process*, Sabatier, P.A. (ed.). Cambridge, Westview.

Sutter, P. (2016). *Évaluation des besoins pastoraux suite à la crise Boko-Haram*. FAO, Cameroon-Chad.

UNEP (2004). Fortnam, M.P. and Oguntola, J.A. (eds), Lake Chad Basin, GIWA Regional assessment 43, University of Kalmar, Kalmar.

van Vliet, G. and Magrin, G. (2012). "L'écorce et le noyau" : Les relations entre Banque mondiale. État, ONG et entreprises pétrolières au Tchad. In *L'État, acteur du développement*, Leloup, F., Brot, J., Gerardin, H. (eds). Karthala, Paris.

List of Authors

Brice ANSELME
Prodig
Université Paris 1
Panthéon-Sorbonne
Aubervilliers
France

Gilles ARNAUD-FASSETTA
Prodig
Université Paris Cité
France

Anaïs BÉJI
Université Paris 1
Panthéon-Sorbonne
Aubervilliers
France

Martine BERGER
Prodig
Université Paris 1
Panthéon-Sorbonne
Aubervilliers
France

Jean-Claude BERGÈS
Prodig
Université Paris 1
Panthéon-Sorbonne
Aubervilliers
France

Frédéric BERTRAND
Prodig
Sorbonne Université
Paris
France

Julie BETABELET
Université de Bangui
Central African Republic

Guillaume BROUSSE
EDF R&D
Chatou
France

Benoît CARLIER
EPTB Seine Grands Lacs
Paris
France

Jean-Louis CHALÉARD
Prodig
Université Paris 1
Panthéon-Sorbonne
Aubervilliers
France

Raphaëlle CHEVRILLON-GUIBERT
Prodig
IRD
Aubervilliers
France

Hubert COCHET
Prodig
AgroParisTech
France

Lisa COULAUD
Prodig
Université Paris 1
Panthéon-Sorbonne
Aubervilliers
France

Axelle CROISÉ
Prodig
Université Paris 1
Panthéon-Sorbonne
Aubervilliers
France

Anna DESSERTINE
Prodig
IRD
Aubervilliers
France

Lamine DIALLO
M2TA
Université Cheikh-Anta-Diop
de Dakar
Senegal

Cécile FALIÈS
Prodig
Université Paris 1
Panthéon-Sorbonne
Aubervilliers
France

Laurent GAGNOL
EA Discontinuités
Université d'Artois
Arras
France

Cyriaque HATTEMER
Prodig
Université Paris 1
Panthéon-Sorbonne
Aubervilliers
France

Sébastien JACQUOT
Prodig
Université Paris 1
Panthéon-Sorbonne
Aubervilliers
France

Audrey KOUMRAÏT MBAGOGO
Université des sciences et de
technologie d'Ati
Chad
and
Université Paris 1
Panthéon-Sorbonne
France

Émilie LAVIE
Prodig
Université Paris Cité
France

Jacques LEMOALLE
IRD
Montpellier
France

Jérôme LOMBARD
Prodig
IRD
Aubervilliers
France

Malika MADELIN
Prodig
Université Paris Cité
France

Géraud MAGRIN
Prodig
Université Paris 1
Panthéon-Sorbonne
Aubervilliers
France

Abdourahamani MAHAMADOU
Prodig
Université Abdou Moumouni
Niamey
Niger

Nora MAREÏ
Prodig
CNRS
Aubervilliers
France

Évelyne MESCLIER
Prodig
IRD
Aubervilliers
France

Pascale METZGER
Prodig
IRD
Aubervilliers
France

Luc MICHLER
Aquabio
Chambéry
France

Marie MORELLE
Prodig
Université Paris 1
Panthéon-Sorbonne
Aubervilliers
France

Olivier NINOT
Prodig
CNRS
Aubervilliers
France

Angélique PALLE
IRSEM
Paris
France

Robin PETIT-ROULET
Prodig
Université Paris 1
Panthéon-Sorbonne
Aubervilliers
France

Élisabeth PEYROUX
Prodig
CNRS
Aubervilliers
France

Marie PIGEOLET
Prodig
Université Paris 1
Panthéon-Sorbonne
Aubervilliers
France

Angèle PROUST
Prodig
Université Paris 1
Panthéon-Sorbonne
Aubervilliers
France

Christine RAIMOND
Prodig
CNRS
Aubervilliers
France

Charline RANGÉ
GRET
Paris
France

Mathilde RESCH
Prodig
METIS
Sorbonne Université
Paris
France

Yann RICHARD
Prodig
Université Paris 1
Panthéon-Sorbonne
Aubervilliers
France

Muriel SAMÉ EKOBO
FPAE
Yaoundé
Cameroon

Edith SAWADOGO
Prodig
Université Paris 1
Panthéon-Sorbonne
Aubervilliers
France

Gashin SHAHSAVARI
Hydroconseil
Chateauneuf-de-Gadagne
France

Alexis SIERRA
Prodig
INSPE
CY Cergy Paris Université
France

Bernard TALLET
CEMCE
Mexico City
Mexico
and
Université Paris 1
Panthéon-Sorbonne
France

Kei TANIKAWA OBREGÓN
Prodig
Université Paris 1
Panthéon-Sorbonne
Aubervilliers
France

Irene VALITTUTO
Prodig
Université Paris 1
Panthéon-Sorbonne
Aubervilliers
France

Vincent VIEL
Prodig
Université Paris Cité
France

Tongnoma ZONGO
CNRST
Ouagadougou
Burkina Faso

Index

Other titles from

in

Innovation, Entrepreneurship and Management

2022

AOUINAÏT Camille
Open Innovation Strategies (Smart Innovation Set – Volume 39)

BOUCHÉ Geneviève
Productive Economy, Contributory Economy: Governance Tools for the Third Millennium (Innovation and Technology Set – Volume 15)

BRUYÈRE Christelle
Caring Management in Health Organizations: A Lever for Crisis Management (Health and Innovation Set – Volume 3)

HELLER David
Valuation of the Liability Structure by Real Options (Modern Finance, Management Innovation and Economic Growth Set – Volume 5)

MATHIEU Valérie
A Customer-oriented Manager for B2B Services: Principles and Implementation

MORALES Lucía, DZEVER Sam, TAYLOR Robert
Asia-Europe Industrial Connectivity in Times of Crisis (Innovation and Technology Set – Volume 16)

NOËL Florent, SCHMIDT Géraldine
Employability and Industrial Mutations: Between Individual Trajectories and Organizational Strategic Planning (Technological Changes and Human Resources Set – Volume 4)

DE SAINT JULIEN Odile
The Innovation Ecosystem as a Source of Value Creation: A Value Creation Lever for Open Innovation (Diverse and Global Perspectives on Value Creation Set – Volume 4)

SALOFF-COSTE Michel
Innovation Ecosystems: The Future of Civilizations and the Civilization of the Future (Innovation and Technology Set – Volume 14)

VAYRE Emilie
Digitalization of Work: New Spaces and New Working Times (Technological Changes and Human Resources Set – Volume 5)

ZAFEIRIS Konstantinos N, SKIADIS Christos H, DIMOTIKALIS Yannis, KARAGRIGORIOU Alex, KARAGRIGORIOU-VONTA Christina
Data Analysis and Related Applications 1: Computational, Algorithmic and Applied Economic Data Analysis (Big Data, Artificial Intelligence and Data Analysis Set – Volume 9)
Data Analysis and Related Applications 2: Multivariate, Health and Demographic Data Analysis (Big Data, Artificial Intelligence and Data Analysis Set – Volume 10)

2021

ARCADE Jacques
Strategic Engineering (Innovation and Technology Set – Volume 11)

BÉRANGER Jérôme, RIZOULIÈRES Roland
The Digital Revolution in Health (Health and Innovation Set – Volume 2)

BOBILLIER CHAUMON Marc-Eric
Digital Transformations in the Challenge of Activity and Work: Understanding and Supporting Technological Changes (Technological Changes and Human Resources Set – Volume 3)

BUCLET Nicolas
Territorial Ecology and Socio-ecological Transition
(Smart Innovation Set – Volume 34)

DIMOTIKALIS Yannis, KARAGRIGORIOU Alex, PARPOULA Christina,
SKIADIS Christos H
Applied Modeling Techniques and Data Analysis 1: Computational Data
Analysis Methods and Tools (Big Data, Artificial Intelligence and Data
Analysis Set - Volume 7)
Applied Modeling Techniques and Data Analysis 2: Financial,
Demographic, Stochastic and Statistical Models and Methods (Big Data,
Artificial Intelligence and Data Analysis Set – Volume 8)

DISPAS Christophe, KAYANAKIS Georges, SERVEL Nicolas,
STRIUKOVA Ludmila
Innovation and Financial Markets
(Innovation between Risk and Reward Set – Volume 7)

ENJOLRAS Manon
Innovation and Export: The Joint Challenge of the Small Company
(Smart Innovation Set – Volume 37)

FLEURY Sylvain, RICHIR Simon
Immersive Technologies to Accelerate Innovation: How Virtual and
Augmented Reality Enables the Co-Creation of Concepts
(Smart Innovation Set – Volume 38)

GIORGINI Pierre
The Contributory Revolution (Innovation and Technology Set – Volume 13)

GOGLIN Christian
Emotions and Values in Equity Crowdfunding Investment Choices 2:
Modeling and Empirical Study

GRENIER Corinne, OIRY Ewan
Altering Frontiers: Organizational Innovations in Healthcare (Health and
Innovation Set – Volume 1)

GUERRIER Claudine
Security and Its Challenges in the 21st Century (Innovation and Technology Set – Volume 12)

HELLER David
Performance of Valuation Methods in Financial Transactions (Modern Finance, Management Innovation and Economic Growth Set – Volume 4)

LEHMANN Paul-Jacques
Liberalism and Capitalism Today

SOULÉ Bastien, HALLÉ Julie, VIGNAL Bénédicte, BOUTROY Éric, NIER Olivier
Innovation in Sport: Innovation Trajectories and Process Optimization (Smart Innovation Set – Volume 35)

UZUNIDIS Dimitri, KASMI Fedoua, ADATTO Laurent
Innovation Economics, Engineering and Management Handbook 1: Main Themes
Innovation Economics, Engineering and Management Handbook 2: Special Themes

VALLIER Estelle
Innovation in Clusters: Science–Industry Relationships in the Face of Forced Advancement (Smart Innovation Set – Volume 36)

2020

ACH Yves-Alain, RMADI-SAÏD Sandra
Financial Information and Brand Value: Reflections, Challenges and Limitations

ANDREOSSO-O'CALLAGHAN Bernadette, DZEVER Sam, JAUSSAUD Jacques, TAYLOR Robert
Sustainable Development and Energy Transition in Europe and Asia (Innovation and Technology Set – Volume 9)

BEN SLIMANE Sonia, M'HENNI Hatem
Entrepreneurship and Development: Realities and Future Prospects (Smart Innovation Set – Volume 30)

LATOUCHE Pascal
Open Innovation: Human Set-up
(Innovation and Technology Set – Volume 10)

LIMA Marcos
Entrepreneurship and Innovation Education: Frameworks and Tools
(Smart Innovation Set – Volume 32)

MACHADO Carolina, DAVIM J. Paulo
Sustainable Management for Managers and Engineers

MAKRIDES Andreas, KARAGRIGORIOU Alex, SKIADAS Christos H.
Data Analysis and Applications 3: Computational, Classification, Financial,
Statistical and Stochastic Methods
(Big Data, Artificial Intelligence and Data Analysis Set – Volume 5)
Data Analysis and Applications 4: Financial Data Analysis and Methods
(Big Data, Artificial Intelligence and Data Analysis Set – Volume 6)

MASSOTTE Pierre, CORSI Patrick
Complex Decision-Making in Economy and Finance

MEUNIER François-Xavier
Dual Innovation Systems: Concepts, Tools and Methods
(Smart Innovation Set – Volume 31)

MICHAUD Thomas
Science Fiction and Innovation Design (Innovation in Engineering and
Technology Set – Volume 6)

MONINO Jean-Louis
Data Control: Major Challenge for the Digital Society
(Smart Innovation Set – Volume 29)

MORLAT Clément
Sustainable Productive System: Eco-development versus Sustainable
Development (Smart Innovation Set – Volume 26)

SAULAIS Pierre, ERMINE Jean-Louis
Knowledge Management in Innovative Companies 2: Understanding and
Deploying a KM Plan within a Learning Organization
(Smart Innovation Set – Volume 27)

2019

AMENDOLA Mario, GAFFARD Jean-Luc
Disorder and Public Concern Around Globalization

BARBAROUX Pierre
Disruptive Technology and Defence Innovation Ecosystems
(Innovation in Engineering and Technology Set – Volume 5)

DOU Henri, JUILLET Alain, CLERC Philippe
Strategic Intelligence for the Future 1: A New Strategic and Operational
Approach
Strategic Intelligence for the Future 2: A New Information Function
Approach

FRIKHA Azza
Measurement in Marketing: Operationalization of Latent Constructs

FRIMOUSSE Soufyane
Innovation and Agility in the Digital Age
(Human Resources Management Set – Volume 2)

GAY Claudine, SZOSTAK Bérangère L.
Innovation and Creativity in SMEs: Challenges, Evolutions and Prospects
(Smart Innovation Set – Volume 21)

GORIA Stéphane, HUMBERT Pierre, ROUSSEL Benoît
Information, Knowledge and Agile Creativity
(Smart Innovation Set – Volume 22)

HELLER David
Investment Decision-making Using Optional Models
(Economic Growth Set – Volume 2)

HELLER David, DE CHADIRAC Sylvain, HALAOUI Lana, JOUVET Camille
The Emergence of Start-ups
(Economic Growth Set – Volume 1)

HÉRAUD Jean-Alain, KERR Fiona, BURGER-HELMCHEN Thierry
Creative Management of Complex Systems
(Smart Innovation Set – Volume 19)

SAULAIS Pierre, ERMINE Jean-Louis
Knowledge Management in Innovative Companies 1: Understanding and Deploying a KM Plan within a Learning Organization
(Smart Innovation Set – Volume 23)

SERVAJEAN-HILST Romaric
Co-innovation Dynamics: The Management of Client-Supplier Interactions for Open Innovation
(Smart Innovation Set – Volume 20)

SKIADAS Christos H., BOZEMAN James R.
Data Analysis and Applications 1: Clustering and Regression, Modeling-estimating, Forecasting and Data Mining
(Big Data, Artificial Intelligence and Data Analysis Set – Volume 2)
Data Analysis and Applications 2: Utilization of Results in Europe and Other Topics
(Big Data, Artificial Intelligence and Data Analysis Set – Volume 3)

UZUNIDIS Dimitri
Systemic Innovation: Entrepreneurial Strategies and Market Dynamics

VIGEZZI Michel
World Industrialization: Shared Inventions, Competitive Innovations and Social Dynamics
(Smart Innovation Set – Volume 24)

2018

BURKHARDT Kirsten
Private Equity Firms: Their Role in the Formation of Strategic Alliances

CALLENS Stéphane
Creative Globalization
(Smart Innovation Set – Volume 16)

CASADELLA Vanessa
Innovation Systems in Emerging Economies: MINT – Mexico, Indonesia, Nigeria, Turkey
(Smart Innovation Set – Volume 18)

PANSERA Mario, OWEN Richard
Innovation and Development: The Politics at the Bottom of the Pyramid
(Innovation and Responsibility Set – Volume 2)

RICHEZ Yves
Corporate Talent Detection and Development

SACHETTI Philippe, ZUPPINGER Thibaud
New Technologies and Branding
(Innovation and Technology Set – Volume 4)

SAMIER Henri
Intuition, Creativity, Innovation

TEMPLE Ludovic, COMPAORÉ SAWADOGO Eveline M.F.W.
Innovation Processes in Agro-Ecological Transitions in Developing Countries
(Innovation in Engineering and Technology Set – Volume 2)

UZUNIDIS Dimitri
Collective Innovation Processes: Principles and Practices
(Innovation in Engineering and Technology Set – Volume 4)

VAN HOOREBEKE Delphine
The Management of Living Beings or Emo-management

2017

AÏT-EL-HADJ Smaïl
The Ongoing Technological System
(Smart Innovation Set – Volume 11)

BAUDRY Marc, DUMONT Béatrice
Patents: Prompting or Restricting Innovation?
(Smart Innovation Set – Volume 12)

BÉRARD Céline, TEYSSIER Christine
Risk Management: Lever for SME Development and Stakeholder Value Creation

UZUNIDIS Dimitri, SAULAIS Pierre
Innovation Engines: Entrepreneurs and Enterprises in a Turbulent World
(Innovation in Engineering and Technology Set – Volume 1)

2016

BARBAROUX Pierre, ATTOUR Amel, SCHENK Eric
Knowledge Management and Innovation
(Smart Innovation Set – Volume 6)

BEN BOUHENI Faten, AMMI Chantal, LEVY Aldo
Banking Governance, Performance And Risk-Taking: Conventional Banks
Vs Islamic Banks

BOUTILLIER Sophie, CARRÉ Denis, LEVRATTO Nadine
Entrepreneurial Ecosystems (Smart Innovation Set – Volume 2)

BOUTILLIER Sophie, UZUNIDIS Dimitri
The Entrepreneur (Smart Innovation Set – Volume 8)

BOUVARD Patricia, SUZANNE Hervé
Collective Intelligence Development in Business

GALLAUD Delphine, LAPERCHE Blandine
Circular Economy, Industrial Ecology and Short Supply Chains
(Smart Innovation Set – Volume 4)

GUERRIER Claudine
Security and Privacy in the Digital Era
(Innovation and Technology Set – Volume 1)

MEGHOUAR Hicham
Corporate Takeover Targets

MONINO Jean-Louis, SEDKAOUI Soraya
Big Data, Open Data and Data Development
(Smart Innovation Set – Volume 3)

MOREL Laure, LE ROUX Serge
Fab Labs: Innovative User
(Smart Innovation Set – Volume 5)

PICARD Fabienne, TANGUY Corinne
Innovations and Techno-ecological Transition
(Smart Innovation Set – Volume 7)

2015

CASADELLA Vanessa, LIU Zeting, DIMITRI Uzunidis
Innovation Capabilities and Economic Development in Open Economies
(Smart Innovation Set – Volume 1)

CORSI Patrick, MORIN Dominique
Sequencing Apple's DNA

CORSI Patrick, NEAU Erwan
Innovation Capability Maturity Model

FAIVRE-TAVIGNOT Bénédicte
Social Business and Base of the Pyramid

GODÉ Cécile
Team Coordination in Extreme Environments

MAILLARD Pierre
Competitive Quality and Innovation

MASSOTTE Pierre, CORSI Patrick
Operationalizing Sustainability

MASSOTTE Pierre, CORSI Patrick
Sustainability Calling

2014

DUBÉ Jean, LEGROS Diègo
Spatial Econometrics Using Microdata

LESCA Humbert, LESCA Nicolas
Strategic Decisions and Weak Signals

Printed by BoD™in Norderstedt, Germany

9 781786 306531